SPEAKING OF WORDS

JAMES MacKILLOP
DONNA WOOLFOLK CROSS

Onondaga Community College

HOLT, RINEHART AND WINSTON
New York   Chicago   San Francisco
Atlanta   Dallas
Montreal   Toronto

SPEAKING OF WORDS
A Language Reader

Library of Congress Cataloging in Publication Data

Main entry under title:

Speaking of words.

   1. College readers. 2. English language—Addresses, essays, lectures. I. MacKillop, James. II. Cross, Donna Woolfolk.
PE1122.S6   808'.042   77-14952
ISBN 0-03-018056-2

Acknowledgments

For the "Grammar" cartoon on page 16: Copyright © 1977 Stuart Leeds, *Saturday Review*.

For the figure on page 42: From *An Introduction to Descriptive Linguistics, Revised Edition* by H. A. Gleason, Jr. Copyright 1955, ©, 1961 by Holt, Rinehart and Winston, Inc. Reprinted by permission of Holt, Rinehart and Winston.

For the cartoons on pages 110 and 146: Reprinted courtesy of P. Kahan.

For the dictionary entry on pages 240–241: © 1969, 1970, 1973, 1975, 1976, Houghton Mifflin Company. Reprinted by permission from *The American Heritage Dictionary of the English Language*.

For the dictionary entry on pages 289–292: From the *Oxford English Dictionary*, vol. 3, p. 122, by permission of the Oxford University Press.

CHAPTER 1

"Students' Right to Their Own Language": Copyright © 1974 by the National Council of Teachers of English. Reprinted by permission of the publisher and the author. Copies of this statement are available from NCTE.

"Riting Inglish Real Good" by J. Mitchell Morse: © 1976 by the New York Times Company. Reprinted by permission.

"What Makes Freshman English Such a Hard Course" (Original title, "The Multiple Meanings of 'To Write' ") by Elizabeth Wooten Cowen: From the Spring 1976 issue of *Freshman English News*. Reprinted by permission of the author.

Selections from *Telling Writing* and *Uptaught*: Reprinted from Ken Macrorie's *Telling Writing*, Copyright © 1976, and *Uptaught*, Copyright © 1970, with the permission of the publisher, Hayden Book Company, Inc.

"The Case for Standard English" by David Eskey; "Doublespeak: Dialectology in the Service of Big Brother" by James Sledd; "Correctness and Style in College Composition" by A. A. Hill: Reprinted by permission of the National Council of Teachers of English and the author.

"Why Young People Today Can't Write" by A. Bartlett Giamatti: Reprinted with permission from the January 1976 issue of the Yale Alumni Magazine; copyright by Yale Alumni Publications, Inc.

CHAPTER 2

"How Language Shapes Our Thoughts": Copyright 1954 Stuart Chase.

"The Gift of Tongues": From *Mirror for Man* by Clyde Kluckhohn. Copyright 1949 by McGraw-Hill, Inc. Used with permission of McGraw-Hill Book Company.

Word Play: What Happens When People Talk: From *Word Play: What Happens When People Talk*, by Peter Farb. Copyright © 1973 by Peter Farb. Reprinted by permission of Alfred A. Knopf, Inc.

"Signs and Symbols in Language and Thought" by Susanne K. Langer: Excerpts from 'The Lord of Creation' by Susanne K. Langer which originally appeared in the January 1944 Fortune Magazine. And from "If I say 'Napoleon . . ." (p. 50): Reprinted by permission of the publishers from *Philosophy in a New Key: A Study in the Symbolism of Reason, Rite and Art*, 3rd Edition, by Susanne K. Langer, Cambridge, Mass.: Harvard University Press, Copyright © 1942, 1951, 1957 by the President and Fellows of Harvard College; © 1970 by Susanne K. Langer.

"Classification" by S. I. Hayakawa: From *Language in Thought and Action*, 3rd Edition, by S. I. Hayakawa, copyright © 1972 by Harcourt Brace Jovanovich, Inc., and reprinted with their permission.

"Selection, Slanting, and Charged Language" by Newman P. Birk and Genevieve B. Birk: From *Understanding and Using English*, 5th edition by Newman P. Birk and Genevieve B. Birk, copyright © 1949, 1951, 1958, 1965 by Odyssey Press, 1972 by The Bobbs-Merrill Company, Inc., used by permission of the publisher.

"The Day" by Seymour M. Hersh: From *My Lai 4*, by Seymour M. Hersh. Copyright © 1970 by Seymour M. Hersh. Reprinted by permission of Random House, Inc.

"Science and Linguistics" by Benjamin Lee Whorf: Reprinted by permission of the MIT Press, from *Language, Thought and Reality*, 1956.

From *Don Juan in Hell* and *Man and Superman* by George Bernard Shaw: Reprinted from *Don Juan in Hell* and *Man and Superman* by permission of The Society of Authors on behalf of the Bernard Shaw Estate.

From *A Preface to Critical Reading* by Richard Altick: From *A Preface to Critical Reading* by Richard Altick. Copyright © 1969 by Holt, Rinehart and Winston, Inc. Reprinted by permission of Holt, Rinehart and Winston.

CHAPTER 3

"The English Language Is My Enemy" by Ossie Davis: Reprinted by permission of The Association for the Study of Afro-American Life and History, Inc.

"Defining the 'American Indian': A Case Study in the Language of Suppression" by Haig A. Bosmajian: Reprinted by permission of the author, from the March 1973 edition of *The Speech Teacher*.

For Pat
and
For Richard,
Who Saw It Through . . .

Preface

Neither the editors nor the publisher of *Speaking of Words* presumes to tell you how to teach freshman composition. The crushing number of texts already on our shelves as well as the diversity of approaches we find in our own department are enough to tell us that most of us want to do it our own way. Each class we face is different, not only because our students come from different parts of the country and different social and ethnic groups, but also because each student's educational history—indeed, each Person—is different. For these reasons we have found that we have had to keep our own syllabi flexible to account for the unexpected that turns up every year.

We have tried to assemble a text which can be of use to instructors with different educational philosophies and methods. Some instructors will want to follow the order we have implied in the table of contents; others may choose to ignore it. Some will want to make use of our writing suggestions for essay papers or journal keeping; others may want to create different assignments from the readings. The readings and assignments are adaptable to your own tastes and philosophies as well as to the interests, strengths, and limitations of your students.

A word about the exercises in each chapter. We have placed them *before* the reading selections, rather than after them, as is usually the case. By doing this, we hope to give students a chance to experience language before they read or write about it—to discover new information for themselves rather than simply reinforce information provided by someone else. As with the writing suggestions, this format can be followed or ignored. Another aid in the use of *Speaking of Words* is the Instructor's Manual. For more information, write to the English Editor, Holt, Rinehart and Winston, 383 Madison Avenue, New York, New York 10017.

We have tried to avoid pedantic minutiae and concentrate on broader, more basic issues important to enlightened living in a difficult age. We want to help students of all curricula—liberal arts in a large, elite university or a career program in a two-year college—gain some understanding of the ways language affects their beliefs, habits, actions, and relationships every day. We want to help them to be the masters, not the victims, of their native tongue.

In the theory about teaching writing, a few pieces of advice are mentioned repeatedly. People write best when they are writing about something they know and when they can sense a purpose in their writing. With these in mind we think that language itself is the best subject for freshman writing because it is already a part of the students' experience and because it can be made relevant to everything: personal history, politics, the media, love, science, and sex. Language may be the subject of this text, but writing and rewriting is the meat of the course.

No editor is an island, and we could not have completed this book without the help of many people. All the members of our department have contributed to *Speaking of Words* in ways each one could not calculate. Our disagreements, sometimes divisive at the moment, have helped us to broaden our understanding of the scope of the course. Colleagues who have been immediately helpful have been Norma Foody, Doug Brode, and David Feldman. Instructors from other institutions who have been generous with their advice have been David Bergdahl of Ohio University, Ellen P. Wiese and Morton Bloomfield of Harvard University, Russell A. Hunt of Saint Thomas University in New Brunswick, Don W. Melander of New England College, Harley Sachs of Michigan Technological University, and Edward H. Kelly of the State University of New York at Oneonta. For their help, we would like to thank Professors Ken Burrows, West Virginia Institute of Technology; Donald Emblen, Santa Rosa Junior College; William Herman, City University of New York, City College; David Skwire, Cuyahoga Community College, Metropolitan Campus; Norman Stageberg, University of Northern Iowa; Merle Thompson, Northern Virginia Community College; Eve Vanouse, State University of New York at Oswego; Evelyn Wood, University of Northern Iowa. We would like to give the warmest thanks to the staff of the Onondaga Community College Library, all of whom have been unfailing in their generosity. Lastly, we would like to thank Harriett Prentiss of Holt, Rinehart, and Winston, without whom, quite literally, this book would have been impossible.

JAMES MACKILLOP   *Syracuse, New York*
DONNA WOOLFOLK CROSS   *December 1977*

To The Student

This book is about language, not just any language, but English, the native tongue of just about every one of you. You learned to speak it well enough to order a meal in a restaurant before you ever went to school. You have been learning to write it, chances are, for about twelve years, but if you are anything like most of your fellow students, you still feel ill at ease when putting it down on paper. And now you are about to try to learn more about language and writing in a course called "freshman composition" (disguised under other names in many colleges). Most students complain about the course for one reason or another, but many of them do learn how to write well. We hope this book will help you to be one of the latter.

Learning about language, it must be admitted, will not automatically improve your writing. Writing is a performance like making pizza, playing tennis, dancing, or even driving. Some people will naturally be more talented than others, but almost anyone can become competent with practice and guidance. There is no substitute for practice: the way to learn to write is to write.

Writing about language, we believe, is the most relevant kind of writing you could do. We see the language journal as an important part of this course. The journal assignments are different from the essay writing assignments in that they are meant to be continuing, that is, you should keep writing down new examples and ideas that fit the assignments as they occur to you throughout the semester. After all, you are going to be using language no matter what you do in life, and as long as you stay in society, it is going to be used *on* you, even against you. But if you understand language and its uses, you are less likely to be victimized by politicians, advertisers, journalists, lawyers, bureaucrats—by all those who know the power and purposes of language and who are not above using it as a weapon against those who don't. In short, learning about language can help you become its master, not its slave.

"Freshman composition," as many people both inside and outside college think, is an impossible course. One impossibility is that you cannot learn all there is to know about writing or language in one term, no matter how demanding the syllabus. Another is the possible varieties of "good writing." As you go through the course try to think about what *you* expect to get out of it, what it demands of you, and what is happening to you as you try to meet the course demands. These are some of the reasons that we begin Chapter 1 by talking about the course itself.

Lastly, you should know that there are few "right" answers to the questions in the book. Indeed, getting the "right" answers is not the point of this text. The point is to help you start thinking about your language, about the way you use it and it uses you.

Contents

Preface   ix
To the Student   xi

Chapter 1. "But the Registrar Said I *Have* to Take This Course": Language in the Classroom   1

Classroom Exercise   1
Merrill Sheils, "Why Johnny Can't Write"   2
Committee of the CCCC Language Statement, "Students' Right to Their Own Language"   8
J. Mitchell Morse, "Riting Inglish Real Good"   12
Elizabeth Wooten Cowan, "What Makes Freshman English Such ' Hard Course?"   14
Student Essay: "English Classes and Me"   19
Points of Departure: 21
   A. Ken Macrorie, "Engfish," from *Telling Writing*   21
   B. Ken Macrorie, from *Uptaught*   22
   C. David Eskey, "The Case for Standard English   22
   D. James Sledd, "Doublespeak: Dialectology in the Service of Big Brother   23
   E. Anthony Burgess, [a letter to] "My Dear Students"   24
   F. Archibald A. Hill, "Correctness and Style in College Composition"   24
   G. A. Bartlett Giamatti, "Why Young People Today Can't Write"   25
   H. *Newsweek*, "Newsmakers": "George Washington's Language"   26
Writing Assignments   27
Journal Keeping   28

Chapter 2. "Let Me Give You a Piece of My Mind": How Language Shapes Our Thoughts and Reality   29

Classroom Exercise: How Much Do We Think Without Words?   29
Stuart Chase, "How Language Shapes Our Thoughts   29
Jane Otten, "Living in Syntax"   34
Clyde Kluckhohn, "The Gift of Tongues"   37

Peter Farb, from *World Play: What Happens When People Talk*   43
Mark Twain, from "The Awful German Language"   46
Susanne K. Langer, "Signs and Symbols in Language and
    Thought"   49
Class-oom Exercise, on Classification   54
S. I. Hayakawa, "Classification"   54
Classroom Exercise, on Selection, Slanting, and Charged Language   63
Newman P. Birk and Genevieve B. Birk, "Selection, Slanting, and
    Charged Language"   64
Classroom Exercise   73
Seymour Hersh, from "The Day"   76
Student Essay: "Tree"   79
Points of Departure: 81
   A. Benjamin Lee Whorf, from *Science and Linguistics*   81
   B. Charlton Laird, from *The Miracle of Language*   81
   C. Edward Sapir, from *Language*   82
   D. Alan Watts, from *The Way of Zen*   82
   E. George Bernard Shaw, from *Don Juan in Hell*   83
   F. Richard Altick, from *A Preface to Critical Reading*   83
Writing Assignments   84

Chapter 3. "How Do I Know What I Think Till I See What I Say?": Language and Belief—How Language Reinforces Racial, Ethnic, and Sexual Discrimination   87

Classroom Exercise   87
Ossie Davis, "The English Language Is My Enemy!"   88
Gordon W. Allport, "Linguistic Factors in Prejudice"   89
Haig A. Bosmajian, "Defining the 'American Indian': A Case Study in
    the Language of Suppression"   95
Classroom Exercise   100
Casey Miller and Kate Swift, "Is Language Sexist? One Small Step for
    Genkind"   101
Louis Foley, "You Can Overdo Being 'A Real *Person*'"   111
Barbara Lawrence, "Four-Letter Words Can Hurt You—If You're a
    Woman"   113
Muriel R. Schulz, "Is the English Language Anybody's
    Enemy?"   115
Student Essay: "Don't Call Me a 'Wop'!"   118
Points of Departure: 121
   A. Norman Cousins, "The Environment of Language"   121
   B. Louie Crews, "A Black Addendum to Roget"   121
   C. "When Does Sex Stereotyping Begin?"   122
   D. J. J. MacKillop and D. W. Cross, Compiled from
    news reports   122

   E.   Summary from J. J. MacKillop and D. W. Cross, " 'Man': Memo
          from a Publisher"   123
   F.   From *English Highlights*, "Does Language Libel the
          Left-Handed?"   124
Writing Assignments   125

Chapter 4. "I Want to Make One Thing Perfectly Clear": The Misuse of Language   129

Classroom Exercise   129
Stuart Chase, "Gobbledygook"   130
Melvin Maddocks, "The Limitations of Language"   138
Editors of *Time Magazine*, "The Euphemism: Telling It Like It
      Isn't"   141
Judith Kaplan, "Catch Phrases Don't Communicate"   146
James P. Degnan, "Masters of Babble: Turning Language into
      Stone   149
Richard K. Redfern, "A Brief Lexicon of Jargon"   153
R. D. Rosen, "Psychobabble"   157
Francine Hardaway, "Foul Play: Sports Metaphors and Public
      Doublespeak"   163
Student Essay: "Truckers—Keep on Truckin', Away from
      Me"   168
Points of Departure: 170
   A.   George Orwell, from "Politics and the English Language"   170
   B.   Edwin Newman, "Howard Cosell," from *Strictly Speaking*   171
   C.   J. J. MacKillop and D. W. Cross, "How to Tell Mommy
          Her Child Is . . . ."   171
   D.   Editors of *Time Magazine*, "Doctor's Jargon"   172
   E.   *The Syracuse Herald-Journal*, "A Language of Their
          Own"   173
   F.   Mario Pei, "Scientese," from *Doublespeak in America*   173
   G.   William D. Lutz, "Doublespeak or the Forked Tongue"   174
Writing Assignments   175

Chapter 5. "That's What I Think Too—Isn't It?" The Analysis of Propaganda   178

Classroom Exercise   178
D. W. Cross, "Propaganda: How Not to Be Bamboozled"   180
Richard M. Nixon, "The Checkers Speech"   190
James E. (Jimmy) Carter, "In Changing Times, Eternal Values"·
      Inaugural Address, January 20, 1977   196
Aldous Huxley, "Propaganda in a Democratic Society"   199
William Safire, "Political Labels: Conservative, Liberal, Democrat,
      Republican"   202

Bill Garvin, "Mad's Guaranteed Effective All-Occasion
    Non-Slanderous Political Smear Speech"   207
Morris K. Udall, "Affective Language in Political Propaganda:
    'Federal Spending' "   209
David Ogilvy, "How to Write Potent Copy"   212
Carl P. Wrighter, "Weasel Words: God's Little Helpers"   214
John D. Lofton, Jr., "Does the Consumer Really Care?"   224
Dawn Ann Kurth, "Bugs Bunny Says They're Yummy"   226
Student Essay: "What Is Avon Calling to Me?"   229
Points of Departure: 231
    A.   Kevin Casn, *Who the Hell Is William Loeb?*   231
    B-K.   Anonymous. A Propaganda Sampler   232-236
Writing Assignments   237

Chapter 6. "How Can I Look It Up If I Don't Know How To Spell?": Dictionaries—Etymology, Levels of Usage, and the Fluctuating Meanings of Words   239

Classroom Exercise   239
Paul Roberts, "How to Find Fault with a Dictionary"   243
Dwight Macdonald, "The String Untuned"   255
Patrick E. Kilburn, "The Gentlemen's Guide to Linguistic
    Etiquette'   265
B. Isaac Chisholm, "The Background of Words: A Short Guide to
    Etymology"   270
Lawrence Van Gelder, "The Ketchup Connection"   283
Student Essay: "Hunting a 'Deer' "   285
Points of Departure: 287
    A.   Putting Your Hands into The *Oxford English Dictionary*.   287
    B.   How to Pick Your Own Dictionary of Usage.   293
Writing Assignments   300

SPEAKING OF WORDS

1 "But the Registrar Said I *Have* to Take This Course" Language in the Classroom

CLASSROOM EXERCISE

It is *right* for Boy Scouts to help old ladies across the street.

It is *right* for schools to vaccinate children against measles.

It is *right* to say "I haven't got any" instead of "I don't got none."

1. What does the word "right" mean in each of the sentences above? Is the meaning the same, or does it change?

2. In particular, what does it mean when we speak about being "right" in English class? Who determines what is "right" and what is not? How do you know?

3. What do you think about the following sentence? Is this good writing or not? Discuss.

It's obvious, in our modern world of today theirs a lot of impreciseness in expressing thoughts we have.

(written by an 18-year-old college freshman)

4. In judging whether a piece of writing is good or bad, what things do you usually consider? What things do English teachers consider? Employers? Book reviewers? People who receive letters?

5. Do you find it hard to tell whether something you have written is good or bad? Is it easier to judge someone else's writing? Why or why not?

6. Is the following sentence better than the one in question 3? Or not as good? What criteria do you use for judgment?

From this course I hope to attain a working knowledge of English in the full sense of what the author wants.

(written by college freshman at first class meeting)

7. What does this sentence mean? If you're not sure what it means, whose fault is it—yours or the writer's?

8. Do you think the student really means what he says here? If not, why did he write it?

MERRILL SHEILS
Why Johnny Can't Write

Freshman composition has been short on friends for a long time, but only recently has it become the subject of a rather heated bad press. In the past few years there have been hundreds of newspaper accounts of declining national scores on the Scholastic Achievement Tests and, sometimes, a possible decline in genuine literacy among educated people. The following account, a cover story in a national news-magazine, has been one of the most widely read of these. Although it has been angrily attacked by many teachers of English, it is valuable on two counts: it does not try to sell one analysis over another, and it points a finger of blame at other people besides "Johnny." (Copyright 1975 by Newsweek, Inc. All rights reserved. Reprinted by permission.)

If your children are attending college, the chances are that when they graduate they will be unable to write ordinary, expository English with any real degree of structure and lucidity. If they are in high school and planning to attend college, the chances are less than even that they will be able to write English at the minimal college level when they get there. If they are not planning to attend college, their skills in writing English may not even qualify them for secretarial or clerical work. And if they are attending elementary school, they are almost certainly not being given the kind of required reading material, much less writing instruction, that might make it possible for them eventually to write comprehensible English. Willy-nilly, the U.S. educational system is spawning a generation of semiliterates.

Nationwide, the statistics on literacy grow more appalling each year. In March, the Department of Health, Education and Welfare revealed the results of a special study that showed a steady erosion of reading skills among American students since 1965. Last month, the College Entrance Examination Board announced the formation of a panel of top educators who will study the twelve-year-long decline in Scholastic Aptitude Test scores; the fall-off has been especially sharp in verbal skills. Students' SAT scores this year showed the biggest drop in two decades. According to the National Assessment of Educational Progress, the majority of Americans of all ages tend to use only the simplest sentence structure and the most elementary vocabulary when they write. Among teen-agers, writing performance appears to be deteriorating at the most alarming rate of all. The NAEP's latest studies show that the essays of 13- and 17-year-olds are far more awkward, incoherent and disorganized than the efforts of those tested in 1969.

. . .

The cries of dismay sound [loud] in the halls of commerce, industry and the 3 professions, where writing is the basis for almost all formal business communication. Computer print-outs and the conference call may have altered forever the pace and nature of information exchanged, but transactions for the record—from interoffice memorandums to multinational corporate contracts—all depend on the precision and clarity of the written word.

Increasingly, however, officials at graduate schools of law, business and 4 journalism report gloomily that the products of even the best colleges have failed to master the skills of effective written communication so crucial to their fields. At Harvard, one economics instructor has been so disturbed at the inability of his students to write clearly that he now offers his own services to try to teach freshmen how to write. Businessmen seeking secretaries who can spell and punctuate or junior executives who can produce intelligible written reports complain that college graduates no longer fill the bill. "Errors we once found commonly in applications from high school graduates are now cropping up in forms from people with four-year college degrees," says a personnel official for the Bank of America. Even the Civil Service Commission, the Federal government's largest employer, has recently doubled its in-house writing programs in order to develop adequate civil servants.

The colleges and universities complain that many of the most intelligent 5 freshmen, in some ways more articulate and sophisticated than ever before, are seriously deficient when it comes to organizing their thoughts on paper. By the time they reach college, the professors complain, it is almost too late to help them. The breakdown in writing has been in the making for years, they say, and the causes for it range from inadequate grounding in the basics of syntax, structure and style to the popularity of secondary-school curriculums that no longer require the wide range of reading a student must have if he is to learn to write clearly.

There is no question in the minds of educators that a student who cannot 6 read with true comprehension will never learn to write well. "Writing is, after all, book-talk," says Dr. Ramon Veal, associate professor of language education at the University of Georgia's College of Education. "You learn book-talk only by reading." But as the standard tests suggest, students' reading ability is declining—and the effects of this erosion are readily apparent. For example, when the Association of American Publishers prepared a pamphlet to help college freshmen get the most from their textbooks, they found that its "readability level"—calculated for twelfth-grade skills—was far too high for students entering college. The pamphlet had to be rewritten at the ninth-grade level.

. . .

. . . [A] panel of English teachers and scholars from across the country 7 suggests that [students] . . . have been strongly influenced by the simplistic spoken style of television. E. B. White, essayist emeritus of *The New Yorker*, puts it this way: "Short of throwing away all the television sets, I really don't know what we can do about writing." No one has yet produced a thorough study of the effect of TV on a generation of students raised in its glare, but on at least two points most language experts agree: time spent watching television is time that might otherwise be devoted to reading; and the passiveness of the viewing—"letting the television just sink into one's environment," in the words of Barzun—seems to have a markedly bad effect on a child's active pursuit of written skills. "The TV keeps children entertained," complains Albert Tillman, director of a writing clinic at the University of Illinois. "It does not demand that they take active part in their learning."

Even the effects of television might be counteracted if students were required 8 to learn the language in the classroom. There, however, the past decade has produced a number of changes that in some school systems have all but terminated the teaching of the written language. Overcrowded classrooms and increased workloads have led many teachers to give up assigning essays and to rely, instead, on short-answer exercises that are easier to mark. As a result, many students now graduate from high school without ever having had any real practice in writing.

The 1960s also brought a subtle shift of educational philosophy away from 9 the teaching of expository writing. Many teachers began to emphasize "creativity" in the English classrooms and expanded their curriculums to allow students to work with contemporary media of communication such as film, videotape and photography. In the process, charges Dorothy Matthews, director of undergraduate English at Illinois, they often shortchanged instruction in the written language. "Things have never been good, but the situation is getting a lot worse," she complains. "What really disturbs us is the students' inability to organize their thoughts clearly." An essay by one of Matthews's Illinois freshmen stands as guileless testimony to the problem: "It's obvious in our modern world of today theirs a lot of impreciseness in expressing thoughts we have."

Even where writing still is taught, the creative school discourages insistence 10 on grammar, structure and style. Many teachers seem to believe that rules stifle spontaneity. Dr. Eliott Anderson, professor of English at Northwestern University, reports that many high-school teachers have simply stopped correcting poor grammar and sloppy construction, and he is inclined to think that these creative teachers have subverted their own goals. "You don't get very interesting creative results," he notes, "from students who can't use the language as a tool in the first place."

In the opinion of many language experts, another major villain is the school 11 of "structural linguistics." Writing is far less important than speech, the structural linguists proclaim, because only about 4 per cent of the world's languages have a written form; they believe that there are no real standards for any language, apart from the way it is commonly spoken. Philologist Pei traces the predominance of this school to the 1961 publication of Webster's Third International Dictionary, the first English dictionary that did not give preference to the way the language is used by its best-educated writers. Since then, he suggests, teachers in the classrooms have come increasingly under the sway of the structural-linguistic dogma: that the spoken idiom is superior to the written, and that there is no real need for students to study the rules of their language at all. "If you will scoff at language study," asks Pei, "how, save in terms of language, will you scoff?"

The pervasive influence of the structural linguists, coupled with the political 12 activism of the past decade, has led many teachers to take the view that standard English is just a "prestige" dialect among many others, and that insistence on its predominance constitutes an act of repression by the white middle class. Last year, after a bitter dispute within its own ranks, the Conference on College composition of the National Council of Teachers of English adopted an extraordinary policy statement embodying that philosophy. Entitled ["Students' Rights to Their Own Language,"] the document is more a political tract than a set of educational precepts. "Linguistic snobbery was tacitly encouraged by a slavish reliance on rules," it argues, "and these attitudes had consequences far beyond the realm of language. People from different language and ethnic backgrounds were denied social privileges, legal rights and economic opportunity, and their inability to manipulate the dialect used by the privileged group was used as an excuse for this denial."

The supporters of this argument reject the notion that public education is 13 designed to help those who do not use standard English to survive in a society that does. "We tend to exaggerate the need for standard English," insists Elisabeth McPherson, an English teacher at a St. Louis community college who helped draft the declaration. "You don't need much standard English skill for most jobs in this country." True enough. But won't students, denied the opportunity to master standard English because their teachers refuse to teach it, also lose the chance at higher-ranking jobs where standard English does prevail? McPherson, who calls herself "idealistic," replies that "the important thing is that people find themselves through their own language."

But, "prestige dialect" or not, standard English is in fact the language of 14 American law, politics, commerce and the vast bulk of American literature—and the traditionalists argue that to deny children access to it is in itself a pernicious form of oppression. They also emphasize that the new attempt to stress the language as it is spoken rather than as it is written has significance far beyond the basics of jobs or social mobility. "Learning to write is the hardest, most important thing any child does," says Dr. Carlos Baker, chairman of the English department at Princeton University and author of a best-selling biography of Ernest Hemingway. "Learning to write is learning to think."

Baker and like-minded colleagues stress that setting down thoughts in writing 15 forces students to examine the actual meaning of their words and the logic—or the lack of it—that leads from one statement to another. "You just don't know anything unless you can write it," says semanticist S. I. Hayakawa. "Sure, you can argue things in your head and bring them out at cocktail parties, but in order to argue anything thoroughly, you must be able to write it down on paper."

· · ·

Shakespeare	Standard English	Dialect
Alas! Poor Yorick. I knew him, Horatio; a fellow of infinite jest of most excellent fancy; he hath borne me on his back a thousand times; and now, how abhorred in my imagination it is!	Poor Yorick! I really knew him, Horatio—a man of great good humor, of fantastic imagination; he helped me through many hard times, and I feel just terrible about this.	My man Yorick. We was real tight, Horatio. I mean, the dude be crazy but he saved my ass many times. What you think, man? It really took me on out.

Educators agree that it is absolutely essential to make students write. "That's 16 the only way they learn," says Eunice Sims, coordinator of English for the Atlanta school system. "Let them write about whatever interests them and teach from that. You can always move a student from essays on street fighting to essays on Shelley." Sims thinks that even in overcrowded classrooms where teachers cannot possibly analyze every single paper, the students still should write as often as possible. "If a teacher reads every fifth paper a child writes, he or she knows pretty well how the student's doing."

Most of the experts, in fact, applaud the modern notion that grammar and 17 syntax are most successfully taught through a child's own writing, not by handing him a set of abstract rules and expecting him to conform once he has learned them by rote. "The main principle is to get a student deeply involved in the materials of his past and memory and have him write about them," says James Dickey, resident poet at the University of South Carolina. "Then the teacher must become a kind of coach. In football, if someone is slow of foot the coach makes him do wind sprints. In writing, if a student is weak on how the language is put together I have him get an elementary grammar book and *exercise*."

Despite the laudable coaching efforts of some individual teachers, however, 18 very little improvement in the writing skills of American students is likely unless the educational establishment recaptures the earlier conviction that the written language is important. . . .

The spoken word, while adding indisputable richness and variety to the 19 language as a whole, is by its very nature ephemeral. The written language remains the only effective vehicle for transmitting and debating a culture's ideas, values and goals. "Every lover of the language knows that its glory resides in the recurring infusions of new elements . . . and that change is constant, continual, and will never cease," wrote Lincoln Barnett in his classic work "The Treasure of Our Tongue." "But the written word is the brake on the spoken word. The written word is the link between the past and the future."

The point is that there have to be some fixed rules, however tedious, if the 20 codes of human communication are to remain decipherable. If the written language is placed at the mercy of every new colloquialism and if every fresh dialect demands and gets equal sway, then we will soon find ourselves back in Babel. In America today, as in the never never world Alice discovered on her trip through the looking-glass, there are too many people intent on being masters of their language and too few willing to be its servants.

> "There's glory for you!" 21
> "I don't know what you mean by 'glory'," Alice said.
> Humpty Dumpty smiled contemptuously. "Of course you don't—till I tell you. I meant 'there's a nice knock-down argument for you'!"
> "But 'glory' doesn't mean 'a nice knock-down argument'," Alice objected.
> "When I use a word," Humpty Dumpty said in rather a scornful tone, "it means just what I choose it to mean, neither more nor less."
> "The question is," said Alice, "whether you can make words mean so many different things."
> "The question is," said Humpty Dumpty, "which is to be Master —that's all."

DISCUSSION QUESTIONS

1. What are some of the principal reasons given why Johnny can't write? Which does the article think is most important? Which do you think? What has been left out?

2. Does it change your perspective on this article to know that the now defunct *Look* magazine published an article in 1961 also titled "Why Johnny Can't Write"?

3. One reason for growing concern over students' inability to write is the falling scores on standardized tests such as the Scholastic Aptitude Test (SAT) over the last few years. Do you remember taking such tests? Do you feel they were a good measure of your ability to write? Why or why not?

4. Many authorities feel that today's students are limited by the kind of language spoken on television. How do you feel? Is television bad? What do you think of Barzun's statement (paragraph 7) that the "passiveness" of TV viewing discourages children from taking an active part in their learning?

5. The article says that crowded classrooms and increased workloads have led many teachers to give up assigning essays and rely on short-answer exercises instead. Was this true of your experience in high school? How much essay writing did you actually have to do? Do you think you learn as much from short answer exercises as from essays? Why or why not?

6. In paragraph 9, the article implies that the educational establishment no longer considers the written language important. How important do you think it is? Is it "relevant"? Or will the letter be replaced by the telephone?

7. In paragraph 10, the article says there are many teachers who feel that insistence on rules of grammar and style stifle spontaneity and creativity. It also quotes Dr. Anderson, an opponent of this viewpoint, who says, "You don't get very interesting creative results from students who can't use language as a tool in the first place." Which opinion do you agree with? Why?

8. The article quotes Elisabeth McPherson (paragraph 13), one of the people who helped draft the CCCC Language Statement that follows, as saying that "the important thing is that people find themselves through their own language." What do you think she means by this?

9. Do you agree with Hayakawa that "you just don't know anything unless you can write it"? Why or why not?

10. What do you think of the suggestion that a student should write as often as possible even if the teacher cannot read every paper the student writes? Do you think that writing without a teacher's guidance or criticism is helpful? Why or why not?

COMMITTEE OF THE CCCC LANGUAGE STATEMENT[1]
Students' Right to Their Own Language

Here, somewhat abridged, is the document described in paragraph 12 of "Why Johnny Can't Write." The product of several years of study, it was presented to the CCCC convention in Anaheim, California, in April 1974, where it passed by a vote of 79 to 20.

Although the statement has been distributed in the two college-level journals of the National Council of Teachers of English, *College Composition and Communication* and *College English*, there is no way of knowing just how many English instructors have read it or are heeding it. Among those who have read it, opinion remains hotly divided.

The committee which wrote the statement was headed by the late Dr. Melvin A. Butler of Southern University and included twelve members from diverse large universities and small colleges.

American schools and colleges have, in the last decade, been forced to take a   1
stand on a basic educational question: what should the schools do about the language habits of students who come from a wide variety of social, economic, and cultural backgrounds? . . . Should the schools try to uphold language variety, or to modify it, or to eradicate it?

· · ·

Before these questions can be responsibly answered, English teachers at all   2
levels, from kindergarten through college, must uncover and examine some of the assumptions on which our teaching has rested. Many of us have taught as

---

[1]CCCC stands for Conference on College Composition and Communication, the division of the National Council of Teachers of English most concerned with freshman composition.

though there existed somewhere a single American "standard English" which could be isolated, identified, and accurately defined. We need to know whether "standard English" is or is not in some sense a myth. We have ignored, many of us, the distinction between speech and writing and have taught the language as though the *talk* in any region, even the talk of speakers with prestige and power, were identical to edited *written* English.

We have also taught, many of us, as though the "English of educated speak-   3
ers," the language used by those in power in the community, had an inherent advantage over other dialects as a means of expressing thought or emotion, conveying information, or analyzing concepts. We need to discover whether our attitudes toward "educated English" are based on some inherent superiority of the dialect itself or on the social prestige of those who use it. We need to ask ourselves whether our rejection of students who do not adopt the dialect most familiar to us is based on any real merit in our dialect or whether we are actually rejecting the students themselves, rejecting them because of their racial, social, and cultural origins.

· · ·

. . . Students who come from backgrounds where the prestigious variety of   4
English is the normal medium of communication have built-in advantages that enable them to succeed, often in spite of and not because of their schoolroom training in "grammar." They sit at the head of the class, are accepted at "exclusive" schools, and are later rewarded with positions in the business and social world. Students whose nurture and experience give them a different dialect are usually denied these rewards. As English teachers, we are responsible for what our teaching does to the self-image and the self-esteem of our students. We must decide what elements of our discipline are really important to us, whether we want to share with our students the richness of all varieties of language, encourage linguistic virtuosity, and say with Langston Hughes:

I play it cool and dig all jive
That's the reason I stay alive
My motto as I live and learn
Is to dig and be dug in return.

It was with these concerns in mind that the Executive Committee of the   5
Conference on College Composition and Communication, in 1972, passed the following resolution:

We affirm the students' right to their own patterns and varieties of language—the dialects of their nurture or whatever dialects in which they find their own identity and style. Language scholars long ago denied that the myth of a standard American dialect has any validity. The claim that any one dialect is unacceptable amounts to an attempt of one social group to exert its dominance over another. Such a claim leads to false advice for speakers and writers, and immoral advice for humans. A nation proud of its diverse heritage and its cultural and racial variety will preserve its heritage of dialects. We affirm strongly that teachers must have the experiences and training that will enable them to respect diversity and uphold the right of students to their own language.

· · ·

In a specific setting, because of historical and other factors, certain dialects ₆ may be endowed with more prestige than others. Such dialects are sometimes called "standard" or "consensus" dialects. These designations of prestige are not inherent in the dialect itself, but are *externally imposed*, and the prestige of a dialect shifts as the power relationships of the speakers shift.

. . .

. . . Dialects are all equally serviceable in logic and metaphor. ₇

Perhaps the most serious difficulty facing "non-standard" dialect speakers in ₈ developing writing ability derives from their exaggerated concern for the *least* serious aspects of writing. If we can convince our students that spelling, punctuation, and usage are less important than content, we have removed a major obstacle in their developing the ability to write. Examples of student writing are useful for illustrating this point. In every composition class there are examples of writing which is clear and vigorous despite the use of non-standard forms (at least as described by the handbook)—and there are certainly many examples of limp, vapid writing in "standard dialect." Comparing the writing allows the students to see for themselves that dialect seldom obscures clear, forceful writing. . . .

. . . We do not condone ill-organized, imprecise, undefined, inappropriate ₉ writing in any dialect but we are especially distressed to find sloppy writing approved so long as it appears with finicky correctness in "school standard" while vigorous and thoughtful statements in less prestigious dialects are condemned.

. . .

English teachers should be concerned with the employability as well as the ₁₀ linguistic performance of their students. Students rightly want marketable skills that will facilitate their entry into the world of work. Unfortunately, many employers have narrowly conceived notions of the relationship between linguistic performance and job competence. Many employers expect a person whom they consider for employment to speak whatever variety of American English the employers speak, or believe they speak. Consequently, many speakers of divergent dialects are denied opportunities that are readily available to other applicants whose dialects more nearly approximate the speech of the employer. But a plumber who can sweat a joint can be forgiven confusion between "set" and "sat." In the same way, it is more important that a computer programmer be fluent in Fortran than in EAE. Many jobs that are normally desirable—that are viewed as ways of entering the American middle class—are undoubtedly closed to some speakers of some non-standard dialects, while some of the same jobs are seldom closed to white speakers of non-standard dialects.

Spoken dialect makes little difference in the performance of many jobs, and ₁₁ the failure of employers to hire blacks, Chicanos, or other ethnic minorities is often simply racial or cultural prejudice. . . .

. . . English teachers who feel they are bound to accommodate the linguistic ₁₂ prejudices of current employers perpetuate a system that is unfair to both students who have job skills and to the employers who need them.

. . .

DISCUSSION QUESTIONS

1. Paragraph 12 of "Why Johnny Can't Write" described this statement as "extraordinary," and "more a political tract than a set of educational precepts." How valid, in your judgment, is this criticism? How would the CCCC Committee respond to Sheils' comment?

2. Although the vote to adopt the language statement was lopsided, 79 to 20, argument over its merits have been bitter. Why does the argument over the statement engage people's emotions? If you were attending the session in which it was discussed, would you have voted for it or against it? Explain.

3. Robert C. Pooley, an authority on usage generally favorable to liberalizing standards of "correctness," has said that if the CCCC Language Statement were taken literally no one would ever again teach English usage. What is left for an English teacher to talk about? What do you see as the point of English classes, anyway?

4. How many jobs can you think of where a knowledge of Edited Standard English is not necessary? Are you thinking of such a job or profession right now? What other parts of your college education also prepare you for this job?

5. Do English programs exist to make people employable?

6. In a portion deleted from the CCCC statement, the following example sentence is given:

He had a pain in his neck, the kind you get when you've suffered a bore too long.

The sentence contains an unnecessary shift in person, an error condemned in almost any handbook of English as well as in "Why Johnny Can't Write." Is the sentence hard to understand? Does it imply a lack of grace on the part of its author?

7. How does the Doonesbury cartoon on this page present a commentary on the CCCC language statement? Which speaker is being satirized?

8. Professor Allen N. Smith of Salisbury State College in Maryland has argued that because each writer must write for an audience, no one has a right to his own language. What do you think about this statement? What rights do audiences have?

Copyright 1973, G. B. Trudeau/Distributed by Universal Press Syndicate.

9. Every day we see examples of dialect in print, usually to achieve a specific effect. For example, many of us have seen the bumper sticker "Mafia Staff Car: Keepa You Hands Off." In some parts of the country one often sees "West Virginia: We Ain't Fergittin.' " What would be lost if these were put in Edited Standard English? Would you expect a business letter from the people who produced these bumper stickers to be written in the same dialect?

10. Observe the language habits of people on television interview shows and news programs. How often do you hear what would be described as "mistakes" in a college English class? How many people speak what could be called dialect? Who are they?

J. MITCHELL MORSE
Riting Inglish Real Good

Published reaction to the CCCC Language Statement, both pro and con, began immediately and has continued over the years. J. Mitchell Morse, Professor of English at Temple University and a well-known critic of current trends in the teaching of English, has commented on the CCCC Language Statement several times. The briefest and pithiest of his commentaries is this one, which appeared not in a stuffy professional journal but in the pages of The New York Times. Professor Morse asks how far we can apply the rights the CCCC would allow students.

I see the hand writing on the wall. It reads, "In are times the responcable 1 writer must read the hand writeing on the wall so he can asses the human conditions." It reads, "The modren day literature has it's good merit's as well as it's bad one's but I don't think so." It reads, "Joyce was liveing symotanious to Kafka all though the did not aide each other in utilyzing the same standart of excellent like stream of conscience."

That is the written language of juniors and seniors majoring in English at 2 fully accredited four-year colleges and universities in all parts of the country. We English teachers exchange these things. But don't worry. The Council on College Composition and Communication, in an official policy statement entitled "Students' Right to Their Own Language," says that such "surface features" as spelling, grammar, punctuation and vocabulary have no effect on the "deep structure," "meaning" or "content" of a sentence, and therefore that we should not insist on accuracy in such matters lest we inhibit the students' "creativity and individuality."

"George Orwell makes me feel like I was desserted on some destitute island in   3
Politics and the English language. He points out the destruction of the language, is caused by people, attempting to decieve the writing and using bad speech pratices," says a student majoring in English.

Students have a right to their own language, says the Council.   4

"The victims screems for helping herself was effident thru all the allies   5
around 100 Murch Avenue as if the thick smoke billowing from a factorys exhaust pipe," says a student majoring in English.

Students have a right to their own language, says the Council.   6

The revolutionerys can not ignore the reactionery forces that threaten to   7
undue his work and propel his achievements into preexisting revolutionery conditions," says a student majoring in English.

Students have a right to their own language, says the Council.   8

"The blind and the death suffer unjustly because of there handicaped which   9
are considered as being dim witness and are felt to be in a class for the retarded even when there not," says a student majoring in English.

Students have a right to their own language, says the Council.   10

And this is the language of the Council: "Simply because 'Johnny can't read'   11
doesn't mean 'Johnny is immature' or 'Johnny can't think.' He may be bored. . . . If we can convince our students that spelling, punctuation, and usage are less important than content, we have removed a major obstacle in their developing the ability to write."

That is the hand writeing on the wall.   12

DISCUSSION QUESTIONS

1. What is Professor Morse trying to say here? What, according to him, is "the hand writeing on the wall"?

2. What is the tone of the article? Why do you think Professor Morse chose to present his views this way?

3. What is wrong with the writing in paragraph 1? What does Professor Morse seem to object to most—what the students are trying to express, or the way they express it? Or both? Explain.

4. What would the CCCC Committee think about the writing in paragraph 1? What criteria would they use for judgment?

5. Do the errors in paragraphs 1, 3, 5, 7, and 9 interfere with what the authors were trying to communicate? Do the errors bother you? Why or why not?

6. Do you believe very many students write this way? Are Professor Morse's examples of student writing representative of the writing in your school or in your class?

ELIZABETH WOOTEN COWAN
What Makes Freshman English Such a Hard Course?

All of us, teachers and students, would like to be "better writers." All philosophies of teaching composition seek to improve student writing in some manner. No one, not the most cynical teacher or the least motivated students, ever speaks against "good writing." Still, the goal seems to be beyond the reach of an increasing number of us. Perhaps the question to be asked is, What is "good writing" anyway? How many things do we have to do when we write? Are there a large number of steps—and do we have to take them all at the same time?

In the following essay, written for teachers of freshman composition, Elizabeth Wooten Cowan reviews all the ways she was told to write as she went from grade school through college. Part of the difficulty may be that students are trying to write in too many ways at the same time.

. . . Freshman English is a course in frustration. It often poses more philo-   1
sophical and logistical problems for a department than any other area of the curriculum. It is one of the costliest things we do; worrying about it, trying to re-do it, starting over, under, back and beyond are as perennial as wild onions on the lawn. Although I've spent most of my teaching career thinking about the purpose and the execution of the course, for the past three months, since the enormous surge of national interest in the subject, I have been plagued by the question—what makes this such a hard course? Where does the difficulty lie? Is there anything that could be done, thought, or discovered that would make life easier and success surer for the thousands of dedicated, strained teachers and students of freshman composition? . . .

Here is my hypothesis: 2

In freshman English, the term "good writing" has so many meanings that   3
teachers and students are defeated by the very definition of the term.

If you will allow me to indulge in a piece of personal narrative about my own   4
writing experiences, I will illustrate the changes I see the meaning of the term
writing going through and the ambiguity in the use of that term when a teacher
says, "You must do good writing." . . .

The first experience I can remember with writing was in pre-school when my   5
mother gave me a scrap of paper and a pencil to keep me quiet during my daddy's
long-winded sermons. With what diligence did I scrunch down by the side of the
bench and draw marks which usually were "letters" to important people like
Grandmother Margie or Aunt Blanche. My writing was "good" if I just made
marks on the paper, good enough to get put into envelopes sent off to people I
loved.

Then came first grade. *Writing* then became something else—learning to draw letters correctly from patterns on the blackboard. To learn to write was to learn a brand new skill, how to copy a letter in approximately the same shape every time. There was not much room for experimentation here; *b* and *d* always had the loops on the side they did regardless of what I thought or wished. But getting it right meant I was maturing, learning what big people knew—and there's not much else more important to a six year old. When I got an "A" in writing on my report card that year it was because I could finally print correctly all my letters in the correct shape and in uniform size.

Then there was the second grade where we learned to do cursive writing. Instead of drawing the letters this year, we learned to "write" them. We still had charts on the board to go by, and many penmanship drills. In this grade we discovered that good writing was not just to make the letters right but to hook them together and make them legible and pretty.We would practice our writing by copying the spelling words from the board, writing them 5 or 10 times each (15 if the class had been bad). So, an "A" in writing that year meant that I could hook my letters together, give them the shape they needed for that hooking, and make them attractive.

After these two years of much concentration on learning the literal art of making letters and forming words, I don't remember much about writing per se for the rest of my elementary school years. In those middle years, writing wasn't important in itself; it, for the most part, helped me study other things—to answer geography questions, write book reports, do extra credit encyclopedia assignments.

It was during these middle years, however, that my teachers introduced two activities which they believed would in the future be directly related to my ability to do good writing: learning ancillary grammatical facts about words and learning an elementary pattern of organization of sentences. We began in the third grade to learn the parts of speech and the elements of the sentence, and by the fourth we were taking the *Weekly Reader* tests to check our ability to find topic sentences and main ideas. The teachers, however, saw this learning in a sequence which alleviated our having to know it all at once. There was a limit. I remember wanting to know in the fifth grade where to put the prepositional phrase when we were diagramming sentences, and Mrs. Brock said for me not to worry—I wasn't supposed to know that until next year. What a relief!

These elementary grades were spent learning the "first time things"—things in graduated levels of difficulty about the language we spoke and wrote. The space on the report card became English or language arts, and writing as a subject took a back seat to the other things we were busy learning—the rules of traditional grammar, the names of the parts of speech, things our teachers felt we had to know for the future, things they considered basic to education.

It was in the eighth grade that I learned a new function for writing (you may have learned about it much earlier and in conjunction with other stages), and that was to imagine. I don't think I will ever forget Marjorie McKensie, who gave us an assignment—in civics of all classes—to go to any country we wanted to in our heads and to write her about our trip. What excitement. I "went" to Rio de

Janeiro, and I remember how the writing went on page after page. I probably pretended a longer trip than she could conceivably need or desire, but I was enthralled with using my imagination and turning those dreamings into words which I could read again and again. We didn't exercise this use of writing much in English class those junior high school years, which may be the reason the civics creative writing assignment stands out so delightfully in my mind. If ever so briefly, I had realized a new use for writing words.

Sometime in high school writing became a subject again—this time to learn 12 to write themes. The concentration was placed on how to organize your thoughts, how to practice different approaches (like doing a comparison/contrast paper or a persuasive essay or a classification paragraph). And here writing began to be measured on something other than my grasping the "how to" of the process—I now was also evaluated on how well I thought. Getting an "A" in writing now was not so easy; you didn't have just to do what you did in grade school—get the conventional signs and symbols right—you also had to think

originally and impressively, in the teacher's opinion. The term *good writing* now meant it had to look right, sound right, follow the right form, *and* express a significant, well-stated idea.

Here in this stage the relation seen by my teachers between learning the parts 13 of speech in middle school and being able to write well later became apparent. When the corrections on the paper read "Don't split the infinitive," a lucky remembrance of what an infinitive was made the revision process much quicker. If you couldn't remember, you had double duty to pull—write the rule out of the grammar book and correct the paper. And you wished then if you had never wished it before that you had paid a little better attention to those earlier lessons.

Finally, there came one last purpose that writing had to serve in my pre- 14 college schooling, and that was to illustrate that I understood literature. We began learning about irony and point of view and characterization. In this stage the writing had to be correct and have an idea, and the idea had to show that I could interpret stories and poems. It was just a kind of introduction, a kind of glimpse into the future which conveyed to me as a twelfth grader that "good writing" at its best was all the things it had been before *and* on the subject of literature. It was, then, in the high school grades that the various components of what my teachers over the years considered to be good writing began to come together. Yet I was still seen in a "just learning" light and was not graded against a standard that demanded that I know previously how to do the work.

I think I can now draw for you the continuum I see on the multiple meanings 15 of the term, *good writing*, the various, often unconnected things the words mean at different stages in our learning.

| TO WRITE | | | | | | | |
means							
to draw letters	to hook letters	to learn terms	to imagine	to see structure	to organize	to have ideas	to know literature

I propose that perhaps the greatest difficulty in freshman English is that this is 16 the first time in the students' education that they are expected to perform *all* the meanings of *good writing* initially, simultaneously, and never failingly. . . .

• • •

The difficulty in freshman English really has little to do with how strongly 17 one believes that a good writer must be able to perform all these meanings of the term at random and at all times. Believing this firmly and striving for it assiduously seem only to affect how bad one feels when it's not accomplished. I would like to ask if it is fair for the freshman English course to bear all the weight of the learning or the lack of learning of the multiple meanings of "good writing" down through the years? No wonder college teachers turn to the high schools and say, "What have you been doing?" who turn to the elementary schools and say, "What's wrong with you?" who turn to the television and say, "You devil, you."

Just another exercise in futility. So long as we see good writing possible only if the student can leap from one meaning of the term to another in a single bound and pull together a performance of all the meanings assigned in the educational process, there will be no way that a one-year course in freshman English can be successful. I would have us ask—*who* determined that X comes before Y in the process of good writing? Is there possibly a new space on the continuum—a brand new space—one which is not merely a telescoping of the spaces already there? . . . We have the right as a discipline to take a new look at what produces good writing—even at a definition of good writing—and see if, in truth, there is another space on the continuum, an additional meaning of good writing, particularly taking a good look at the things we've been told a student must do *before* she or he can write.

We're assured of fifty more years like the last and hundreds of textbooks like 18 the past, assured of frustrations and signs and strivings and failings, as long as we accept unchallenged the current meanings of "good writing" and the previous methods of achieving those meanings. Fritz Perls in one of his books tells about an expert swordsman. This man was so skillful with his sword that when he went out into the rain he didn't even need an umbrella. He could with the speed of light and the dexterity of an eagle hit every raindrop with the tip of his sword before the raindrop hit his head. We're trying to achieve this in freshman English—and we're not expert swordsmen. It's no wonder we are tired.

DISCUSSION QUESTIONS

1. How does your experience in different English classes throughout grade school and high school compare with Cowan's? Did your teachers put the same kind of demands on you?

2. Have your instructors had as many different definitions of "to write"? Have those different definitions been presented simultaneously?

3. Are most of these pressures on your mind as you try to write?

4. Elsewhere Cowan has described Freshman English—meaning freshman composition—as a headache without remedy. Do you and your fellow students consider it more of a headache than, say, a freshman course in mathematics, a laboratory science, or a foreign language?

5. Of the eight meanings of "to write" discussed in the essay (and spelled out after paragraph 15), which do you feel is most important? Which is least important?

6. Are there other meanings of "to write" that Cowan has not included?

7. Can one be a "good writer" while ignoring any of these definitions of "to write"?

8. Which aspect of writing is the most difficult to master? Either now, in this class, or in the long run of your career?

Student Essay
English Classes and Me

Although I have taken English every year I have been in school, it was never   1
one of my most outstanding courses, either good or bad. Writing has never been
a special problem for me, but I am not sure how much my different teachers
have to do with that. If I had to sum up what my past twelve years taking English
courses have been like I am afraid I would have to say that although I was kept
busy all the time I was never taught very much substantial or memorable.

Most of the grade school years are a blur now, although that is not necessarily   2
the fault of the different schools I attended. As my father was a serviceman, we
moved around the world while I was growing up. In the eight years of grade
school I was a student in four different states as well as West Germany. Each
year, it seemed, my new teacher would contradict much of what I had learned
the previous year. One wanted us to pay a penny fine for saying "guy" or "ain't,"
and another would use "guy" or "ain't" in class. I can't recall writing many
papers, but I do recall writing exercises on the tear-out sheets of workbooks.
Sometimes we would copy these exercises on the board. Once, in Oklahoma, the
whole class copied an exercise on the differences between "brothers-in-law" and
"brother-in-*law*'s"; it must have been worthwhile, because I will remember it
forever.

Of the few papers I had to write in grade school, at least two were the   3
"Peanuts" classic, "What I Did on My Summer Vacation." Our summer vaca-
tions were usually exciting, but I can't remember just why I was supposed to write
about them. Somehow spelling always seemed like the most important part. One
year this was particularly difficult as I was trying to recall the spellings of different
German cities, *Wiesbaden, Würzburg*, etc., and my teacher at Kincheloe Air
Force had not heard of them.

One advantage of moving every twenty months or so was that I had to keep   4
writing letters. From the third grade on I wrote at least two a week, first to my
grandparents, and later to the different friends I was always leaving behind. I
have been able to stick with this over the years so that two of my old girlfriends,
whom I know mostly by mail, are really two of my best friends. Later, I tried
keeping a journal in a spiral notebook several times, but I could never stick with
it. I was afraid of saying anything too secretive in it, and I was not sure I wanted
to spend time writing something no one was going to read. But if I had all my old
letters stapled together, they would make a fairly fat journal.

When I finished grade school, my parents separated and my mother and I   5
settled with my grandparents here. The yearly change in what English was
supposed to be continued, however. In my freshman year of high school I had
the infamous Miss Claypool, who told us all what bad writers we all were. This
was the only course I ever had, until now, that was mostly devoted to composition. By her standards I must have been poor, because she gave me mostly C's
and D's. She took off one grade for every comma mistake or usage mistake, such

as "different than" for "different from." She had us writing every week, and I hated it: "Who would we nominate as American of the Year?" or "Pro and con: The dress code is in the interest of all students." Perhaps Miss Claypool was a success; I'll never write "different than" again, although I am still not sure about the differences between "lay" and "lie."

Sophomore year was entirely different, first, because it was a literature 6 course, but more, second, because of Larry Benson, the teacher. The differences between the names of the two teachers tells it all: "Miss" Claypool and "Larry" Benson. Larry wore a Levi leisure suit, although sometimes with a tie, as the principal commanded. He had us sit in a circle and always called us by our first names. He had us read what everyone else read, *The Merchant of Venice* and *The Separate Peace*, but he never gave us actual papers to write. Instead we kept journals of our impressions in reading. His comments on the journals always seemed to say that we were doing everything right, which certainly made writing less of a bind. He stayed only another year at the high school. I never knew for sure why he left, but everyone said he was fired.

Eleventh and twelfth grade English classes were both surveys of literature, 7 first American and then British. I did not have to write many papers either year. And in both years the teachers seemed more interested in what I had to say about Washington Irving or Charlotte Brontë than about the way I said it. I did not have to write a term paper either year, but, then again, I did have to write one in history—on the causes of the Industrial Revolution. I did, however, write essay exams in English.

My best experience in learning how to write in high school came in working 8 on our student newspaper. I was extremely nervous about writing for the newspaper at first, and many of my news stories came out in a kind of garbled language. But no teacher slapped me down for this. Instead, I found out what my problems were from other kids on the newspaper staff or by seeing my writing in print. Unfortunately, I could not stick with this for more than a year and a half as I had to start working in the middle of my junior year.

Taking Freshman Composition now after twelve years of English courses 9 feels like starting all over again in the same place. I have spoken English all my life, even when I lived in Germany, and I feel I can handle it pretty well, in most instances. But, then again, I suppose I need some more work in organization for the other classes I am going to be taking between now and law school.

RHETORICAL ANALYSIS

1. What aspects of this essay mark it as a student's instead of a professional writer's? Be specific: voice, tone, vocabulary, sentence length, etc.
2. Would the paper be more or less effective if it had been written in a more professional way?
3. Although this paper does not present an argument, it does include one

sentence that summarizes the whole paper, much like a "thesis" sentence. Which sentence is that? Do you think it is effectively placed?

4. Look at the second sentence in paragraph 2, beginning "As my father . . ." Is it constructed as most students would write it? Is it better this way? Or could it be improved?

5. What did the author gain by being specific about the places where she lived and attended school?

6. What are the differences between "lay" and "lie"? (See paragraph 5.)

POINTS OF DEPARTURE

There is much more to be said about some of the questions raised in this chapter, and, indeed, it *has* been said and published. Rather than swell the pages of this book with additional full essays on the subject, the editors decided to give you selected points of view from a variety of authors. The instructor and student may decide to read all of them, none of them, or some of them. We call them "points of departure" because they raise points you may want to develop or challenge. If they help you to get started, they have served their purpose.

A

One day a college student stopped a professor in the hall and said, "I have this terrible instructor who says I can't write. Therefore I shouldn't teach English. He really grinds me. In another class I've been reading James Joyce, so I wrote this little comment on the instructor in Joyce's style. Do you think I should submit it to *The Review?*"

The professor looked at the lines she had written about her instructor:

> . . . the stridents in his glass lisdyke him immersely. Day each that we tumble into the glass he sez to mee, "Eets too badly that you someday fright preach Engfish."

and he knew the girl had found a name for the phony, pretentious language of the schools—Engfish.

Most English teachers have been trained to correct students' writing, not to read it; so they put down those bloody correction marks in the margins. When the students see them, they think they mean the teacher doesn't care what students write, only how they punctuate and spell. So they give him Engfish. He calls the assignments by their traditional name—*themes*. The students know theme writers seldom put down anything that counts for them. No one outside school ever writes anything called *themes*. Apparently they are teacher's exercises, not really a kind of communication. On the first assignment in a college class a student begins his theme like this:

I went downtown for the first time. When I got there I was completely astonished by the hustle and the bustle that was going on. My first impression of the downtown area was quite impressive.

Beautiful Engfish. The writer said not simply that he was astonished, but 4 completely astonished, as if the word *astonished* had no force of its own. The student reported (*pretended* would be a truer word) to have observed hustle and bustle, and then explained in true Engfish that the hustle and bustle was going on. He managed to work in the academic word *area*, and finished by saying the impression was impressive.

Ken Macrorie, "Engfish," from *Telling Writing*

B

A Force

Engfish professors call students who write "He don't" or "We was" illiterate. 1 Frequently black students write that dialect of American-English. The professors call it *an error*.

Few black students major in English or take courses in literature or writing. 2 They're not prepared for them. They don't know Engfish.

Sensitivity to Language

For decades white Americans have livened their language by introducing into 3 it expressions from the streets and nightspots of Harlem, part of the dialect of supposedly ill-educated black Americans.

The Purpose of Engfish

The grade school student is told by his teacher that he must learn engfish 4 because the high school teacher will expect mastery of it. The high school student is told by his teacher that he must learn it because the college professor will expect mastery of it. The college undergraduate is told by his professor that he must learn it so he can go to graduate school and write his Ph.D. thesis in it.

Almost no one reads Ph.D. theses. 5

Ken Macrorie, from *Uptaught*

C

In defending standard English and the teaching of standard English, I am 1 certainly not . . . suggesting that we should just go on doing what we have been doing. On the contrary, I would argue that the teaching of standard English, though it must not be abandoned, should be radically overhauled. If American students had ever been exposed to the facts about language and varieties of language there might never in my opinion, have been any problem. We should, as responsible professionals, thus insist that no English teacher be turned loose in the classroom until he has mastered at least the fundamentals of social and regional dialectology. Such a teacher will know better than to try to sell his students a single brand of English as the one and only English for all times and places. He will deal with the many dialects of the language, and the natural shifting of styles within dialects, as the typical situation it is. And he will waste no time in class running down nonstandard forms or making transparently fraudulent claims for the natural superiority of the standard dialect. He will, however, continue to teach it and, given a rational description of the facts, his students may in turn come to understand the true function and value of standard English in our society.

Standard English is essentially a complex set of rules (albeit a loosely struc- 2 tured set), much like the rules of football or chess and, just as in these sports, abandoning the rules or stretching them too far can result in a total breakdown of the game in which nobody wins and everybody loses. That the rules of standard English are an arbitrary set intrinsically no better than those of nonstandard dialects in no way detracts from their immeasurable value as the agreed upon rules of the game. To some extent the drive for social justice depends on certain kinds of education, and teaching the facts about languages and dialects may help to dispel one kind of prejudice. But the schools must also continue to teach our students to read and write the standard language, not as the language of the rich and powerful but as the language of educated speakers everywhere.

David Eskey, "The Case for Standard English"

D

[The biloquialist (one who would force those speaking dialects to learn stand- 1 ard English as a second language), often asks,] "What else would you do?" It's all very well, he will concede, to expose linguistic prejudice as an instrument of repression and to work for social justice, though he himself may not be notably active in either cause; but in the meantime, he asks, what will become of students who don't learn standard English? In the foreseeable future there will always be distinctions in speech between leaders and followers, between workers at different jobs, residents of different areas. And in a healthy society there would be no great harm in that. Millions of people in this country today do not speak standard English, and millions of them, if they are white, have very good incomes. But in job-hunting in America, pigmentation is more important than pronunciation.

There is not, moreover, and there never has been, a serious proposal that 2 standard English should not be taught at all, if for no other reason than because its teaching is inevitable. Most teachers of English speak it (or try to speak it); most books are written in it (somnigraphy being sadly typical); and since every child, if it is possible, should learn to read, schoolchildren will see and hear standard English in the schools as they also see and hear it on TV. Inevitably their own linguistic competence will be affected.

The effect will be best if teachers consciously recognize the frustrations and contradictions which life in a sick world imposes on them. Because our ruling class is unfit to rule, our standard language lacks authority; and because our society has been corrupted by the profit-seeking of technology run wild, an honest teacher cannot exercise his normal function of transmitting to the young the knowledge and values of their elders. In fact, the time may come, and soon come, when an honest teacher can't keep his honesty and keep teaching. At that point, he must make his choice—and take the consequences. So long, however, as he stays in the classroom, he must do his imperfect best while recognizing its imperfection, and must find in that effort itself his escape from alienation.

James Sledd, "Doublespeak: Dialectology in the Service of Big Brother"

E

I find that I myself am permitting a relaxation of standards that I would never have tolerated while I was a professional teacher. One ought not to pass an essay that describes Shakespeare's Cressida as "kind of a C. T." or Ophelia as "going crazy because of her dad's being wiped out." On the other hand, why not? This is the new idiom, and it does not show any less literary perception than what some of my fellow students used to write: "Keats shows a sense of beauty here," or "The blank verse of Marlowe is quite good when he really has something to say." But once I countenance slanginess I am ready to admit imprecision. Soon I must give a pass mark to: "Lady Mackbet says she had a kid not in so many words but she says she remembers what it was like when a kid sucked her tit so I reckon she was a mother sometime and the kid must have died but we don't hear no more about it which is really careless of Shakesper because the real reason why McBeth and his wife are kind of restless and ambitious is because they did not have a baby that lived and perhaps this is all they really want and S. says notin about it." If this becomes a standard worthy of a bachelor's degree, what about the student who writes: "The weakly placed negatives in Dr. Faustus's penultimate line—'Ugly hell, gape not, come not, Lucifer'—may conceivably be taken as expressive of a desire, not implausible in a Renaissance scholar, to dare even the ultimate horrors for the sake of adding to his store of knowledge"?

Anthony Burgess, [a letter to] "My Dear Students"

F

Correctness is not logic, since all languages are largely illogical. English says, "I see him," as if sight were a positive act of will comparable to that in "I hit him." Yet all of us know enough optics to realize that, if there is any action involved, it starts with *him* and reaches and affects *me*. Languages which happen, like Eskimo, to avoid this particular illogicality fall into others as great.

The basis of correctness is not beauty inherent in the forms used. Beauty in linguistic forms is due to the associations they arouse. Such a form as "goil" is ugly only if the hearer happens to dislike Brooklyn. To realize the truth of this statement, one has only to consider variants where we have no such associations. If a child in the New Mexican pueblo of Santa Clara puts the sentence, "I am going to town," in the form *bupiyeummang*, the "ugly" pronunciation is immediately corrected to *bupijeummang*. The Tewa parents are not being merely arbitrary; they are objecting to an unacceptable dialect. I doubt if any English speaker can seriously maintain that he finds one Tewa form more beautiful than the other.

The basis of correctness is not history; such a belief would contradict the ₃ results of linguistic science. Further, the belief that older forms are better than newer can readily be reduced to an absurdity. If only old forms are right, then we do not speak English but bad Old English—or bad Indo-Hittite.

Equally certainly correctness is not the result of an authoritative ruling by an ₄ individual or a book. A neat example of this last view is the statement of a columnist who once said that 98 per cent of Americans mispronounced a given word, since they failed to follow dictionary recommendations. Actually such a statement demonstrates that 2 per cent of America mispronounces the word or that the dictionaries had better catch up on usage.

A final view once widely held is that anything which is impossible in Latin is ₅ incorrect in English. The view hardly needs denial, baleful as its lingering influence may be on the analysis of English grammar. At least, no one would now seriously maintain that "Oh, father!" is a vocative case, incapable of being split into two words.

Archibald A. Hill, "Correctness and Style in English Composition"

G

Never mind the statistics. Ask the students. They will tell you how badly they ₁ need help with their language. Last year at Yale, 185 students applied for 12 places in one small college seminar on expository writing—nothing fancy, just a course on how to write. This is typical of the students' desperate wish to be taught how to handle the fundamental medium in which we live.

What has happened? I believe that of all the institutions attacked in the past ₂ dozen years—governmental, legal, and educational—the one that suffered most was the institution of language itself, that massive, living system of signs that on the one hand limits us and, on the other hand, allows us to decide who we are. This institution—language—was perceived as being repressive. It was thought to be the agent of all other repressive codes—legal, political, and cultural. Language was the barrier that blocked—blocked access to pure feeling, blocked true communal experience of the kind that flowered at Woodstock, blocked the restoration of Eden.

Language was what was circumvented by drugs and music—those agents of ₃ higher states whose main virtue was that they were not verbal but visual or aural, the pure association of pure shape or sound unencumbered by words—which is to say by distinctions, which is to say by meaning. Language disassociated us from primitive impulses. It polluted us with ambiguity; it was not pure. Language impeded freedom.

The first shot in the revolution in 1964 was the Free Speech Movement. It 4 was intended not only to free speech from middle-class constraints about uttering obscenities, for instance. It was also intended to free us from the shackles of syntax, the racism of grammar, the elitism of style. All those corrupt and corrupting elements in American society, those signs that we had fallen from paradise, could be located in an aspect of language. The Free Speech Movement was where we first began to hear language mediated through the bull horn into the formulaic chant of a crowd.

This reductiveness would soon be extended to all kinds of systems that as- 5 serted differentness or pluralism as essential to their workings. But language was where it was first applied. The slogan—like the picket sign, the bumper sticker, the single name by which so many people in The Movement went (surnames being invidious)—all were part of an effort to compress language to a single unambiguous medium of exchange, a coin of the realm that could not be counterfeited or abused. Because what was being sought was not the protean leap of language, but unity of feeling—complete integration of desire and fulfilment.

And here is where language was more of an enemy than anything else. For 6 while language may be a medium for sentimentality, it will not finally yield to it. Try as you can, you can neither wholly avoid words nor wholly make them mean only what you feel. Words resist. But Abbie Hoffman says it better than I can. I quote from Hoffman's speech on the warm evening of May 1, 1970, in the courtyard of Ezra Stiles College at Yale, on the occasion of one of the last great campus gatherings of The Movement:

> Don't listen to people who say we got to be serious, responsible. Everybody's 7 responsible and serious but us. We gotta redefine the————language. Work— W-O-R-K—is a dirty four-letter word. . . . We need a society in which work and play are not separate. We gotta destroy the Protestant ethic as well as capitalism, racism, imperialism—that's gotta go too. We want a society in which dancin' in the streets isn't separate from cuttin' sugar cane. . . . We have picked the Yale lock.

Fascinating. Because the Protestant ethic, capitalism, racism, and im- 8 perialism are almost forgotten, almost mere afterthoughts, as Hoffman proclaimed what he really wants: a garden world where nothing is separate, work and play, cutting cane and dancing, where the togetherness will come by "redefining the language." If only he could redefine the language as easily as he could manipulate a crowd. But language won't change its essential shape for anyone. If you engage it, you must honor its deep tides. The most that Abbie Hoffman can do is make it do tricks, and the pun at the end is his trick.

A. Bartlett Giamatti, "Why Young People Today Can't Write"

H

George Washington could not tell a lye—as he might have spelled it. "The 1 spelling is absolutely chaotic—one might even say *creative*," says a professorial paper on "George Washington's Language" by Louis G. Heller of New York's

City College and James Macris of Clark University in Massachusetts. The authors cite such Washington spellings as "bairskin," "burrying," and "Sonday," as well as examples of his faulty grammar: "I have also wrote to Lord Sterling"; "Went a-hunting with Jacky Custis, and catched a fox after three hours chase." In fairness, Heller and Macris allow for Washington's limited education and some loose spelling rules of his era. Nevertheless, the professors gave him poor marks. If George were in college today, says Heller, "he would need remedial work, massive remediation."

Newsweek, "Newsmakers: George Washington's English"
Copyright 1976 by Newsweek, Inc. All rights reserved. Reprinted by permission.

WRITING ASSIGNMENTS

Essays

1. Write a description of your experiences in composition courses up until now. If you need ideas to expand your paper, compare your experiences with what "Why Johnny Can't Write" says about the teaching of English; after all, you should know more about some English classes than do professional journalists. Has your experience been like that of the student who wrote the essay on pages 19–20?

2. Many important twentieth-century authors did not do well by freshman composition. William Faulkner flunked it at the University of Mississippi, and Ernest Hemingway never took it at all. How is this possible? How much mastery over language can one be expected to learn in ten to fourteen weeks? How much of it is a lifetime job?

3. Professor Elisabeth McPherson, a moving force behind the CCCC Language Statement, defended it in a letter to *Newsweek* two weeks after "Why Johnny Can't Write" was published. She said, in part, ". . . If it is political to fight against language discrimination, to urge that teachers hear and respect what their students are telling them, to stop making people so ashamed of their language that they are afraid to write lest they be 'wrong,' then of course the statement is political. I'd prefer to call it linguistically sound." What is your opinion? Can language and politics be separated?

4. Another letter to *Newsweek*, presumably from two parents, reacted to the CCCC Language Statement this way: "After reading the comments of Ms. McPherson and company, we could just scream. . . ." Pretend you are these unhappy parents and write a letter to the CCCC denouncing its assertion that students' have a right to their own (perhaps nonstandard or substandard) language. Be sure to explain *why* you think the CCCC position is unsound.

5. Archibald Hill gives a list of things that correctness *is not*. Write a short essay defining your idea of what correctness *is*.

6. How important to society is the "Why Johnny Can't Write" question? Do you think the problem deserves the attention it is getting? Write an essay supporting or attacking the public concern over student writing.

JOURNAL KEEPING

In each chapter, we will give you some suggestions for writing in your language journal. The writing in your journal is, by definition, less structured than in formal papers. Some teachers feel that it should never be structured; others feel that it should follow some plan, even a loose one. Your instructor will tell you what she or he wants you to do.

Many of the journal suggestions we give you are meant to be continuing—in other words, one suggestion can be used for several entries throughout the semester, as you find more material or develop new ideas about it. (For example, suggestion 1 asks you to keep a log of the way language is used by public figures. Each time you hear language used in an interesting way by a politician or government spokesman or foreign prime minister, you can record it in your journal.)

In addition to the specific suggestions that we provide, you can include ideas of your own. Some of the things you can write about in your journal are:

Your reactions to ideas brought up in the essays and articles in this book; further thoughts about any of the selections.
Examples of the different ways you see language used around you.
Ads, newspaper clippings, political speeches, dialogues that illustrate some of the ideas about language raised in this book. Tape or staple these into your journal, and *be sure to comment on why you are including them.*

1. Keep a log on the kind of language used by public figures. Do some of the most prominent members of society make "mistakes" in English that might not be allowed on a freshman English paper? Similarly, how many leaders, including those from minorities, speak in dialect? What dialect words or phrases seem to be in widest use?

2. Record examples of "educationese" you hear used by your teachers or see in your textbooks. Do they sometimes use language that communicates nothing to you or anybody? What subjects encourage this kind of language?

3. Record any examples of "Engfish," as defined by Ken Macrorie on pages 21–22. Do you or your fellow students use it? When? Why?

4. Compare the use of language by older and younger people. Are "mistakes" in English more common among older people or younger people? What do your results tell you about what the schools are teaching?

2 "Let Me Give You a Piece of My Mind"
How Language Shapes Our Thought and Reality

Begin 1/24/80

CLASSROOM EXERCISE

How much do we think without words? How often do *you* think without using words? And what kind of "thoughts" do you have apart from thoughts expressed in words?

Take five minutes, now, in class, to try to answer these questions. Have everyone be quiet and then try—*try*—to think without words. Every time words come into your head, deliberately push them out and return to thinking without words. At the end of five minutes, let everyone report on what happened, on how much, if any, thinking she or he did without using words, and on what the nature of the "thinking" was.

Other exercises precede some of the later essays in this chapter. See pages 63 and 73.

STUART CHASE
How Language Shapes Our Thoughts

Which came first, the idea or the word? For many linguists, the word came first—at least as far as our understanding of things and ideas goes. After all, we are surrounded each day with thousands of colors, forces, chemicals, microbes, animals, and ideas—but we can't acknowledge them unless we have a name for them. The human species always breathed oxygen but never knew it until scientists had a word for it. Language gives us the limits of the knowable world.

The notion that language shapes our reality has been suggested by a number of writers, such as Edward Sapir, a scholar of American Indian languages, and Alfred Korzybski, who used the theory in the foundation of a study called General Semantics. But the theory is most associated with a brilliant student of Sapir's, Benjamin Lee Whorf, and is thus known as the "Whorf thesis" or "Sapir-Whorf thesis" today. As Whorf wrote mostly for obscure professional journals and died before he could collect his ideas into one coherent book, his ideas have been inaccessible for many people. Fortunately, Stuart Chase, a journalist and economist who admired Whorf, has provided us with an introduction to the theory.

Language, more than any other human trait, makes us human, distinguishes 1 us from all other creatures. . . .

Of all the tens of thousands of behavior patterns and belief systems we learn 2 from the culture, language is far and away the most important. It has long been recognized that every man alive—or who ever lived for that matter—is culture bound. It remained for [Benjamin Lee] Whorf and his group to demonstrate that every one of us is language-bound. . . .

The metalinguists [followers of Whorf] demonstrate that the forms of a 3 person's thoughts are controlled by patterns learned early, of which he is mostly unconscious. Thinking is a language process, whether in English, Russian, or Hopi. Every language is a complex system, with three main functions:

To communicate with other persons. 4

To communicate with oneself, or, as we say, think. 5

To mold one's whole outlook on life. 6

Thinking follows the tracks laid down in one's own language; these tracks will 7 converge on certain phases of "reality," and completely bypass phases which may be explored in other languages. In English, for instance, we say, "Look at that wave." But a wave in nature never occurs as a single phenomenon. In the Hopi language they say, "Look at that slosh." The Hopi word, whose nearest equivalent in English is "slosh," gives a closer fit to the actual physics of wave motion, connoting movement in a mass.

Most of us were brought up to believe that talking is merely a tool which 8 something deeper called "thinking" puts to work. Thinking, we have assumed, depends on laws of reason and logic common to all mankind. These laws are said to be implicit in the mental machinery of human beings, whether they speak English or Choctaw. Languages, it follows, are simply parallel methods for expressing this universal logic. On this assumption it also follows that any logical idea can be translated unbroken, or even unbent, into any language. A few minutes in the glass palace of the United Nations in New York will quickly disabuse one of this quaint notion. Even such a common concept as "democracy" may not survive translation.

• • •

B. C. by permission of Johnny Hart and Field Enterprises, Inc.

The ancient Greeks, with their belief in a universal rule of reason, neverthe-   9
less did their thinking in Greek, which, like all Indo-European tongues, followed
what is called the "subject-predicate" form. If there is a verb there must be a
noun to make it work; it could not often exist in its own right as pure action. The
ancient Greeks, as well as all Western peoples today, say, "The light flashed."
Something has to be there to make the flash; "light" is the subject; "flash" is the
predicate. The whole trend of modern physics, however, with its emphasis on
the *field*, or the whole process, is away from subject-predicate propositions. A
Hopi Indian, accordingly, is the better physicist when he says, *"Reh-pi"*—
"flash!"—one word for the whole performance, no subject, no predicate, and no
time element. (Children tend to do this too.) In Western languages we are
constantly reading into nature ghostly entities which flash and perform other
acts. Do we supply them because our verbs require substantives in front of them?

• • •

The Paths of Chinese Logic

Speakers of Chinese dissect nature and the universe very differently from
Western speakers, with a profound effect upon their systems of belief. . . .

In the West we say, "This is the front of the car, and that is the rear, and let's   11
have no more nonsense about it!" But in the Chinese view, Westerners are guilty
of considerable nonsense in creating "frontness" and "rearness" as entities. Even
a Westerner can see that if a car is torn in two in a crash, the part with the
radiator grille becomes the "front," and the part toward the now severed
windshield becomes the "rear"—*of that segment*. We can see, if we work hard
enough, that there are no such entities as "frontness" or "rearness," "difficulty"
or "easiness," "longness" or "shortness," by themselves out there. The Chinese
language has this useful correction built in; we Westerners have to sweat it out
with the help of linguistics, semantics, and mathematics.

Linguists have also emphasized that Chinese is a "multi-valued" language,   12
not primarily two-valued like English and Western languages generally. We say
that things must be "good" or "bad," "right" or "wrong," "clean" or "dirty,"
"black" or "white,"—ignoring shades of grey. When an economist talks about a

middle road between "socialism" and "capitalism," both camps vie in their ferocity to tear him apart. (I have been that unhappy economist.)

Speakers of Chinese set up no such grim dichotomies; they see most situa- 13 tions in shades of grey, and have no difficulty in grasping the significance of a variety of middle roads. As a result, Chinese thought has been traditionally tolerant, not given to the fanatical ideologies of the West. Racial, religious, and doctrinal conflicts have been hard to maintain in China, because a Chinese speaker does not possess an unshakable confidence that he is totally right and that his opponent is totally wrong. Observe that this is not a moral judgment, but structural in the language.

. . .

Eskimo breaks our single term "snow" into many words for different kinds of 14 snow—a procedure which all skiers can applaud. Aztec, however, goes in the opposite direction; here we find one word for "snow," "ice," and "cold." In Hopi, "wave," "flame," "meteor," and "lightning" are all verbs, suiting their dynamic quality. Looking into the August sky, a Hopi says: "*Reh-pi!* It meteors." (Observe how in English we need a djin called "it" to power the meteor.)

It is easier and clearer to recite the story of William Tell in the Algonquin 15 language than in English or French, because it is equipped with enough posses- sive pronouns to distinguish easily between "his" as applied to Tell, and as applied to his son. Writing in English I must continually watch my step with pronouns, lest I attach them to the wrong person or thing.

Chichewa, spoken by a tribe of unlettered Negroes in East Africa, has two 16 past tenses, one for events which continue to influence the present, and one for events which do not. With this structure, says Whorf, "a new view of time opens before us. . . . It may be that these primitive folks are equipped with a language which, if they were to become philosophers or mathematicians, could make them our foremost thinkers upon *time*."

LANGUAGE LINKS MANKIND

The metalinguists cause us to realize that language is not a tool with which to 17 uncover a deeper vein of reason, universal to all thinkers, but a shaper of thought itself. Shaping the thought, it helps to shape the culture, as in the Western cult of the Adoration of Time. They are making us realize that we get our view of the world, our *Weltanschauung*, as much from words inside our heads as from independent observation. When, as scientists, we try to become independent observers, the words may distort the readings, unless we take special precautions. Einstein could not accurately talk about relativity in German or English, he had to talk about it in the calculus of tensors. There is no reason to suppose that English, German, Russian, or any Indo-European language, with its two-valued logic, its monster-making subject-predicate form, is the ultimate in communica- tion.

The structure, or grammer, of each language, says Whorf, "is not merely a 18 reproducing instrument for voicing ideas but rather is itself the shaper of ideas, the program and guide for the individual's mental activity, for his analysis of impressions." The world is presented to us in a kaleidoscopic flux of impressions which must be organized by our minds, which means by the linguistic system built into our minds. We cut up the seamless web of nature, gather the pieces into concepts, because, within our speech community, we are parties to an agreement to organize things that way, an agreement codified in the patterns of language. This agreement is, of course, an unstated one, but "its terms are absolutely obligatory"; we cannot talk at all except by subscribing to the rules. People who try to avoid them land in mental hospitals.

* * *

DISCUSSION QUESTIONS

1. The philosopher Wittgenstein once said, "All I know is what I have words for." Do you "know anything" you don't have words for? What is it?

2 In another part of the same essay not included in this selection, Chase says, "No human being is free to describe nature with strict objectivity, for he is a prisoner of his language." In English, we talk of a beautiful "sunrise" or "sunset," even though the sun doesn't really "rise" or "set." Do these words influence the way we perceive these phenomena? Can you think of any other words in English that don't "fit the facts?"

3. In paragraph 8, Chase remarks that even a common concept like "democracy" can be difficult to translate for United Nations members who don't speak English. Rudolph Flesch, in his book *The Art of Clear Thinking*, deals with the same problem and describes some of the difficulties of writing the UN Charter. The Latin American delegation could not translate the phrase "sovereign equality" and preferrred "personality of states"—a phrase that means very little to an English-speaking person. The French had no word-equivalent for "trusteeship," the Chinese had none for "steering committee," and the Spanish-speaking members had no way of expressing the difference between "chairman" and "president." Can you think of any other English words that might be difficult to translate into another language? Why are they so hard to translate?

4. If you had difficulty answering question 3, can you think why? What reason do you think Stuart Chase would give for the difficulty of question 3?

5. One dictionary defines "language" as:

The aspect of human behavior that involves the use of vocal sounds in meaningful patterns and, when they exist, corresponding written symbols to form, express, and communicate thoughts and feelings.

Do you agree with this definition? What, if anything, does it leave out? Under this definition, would the Morse Code be a language? How about Pig Latin?

6. Allen and Beatrice Gardener have taught hundreds of words from the American Sign Language of the Deaf to a chimpanzee named Washoe, who

can combine these signs in creative new ways. Does this mean she "speaks" or knows a language? What are the implications of this experiment? Do you think teaching sign language to chimps on a large scale would be a good idea? Why or why not?

7. The story is told of some Peace Corps Volunteers in an especially poor corner of the third world who were trying to teach the native population to put their garbage in garbage cans. The natives had no word for "garbage," so the volunteers decided to make a film—showing themselves picking up garbage and putting it in cans. When they asked the local population what they had seen in the film, they said, "Chickens." And, sure enough, there were chickens in the backgrounds of many of the shots in the film. How does this relate to what Chase is saying about the way language shapes reality? Can you think of any *other* explanations for the natives' reaction to the film?

JANE OTTEN
Living in Syntax

In years past some subjects were literally "unspeakable' because the words for those subjects could not be uttered in polite conversation without censure for the speaker. Other subjects were "unspeakable" not because they were unpleasant or vulgar, but because words for them could not be taken from past or contemporary experience. Thus in 1895 hemorrhoids were unspeakable but transistors were unthinkable.

The activity Otten discusses was so disapproved of in earlier generations that it could barely be discussed, and it was so uncommon that it was unthinkable for most people. And although many people—perhaps a majority—still disapprove of the activity, Otten has given much thought to the subject but finds she cannot speak of it very well. It may be that she is up against a limit of the English language. (Copyright 1974 by Newsweek Inc. All rights reserved. Reprinted by permission.)

We like to think of ours as a living language—and it is. Successive editions of 1 Webster's Unabridged Dictionary testify to this, as do our own ears—and our own vocabulary—in daily conversation.

We have constructed and adapted words to fit new technologies, situations 2 and events, new kinds of people and attitudes. Hippie was not in our vocabulary fifteen years ago, nor was ombudsman. Nobody had ever heard of glitch or astronaut, ripoff or teach-in. Rap, cat and grass had other connotations then, and a jock was an article of male apparel. Today, when you hear these words, you know exactly what they mean.

But no new word has come into our vocabulary to describe precisely the ₃ parties to a new kind of relationship, one that is becoming more and more common. What do you call the person of the opposite sex who is living with your son or daughter?

I have been struggling with this one for some time now, in conversations with ₄ friends and acquaintances. "My daughter's er," I would start out, or "My daughter's . . . um . . . " But the listener would pin me down, and because my daughter objected to "boyfriend," I began to refer to my daughter's "boy." This went over all right for a time, until one startled neighbor wanted to know when my daughter had had the baby.

Wanted: A Bon Mot

I realized I was not alone with this nomenclature problem when I had a ₅ conversation with a friend whom I hadn't seen in a long time. We had a lot to catch up on, and she began telling me about her son who was living in Cambridge and publishing a little newspaper with his—er—girlfriend. My ears leaped into that "er" and I told her why I found her pause the most interesting part of her narrative. She admitted that she shared my problem.

This spurred me to conduct a small survey. I found many of my peers in the ₆ same predicament, but none close to a solution. Our vocabulary cries out now for a precise word to describe two people of different sex who are living together. None of the old words work. They are fuzzy, beg the question and often have traditional connotations which misrepresent the current situation.

Friend, for example, could be of either sex and doesn't necessarily imply an ₇ intimate relationship. *Boyfriend* or *girlfriend* does suggest a close relationship, but these terms are really too old-hat and don't describe the living arangement. *Roommate*, another possibility, specifies joint living conditions but omits gender identification, and *apartmentmate* is much the same. *Companion* may connote certain kinds of sharing, but it hardly represents the full range that the relationship embraces.

Cohabitor?

Most consistently slighted in all of these terms is the undoubted sexual nature ₈ of the partnership. Here are some which do not convey this aspect, but they, too, are flawed:

Swain—that's all right for him, but what do you call her?   ₉

Suitor—this is most often a totally inaccurate description.   ₁₀

Fiancé (or *fiancée*)—are you out of your mind?   ₁₁

Lover—too romantic and old-world to be applied to many contemporary ₁₂ relationships. The word also implies that one of the persons involved is married and is conducting an adulterous relationship.

Mistress—forget it.   ₁₃

Paramour—this could hardy be applied to couples who do their shopping at 14
the Safeway on Saturday nights.

Consort—far too regal in its overtones and, besides, implies an existing 15
marriage.

Partner—this suggests a close, sharing relationship, all right, but even 16
though Masters and Johnson, David Reuben and others have given it a new
sexual cachet, the word's principal connotation is still commercial.

Mate—this seems to be the official designation adopted by a New York-based 17
group plugging non-parenthood, but the word mostly calls to mind the jungle
and "me Tarzan, you Jane."

My research has brought out several designations by other desperate parents. 18
None is acceptable to me, but here they are anyway.

The first is *lover-in-law*. Just try that in some simple sentences. If you say, 19
"My lover-in-law is coming for dinner tonight," the interpretation is that you are
having an affair with your spouse's parent or sibling. You must therefore attach
the phrase specifically to your son or daughter, but that result is equally misleading. "My daughter's lover-in-law," you say, "is having a play produced off-
Broadway." That means that it's your daughter who is having a meaningful
relationship with one of her in-laws.

Son-in-Common-Law?

Another freshly coined term is *outlaw*. "We are meeting our son-outlaw at 20
the airport," you say, and your listener concludes that he is a Vietnam defector
returning from Canada or that your daughter is married to him and you detest
him. Still another diverting term comes from some friends who are a bit bitter
over the somewhat larger monthly allowance they must now send to their daughter. They refer to her male living companion as her *checkmate*.

In conversations with my spouse (there's no problem about that) I sometimes 21
refer to our child's *spose*, which contains the implicit question, "Do you 'spose
they'll ever get married?" But I prefer to use this only in private conversations.

I hope somebody soon will come up with the precise handle to describe 22
persons involved in this situation because the lack of it is severely limiting my
conversation. I do love to talk about my children and I would like to do so in
accurate terms. In the meantime, I can only make sparing references to my
daughter's er and my son's um.

DISCUSSION QUESTIONS

1. What exactly is Mrs. Otten's problem in describing the relationship
her son or daughter has with a certain member of the opposite sex? Can you
summarize her essay?

2. Does the lack of an appropriate term to describe the relationship
support or refute the thesis that one cannot think without words? After all,
isn't she thinking about the relationship?

3. The title does not refer to actual syntax, of course, but rather makes a pun on the phrase "living in sin," sometimes used to describe the relationship Mrs. Otten refers to in the essay. Although the phrase describes the relationship rather than a person, the phrase "living in sin" never appears in the essay. If Mrs. Otten had mentioned it, what do you think her attitude toward it would have been?

4. Mrs. Otten dismisses such terms as "fiancé" (paragraph 11) and "mistress" (paragraph 13) without explanation. What are the connotations of these words? And why does she think they are inadequate?

5. Sociologists studying these relationships have referred to them by the acronym LTA, for "Living Together Arrangements." On the basis of having read her essay, do you believe Mrs. Otten would find this an acceptable substitute?

6. What other terms from traditional speech might Mrs. Otten have used? Why should she have dismissed or possibly accepted them?

7. Does the essay imply that Mrs. Otten would prefer that her sons and daughters marry the members of the opposite sex they are presently living with?

1/24/80

CLYDE KLUCKHOHN
The Gift of Tongues

Both Edward Sapir and B. L. Whorf gave more of their attention to American Indian languages rather than to the languages of Western Europe. Subsequently, the Sapir-Whorf thesis has been especially interesting to anthropologists, some of whom dispute rather than accept the idea. One anthropologist who admired Whorf and applied his thesis to a wide variety of languages was Clyde Kluckhohn of Harvard University.

Part of what Kluckhohn writes about is familiar to all of us. We ask someone who speaks another language—Polish, Italian, Swedish, Yiddish, whatever—to translate a word or phrase for us, and when they do they include that patronizing phrase, ". . . but it loses so much in translation." That so much lost in translation was one of Robert Frost's definitions of poetry.

In speaking of the difficulty, if not the impossibility, of translating, another poet, Randall Jarrell, made use of a memorable figure of speech. He said that Rilke, writing in German, had produced poems which read like ornately carved ivory chessman. In trying to translate, he, Jarrell, felt as though he were trying to recreate the chessman out of delicate ferns.

. . . Anyone who has struggled with translation is made to realize that there   1
is more to a language than its dictionary. The Italian proverb *"traduttore, tradit-*
tore" (the translator is a betrayer) is all too correct. I asked a Japanese with a fair
knowledge of English to translate back from the Japanese that phrase in the new
Japanese constitution that represents our "life, liberty, and the pursuit of happiness." He rendered, "license to commit lustful pleasure." English to Russian and
Russian back to English transmuted a cablegram "Genevieve suspended for
prank" into "Genevieve hanged for juvenile delinquency."

These are obvious crudities. But look at translations into half-a-dozen lan-   2
guages of the same passage in the Old Testament. The sheer difference in length
will show that translation is not just a matter of finding a word in the second
language that exactly matches a word in the original. Renderings of poetry are
especially misleading. The best metrical translation of Homer is probably the
fragment done by Hawtrey. The final two lines of the famous "Helen on the
wall" passage of the third book in the Iliad goes as follows:

> So said she; but they long since in earth's soft arms
> > were reposing
> There in their own dear land, their fatherland,
> > Lacedaemon

Hawtrey has caught the musical effect of Greek hexameter about as well as it is
possible to do in English. But the Greek says literally, "but them, on the other
hand, the life-giving earth held fast." The original is realistic—Helen's brothers
were dead and that was that. The English is sentimental.

Once in Paris I saw a play called "The Weak Sex." I found it charmingly   3
risqué. A year later in Vienna I took a girl to see a German translation of the
same play. Though she was no prude, I was embarrassed because the play was
vulgar if not obscene in German.

• • •

Really, there are three kinds of translation. There is the literal or word-for-   4
word variety which is always distorted except perhaps between languages that are
very similar in structure and vocabulary. Second, there is the official type where
certain convention as to idiomatic equivalents are respected. The third, a psychological type of translation, where the words produce approximately the same
effects in the speakers of the second language as they did in those of the original,
is next to impossible. At best, the rendering must be extremely free, with elaborate circumlocutions and explanations.

If words referred only to things, translation would be relatively simple. But   5
they refer also to relations between things and the subjective as well as the
objective aspects of these relationships. In different tongues relationships are
variously conceived. The Balinese word *tis* means not to be cold when it is cold.
The Balinese word *paling* designates the state of a trance or drunkenness or a
condition of not knowing where you are, what day it is, where the center of the
island is, the caste of the person to whom you are talking. The subjective aspects
arise from the fact that we use words not only to express things and relationships

but to express ourselves; words refer not only to events but to the attitudes of the speakers toward those events.

• • •

The British and the Americans are still under the delusion that they speak the same language. With some qualifications this is true as far as denotations are concerned, though there are concepts like "sissy" in American for which there are no precise English equivalents. Connotations, however, are often importantly different, and this makes for the more misunderstanding because both languages are still called "English" (treating alike by words thing that are different). An excellent illustration is supplied by Margaret Mead: 6

> . . . in Britain, the word "compromise" is a good word, and one may speak approvingly of any arrangement which has been a compromise, including, very often, one in which the other side has gained more than fifty per cent of the points at issue. On the other hand, in the United States, the minority position is still the position from which everyone speaks: the President *versus* Congress, Congress *versus* the President, The State government *versus* the metropolis and the metropolis *versus* the State Government. This is congruent with the American doctrine of checks and balances, but it does not permit the word "compromise" to gain the same ethical halo which it has in Britain. Where, in Britain, to compromise means to work out a good solution, in America it usually means to work out a bad one, a solution in which all the points of importance (to both sides) are lost. Thus, in negotiations between the United States and Britain, all of which had, in the nature of the case, to be compromises, as two sovereignties were involved, the British could always speak approvingly and proudly of the result, while the Americans had to emphasize their losses.

The words, then, that pass so readily from mouth to mouth are not entirely trustworthy substitutes for the facts of the physical world. The smooth-worn standard coins are slippery stepping-stones from mind to mind. Nor is thinking simply a matter of choosing words to express thoughts. The selected words always mirror social situation as well as objective fact. Two men go into a bar in New York and are overcharged for bad liquor: "This is a gyp joint." The same thing happens in Paris: "The French are a bunch of chiselers." 7

. . . Every language is something more than a vehicle for exchanging ideas and information—more even than a tool for self-expression and for letting off emotional steam or for getting other people to see what we want. 8

Every language is also a special way of looking at the world and interpreting experience. Concealed in the structure of each different language are a whole set of unconscious assumptions about the world and life in it. The anthropological linguist has come to realize that the general ideas one has about what happens in the world outside oneself are not altogether "given" by external events. Rather, up to a point, one sees and hears what the grammatical system of one's language has made one sensitive to, has trained one to look for in experience. This bias is the more insidious because everyone is so unconscious of his native language as a system. To one brought up to speak a certain language it is part of the very nature of things, remaining always in the class of background phenomena. It is as natural that experience should be organized and interpreted in these language- 9 defined classes as it is that the seasons change. In fact the naïve view is that anyone who thinks in any other way is unnatural or stupid, or even vicious—and most certainly illogical.

• • •

From the anthropological point of view there are as many different worlds 10 upon the earth as there are languages. Each language is an instrument which guides people in observing, in reacting, in expressing themselves in a special way. The pie of experience can be sliced in many different ways, and language is the principal directive force in the background. You can't say in Chinese, "answer me yes or no," for there aren't words for yes or no. . . .

In the Haida language of British Columbia there are more than twenty verbal 11 prefixes that indicate whether an action was performed by carrying, shooting, hammering, pushing, pulling, floating, stamping, picking, chopping, or the like. Some languages have different verbs, adjectives, and pronouns for animate and inanimate things. In Melanesia there are as many as four variant forms for each possessive pronoun. One may be used for the speaker's body and mind, another for illegitimate relatives and his loincloth, a third his possessions and gifts. The underlying conceptual images of each language tend to constitute a coherent though unconscious philosophy.

When in English one word, "rough," may equally well be used to describe a 12 road, a rock, or the business surface of a file, the Navaho language finds a need for three different words which may not be used interchangebly. While the general tendency is for Navaho to make finer and more concrete distinctions, this not inevitably the case. The same stem is used for rip, light beam, and echo, ideas which seem diverse to speakers of European languages. One word is used to designate a medical bundle with all its contents, the skin quiver in which the contents are wrapped, the contents as a whole, and some of the distinct items. Sometimes the point is not that the images of Navahos are less fluid and more dilimited but rather just that the external world is dissected along different lines. For example, the same Navaho word is used to describe both a pimply face and a nodule-covered rock. In English a complexion might be termed "rough" or "coarse," but a rock would never, except facetiously, be described as pimply. Navaho differentiates two types of rough rock: the kind which is rough in the manner in which a file is rough and the kind which is nodule-encrusted. In these cases the differences between Navaho and the English ways of seeing the world cannot be disposed of merely by saying that the Navaho language is more precise. The variations rest in the features which the two languages see as essential. Cases can indeed be given where the Navaho is notably less precise. Navaho gets along with a single word for flint, metal, knife, and certain other objects of metal. This, to be sure, is due to the historical accident that, after European contact, metal in general and knives in particular took the place of flint.

The nature of their language forces the Navaho to notice and report many 13 other distinctions in physical events which the nature of the English language allows speakers to neglect in most cases, even though their senses are just as capable as those of the Navaho to register the smaller details of what goes on in the external world. For example, suppose a Navaho range rider and a white supervisor see that a wire fence needs repair. The supervisor will probably write in his notebook, "Fence at such and such a place must be fixed." If the Navaho reports the break, he must choose between forms that indicate whether the damage was caused by some person or by nonhuman agency, whether the fence was of one or several strands of wire.

In general, the difference between Navaho thought and English thought—   14
both as manifested in the language and as forced by the very nature of the linguistic forms into such patterns—is that Navaho thought is ordinarily much more specific. The ideas expressed by the English verb *to go* provide a nice example. When a Navaho says that he went somewhere he never fails to specify whether it was afoot, astride, by wagon, auto, train, airplane, or boat. If it be a boat, it must be specified whether the boat floats off with the current, is propelled by the speaker, or is made to move by an indefinite or unstated agency. The speed of a horse (walk, trot, gallop, run) is expressed by the verb form chosen. He differentiates between starting to go, going along, arriving at, returning from a point. It is not, of course, that these distinctions *cannot* be made in English, but that they *are not* made consistently. They seem of importance to English speakers only under special circumstances.

A cross-cultural view of the category of time is highly instructive. Beginners   15
in the study of classical Greek are often troubled by the fact the word *opiso* sometimes means "behind," sometimes "in the future." Speakers of English find this baffling because they are accustomed to think of themselves as moving through time. The Greeks, however, conceived of themselves as stationary, of time as coming up behind them, overtaking them, and then, still moving on, becoming the "past" that lay before their eyes.

• • •

Any language is more than an instrument of conveying ideas, more even   16
than an instrument for working upon the feelings of others and for self-expression. Every language is also a means of categorizing experience. The events of the "real" world are never felt or reported as a machine would do it. There is a selection process and an interpretation in the very act of response. Some features of the external situation are highlighted; others are ignored or not fully discriminated.

Every people has its own characteristic classes in which individuals   17
pigeonhole their experiences. These classes are established primarily by the language through the types of objects, processes, or qualities which receive special emphasis in the vocabulary and equally, though more subtly, through the types of differentiation or activity which are distinguished in grammatical forms. The language says, as it were, "notice this," "always consider this separate from that," "such and such things belong together." Since persons are trained from infancy to respond in these ways, they take such discriminations for granted as part of the inescapable stuff of life. When we see two people with different social traditions respond in different ways to what appear to the outsider to be identical stimulus situations, we realize that experience is much less an objective absolute than we thought. Every language has an effect upon what the people who use it see, what they feel, how they think. . . .

DISCUSSION QUESTIONS

1. The great German writer Goethe once said, "We only see what we know." Is this what Kluckhohn is saying here? Explain.

2. What does Kluckhohn mean when he says that "everyone is so unconscious of his native tongue as a system" (paragraph 9.)? Do you agree with this idea? How "conscious" are you of your own language as a system of thought?

3. One of the ways in which we can see what Kluckhohn is talking about is the way in which different languages name the colors of the rainbow. Is there a continuous gradation of color from one end of the spectrum to the other? Or are the dividing lines between colors the ones we, or our culture, choose to draw? Explain.

4. The chart below compares the way speakers of English, Shona (a language of Rhodesia), and Bassa (a language of Liberia) see the spectral colors. Where we see six, the Shona speaker sees only three. The Shona word *cips^{w}uka* occurs twice because the Shona speaker classifies the "red" and "purple" ends as similar. The Bassa speaker classifies the spectrum into only two general categories. All three languages, of course, have additional words for gradations within major color groups.

English:	purple	blue	green	yel-low	orange	red

Shona:	cips^{w}uka	citema	cicena	cips^{w}uka

Bassa:	hui	zīza

Is one of these naming systems necessarily correct? Or is none of them? What about "primary colors"?

5. Like Shona and Bassa, English has many words to describe gradations of one color, such as the color red, which can be pink, coral, magenta, scarlet, cerise, vermilion, puce, soliferino, etc. Many of these words seem much unlike the others and are of different origins; how can you account for this? Does the proliferation of these words for color gradation imply that the English word "red" is inadequate?

6. The physical enviroment of most speakers of English is quite different from that of most speakers of Shona and Bassa, which may help to explain the different perceptions of the languages. But English and Irish developed in quite similar physical environments, and Irish has two words which are both translated as "green" in English. They are *uaine*, said of nonliving things or of green eyes, and *glas*, said of the grass or the sea, or "green" in the sense of being raw, incomplete, or inexperienced. How can this difference in the two

languages be explained? Does it support or contradict what Kluckhohn is saying here?

7. Most cuss words of any given language, such as English, have been in the language a long time. Only rarely does a language ever borrow a cuss word from another language, and even if they do such words are extremely difficult to translate. For example, *schweinerhund* is a pretty serious curse in German, but it is only "pig dog" in English. Why is this so? Can someone in your class pronounce this word as it is pronounced in German? What is lost in translation?

8. As the United States and Canada are still nations of immigrants, some of the students in your class should know someone, perhaps a parent or older relative, who is a fluent speaker of another language. Ask those students to bring in words or phrases from another language which are all but impossible to translate. What kinds of words or phrases are they? To what do they relate?

9. What kind of expression in English, other than cuss words, do you think might be impossible to translate into another language? Can you give some examples?

1/24/80

PETER FARB
from Word Play: What Happens When People Talk

As the Sapir-Whorf thesis or hypothesis is impossible to prove, either physically or logically, some linguists have, inevitably, opposed it. Here is a summary of opinion from a recent popular book, the first book on sociolinguistics to become a best seller.

Although a fuller exploration of the Sapir-Whorf hypothesis is the work of experts, our understanding of its implications may be resolved into one of two questions: Does our culture and the stuff of our experience determine our language, or does our language determine the way we perceive and think about our experience and our culture?

Whorf's theories about the relationship between culture and language have been greeted enthusiastically by some scholars and attacked or treated warily by others. The weakness of the Sapir-Whorf Hypothesis, as it has come to be known, is the impossibility of generalizing about entire cultures and then attributing these generalizations to the languages spoken. The absence of clocks, calendars, and written histories obviously gave the Hopis a different view of time from that found among speakers of European languages. But such an observation is not the same thing as proving that these cultural differences were caused by the differences between Hopi and European grammars. In fact, an interest in time-reckoning is not characteristic solely of European cultures but can be found among speakers of languages as different as Egyptian, Chinese, and Maya. And, on the other hand, thousands of unrelated speech communities share with the Hopis a lack of concern about keeping track of time. To attempt to explain cultural differences and similarities as a significant result of the languages spoken is to leave numerous facts about culture unexplained. The great religions of the world—Judaism, Christianity, Hinduism, and Mohammedanism—have flourished among diverse peoples who speak languages with sharply different grammars. Mohammedanism, for example, has been accepted by speakers of languages with grammars as completely different as those of the Hamito-Semitic, Turkish, Indo-Iranian, Tibeto-Burman, and Malayo-Polynesian families. And the reverse is true as well. Cultures as diverse as the Aztec Empire of Mexico and the Ute hunting bands of the Great Basin spoke very closely related tongues.

Nevertheless, attempts have been made to prove the Sapir-Whorf 2 Hypothesis, such as one experiment which used as test subjects bilingual Japanese women, living in San Francisco, who had married American servicemen. The women spoke English to their husbands, children, and neighbors, and in most everyday speech situations; they spoke Japanese whenever they came together to gossip, reminisce, and discuss the news from home. Each Japanese woman thus inhabited two language worlds—and according to the predictions of the hypothesis, the women should think differently in each of these worlds. The experiment consisted of two visits to each woman by a bilingual Japanese interviewer. During the first interview he chatted with them only in Japanese; during the second he carried on the same discussion and asked the same questions in English. The results were quite remarkable; they showed that the attitudes of each woman differed markedly, depending upon whether she spoke Japanese or English. Here, for example, is the way the same woman completed the same sentences at the two interviews:

"When my wishes conflict with my family's . . .
    . . . it is a time of great unhappiness." (Japanese)
    . . . I do what I want." (English)

"Real friends should . . .
    . . . help each other." (Japanese)
    . . . be very frank." (English)

Clearly, major variables in the experiment had been eliminated—since the women were interviewed twice by the same person in the same location of their homes, and they discussed the same topics—with but one exception. And that sole exception was language. The drastic differences in attitudes of the women could be accounted for only by the language world each inhabited when she spoke.

The Sapir-Whorf Hypothesis also predicts that language makes its speakers 3 intellectually lazy. They will categorize new experiences in the well-worn channels they have been used to since birth, even though these channels might appear foolish to an outsider. The language spoken by the Western Apaches of Arizona, for example, has long had its own channels for classifying the parts of the human body, a system which ignores certain distinctions made in other languages and which makes different ones of its own. Then, about 1930, a new cultural item, the automobile, was introduced into the Apache reservation. An automobile, surely, is different from a human body, yet the Apaches simply applied their existing classification for the human body to the automobile. The chart . . . lists approximate pronunciations of the Apache words for the parts of the human body, the way they are categorized—and the way their meanings were extended to classify that new cultural item, the automobile.

Many linguists nowadays are wary of the Sapir-Whorf Hypothesis. Research that has attempted to confirm the hypothesis, such as the experiment with the Japanese women or the study of the Apache terms for the automobile, is usually regarded as fascinating examples rather than as universal truths about the way speech communities view the world. Neither Whorf nor any of his followers has proven to everyone's satisfaction that differences between two speech communities in their capacity to understand external reality are based entirely or even overwhelmingly on differences in their languages. Whorf overemphasized one point (that languages differ in what *can* be said in them) at the expense of a greater truth (that they differ as to what is *relatively easy* to express in them). Languages, rather than causing cultural differences between speech communities, seem instead to reflect the different cultural concerns of their speakers. The history of language is not so much the story of people misled by their languages as it is the story of a successful struggle against the limitations built into all language systems. The Western Apache system for classifying the human body did not lock them into certain habitual patterns of thought that prevented them from understanding the automobile. In fact, the existence of these patterns may have aided the Apaches in making sense out of that new cultural item.

APACHE WORDS
FOR PARTS OF THE HUMAN BODY
AND THE AUTOMOBILE

Human Anatomical Terms		Extended Auto Meanings
External Anatomy:		
daw	"chin and jaw"	"front bumper"
wos	"shoulder"	"front fender"
gun	"hand and arm"	"front wheel"
kai	"thighs and buttocks"	"rear fender"
ze	"mouth"	"gas-pipe opening"
ke	"foot"	"rear wheel"
chun	"back"	"chassis"
inda	"eye"	"headlight"
Face:		
chee	"nose"	"hood"
ta	"forehead"	"auto top"
Entrails:		
tsawa	"vein"	"electrical wiring"

DISCUSSION QUESTIONS

1. What is Farb's objection to the Sapir-Whorf hypothesis? How does the evidence he cites support his views?

2. In paragraph 1, Farb mentions that the great religions of the world have often been followed by peoples who speak very different languages. Are there any differences in the way a given religion is practiced by different nations or peoples? Do you know, for example, how Christianity is practiced in Russia, Holland, northern Germany?

3. Commenting on the interviews with the Japanese-American housewives (see paragraph 2), Farb says that the only explanation for the difference in their answers was the difference in the language each woman was speaking at the time. Do you agree with this explanation? Can you think of any other explanations for the variation in the answers?

4. Farb uses the example of the Apache words for *car* to attack the Sapir-Whorf hypothesis. Is it possible to use this same example to *support* the Sapir-Whorf hypothese? Explain.

5. Farb says that Whorf was wrong to argue that languages differ in what *can be* said in them, and that it's closer to the truth to say that languages differ as to what is *relatively easy* to express in them. Explain the distinction between these two points of view.

6. What has been the experience of English in accommodating new phenomena? Have we more often called new things by old names, as when we incorrectly called the bison a "buffalo"? Or have we borrowed words from other languages, as when we found new kinds of storms in different climates and called them "typhoons" (from Chinese) or "hurricanes" (from Carib)? What about when we saw unanticipated quasistellar objects and called them "quasars"?

MARK TWAIN
from The Awful German Language

Anyone who has ever studied a foreign language knows some of the problems Professor Kluckhohn speaks of in a previous essay. Not only is absolute translation—with every connotation and nuance intact—impossible, but each new language presents the learner with a mass of rules and structures which seem, initially, without reason for their existence. This was the experience of the young Mark Twain, who toured Europe when he was first building his reputation as a satirist. Had he the opportunity to try to learn some other languages, he might not have found German such an awful language to learn. Still, his difficulties were enough to prod this minor classic in American literature.

In German every noun has a gender, and there is no sense or system in the distribution; so the gender of each must be learned separately and by heart. There is no other way. To do this one has to have a memory like a memorandum-book. In German, a young lady has no sex, while a turnip has. Think what over-wrought reverence that shows for the turnip, and what callous disrespect for the girl. See how it looks in print—I translate this from a conversation in one of the best of the German Sunday school books:

"*Gretchen*—Wilhelm, where is the turnip?"
"*Wilhelm*—She has gone to the kitchen."
"*Gretchen*—Where is the accomplished and beautiful English maiden?"
"*Wilhelm*—It has gone to the opera."

To continue with the German genders: a tree is male, its buds are female, its leaves are neuter; horses are sexless, dogs are male, cats are female—tomcats included, of course; a person's mouth, neck, bosom, elbows, fingers, nails, feet, and body are of the male sex, and his head is male or neuter according to the word selected to signify it, and *not* according to the sex of the individual who wears it—for in Germany all the women wear either male heads or sexless ones; a person's nose, lips, shoulders, breast, hands, and toes are of the female sex; and his hair, ears, eyes, chin, legs, knees, heart, and conscience haven't any sex at all. The inventor of the language probably got what he knew about a conscience from hearsay.

Now, by the above dissection, the reader will see that in Germany a man many *think* he is a man, but when he comes to look into the matter closely, he is bound to have his doubts; he finds that in sober truth he is a most ridiculous mixture; and if he ends by trying to comfort himself with the thought that he can at least depend on a third of this mess as being manly and masculine, the humiliating second thought will quickly remind him that in this respect he is no better off than any woman or cow in the land.

In the German it is true that by some oversight of the inventor of the language, a Woman is a female; but a Wife *(Weib)* is not—which is unfortunate. A Wife, here, has no sex; she is neuter; so, according to the grammar, a fish is *he*, his scales are *she*, but a fishwife is neither. To describe a wife as sexless may be called under-description; that is bad enough, but over-description is surely worse. A German speaks of an Englishman as the *Engländer*; to change the sex, he adds *inn*, and that stands for Englishwoman—*Engländerinn*. That seems descriptive enough, but still it is not exact enough for a German; so he precedes the word with that article which indicates that the creature to follow is feminine, and writes down thus: "*die* Engländer*inn*,"—which means "the *she-Englishwoman*." I consider that that person is over-described.

Well, after the student has learned the sex of a great number of nouns, he is still in a difficulty, because he finds it impossible to persuade his tongue to refer to things as "*he*" and "*she*," and "*him*" and "*her*," which it has been always accustomed to refer to as "*it*." When he even frames a German sentence in his mind, with the hims and hers in the right places, and then works up his courage to the utterance-point, it is no use—the moment he begins to speak his tongue flies the track and all those labored males and females come out as *"its."* And even when he is reading German to himself, he always calls those things *"it,"* whereas he ought to read this way:

Tale of the Fishwife and Its Sad Fate[1]

It is a bleak Day. Hear the Rain, how he pours, and the Hail, how he rattles; and see the Snow, how he drifts along, and oh the Mud, how deep he is! Ah the poor Fishwife, it is stuck fast in the Mire; it has dropped its Basket of Fishes; and its Hands have been cut by the Scales as it seized some of the falling Creatures; and one Scale has even got into its Eye, and it cannot get her out. It opens its Mouth to cry for Help; but if any Sound comes out of him, alas he is drowned by the raging of the Storm. And now a Tomcat has got one of the Fishes and she will surely escape with him. No, she bites off a Fin, she holds her in her Mouth—will she swallow her? No, the Fishwife's brave Mother-dog deserts his Puppies and rescues the Fin—which he eats, himself, as his Reward. O, horror, the Lightning has struck the Fish-basket; he sets him on Fire; see the Flame, how she licks the doomed Utensil with her red and angry Tongue; now she attacks the helpless Fishwife's Foot—she burns him up, all but the big Toe, and even *she* is partly consumed; and still she spreads, still she waves her fiery Tongues; she attacks the Fishwife's Leg and destroys *it*; she attacks its Hand and destroys *her*; she attacks its poor worn Garment and destroys *her* also; she attacks its Body and consumes *him*; she wreathes herself about its Heart and *it* is consumed; next along its Breast, and in a Moment *she* is a Cinder; now she reaches its Neck—*he* goes; now its Chin—*it* goes; now its Nose—*she* goes. In another Moment, except Help come, the Fishwife will be no more. Time presses—is there none to succor and save? Yes! Joy, joy, with flying Feet the she-Englishwoman comes! But alas, the generous she-Female is too late: where now is the fated Fishwife? It has ceased from its Sufferings, it has gone to a better Land; all that is left of it for its loved Ones to lament over, is this poor smoldering Ash-heap. Ah, woeful, woeful Ash-heap! Let us take him up tenderly, reverently, upon the lowly Shovel, and bear him to his long Rest, with the Prayer that when he rises again it will be in a Realm where he will have one good square responsible Sex, and have it all to himself, instead of having a mangy lot of assorted Sexes scattered all over him in Spots.

DISCUSSION QUESTIONS

1. What is the problem with Twain's "translation" in paragraph 1? Why don't Germans see the absurdity he indicates?
2. When an English-speaking man says of his automobile, "Good old Betsy; she's been good to me," is he doing the same thing the Germans do? Why or why not?

---

[1] I capitalize the nouns, in the German (and ancient English) fashion. [*Twain's note*—eds.]

3. If you are taking German now, ask your instructor about Twain's essay. How do native-speaking Germans remember the different noun genders? Do they, as Twain suggests in paragraph 1, simply have better memories than we do?

4. Can you follow the "Tale of the Fishwife and Its Sad Fate"? If not, where does it become difficult to follow? Would a native German have the same difficulty?

5. Can you think of anything in the English language that would be as difficult for a German-speaking person to learn as the German noun-gender system is to us? Why don't we have difficulty with these things?

SUSANNE K. LANGER
Signs and Symbols in Language and Thought

A familiar thumbnail definition of language is "a symbolic system." We would like to believe that our symbol-making capacity is what distinguishes us from animals who respond only to signs. Yet humans respond to signs too, often more emphatically than to symbols. We answer bells, watch the clock, obey warning signals, follow arrows, take off the kettle when it whistles, and so on. If we are to know how much of our language is purely symbolic we should have a clear idea of what signs and symbols are. The following selection, taken from two different writings by German émigré philosopher Susanne K. Langer, gives us dozens of examples to help show us the way.

A symbol is not the same thing as a sign; that is a fact that psychologists and   1
philosophers often overlook. All intelligent animals use signs; so do we. To them as well as to us sounds and smells and motions are signs of food, danger, the presence of other beings, or of rain or storm. Furthermore, some animals not only attend to signs but produce them for the benefit of others. Dogs bark at the door to be let in; rabbits thump to call each other; the cooing of doves and the growl of a wolf defending his kill are unequivocal signs of feelings and intentions to be reckoned with by other creatures.

We use signs just as animals do, though with considerably more elaboration.   2
We stop at red lights and go on green; we answer calls and bells, watch the sky for coming storms, read trouble or promise or anger in each other's eyes. That is animal intelligence raised to the human level. Those of us who are dog lovers can probably all tell wonderful stories of how high our dogs have sometimes risen in the scale of clever sign interpretation and sign using.

A sign is anything that announces the existence or the imminence of some   3
event, the presence of a thing or a person, or a change in a state of affairs. There

are signs of the weather, signs of danger, signs of future good or evil, signs of what the past has been. In every case a sign is closely bound up with something to be noted or expected in experience. It is always a part of the situation to which it refers, though the reference may be remote in space and time. In so far as we are led to note or expect the signified event we are making correct use of a sign. This is the essence of rational behavior, which animals show in varying degrees. It is entirely realistic, being closely bound up with the actual objective course of history—learned by experience, and cashed in or voided by further experience.

If man had kept to the straight and narrow path of sign using, he would be   4 like the other animals, though perhaps a little brighter. He would not talk, but grunt and gesticulate and point. He would make his wishes known, give warn- ings, perhaps develop a social system like that of bees and ants, with such a wonderful efficiency of communal enterprise that all men would have plenty to eat, warm apartments—all exactly alike and perfectly convenient—to live in, and everybody could and would sit in the sun or by the fire, as the climate demanded, not talking but just basking, with every want satisfied, most of his life. The young would romp and make love, the old would sleep, the middle-aged would do the routine work almost unconsciously and eat a great deal. But that would be the life of a social, superintelligent, purely sign-using animal.

To us who are human, it does not sound very glorious. We want to go places   5 and do things, own all sorts of gadgets that we do not absolutely need, and when we sit down to take it easy we want to talk. Rights and property, social position, special talents and virtues, and above all our ideas, are what we live for. We have gone off on a tangent that takes us far away from the mere biological cycle that animal generations accomplish; and that is because we can use not only signs but symbols.

A symbol differs from a sign in that it does not announce the present of the   6 object, the being, condition, or whatnot, which is its meaning, but merely brings this thing to mind. It is not a mere "substitute sign" to which we react as though it were the object itself. The fact is that our reaction to hearing a person's name is quite different from our reaction to the person himself. . . .

• • •

If I say: "Napoleon," you do not bow to the conqueror of Europe as though I   7 had introduced him, but merely think of him. If I mention a Mr. Smith of our common acquaintance, you may be led to tell me something about him "behind his back," which is just what you would *not* do in his presence. Thus the symbol for Mr. Smith—his name—may very well initiate an act appropriate peculiarly to his absence. Raised eyebrows and a look at the door, interpreted as a *sign* that he is coming, would stop you in the midst of your narrative; *that* action would be directed toward Mr. Smith in person.

Symbols are not proxy for their objects, but are *vehicles* for *the conception of*   8 *objects.* To conceive a thing or a situation is not the same thing as to "react toward it" overtly, or to be aware of its presence. In talking *about* things we have conceptions of them, not the things themselves; and *it is the conceptions, not the things, that symbols directly "mean."* Behavior toward conceptions is what words normally evoke; this is the typical process of thinking.

Of course a word may be used as a sign, but that is not its primary role. Its   9 signific character has to be indicated by some special modification — by a tone of voice, a gesture (such as pointing or staring), or the location of a placard bearing the word. In itself it is a symbol, associated with a conception,[1] not directly with a public object or event. The fundamental difference between signs and symbols is this difference of association, and consequently of their *use* by the third party to the meaning function, the subject; signs *announce* their objects to him, whereas symbols *lead him to conceive* their objects. The fact that the same item — say, the little mouthy noise we call a "word" — may serve in either capacity, does not obliterate the cardinal distinction between the two functions it may assume.

Drawing by Stevenson; ©1976 The New Yorker Magazine Inc.

The simplest kind of symbolistic meaning is probably that which belongs to proper names. A personal name evokes a conception of something given as a unit in the subject's experience, something concrete and therefore easy to recall in imagination. Because the name belongs to a notion so obviously and unequivocally derived from an individual object, it is often supposed to "mean" that object as a sign would "mean" it. This belief is reinforced by the fact that a name borne by a living person always is at once a symbol by which we think of the person, and a call-name by which we signal him. Through a confusion of these two functions, the proper name is often deemed the bridge from animal semantic, or sign-using, to human language, which is symbol-using. Dogs, we are told,

---

[1]Note that I have called the terms of our thinking conceptions, not concepts. Concepts are abstract forms embodied in conceptions; their bare presentation may be approximated by so-called "abstract thought," but in ordinary mental life they no more figure as naked factors than skeletons are seen walking the street. Concepts, like decent living skeletons, are always embodied — sometimes rather too much. I shall return to the topic of pure concepts later on, in discussing communication.

understand names — not only their own, but their masters'. So they do, indeed; but they understand them *only in the capacity of call-names*. If you say "James" to a dog whose master bears that name, the dog will interpret the sound as a sign, and *look for* James. Say it to a person who knows someone called thus, and he will ask: "What about James?" That simple question is forever beyond the dog; signification is the only meaning a name can have for him — a meaning which the master's name shares with the master's smell, with his footfall, and his characteristic ring of the door-bell. In a human being, however, the name evokes the *conception* of a certain man so called, and prepares the mind for further conceptions in which the notion of that man figures; therefore the human being naturally asks: "What about James?"

There is a famous passage in the autobiography of Helen Keller, in which 11 this remarkable woman describes the dawn of Language upon her mind. Of course she had used signs before, formed associations, learned to expect things and identify people or places; but there was a great day when all sign-meaning was eclipsed and dwarfed by the discovery that a certain datum in her limited sense-world had a *denotation*, that a particular act of her fingers constituted a *word*. This event had required a long preparation; the child had learned many finger acts, but they were as yet a meaningless play. Then, one day, her teacher took her out to walk — and there the great advent of Language occurred.

"She brought me my hat," the memoir reads, "and I knew I was going out 12 into the warm sunshine. This thought, if a wordless sensation may be called a thought, made me hop and skip with pleasure.

"We walked down the path to the well-house, attracted by the fragrance of 13 the honeysuckle with which it was covered. Some one was drawing water and my teacher placed my hand under the spout. As the cool stream gushed over my hand she spelled into the other the word *water*, first slowly, then rapidly. I stood still, my whole attention fixed upon the motion of her fingers. Suddenly I felt a misty consciousness as of something forgotten — a thrill of returning thought; and somehow the mystery of language was revealed to me. I knew then that w-a-t-e-r meant the wonderful cool something that was flowing over my hand. That living word awakened my soul, gave it light, hope, joy, set it free! There were barriers still, it is true, but barriers that in time could be swept away.

"I left the well-house eager to learn. Everything had a name, and each name 14 gave birth to a new thought. As we returned to the house every object which I touched seemed to quiver with life. That was because I saw everything with the strange, new sight that had come to me."[2]

This passage is the best affidavit we could hope to find for the genuine 15 difference between sign and symbol. The sign is something to act upon, or a means to command action; the symbol is an instrument of thought. Note how Miss Keller qualifies the mental process just preceding her discovery of words — "This thought, *if a wordless sensation may be called a thought."* Real thinking is possible only in the light of genuine language, no matter how limited, how

---

[2]Helen Keller, *The Story of My Life* (1936; 1st ed. 1902), pp. 23-24.

primitive; in her case, it became possible with the discovery that "w-a-t-e-r" was not necessarily a sign that water was wanted or expected, but was the *name* of this substance, by which it could be mentioned, conceived, remembered.

DISCUSSION QUESTIONS

1. Give some examples of expressions you use every day that Professor Langer would classify as signs.

2. What expressions do you use that would be clearly and unambiguously symbols?

3. In paragraph 9 Professor Langer draws her most concise distinction between signs and symbols in their use with a third party. Signs *announce* their objects to a third party, whereas symbols lead the third party to *conceive* or think about, their objects. To see how this works, consider how you might express that you have great wealth. You could do it symbolically with a small but expensive item, a $50 pen, for example. $50 is not, in and of itself, great wealth. But if you were to express this with a sign you would need great wealth itself, such as a wheelbarrow of gold bricks. How would you express, through sign and symbol, your intelligence, your love for another person, your high ideals, your taste in music, or your mechanical skills?

4. Many students think of symbols as strange, mysterious things they are supposed to find in works of literature. How can you counter this impression?

5. Which are more likely to be misinterpreted, signs or symbols? Why?

6. Ralph has a flat tire and has stopped by the side of the road to fix it. Fred is walking along the road, sees Ralph, and would like to help. Fred says, "See you got a flat." Ralph answers, "Yes, I observed that," and throws a tire iron at Fred. How much of the communication of both parties was through sign or symbol? What was misunderstood?

7. The episode from Helen Keller's autobiography, quoted in paragraphs 12-14, in which she describes her first understanding of the word "water," provides the climax in William Gibson's play and film *The Miracle Worker*. Why is it significant?

8. Customs are often continued long after the beliefs they were based on have passed away. Consider, for example, a wedding ceremony. What parts of the ceremony no longer reflect today's values or beliefs? Why do these customs persist?

9. What messages do the following symbols convey: a Greek-letter fraternity pin? A flag decal on a car window? A personalized memo pad ("From the desk of . . . ")? One dozen long-stemmed roses? A single-loop earring worn by a man? A pendant with a peace sign? Ownership of a Volkswagen? A Cadillac? A motorcycle?

CLASSROOM EXERCISE

There is a basic scheme of classification built into our language. This system of classification directs us so that we only see the things we can easily classify with words we have, while we overlook or disregard everything else. As Wendell Johnson said, we see with our categories.

Try now to see if you can learn to classify something in a different way from what you are accustomed to. For example, we classify or divide a person's arm into its definite, concrete categories: finger, hand, wrist, forearm, upper arm, shoulder. But can you *really* tell the exact point at which your wrist ends and your forearm begins? Can you put your finger on the imaginary line between your arm and your shoulder?

In truth, there is no way to tell where the "wrist" ends and the "forearm" begins, because these categories are artificial. The arm is a continuous unit. Now in class, work together in groups to create a *new* way of classifying or "dividing up" an arm. You can base your system of classification on functions, appearance, sensitivity to touch, or anything else you may choose, but try to develop a system you can justify and defend.

S. I. HAYAKAWA
Classification

As we have seen in the previous classroom exercise, the reality around us is more diverse than the categories our languages allow us to divide it into. A more important way in which this classification touches our lives is the way in which we perceive people. Take yourself, for example. When you look into a mirror, you see that familiar face: you. But when other people look at you, they see you in some kind of category: a freshman, a biology major, a motorcycle rider, a granola freak, a guitar player, a redhead, a Methodist, a short person, and a Democrat, all of which you may be. The trouble is that the consequences of the classification you find yourself in may be far-reaching, and something you cannot control. The analysis that Dr. Hayakawa gives to the process is, by now, classic, another kind of category we can use. In January 1977, Dr. Hayakawa became the junior Senator from California.

When a legal distinction is determined . . . between night and day, childhood and maturity, or any other extremes, a point has to be fixed or a line has to be drawn, or gradually picked out by successive decisions, to mark where the change takes place. Looked at by itself without regard to the necessity behind it, the line or point seems arbitrary. It might as well be a little more to the one side or the other. But when it is seen that a line or point there must be, and that there is no mathematical or logical way of fixing it precisely, the decision of the legislature must be accepted unless we can say that it is very wide of any reasonable mark.

Oliver Wendell Holmes

For of course the true meaning of a term is to be found by observing what a man does with it, not by what he says about it.

P. W. Bridgman

Giving Things Names

The figure below shows eight objects, let us say animals, four large and four small, a different four with round heads and another four with square heads, and still another four with curly tails and another four with straight tails. These animals, let us say, are scampering about your village, but since at first they are of no importance to you, you ignore them. You do not even give them a name.

One day, however, you discover that the little ones eat up your grain, while the big ones do not. A differentiation sets itself up, and abstracting the common characteristics of A, B, C, and D, you decide to call these *gogo*; E, F, G, and H you decide to call *gigi*. You chase away the *gogo*, but leave the *gigi* alone.

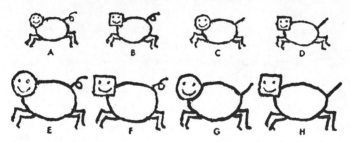

Your neighbor, however, has had a different experience; he finds that those with square heads bite, while those with round heads do not. Abstracting the common characteristics of B, D, F, and H, he calls them *daba*, and A, C, E, and G he calls *dobo*. Still another neighbor discovers, on the other hand, that those with curly tails kill snakes, while those with straight tails do not. He differentiates them, abstracting still another set of common characteristics: A, B, E, and F are *busa*, while C, D, G, and H are *busana*.

Now imagine that the three of you are together when E runs by. You say, "There goes the *gigi*"; your first neighbor says, "There goes the *dobo*"; your other neighbor says, "There goes the *busa*." Here immediately a great controversy arises. What is it really, a *gigi*, a *dobo*, or a *busa*? What is its *right name*? You are quarreling violently when along comes a fourth person from another village who calls it a *muglock*, an edible animal, as opposed to *uglock* an inedible animal— which doesn't help matters a bit.

Of course, the question, "What is it *really*? What is its *right name*?" is a nonsense question. By a nonsense question is meant one that is not capable of being answered. Things can have "right names" only if there is a necessary connection between symbols and things symbolized, and we have seen that there is not. That is to say, in the light of your interest in protecting your grain, it may be necessary for you to distinguish the animal E as a *gigi*; your neighbor, who doesn't like to be bitten, finds it practical to distinguish it as a *dobo*; your other neighbor, who likes to see snakes killed, distinguishes it as a *busa*. What we call things and where we draw the line between one class of things and another depend upon the interests we have and the purposes of the classification. For example, animals are classified in one way by the meat industry, in a different way by the leather industry, in another different way by the fur industry, and in a still different way by the biologist. None of these classifications is any more final than any of the others; each of them is useful for its purpose.

This holds, of course, for everything we perceive. A table "is" a table to us, 5 because we can understand its relationship to our conduct and interests; we eat at it, work on it, lay things on it. But to a person living in a culture where no tables are used, it may be a very big stool, a small platform, or a meaningless structure. If our culture and upbringing were different, that is to say, our world would not even look the same to us.

Many of us, for example, cannot distinguish between pickerel, pike, salmon, 6 smelts, perch, crappies, halibut, and mackerel; we say that they are "just fish, and I don't like fish." To a seafood connoisseur, however, these distinctions are real, since they mean the difference to him between one kind of good meal, a very different kind of good meal, or a poor meal. To a zoologist, even finer distinctions become of great importance, since he has other and more general ends in view. When we hear the statement, then, "This fish is a specimen of the pompano, *Trachinotus Carolinus*," we accept this as being "true," even if we don't care, not because that is its "right name," but because that is how it is classified in the most complete and most general system of classification which people most deeply interested in fish have evolved.

When we name something, then, we are classifying. *The individual object or* 6 *event we are naming, of course, has no name and belongs to no class until we put it in one.* To illustrate again, suppose that we were to give the extensional meaning of the word "Korean." We would have to point to all "Koreans" living at a particular moment and say, "The word 'Korean' denotes at the present moment these persons: A_1, A_2, A_3, . . . A_n." Now, let us say, a child, whom we

Labeling "I don't see it real clear till I label it"

shall designate as Z, is born among these "Koreans." *The extensional meaning of the word "Korean," determined prior to the existence of Z, does not include Z.* Z is a new individual belonging to no classification, since all classifications were made without taking Z into account. Why, then, is Z also a "Korean"? *Because we say so.* And, saying so—fixing the classification—we have determined to a considerable extent future attitudes toward Z. For example, Z will always have certain rights in Korea; he will always be regarded in other nations as an "alien" and will be subject to laws applicable to "aliens."

In matters of "race" and "nationality," the way in which classifications work   7 is especially apparent. For example, I am by birth a "Canadian," by "race" a "Japanese," and am now an "American." Although I was legally admitted to the United States on a Canadian passport as a "non-quota immigrant," I was unable to apply for American citizenship until after 1952. According to American immigration law (since 1952 as well as before), a Canadian entering the United States as a permanent resident has no trouble getting in, unless he happens to be of Oriental extraction, in which case his "nationality" becomes irrelevant and he is classified by "race." If the quota for his "race"—for example, Japanese—is filled (and it usually is), and if he cannot get himself classified as a non-quota immigrant, he is not able to get in at all. Are all these classifications "real"? Of course they are, and *the effect that each of them has upon what he may and may not do constitutes their "reality."*

I have spent my entire life, except for short visits abroad, in Canada and the   8 United States. I speak Japanese haltingly, with a child's vocabulary and an American accent; I do not read or write it. Nevertheless, because classifications seem to have a kind of hypnotic power over some people, I am occasionally credited with (or accused of) having an "Oriental mind." Since Buddha, Confucius, General Tojo, Mao Tse-tung, Pandit Nehru, Syngman Rhee, and the proprietor of the Golden Pheasant Chop Suey House all have "Oriental minds," it is difficult to know whether to feel complimented or insulted.

When is a person a "Negro"? By the definition accepted in the United States,   9 any person with even a small amount of "Negro blood"—that is, whose parents or ancestors were classified as "Negroes"—is a "Negro." *It would be exactly as justifiable to say that any person with even a small amount of "White blood" is "white."* Why do they say one rather than the other? Because the former system of classification *suits the purposes of those making the classification.* Classification is not a matter of identifying "essences," as is widely believed. It is simply a reflection of social convenience and necessity—and different necessities are always producing different classifications.

There are few complexities about classifications at the level of dogs and cats,   10 knives and forks, cigarettes and candy, but when it comes to classifications at high levels of abstraction—for example, those describing conduct, social institutions, philosophical and moral problems—serious difficulties occur. When one person kills another, is it an act of murder, an act of temporary insanity, an act of homicide, an accident, or an act of heroism? As soon as the process of classification is completed, our attitudes and our conduct are to a considerable degree determined. We hang the murderer, we lock up the insane man, we free the victim of circumstances, we pin a medal on the hero.

The Blocked Mind

Unfortunately, people are not always aware of the way in which they arrive at 11
their classifications. Unaware of those characteristics of the extensional Mr.
Miller not covered by classifying him as "a Jew," and attributing to Mr. Miller all
the characteristics suggested by the affective connotations of the term with which
he has been classified, they pass final judgment on Mr. Miller by saying, "Well,
a Jew's a Jew. There's no getting around it!"

We need not concern ourselves here with the injustices done to "Jews," 12
"Roman Catholics," "Republicans," "red-heads," "chorus girls," "sailors,"
"brass-hats," "Southerners," "Yankees," "school teachers," "government regu-
lations," "socialistic proposals," and so on by such hasty judgments or, as it is
better to call them, fixed reactions. "Hasty judgments" suggests that such errors
can be avoided by thinking more slowly; this, of course, is not the case, for some
people think very slowly with no better results. What we are concerned with is
the way in which we block the development of our own minds by such automatic
reactions.

To continue with our example of the people who say, "A Jew's a Jew. There's 13
no getting around that!"—they are, as we have seen, confusing the denoted,
extensional Jew with the fictitious "Jew" inside their heads. Such persons, the
reader will have observed, can usually be made to admit, on being reminded of
certain "Jews" whom they admire—perhaps Albert Einstein, perhaps former
Associate Justice Arthur Goldberg, perhaps Jascha Heifetz, perhaps Sandy
Koufax—that "there are exceptions, of course." They have been compelled by
experience, that is to say, to take cognizance of at least a few of the multitude of
"Jews" who do not fit their preconceptions. At this point, however, they continue
triumphantly, "But exceptions only prove the rule!"[1]—which is another way of
saying, "Facts don't count."

In Marin County, California, I once attended hearings at the county 14
courthouse concerning a proposed ordinance to forbid racial discrimination in
the rental and sale of housing. (Such discrimination in Marin is chiefly directed
against Negroes.) I was impressed by the fact that a large majority of those who
rose to speak were in favor of the ordinance; but I was also impressed by the
number who, though maintaining that they counted Negroes among their best
and most admired friends, still spoke heatedly against a law that would, by
forbidding racial discrimination in the sale and rental of housing, enable Negroes
to live anywhere in the county. Presumably, all the Negroes whom they loved
and admired were "exceptions," and the stereotyped "Negro" remained in their
heads in spite of their experience.

People like this may be said to be impervious to new information. They 15
continue to vote for their party *label*, no matter what mistakes their party makes.
They continue to object to "socialists," no matter what the socialists propose.

---

[1]This extraordinarily fatuous saying originally meant, "The exception tests the rule"—Exceptio
probat regulam. This older meaning of the word "prove" survives in such an expression as "automobile proving ground."

They continue to regard "mothers" as sacred, no matter which mother. A woman who had been given up both by physicians and psychiatrists as hopelessly insane was being considered by a committee whose task it was to decide whether or not she should be committed to an asylum. One member of the committee doggedly refused to vote for commitment. "Gentlemen," he said in tones of deepest reverence, "you must remember that this woman is, after all, a mother."[2] Similarly such people continue to hate "Protestants," no matter which Protestant. Unaware of characteristics left out in the process of classification, they overlook, when the term "Republican" is applied to the party of Abraham Lincoln, the party of Warren Harding, the party of Herbert Hoover, the party of Dwight Eisenhower, and the party of Richard M. Nixon, the rather important differences between them.

Cow₁ Is Not Cow₂

How do we prevent ourselves from getting into such intellectual blind alleys, or, 16 finding we are in one, how do we get out again? One way is to remember that practically all statements in ordinary conversation, debate and public controversy taking the form, "Republicans are Republicans," "Business is business," "Boys will be boys," "Women drivers are women drivers," and so on, are *not* true. Let us put one of these back into a context in life.

> "I don't think we should go through with this deal, Bill. Is it altogether fair to the railroad company?
>
> "Aw, forget it! *Business is business*, after all."

Such an assertion, although it looks like a "simple statement of fact," is not simple and is not a statement of fact. The first "business" *denotes* the transaction under discussion; the second "business" invokes the *connotations* of the word. The sentence is a *directive*, saying,"Let us treat this transaction with complete disregard for considerations other than profit, as the word 'business' suggests." Similarly, when a father tries to excuse the mischief done by his sons, he says, "Boys will be boys"; in other words, "Let us regard the actions of my sons with that indulgent amusement customarily extended toward those whom we call 'boys,' " though the angry neighbor will say, of course, "Boys, my eye! They're little hoodlums; that's what they are!" These too are not informative statements but directives, directing us to classify the object or event under discussion in given ways, in order that we may feel or act in the ways suggested by the terms of the classification.

There is a simple technique for preventing such directives from having their 17 harmful effect on our thinking. It is the suggestion made by Korzybski that we add "index numbers" to our terms, thus: Englishman₁, Englishman₂, En-

---

[2]One wonders how this committee member would have felt about Elizabeth Duncan, executed for murder in San Quentin in 1962, whose possessive love of her son led her to hire assassins to kill her pregnant daughter-in-law.

glishman₃, . . . ; cow₁, cow₂, cow₃, . . ; Frenchman₁, Frenchman₂, French-man₃, . . .; communist₁, communist₂, communist₃, . . . The terms of the classification tell us what the individuals in that class have in common; *the index numbers remind us of the characteristics left out.* A rule can then be formulated as a general guide in all our thinking and reading: *Cow₁ is not cow₂; Jew₁ is not Jew₂; politician₁ is not politician₂; and so on.* This rule, if remembered, prevents us from confusing levels of abstraction and forces us to consider the facts on those occasions when we might otherwise find ourselves leaping to conclusions which we might later have caused to regret.

"Truth"

Most intellectual problems are ultimately problems of classification and nomenclature. Some years ago there was a dispute between the American Medical Association and the Antitrust Division of the Department of Justice as to whether the practice of medicine was a "profession" or "trade." The American Medical Association *wanted* immunity from laws prohibiting "restraint of trade"; therefore, it insisted that medicine is a "profession." The Antitrust Division *wanted* to stop certain economic practices connected with medicine, and therefore it insisted that medicine *is* a "trade." Partisans of either side accused the other of perverting the meanings of words and of not being able to understand plain English. 18

Can farmers operate oil wells and still be "farmers"? In 1947 the attorney general of the state of Kansas sued to dissolve a large agricultural cooperative, Consumers Cooperative Association, charging that the corporation, in owning oil wells, refineries, and pipe-lines, was exceeding the statutory privileges of purchasing cooperatives under the Cooperative Marketing Act, which permits such organizations to "engage in any activity in connection with manufacturing, selling, or supplying to its members machinery, equipment or supplies." The attorney general held that the cooperative, under the Act, could not handle, let alone process and manufacture, general farm supplies, but only those supplies used in the marketing operation. The Kansas Supreme Court decided unanimously in favor of the defendant (CCA). In so deciding, the court held that gasoline and oil are "farm supplies," and producing crude oil is "part of the business of farming." The decision which thus enlarged the definition of "farming" read, 19

> This court will take judicial notice of the fact that in the present state of the art of farming, gasoline . . . is one of the costliest items in the production of agricultural commodities. . . . Anyway, gasoline and tractors are here, and this court is not going to say that motor fuel is not a supply necessary to carrying on of farm operations . . . . Indeed it is about as well put as can be on Page 18 of the state's Exhibit C where the defendant (CCA) says: "*Producing crude oil, operating pipe-lines and refineries, are also part of the business of farming. It is merely producing synthetic hay for iron horses. It is off-the-farm farming' which the farmer, in concert with his neighbors, is carrying on.* . . . Production of power farming equipment, then, is logically an extension of the farmers' own operations." (Italics supplied.)

Is a harmonica player a "musician"? Until 1948, the American Federation of 20
Musicians had ruled that the harmonica was a "toy." Professional harmonica
players usually belonged, therefore, to the American Guild of Variety Artists.
Even as distinguished a musician as Larry Adler, who has often played the
harmonica as a solo instrument with symphony orchestras, was by the union's
definition, "not a musician." In 1948, however, the AFM, finding that harmonica players were getting popular and competing with members of the union,
decided that they were "musicians" after all—a decision that did not sit well with
the president of AGVA, who promptly declared jurisdictional war on the AFM.[3]

Thurman Arnold tells of another instance of a problem in classification: 21

> A plaster company was scraping gypsum from the surface of the ground. If it was a
> mine, it paid one tax; if a manufacturing company, it paid another. Expert witnesses
> were called who almost came to blows, such was their disgust at the stupidity of those
> who could not see that the process was essentially mining, or manufacturing. A great
> record was built up to be reviewed by the State Supreme Court on this important
> question of "fact."[4]

Is aspirin a "drug" or not? In some states, it is legally classified as a "drug," 22
and therefore, it can be sold only by licensed pharmacists. If people want to be
able to buy aspirin in groceries, lunchrooms, and pool halls (as they can in other
states), they must have it reclassified as "not a drug."

Is medicine a "profession" or a "trade"? Is the production of crude oil "a part 23
of farming"? Is a harmonica player a "musician"? Is aspirin a "drug"? Such
questions are commonly settled by appeals to dictionaries to discover the "real
meanings" of the words involved. It is also common practice to consult past legal
decisions and all kinds of learned treatises bearing on the subject. The decision
finally rests, however, not upon appeals to past authority, but upon *what people
want*. If they want the AMA to be immune from antitrust action, they will go to
the Supreme Court if necessary to get medicine "defined" as a "profession." If
they want the AMA prosecuted, they will get a decision that it is a "trade." (They
got, in this case, a decision from the Court that it did not matter whether the
practice of medicine was a "trade" or not; what mattered was that the AMA had,
as charged, *restrained* the trade of Group Health Association, Inc., a cooperative
which procured medical services for its members. The antitrust action was up-
held.)

If people want agricultural cooperatives to operate oil wells, they will get the 24
courts to define the activity in such a way as to make it possible. If the public
doesn't care, the decision whether a harmonica player is or is not a "musician"
will be made by the stronger trade union. The question whether aspirin is or is
not a "drug" will be decided neither by finding the dictionary definition of "drug"
nor by staring long and hard at an aspirin tablet. It will be decided on the basis of
where and under what conditions people want to buy their aspirin.

---

[3]The S.F. Police Dept. Bagpipe Band . . . will soon be decked out in the traditional finery of
bagpipers. Pan-Am is flying over from Scotland 21 uniforms. . . . The pipers, by the way, don't have
to belong to the Musicians Union since the bagpipe is classified as an instrument of war. "Has there
ever been any doubt?" Herb Caen in the San Francisco Chronicle.

[4]The Folklore of Capitalism (1938), p. 182.

In any case, society as a whole ultimately gets, on all issues of wide public 25 importance, the classifications it wants, even if it has to wait until all the members of the Supreme Court are dead and an entirely new court is appointed. When the desired decision is handed down, people say, "Truth has triumphed." *In short, society regards as "true" those systems of classification that produce the desired results.*

The scientific test of "truth," like the social test, is strictly practical, except for 26 the fact that the "desired results" are more severely limited. The results desired by society may be irrational, superstitious, selfish, or humane, but the results desired by scientists are only that our systems of classification produce predictable results. Classifications, as amply indicated already, determine our attitudes and behavior toward the object or event classified. When lightning was classified as "evidence of divine wrath," no courses of action other than prayer were suggested to prevent one's being struck by lightning. As soon, however, as it was classified as "electricity," Benjamin Franklin achieved a measure of control over it by his invention of the lightning rod. Certain physical disorders were formerly classified as "demonic possession," and this suggested that we "drive the demons out" by whatever spells or incantations we could think of. The results were uncertain. But when those disorders were classified as "bacillus infections," courses of action were suggested that led to more predictable results.

Science seeks only the *most generally* useful systems of classification; these it 27 regards for the time being, until more useful classifications are invented, as "true."

DISCUSSION QUESTIONS

1. Putting labels on people is the way we stereotype them, ceasing to think of them as whole people. For example, when Eric Crone became the first Harvard quarterback ever drafted by a National Football League, he kept quiet about it around school. As he told an interviewer, many Harvard students looked upon a football player as "someone who doesn't have a mind." Setting aside ethnic, social, and religious stereotypes for a moment, consider what classifications make a real difference in the way a person— perhaps you—can be perceived. Start with amateur/professional, undergraduate/graduate, sane/insane, etc.

2. Elsewhere, Professor Hayakawa has written that one of the basic techniques for producing humor involves unexpected shifts in classification leading to incongruities that strike us as funny. Think, for example, how we might immediately reclassify a high-fashion model if she were hit in the face with a cream pie. Examine cartoons or the joke page of a newspaper, or recount an episode from a television situation comedy to explain how the principle would work. Here are some starters:

    A. "Billy," said the teacher, "why are you late?"
        "I had to take the bull to the cows," he replied.

"Couldn't your father do that?" she asked?
"No," said Billy, "you have to have a bull."

B. Said a monk as he swung by his tail
To the little monks, male and female,
"From your offspring, my dears,
In a few million years,
May evolve a professor at Yale."

C. A woman of the world was speaking to her social worker.
"For ten years I led a life of shame. . . . "
"Yes," replied the eager social worker. "Then what?"
"Then I got over being ashamed!"

3. How practical do you think Korzybski's suggestion (in paragraph 17) is to assign index numbers to our terms? Do you think it would help *you* avoid unfair or faulty generalizations? What do you think would help people better understand their own stereotyping and prejudice?

4. William Faulkner often wrote of people who were "octoroons"—that is, people who were of one-eighth Negro ancestry. In Faulkner's Yoknapatawpha County, the setting for his novels, octoroons were considered—and treated—as "blacks." Does this seem reasonable to you? How do you classify people as "black" or "white"? Would someone who was one-eighth Jewish be classified as a Jew? How about someone who was one-eighth Estonian? What accounts for the difference in the way we classify people?

5. In paragraph 13, Professor Hayakawa speaks of the difference between the "denoted, extensional Jew" and the "fictitious Jew" inside our heads. What are some of the common stereotypes of Jews? Can you think of any words or expressions that help perpetuate this stereotype?

6. "Words don't mean; people mean." Relate this sentence to what Professor Hayakawa says in paragraphs 6 and 7 about Koreans.

7. In paragraph 6, Professor Hayakawa explains the "extensional" meaning of a word. Is purely "extensional" thinking always possible? *Ever* possible? Explain.

8. Professor Hayakawa says that "people are not always aware of the way in which they arrive at their classifications." How aware are you of the reasons for your classifications? Is *your* mind "blocked" by "automatic reactions?" Discuss.

9. In paragraph 25, Professor Hayakawa says that "society regards as 'true' those systems of classification that produce the desired results." What are the dangers of this attitude? What are the advantages?

CLASSROOM EXERCISES

1. To see how the choice of words can influence the way you perceive things, try your hand at this multiple-choice press release. First circle the positive or approving word within each pair of parentheses. Then read the

release, using only the circled words. Next read the release again using the words that are not circled and see how differently the press release can sound: Same senator, same policies, same facts—only the words to describe them have changed.

Senator Zorch is a man of (firm/stubborn) (prejudices/convictions) with the (courage/gall) to (speak out/mouth off) about them. He has a (gentle/weak) disposition and is very (fussy/meticulous) in his habits. Mrs. Zorch is (notorious/famous) for her (outgoing/interfering) nature and her (articulate speech/glib chatter) as well as her (relaxed/dull) dinner parties. The Senator and Mrs. Zorch (spoil/dote upon) their 6-year-old son, an (energetic/hyperactive) (brat/child) with his father's (obliging/officious) (smirk/grin).

The Senator is known for his (foolhardy/daring) support of the (progressive/radical) State Parks program. He also introduced a bill to (increase/hike) government (payments/handouts) to the (disabled/incompetent). His re-election to the Senate will (subject/treat) his constituents to four more years of (strong leadership/heavy-handed dictatorship).

2. We do not always learn words by looking them up in the dictionary; we learn them by hearing them in *context*. We hear a word used in thousands of different contexts, and each context adds something new to our understanding of the meaning of the word. Working in groups, try to arrive at a definition of the nonsense word "mumsy" based on your understanding of it as it is used in the following contexts. Do *not* stop at a simple, one-word definition; work for a definition that will include the feelings you get about this word (those vague, often hard-to-define feelings are *connotations* of the word).

A. Tired of waking up each morning with that mumsy feeling? Take Geritol and feel more alive.

B. The mumsy lines around her lovely mouth only added to her beauty.

C. I'm not tired or sad, just mumsy.

D. They kissed, and walked together, hand in hand, under the peaceful, mumsy, evening sky.

E. The mumsy notes of the nightingale's song pierced the still night air.

NEWMAN P. BIRK AND GENEVIEVE B. BIRK
Selection, Slanting, and Charged Language

The use of labels or stereotypes is only one way in which language can shape our perception of people and things. As the Classroom Exercise should have demonstrated, the words we use in portraying our subjects help to shape our listener's or reader's perception of them. Although the exercise on the previous pages was intended to be as clear—even obvious—as possible, the techniques can be exceedingly subtle and insidious. They can also be more effective than the mere manipulation of a stereotype.

Consider the effect of the simple little phrase "so-called." Never libelous, never quite a contradiction, they undercut the meaning of any statement in which they appearm See what happens to the harmless nursery-rhyme when you say, "Mary had a little *so-called* lamb . . . "

A. The Principle of Selection

Before it is expressed in words, our knowledge, both inside and outside, is   1
influenced by the principle of selection. What we know or observe depends on what we notice; that is, what we select, consciously or unconsciously, as worthy of notice or attention. As we observe, the principle of selection determines which facts we take in.

Suppose, for example, that three people, a lumberjack, an artist, and a tree   2
surgeon, are examining a large tree in a forest. Since the tree itself is a complicated object, the number of particulars or facts about it that one could observe would be very great indeed. Which of these facts a particular observer will notice will be a matter of selection, a selection that is determined by his interests and purposes. A lumberjack might be interested in the best way to cut the tree down, cut it up and transport it to the lumber mill. His interest would then determine his principle of selection in observing and thinking about the tree. The artist might consider painting a picture of the tree, and his purpose would furnish his principle of selection. The tree surgeon's professional interest in the physical health of the tree might establish a principle of selection for him. If each man were now required to write an exhaustive, detailed report on every thing he observed about the tree, the facts supplied by each would differ, for each would report those facts that his particular principle of selection led him to notice.[1]

The principle of selection holds not only for the specific facts that people   3
observe but also for the facts they remember. A student suddenly embarrassed may remember nothing of the next ten minutes of class discussion but may have a vivid recollection of the sensation of the blood mounting, as he blushed, up his face and into his ears. In both noticing and remembering, the principle of selection applies, and it is influenced not only by our special interest and point of view but by our whole mental state of the moment.

The principle of selection then serves as a kind of sieve or screen through   4
which our knowledge passes before it becomes our knowledge. Since we can't notice everything about a complicated object or situation or action or state of our

---

[1]Of course all three observers would probably report a good many facts in common—the height of the tree, for example, and the size of the trunk. The point we wish to make is that each observer would give us a different impression of the tree because of the different principle of selection that guided his observation.

own consciousness, what we do notice is determined by whatever principle of selection is operating for us at the time we gain the knowledge.

It is important to remember that what is true of the way the principle of selection works for us is true also of the way it works for others. Even before we or other people put knowledge into words to express meaning, that knowledge has been screened or selected. Before an historian or an economist writes a book, or before a reporter writes a news article, the facts that each is to present have been sifted through the screen of a principle of selection. Before one person passes on knowledge to another, that knowledge has already been selected and shaped, intentionally or unintentionally, by the mind of the communicator.

B. The Principle of Slanting

When we put our knowledge into words, a second process of selection, the process of slanting, takes place. Just as there is something, a rather mysterious principle of selection, which chooses for us what we will notice, and what will then become our knowledge, there is also a principle which operates, with or without our awareness, to select certain facts and feelings from our store of knowledge, and to choose the words and the emphasis that we shall use to communicate our meaning.[2] Slanting may be defined as the process of selecting (1) knowledge—factual and attitudinal; (2) words; and (3) emphasis, to achieve the intention of the communicator. Slanting is present in some degree in all communication: one may *slant for* (favorable slanting), *slant against* (unfavorable slanting), or *slant both ways* (balanced slanting).

· · ·

C. Slanting by Use of Emphasis

Slanting by use of the devices of emphasis is unavoidable,[3] for emphasis is simply the giving of stress to subject matter, and so indicating what is important and what is less important. In speech, for example, if we say that Socrates was *a wise old man*, we can give several slightly different meanings, one by stressing *wise*, another by stressing *old*, another by giving equal stress to *wise* and *old*, and still another by giving chief stress to *man*. Each different stress gives a different slant (favorable or unfavorable or balanced) to the statement because it conveys a different attitude toward Socrates or a different judgment of him. Connectives and word order also slant by the emphasis they give: consider the difference in slanting or emphasis produced by *old but wise, old and wise, wise but old*. In

---

[2]Notice that the "principle of selection" is at work as we *take in* knowledge, and that slanting occurs as we *express* our knowledge in words.

[3]When emphasis is present—and we can think of no instance in the use of language in which it is not—it necessarily influences the meaning by playing a part in the favorable, unfavorable, or balanced slant of the communicator. We are likely to emphasize by voice stress, even when we answer *yes* or *no* to simple questions.

writing, we cannot indicate subtle stresses on words as clearly as in speech, but we can achieve our emphasis and so can slant by the use of more complex patterns of word order, by choice of connectives, by underlining heavily stressed words, and by marks of punctuation that indicate short or long pauses and so give light or heavy emphasis. Question marks, quotation marks, and exclamation points can also contribute to slanting.[4] It is impossible either in speech or in writing to put two facts together without giving some slight emphasis or slant. For example, if we have in mind only two facts about a man, his awkwardness and his strength, we subtly slant those facts favorably or unfavorably in whatever way we may choose to join them:

More Favorable Slanting	Less Favorable Slanting
He is awkward and strong.	He is strong and awkward.
He is awkward but strong.	He is strong but awkward.
Although he is somewhat awkward, he is very strong.	He may be strong, but he's very awkward.

With more facts and in longer passages it is possible to maintain a delicate balance by alternating favorable and unfavorable emphasis and so producing a balanced effect.

All communication, then, is in some degree slanted by the *emphasis* of the   8 communicator.

D. Slanting by Selection of Facts

To illustrate the technique of slanting by selection of facts, we shall examine   9 three passages of informative writing which achieve different effects simply by the selection and emphasis of material. Each passage is made up of true statements or facts about a dog, yet the reader is given three different impressions. The first passage is an example of objective writing or balanced slanting, the second is slanted unfavorably, and the third is slanted favorably.

A. *Balanced Presentation*

Our dog, Toddy, sold to us a cocker, produces various reactions in various   10 people. Those who come to the back door she usually growls and barks at (a milkman has said that he is afraid of her); those who come to the front door, she whines at and paws; also she tries to lick people's faces unless we have forestalled her by putting a newspaper in her mouth. (Some of our friends encourage these actions; others discourage them. Mrs. Firmly, one friend, slaps the dog with a newspaper and says, "I know how hard dogs are to train.") Toddy knows and responds to a number of words and phrases, and guests sometimes remark that she is a "very intelligent dog." She has fleas in the summer, and she sheds, at times copiously, the year round. Her blonde hairs are conspicuous when they are

---

[4]Consider the slanting achieved by punctuation in the following sentences: He called the Senator an honest man? *He* called the Senator an honest man? He called the Senator an honest man! He said one more such "honest" senator would corrupt the state.

on people's clothing or on rugs or furniture. Her color and her large brown eyes frequently produce favorable comment. An expert on cockers would say that her ears are too short and set too high and that she is at least six pounds too heavy.

The passage above is made up of facts, verifiable facts,[5] deliberately selected   11 and emphasized to produce a *balanced* impression. Of course not all the facts about the dog have been given—to supply *all* the facts on any subject, even such a comparatively simple one, would be an almost impossible task. Both favorable and unfavorable facts are used, however, and an effort has been made to alternate favorable and unfavorable details so that neither will receive greater emphasis by position, proportion, or grammatical structure.

B. *Facts Slanted* Against

That dog put her paws on my white dress as soon as I came in the door, and she   12 made so much noise that it was two minutes before she had quieted down enough for us to talk and hear each other. Then the gas man came and she did a great deal of barking. And her hairs are on the rug and on the furniture. If you wear a dark dress they stick to it like lint. When Mrs. Firmly came in, she actually hit the dog with a newspaper to make it stay down, and she made some remark about training dogs. I wish the Birks would take the hint or get rid of that noisy, short-eared, overweight "cocker" of theirs.

This unfavorably slanted version is based on the same facts, but now these   13 facts have been selected and given a new emphasis. The speaker, using her selected facts to give her impression of the dog, is quite possibly unaware of her negative slanting.

Now for a favorably slanted version:

C. *Facts Slanted* For

What a lively and responsive dog! When I walked in the door, there she was with   14 a newspaper in her mouth, whining and standing on her hind legs and wagging her tail all at the same time. And what an intelligent dog. If you suggest going for a walk, she will get her collar from the kitchen and hand it to you, and she brings Mrs. Birk's slippers whenever Mrs. Birk says she is "tired" or mentions slippers. At a command she catches balls, rolls over, "speaks," or stands on her hind feet and twirls around. She sits up and balances a piece of bread on her nose until she is told to take it; then she tosses it up and catches it. If you are eating something, she sits up in front of you and "begs" with those big dark brown eyes set in that light, buff-colored face of hers. When I got up to go and told her I was leaving, she rolled her eyes at me and sat up like a squirrel. She certainly is a lively and an intelligent dog.

Speaker C, like Speaker B, is selecting from the "facts" summarized in   15 balanced version A, and is emphasizing his facts to communicate his impression.

All three passages are examples of *reporting* (i.e., consist only of verifiable   16 facts), yet they give three very different impressions of the same dog because of the different ways the speakers slanted the facts. Some people say that figures

---

[5]*Verifiable facts* are facts that can be checked and agreed upon and proved to be true by people who wish to verify them. That a particular theme received a failing grade is a verifiable fact; one needs merely to see the theme with the grade on it. That the instructor should have failed the theme is not, strictly speaking, a verifiable fact, but a matter of opinion. That women on the average live longer than men is a verifiable fact; that they live better is a matter of opinion, a *value judgment*.

don't lie, and many people believe that if they have the "facts," they have the "truth." Yet if we carefully examine the ways of thought and language, we see that any knowledge that comes to us through words has been subjected to the double screening of the principle of selection and the slanting of language. . . .

Wise listeners and readers realize that the double screening that is produced 17 by the principle of selection and by slanting takes place even when prople honestly try to report the facts as they know them. (Speakers B and C, for instance, probably thought of themselves as simply giving information about a dog and were not deliberately trying to mislead.) Wise listeners and readers know too that deliberate manipulators of language, by mere selection and emphasis, can make their slanted facts appear to support almost any cause.

In arriving at opinions and values we cannot always be sure that the facts that 18 sift into our minds through language are representative and relevant and true. We need to remember that much of our information about politics, governmental activities, business conditions, and foreign affairs comes to us selected and slanted. More than we realize, our opinions on these matters may depend on what newspaper we read or what news commentator we listen to. Worth-while opinions call for knowledge of reliable facts and reasonable arguments for and against—and such opinions include beliefs about morality and truth and religion as well as about public affairs. Because complex subjects involve knowing and dealing with many facts on both sides, reliable judgments are at best difficult to arrive at. If we want to be fair-minded, we must be willing to subject our opinions to continual testing by new knowledge, and must realize that after all they *are* opinions, more or less trustworthy. Their trustworthiness will depend on the representativeness of our facts, on the quality of our reasoning, and on the standard of values that we choose to apply.

We shall not give here a passage illustrating the unscrupulous slanting of 19 facts. Such a passage would also include irrelevant facts and false statements presented as facts, along with various subtle distortions of fact. Yet to the uninformed reader the passage would be indistinguishable from a passage intended to give a fair account. If two passages (B and C) of casual and unintentional slanting of facts about a dog can give such contradictory impressions of a simple subject, the reader can imagine what a skilled and designing manipulation of facts and statistics could do to mislead an uninformed reader about a really complex subject. An example of such manipulation might be the account of the United States that Soviet propaganda has supplied to the average Russian. Such propaganda, however, would go beyond the mere slanting of the facts: it would clothe the selected facts in charged words and would make use of the many other devices of slanting that appear in charged language.

E. Slanting by Use of Charged Words

In the passages describing the dog Toddy, we were illustrating the technique 20 of slanting by the selection and emphasis of facts. Though the facts selected had to be expressed in words, the words chosen were as factual as possible, and it was the selection and emphasis of facts and not of words that was mainly responsible for the two distinctly different impressions of the dog. In the passages below we are demonstrating another way of slanting—by the use of charged words. This time the accounts are very similar in the facts they contain; the different impressions of the subject, Corlyn, are produced not by different facts but by the subtle selection of charged words.

The passages were written by a clever student who was told to choose as his 21 subject a person in action, and to write two descriptions, each using the "same facts." The instructions required that one description be slanted positively and the other negatively, so that the first would make the reader favorably inclined toward the person and the action, and the second would make him unfavorably inclined.

MOMMA, Courtesy of Mell Lazarus and Field Newspaper Syndicate. Copyright Field Enterprises.

Here is the favorably charged description. Read it carefully and form your 22 opinion of the person before you go on to read the second description.

Corlyn

Corlyn paused at the entrance to the room and glanced about. A well-cut black 23 dress draped subtly about her slender form. Her long blonde hair gave her chiseled features the simple frame they required. She smiled an engaging smile as she accepted a cigarette from her escort. As he lit it for her she looked over the flame and into his eyes. Corlyn had that rare talent of making every male feel that he was the one man in the world.

She took his arm and they descended the steps into the room. She walked with an 24 effortless grace and spoke with equal ease. They each took a cup of coffee and joined a group of friends near the fire. The flickering light danced across her face and lent an ethereal quality to her beauty. The good conversation, the crackling logs, and the stimulating coffee gave her a feeling of internal warmth. Her eyes danced with each leap of the flames.

Taken by itself this passage might seem just a description of an attractive girl. 25 The favorable slanting by use of charged words has been done so skillfully that it is inconspicuous. Now we turn to the unfavorably slanted description of the "same" girl in the "same" actions:

Corlyn

Corlyn halted at the entrance to the room and looked around. A plain black dress 26 hung on her thin frame. Her stringy bleached hair accentuated her harsh features. She smiled an inane smile as she took a cigarette from her escort. As he lit it for her she stared over the lighter and into his eyes. Corlyn had a habit of making every male feel that he was the last man on earth.

She grasped his arm and they walked down the steps and into the room. Her pace 27 was fast and ungainly, as was her speech. They each reached for some coffee and broke into a group of acquaintances near the fire. The flickering light played across her face and revealed every flaw. The loud talk, the fire, and the coffee she had gulped down made her feel hot. Her eyes grew more red with each leap of the flames.

When the reader compares these two descriptions, he can see how charged 28 words influence the reader's attitude. One needs to read the two descriptions several times to appreciate all the subtle differences between them. Words, some rather heavily charged, others innocent-looking but lightly charged, work together to carry to the reader a judgment of a person and a situation. If the reader had seen only the first description of Corlyn, he might well have thought that he had formed his "own judgment on the basis of the facts." And the examples just given only begin to suggest the techniques that may be used in heavily charged language. For one thing, the two descriptions of Corlyn contain no really good example of the use of charged abstractions; for another, the writer was obliged by the assignment to use the same set of facts and so could not slant by selecting his material.

F. Slanting and Charged Language

. . . When slanting of facts, or words, or emphasis, or any combination of 29 the three *significantly influences* feelings toward, or judgments about, a subject, the language used is charged language.

• • •

Of course communications vary in the amount of charge they carry and in 30 their effect on different people; what is very favorably charged for one person may have little or no charge, or may even be adversely charged, for others. It is sometimes hard to distinguish between charged and uncharged expression. But it is safe to say that whenever we wish to convey any kind of inner knowledge— feelings, attitudes, judgments, values—we are obliged to convey that attitudinal meaning through the medium of charged language; and when we wish to understand the inside knowledge of others, we have to interpret the charged language that they choose, or are obliged, to use. Charged language, then, is the natural and necessary medium for the communication of charged or attitudinal meaning. At times we have difficulty in living with it, but we should have even greater difficulty in living without it.

Some of the difficulties in living with charged language are caused by its use 31 in dishonest propaganda, in some editorials, in many political speeches, in most advertising, in certain kinds of effusive salesmanship, and in blatantly insincere, or exaggerated, or sentimental expressions of emotion. Other difficulties are caused by the misunderstandings and misinterpretations that charged language produces. A charged phrase misinterpreted in a love letter; a charged word spoken in haste or in anger; an acrimonious argument about religion or politics or athletics or fraternities; the frustrating uncertainty produced by the effort to understand the complex attitudinal meaning in a poem or play or a short story—

these troubles, all growing out of the use of charged language, may give us the feeling that Robert Louis Stevenson expressed when he said, "The battle goes sore against us to the going down of the sun."

But however charged language is abused and whatever misunderstandings it 32 may cause, we still have to live with it—and even by it. It shapes our attitudes and values even without our conscious knowledge; it gives purpose to, and guides, our actions; through it we establish and maintain relations with other people and by means of it we exert our greatest influence on them. Without charged language, life would be but half life. The relatively uncharged language of bare factual statement, though it serves its informative purpose well and is much less open to abuse and to misunderstanding, can describe only the bare land of factual knowledge; to communicate knowledge of the turbulencies and the calms and the deep currents of the sea of inner experience we must use charged language.

DISCUSSION QUESTIONS

1. Bring a copy of your local newspaper's editorial page to class. It should contain several editorials from the newspaper itself, letters to the editor, and a selection of syndicated columnists. As a class exercise, see how many examples of slanting and charged language you can find. Examples will probably be easier to find in those opinions you are opposed to, but they will appear in the writings of all political persuasions. How can the "verifiable facts" be separated from the rest of the language in the rest of the article, letter, or editorial?

2. As an example of slanting by emphasis, read aloud in class the sentence "The worm will turn," a sentence sometimes used in the training of actors. You should be able to make it mean four different statements.

3. How do the examples in paragraph 7 work and why?

4. Following the example of Toddy, the dog, pick a thoroughly inoffensive or neutral object—the blackboard eraser, a table, a wastebasket, or whatever—and sort out what can be said about it. List first the verifiable facts, weight, color, texture, etc., and then list the favorable or unfavorable judgments that could be made about it: quality of workmanship, smell, cleanliness, etc. Do you find that the judgment will tend to overweigh the verifiable facts in your perception of the object?

5. What are the charged words in the description of Corlyn? Pick out the precise words that influence your view of her.

6. What are some of the "charged abstractions" about Corlyn, as explained in paragraph 28?

7. Gilbert Highet once said that "to simplify history is to falsify it." Have you ever known a situation where omitting details distorted the facts? Explain.

8. Why does a given word mean different things to different people?

CLASSROOM EXERCISE

In one sense, as Hayakawa points out, all words are abstractions, since they are not the things themselves; that is, words are not the things they refer to. But it is also true that some words are more abstract than others. The word "philosophy," for example, is more abstract, more removed from the concrete world of things we perceive through the senses, than is the word "bacon." "Bacon" is something we can touch, smell, crumble, eat, and hold in our hands; it has a *concrete* manifestation that the abstraction "philosopy" lacks. (Where can you get a half-pound of philosophy?)

Here is a scale of words ranged in order of decreasing levels of abstraction:

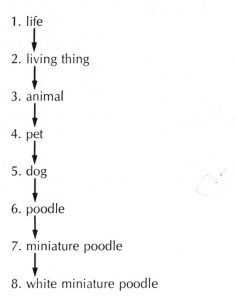

1. life

2. living thing

3. animal

4. pet

5. dog

6. poodle

7. miniature poodle

8. white miniature poodle

Notice how the downward step focuses your perception of the thing referred to a bit more clearly at the same time as it narrows the range of things referred to. "Life" is a more general and inclusive concept than "white miniature poodle," which is fairly narrow and specific.

See if you can work out your own abstract-concrete scale, using these relatively abstract terms as starting points. Work your way downward until you have arrived at a word that is very concrete, trying to use at least 6 steps, more if you can.

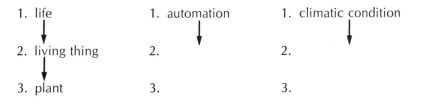

1. life	1. automation	1. climatic condition
2. living thing	2.	2.
3. plant	3.	3.

Now try to work your way back up the scale, using the concrete terms on the bottom as starting points and ending on top with a word that is very abstract.

1.	1.
2.	2.
3.	3.
4.	4.
5.	5.
6.	6.

7. baby broccoli spears   7. brown shag carpet

G.I.'s, in Pincer Move, Kill 128 in a Daylong Battle

Special to The New York Times

SAIGON, South Vietnam, Sunday, March 17—American troops caught a North Vietnamese force in a pincer movement on the central coastal plain yesterday, killing 128 enemy soldiers in daylong fighting.

Two American soldiers were killed and 10 wounded, according to an American spokesman.

The fighting erupted six miles northeast of Quangngai in an area of sand dunes and scrub brush between Highway 1 and the South China Sea.

At the same time, South Vietnamese rangers backed by a company of United States armor from the 11th Armored Cavalry Regiment were reported to have killed 95 of the enemy in a six-and-a-half-hour fight 16 miles northwest of Saigon.

The American headquarters said there were no United States casualties. South Vietnamese casualties were described as light.

The action was part of a vast operation under way in five provinces around Saigon to eliminate the enemy threat against the capital.

SEYMOUR HERSH
The Day

Look at the copy of the original news account of the My Lai mas-
sacre. Before you read further, go back and see—actually underline—all
the concrete words you can find in it.
Then read on in Seymour Hersh's account of that day. How much of
what he gives you is concrete, verifiable fact?

It was sunny and already hot when the first helicopter started its noisy flight to   1
My Lai 4. The time was 7:22 A.M.; it was logged by a tape recorder at brigade
headquarters. A brief artillery barrage had already begun; the My Lai 4 area was
being "prepped" in anticipation of that day's search-and-destroy mission. A few
heavily armed helicopters were firing thousands of small-caliber bullets into the
area by the time Calley and his men landed in a soggy rice paddy 150 meters west
of the hamlet. It was harvest season; the green fields were thick with growth.

· · ·

The hamlet itself had a population of about 700 people, living either in   2
flimsy thatch-covered huts—"hootches," as the GIs called them—or in solidly
made red-brick homes, many with small porches in front. . . . The foliage was
dense: there were high bamboo trees, hedges and plant life everywhere. Medina
couldn't see thirty feet into the hamlet from the landing zone.
The first two platoons of Charlie Company, still unfired upon, entered the   3
hamlet. . . . Calley and some of his men walked into the plaza area in the
southern part of the hamlet. None of the people was running away; they knew
that U. S. soldiers would assume that anyone running was a Viet Cong and
would shoot to kill. There was no immediate sense of panic. The time was about
8 A.M. . . . Grzesik and his men began their usual job of pulling people from
their homes, interrogating them, and searching for Viet Cong. The villagers
were gathered up, and Grzesik sent Meadlo, who was in his unit, to take them to
Calley for further questioning. . . .
Some of Calley's men thought it was breakfast time as they walked in; a few   4
families were gathered in front of their homes cooking rice over a small fire.
Without a direct order, the first platoon also began rounding up the villagers.
There still was no sniper fire, no sign of a large enemy unit. Sledge remembered
thinking that "if there were VC around, they had plenty of time to leave before
we came in. We didn't tiptoe in there."
The killings began without warning. Harry Stanley told the C.I.D. that one   5
young member of Calley's platoon took a civilian into custody and then "pushed
the man up to where we were standing and then stabbed the man in the back
with his bayonet. . . . The man fell into the ground and was gasping for breath."
The GI then "killed him with another bayonet thrust or by shooting him with a
rifle. . . . There was so many people killed that day it is hard for me to recall
exactly how some of the people died." The youth next "turned to where some
soldiers were holding another forty- or fifty-year-old man in custody." He

"picked this man up and threw him down a well. Then [he] pulled the pin from a M26 grenade and threw it in after the man." Moments later Stanley saw "some old women and some little children—fifteen or twenty of them—in a group around a temple where some incense was burning. They were kneeling and crying and praying, and various soldiers . . . walked by and executed these women and children by shooting them in the head with their rifles. The soldiers killed all fifteen or twenty of them. . . . "

There were few physical protests from the people; about eighty of them were 6
taken quietly from their homes and herded together in the plaza area. A few hollered out, "No VC. No VC." But that was hardly unexpected. Calley left Meadlo, Boyce and a few others with the responsibility of guarding the group. "You know what I want you to do with them," he told Meadlo. Ten minutes later—about 8:15 A.M.—he returned and asked, "Haven't you got rid of them yet? I want them dead." Radioman Sledge, who was trailing Calley, heard the officer tell Meadlo to "waste them." Meadlo followed orders: "We stood about ten to fifteen feet away from them and then he [Calley] started shooting them. Then he told me to start shooting them. I started to shoot them. So we went ahead and killed them. I used more than a whole clip—used four or five clips." There are seventeen M16 bullets in each clip. . . . Women were huddled against their children, vainly trying to save them. Some continued to chant, "No VC." Others simply said, "No. No. No."

• • •

Brooks and his men in the second platoon to the north had begun to sys- 7
tematically ransack the hamlet and slaughter the people, kill the livestock and destroy the crops. Men poured rifle and machine-gun fire into huts without knowing—or seemingly caring—who was inside.

• • •

Roberts and Haeberle also moved in just behind the third platoon. Haeberle 8
watched a group of ten to fifteen GIs methodically pump bullets into a cow until it keeled over. A woman then poked her head out from behind some brush; she may have been hiding in a bunker. The GIs turned their fire from the cow to the woman. "They just kept shooting at her. You could see the bones flying in the air chip by chip." No one had attempted to question her; GIs inside the hamlet also were asking no questions. . . .

• • •

Herbert Carter also remembered seeing Medina inside the hamlet well after 9
the third platoon began its advance: "I saw all those dead people laying there. Medina came right behind me." At one point in the morning one of the members of Medina's CP joined in the shooting. "A woman came out of a hut with a baby in her arms and she was crying," Carter told the C.I.D. "She was crying because her little boy had been in front of their hut and . . . someone had killed the child by shooting it." When the mother came into view, one of Medina's men "shot her with an M16 and she fell. When she fell, she dropped the baby." The GI next "opened up on the baby with his M16." The infant was also killed. Carter also saw an officer grab a woman by the hair and shoot her with a .45-caliber pistol: "He held her by the hair for a minute and then let go and she

fell to the ground. Some enlisted man standing there said, "Well, she'll be in the big rice paddy in the sky.' "

. . .

Those Vietnamese who were not killed on the spot were being shepherded by   10
the first platoon to a large drainage ditch at the eastern end of the hamlet. After Grzesik left, Meadlo and a few others gathered seven or eight villagers in one hut and were preparing to toss in a hand grenade when an order came to take them to the ditch. There he found Calley, along with a dozen other first platoon members, and perhaps seventy-five Vietnamese, mostly women, old men and children.

Calley turned his attention back to the crowd of Vietnamese and issued an   11
order: "Push all those people in the ditch." Three or four GIs complied. Calley struck a woman with a rifle as he pushed her down. Stanley remembered that some of the civilians "kept trying to get out. Some made it to the top. . . . " Calley began the shooting and ordered Meadlo to join in. Meadlo told about it later: "So we pushed our seven to eight people in with the big bunch of them. And so I began shooting them all. So did Mitchell, Calley. . . . I guess I shot maybe twenty-five or twenty people in the ditch . . . men, women and children. And babies." Some of the GIs switched from automatic fire to single-shot to conserve ammunition. Herbert Carter watched the mothers "grabbing their kids and the kids grabbing their mothers. I didn't know what to do."

William C. Lloyd of Tampa, Florida, told the C.I.D. that some grenades   12
were also thrown into the ditch. Dennis Conti noticed that "a lot of women had thrown themselves on top of the children to protect them, and the children were alive at first. Then the children who were old enough to walk got up and Calley began to shoot the children."

One further incident stood out in many GIs' minds: seconds after the shoot-   13
ing stopped, a bloodied but unhurt two-year-old boy miraculously crawled out of the ditch, crying. He began running toward the hamlet. Someone hollered, "There's a kid." There was a long pause. Then Calley ran back, grabbed the child, threw him back in the ditch and shot him.

. . .

Nineteen-year-old Nguyen Thi Ngoc Tuyet watched a baby trying to open   14
her slain mother's blouse to nurse. A soldier shot the infant while it was struggling with the blouse, and then slashed at it with his bayonet. Tuyet also said she saw another baby hacked to death by GIs wielding their bayonets.

In the early afternoon the men of Charlie Company mopped up to make sure   15
all the houses and goods in My Lai 4 were destroyed. Medina ordered the underground tunnels in the hamlet blown up; most of them already had been blocked. Within another hour My Lai 4 was no more: its red-brick buildings demolished by explosives, its huts burned to the ground, its people dead or dying.

Michael Bernhardt later summarized the day: "We met no resistance and I   16
only saw three captured weapons. We had no casualties. It was just like any other Vietnamese village—old papa-sans, women and kids. As a matter of fact, I don't remember seeing one military-age male in the entire place, dead or alive. The only prisoner I saw was in his fifties."

When Army investigators reached the barren area in November, 1969, in 17 connection with the My Lai probe in the United States, they found mass graves at three sites, as well as a ditch full of bodies. It was estimated that between 450 and 500 people—most of them women, children and old men—had been slain and buried there.

DISCUSSION QUESTIONS

1. After reading the *New York Times* article on My Lai, do you see a danger in abstract language? Do you see any advantages? Explain.

2. The *Times* article speaks about "eliminating the enemy threat." Can you think of a more concrete way to say this? Can you say it using even more abstract language?

3. It has been claimed that military accounts of events use abstract language to conceal the concrete realities of warfare: 100 "casualties" is certainly more abstract than 100 "dead soldiers." Do you know any other military terms that hide reality in the same way?

4. Would it be a good idea to eliminate abstract words altogether? Would this be possible?

5. After fuller reports of what happened at My Lai 4 were publicized, the army conducted an investigation, after which a court-martial was held. Lieutenant Calley was tried and found guilty, a decision which remains controversial. If you were a defender of Lieutenant Calley, in court or out, how would you present the details of Hersh's descriptions so that they would portray the defendant in the best possible light?

6. Can you find examples where Hersh has used slanted or charged language? Or do the events he describes speak for themselves?

7. How would you characterize Hersh's tone in presenting the description of the events at My Lai 4? What is the evidence of that tone? What other tone might he have taken in talking about these events? How could he have taken another tone?

Student Essay
Tree

I buy the idea that we learn the meaning of words by hearing them in our 1 every day lives, rather than by looking them up in the dictionary. For example, I just looked up the word "tree" in a dictionary, and the entry read like a botany lesson. It didn't tell me anything of what I already know about trees. But I am not thinking about "trees" in general or all the trees in the forest, but just the word "tree" itself. The word never means to me what it did to that clown who wrote,

"Poems are made by fools like me, but only God can make a tree." Not at all. The idea of a tree scares me a little.

When I was little my father used to take me fishing every summer. We always went to the farm of my uncle Emil, who lived at the end of a long backroad called the "Bootjack Road." Most of the farms on the Bootjack Road had been abandoned, and the farmland had turned to scrub. Right in the middle of this waste land there was one, lonely, tall, tree. It looked diseased, as though it had termites, but it was so big that no wind could blow it down. It had only a few leaves toward the top, and it had only one lower branch about fifteen feet off the ground—just perfect for a hanging. The bark was black so that it looked menacing, even on a bright, sunny day. The tree always made me uneasy. When I was seven or eight I used to get down in the back seat so I wouldn't have to look at it, and the grown men in the front didn't pay any attention to me. When I got older my father told me it was stupid not to look at the tree, and so I would pretend not to notice it. But I usually fiddled with the radio about the time we passed it.

I suppose my uncle Emil had something to do with the way I felt about the tree. His wife had left him before I was born, and his house was usually a mess when we came there to fish. He could never make up his mind between whisky and some kind of crazy religion. Some summers we would have to sober him up when we came to fish. Other summers he would just want to read the Bible at us, even when we were out in the boat, so that he would scare away the fish. He was killed two winters ago in a car crash. The neighbors said he was on his way to church, so I suppose he wasn't drinking. But he was hit while driving the Bootjack Road, not far from my least favorite tree. I don't think the tree is spooked, but, then again, I wasn't surprised either.

One of the things that brought all of this back into my head was seeing an old Gary Cooper movie, *The Hanging Tree*, on television. George C. Scott is also in the movie, playing a kind of crazed religious fanatic. He acts a little bit like my uncle Emil. And as you can tell from the title of the movie, part of it deals with a hanging. A lynch mob wants to string up Gary Cooper. Watching the movie I felt it had been made out of my dreams and memories.

RHETORICAL ANALYSIS

1. Does any one sentence in this short essay summarize the sentiment of the whole? Where is it?

2. Look again at the last three sentences in the first paragraph. The first of those three sentences has twenty-eight words in it, the second has three, and the third has nine. Is this contrast in sentence length a good idea? Which of the sentences is the most important?

3. How would you characterize the student's use of concrete language?

4. Does he employ examples of slanted language?

5. Is this paper really more about the student's uncle rather than about the tree?

6. Would the paper have been more effective if the student had given a closer description of the mysterious tree? All of his descriptions are given from the point of view of someone driving by.

POINTS OF DEPARTURE

A ✓ 1/24/80

. . . if a race of people had the physiological defect of being able to see only 1
the color blue, they would hardly be able to formulate the rule that they saw only
blue. The term blue would convey no meaning to them, their language would
lack color terms, and their words denoting their various sensations of blue would
answer to, and translate, our words light, dark, white, black, and so on, not our
word blue. In order to formulate the rule or norm of seeing only blue, they
would need exceptional moments in which they saw other colors. The
phenomenon of gravitation forms a rule without exceptions; needless to say, the
untutored person is utterly unaware of any law of gravitation, for it would never
enter his head to conceive of a universe in which bodies behaved otherwise than
they do at the earth's surface. Like the color blue with our hypothetical race, the
law of gravitation is a part of the untutored individual's background, not something he isolates from that background. The law could not be formulated until
bodies that always fell were seen in terms of a wider astronomical world in which
bodies moved in orbits or went this way and that.

. . .

Formulation of ideas is not an independent process, strictly rational in the 2
old sense, but is part of a particular grammar and differs, from slightly to greatly,
as between different grammars. We dissect nature along lines laid down by our
native languages. The categories and types that we isolate from the world of
phenomena we do not find there because they stare every observer in the face; on
the contrary, the world is presented in a kaleidoscopic flux of impressions which
has to be organized by our minds—and this means largely by the linguistic
systems in our minds. We cut nature up, organize it into concepts, and ascribe
significances as we do, largely because we are parties to an agreement to organize
it in this way—an agreement that holds throughout our speech community and
is codified in the patterns of our language. The agreement is, of course, an
implicit and unstated one, *but its terms are absolutely obligatory*; we cannot talk
at all except by subscribing to the organization and classification of data which
the agreement decrees.

Benjamin Lee Whorf, from *Science and Linguistics*

B ✓

. . . Brains think with words. Perhaps they need not. Supposedly if we had 1
no words, we should still be able to think. But it is the nature of human brains
that they think so much better with words than with any other medium—with
mental pictures, for instance—that, words being available, we learn to think with
them, and rely upon them so much that for practical purposes most people think
only about things for which they have words and can think only in the directions
for which they have words.

Perhaps an analogy may help. Most people can swim a narrow river. Water is 2
an alien element, but with labor we can force ourselves through it. A good

swimmer can cross a wide river, a lake, even the English Channel; no one, as far as we know, has ever swum the Atlantic Ocean, or is likely to do so. Even a champion swimmer, if he had business which required him to spend alternate weeks in Paris and London, would not expect to make the trip regularly by swimming the English Channel. Although we can force ourselves through water by skill and main strength, for all practical purposes our ability to traverse water is only as good as our ships or our airplanes. And so with the activities of our brains. Thinking is probably as foreign to human nature as is water; it is an unnatural element into which we throw ourselves with hesitation, and in which we flounder once we are there. We have learned, during the millenniums, to do rather well with thinking, but only if we buoy ourselves up with words. Some thinking of a simple sort we can do without words, but difficult and sustained thinking, presumably, is completely impossible without their aid, as traversing the Atlantic Ocean is presumably impossible without instruments of marine or supramarine transportation.

Charlton Laird, from *The Miracle of Language*

C

Human beings do not live in the objective world alone, nor alone in the world of social activity as ordinarily understood, but are very much at the mercy of the particular language which has become the medium of expression for their society. It is quite an illusion to imagine that one adjusts to reality essentially without the use of language and that language is merely an incidental means of solving specific problems of communications or reflection. The fact of the matter is that the "real world" is to a large extent unconsciously built up on the language habits of the group. . . . We see and hear and otherwise experience very largely as we do because the language habits of our community predispose certain choices of interpretation.

Edward Sapir, from *Language*

D

Thus the task of education is to make children fit to live in a society by persuading them to learn and accept its codes—the rules and conventions of communication whereby the society holds itself together. There is first the spoken language. The child is taught to accept "tree" and not "boojum" as the agreed sign for that (pointing to the object). We have no difficulty in understanding that the word "tree" is a matter of convention. What is much less obvious is that convention also governs the delineation of the thing to which the word is assigned. For the child has to be taught not only what words are to stand for what things, but also the way in which his culture has tacitly agreed to divide things from each other, to mark out the boundaries within our daily experience. Thus, scientific convention decides whether an eel shall be a fish or a snake, and grammatical convention determines what experiences shall be called objects and what shall be called events or actions. How arbitrary such conventions may be can be seen from the question, "What happens to my fist (noun-object) when I open my hand?" The object miraculously vanishes because an action was disguised by a part of speech usually assigned to a thing! In English the differences between things and actions are clearly, if not always logically, distinguished but a great number of Chinese words do duty for both nouns and verbs—so that one who thinks in Chinese has little difficulty in seeing that objects are also events, that our world is a collection of processes rather than entities.

Stop   1/24/80

Alan Watts, from *The Way of Zen*

E

> In Shaw's *Don Juan in Hell,* a play-within-the-play in *Man and Superman,* the fabled Juan finds himself with some distasteful company, not only the Devil himself, but worse, his friends—who bear a distinct relationship to those elements in English society that the playwright most despised.

DON JUAN. Pooh! why should I be civil to them or to you? In this Palace of Lies a truth or two will not hurt you. Your friends are all the dullest dogs I know. They are not beautiful: they are only decorated. They are not clean: they are only shaved and starched. They are not dignified: they are only fashionably dressed. They are not educated: they are only college passmen. They are not religious: they are only pewrenters. They are not moral: they are only conventional. They are not virtuous: they are only cowardly. They are not even vicious: they are only "frail." They are not artistic: they are only lascivious. They are not prosperous: they are only rich. They are not loyal, they are only servile; not dutiful, only sheepish; not public spirited, only patriotic; not courageous, only quarrelsome; not determined, only obstinate; not masterful, only domineering; not self-controlled, only obtuse; not self-respecting, only vain; not kind, only sentimental; not social, only gregarious; not considerate, only polite; not intelligent, only opinionated; not progressive, only factious; not imaginative, only superstitious, not just, only vindictive; not generous, only propitiatory; not disciplined, only cowed; and not truthful at all—liars every one of them, to the very backbone of their souls.

George Bernard Shaw, from *Don Juan in Hell*

F

. . . take the word *tabloid*, the denotation of which refers to small size. For that reason, newspapers with pages that are half as large as regular ones and which specialize in very brief news articles are regularly called tabloids. But because the average tabloid newspaper emphasizes the racy and the bizarre in its attempt to appeal to a certain class of readers, the word's connotation introduces the idea of sensationalism, of "yellow journalism." Thus *tabloid*, not surprisingly, is applied to newspapers in a negative, or pejorative, sense. In such a fashion many words acquire additional meanings which are derived from common experience and usage. (Similarly, the term *prima donna* refers, strictly speaking, to the leading woman in an opera company. By what process has it come to be applied to a certain kind of man or woman, with no reference to opera?)

Nothing is more essential to intelligent, profitable reading than sensitivity to connotation. Only when we possess such sensitivity can we understand both what the author *means*, which may be quite plain, and what he wants to *suggest*, which may actually be far more important than the superficial meaning. The difference between reading a book, a story, an essay, or a poem for surface meaning and reading it for implication is the difference between listening to the New York Philharmonic Symphony Orchestra on a battered old transister radio and listening to it on a high-fidelity stereophonic record player. Only the latter brings out the nuances that are often more significant than the obvious, and therefore easily comprehended, meaning.

Richard Altick, from *A Preface to Critical Reading*

WRITING ASSIGNMENTS

Essays

1. Choose a word that you think has strong connotations for you. Then write about that word so that others can understand, as much as possible, exactly what it means to you. You will have to discuss some of the experiences (contexts) associated with the word to do this.

2. Take any one of the questions posed by Hayakawa in paragraph 23 of his essay "Classification" on classifying professions and answer it in a short essay. Be sure you give the *reasons* for the classification you choose.

3. One serious problem in classification that affects many students is how to classify marijuana. Should it be classed as a "dangerous drug" as are heroin and LDS, or should it be considered legally in the same class with alcohol? Many judges today have the power to rule whether possession or use of this drug is a misdemeanor or a felony—a difference of classification which could mean the difference between a stiff prison sentence and a small fine with probation. Write an essay defending or attacking a hypothetical law that would classify marijuana as a harmless stimulant and would make any possessor of it subject to a light fine. Do your classifications have an extensional validity founded on reports?

4. If you are presently studying a language other than English, write an essay on how the vocabulary of that language views the world differently from English. What expressions from English cannot be translated well into that language? And what idioms from that language cannot be put well into English? What does your experience tell you about the Sapir-Whorf thesis?

5. Choose at least two generalizations and evaluate them for their usefulness and accuracy. How about "Blonds have more fun," "All politicians are crooks," "Football players are dumb," or "All generalizations are false."

6. Choose a term used to classify a group of people—hippie, women's libber, etc.—and write a short essay defining the stereotype. How fair or how accurate is the stereotype, in your experience?

7. Remember the "Happiness Is a Warm Puppy" series of "Peanuts" cartoon books? What that series did was try to define an abstract term (happiness) by giving concrete examples of things it could refer to (a warm puppy, a martini, etc.). You try the same thing. Define or explain an abstract term by giving some *concrete* illustrations of its meaning. Do not simply list things as the "Peanuts" series do; expand and develop your concrete examples into paragraph descriptions. Some suggestions for abstract terms you could use: love, faith, trust, sorrow, misery, freedom, brotherhood.

8. Describe an actual situation (or invent an imaginary one) in which two people misunderstood each other because they attached different meanings to the same word. Was the misunderstanding over the denotation or the connotation of the word? Explain.

9. Think of some argument, accident, or other event you witnessed recently. Describe what happened, being careful to stick to the facts, but using words with very favorable connotations. Then write a second description of the *same* story, using words with negative connotations. Be careful *not* to change the facts of the story or anything else except the connotations of the words you use to relate it. For example, in one version a person could be "firm" in "sticking" to his "principles." In another he could be "obstinate" in "clinging" to his "prejudices."

10. After re-examining the short selections on language at the end of the chapter, write an essay giving your own definition of what language is.

11. Describe the system of communication you have had with an animal. Was this communication by sign or symbol? Discuss.

JOURNAL KEEPING   1/24/80

1. Think of some thing or group of things for which we have an elaborate system of classifications (such as cars, buildings, or music). Then think of an *alternate system of classification*—simpler, with fewer distinctions. What kind of society might use your new system of classification? Do you see any advantages to it?

2. The philosopher Bertrand Russell used to play a verbal game that went like this: "I am firm/You are stubborn/He is a pig-headed fool." As you are reading the material in this chapter, jot down in your journal some variations on this. Make them all denote the same thing, e.g., "I am pretty/You are attractive/She is nice-looking." You're not playing the game if you write "her face would stop a horse."

3. Clip out articles from newspapers or news magazines that you think reveal a decided bias or slant. Paste them in your journal and underline those words that have strong favorable or unfavorable connotations. Try to think of other words the writer could have used which would have carried

roughly the same denotative meaning, but a vastly different connotation. Explain why you think the newspaper or news magazine used the words they did. What were they driving at?

4. Write your own "Letter to the Editor" on some issue you feel strongly about. Choose words that are highly charged to describe your feelings. Now write a *second* letter on the same topic, trying to use language that is more objective and neutral. Which version would someone opposed to your way of thinking be more likely to be swayed by?

5. Check the denotative meaning of some highly charged words, like "love," "freedom," "mother," and "home," in the dictionary. Discuss the differences between these definitions and your connotations of these words.

6. Write a short evaluation of yourself and the kind of person you think you are. Show it to a person who knows you well and let him or her comment on your selection of detail and slanting.

3 "How Do I Know What I Think Till I See What I Say?"
Language and Belief—How Language Reinforces Racial, Ethnic, and Sexual Discrimination

CLASSROOM EXERCISE

In the previous chapter we considered the ways in which language can act as a sign and as a symbol. We also gave some attention to the theory that language is the instrument of our thinking and that it may shape or at least deeply influence the way we think. In this chapter we shall consider some practical applications of the effect language may have on thought. One way of measuring this is to see what associations different, random words have before we apply them to a subject. Try something neutral, like colors. Take five minutes, now, in class, and jot down all the associations that occur to you when you think of different colors, such as "brown," "red," "yellow," "black," and "white." Don't worry about whether your list is correct or "good," just expand the list as far as you can, preferably without too much premeditation.

When you are done, compare your word associations with the rest of the class. Which words have more associations? What kinds of associations are they?

Brown	*Red*	*Yellow*	*White*	*Black*

OSSIE DAVIS
The English Language Is My Enemy!

The earliest form of what could be called the English language began when the Angles, Saxons, and Jutes invaded the British Isles in the fifth century. Thus it was more than ten centuries before English-speaking peoples came in touch with large numbers of dark-skinned peoples from sub-Saharan Africa. It may be, however, that white-skinned English-speakers were predisposed, because of their language, to think ill of black-skinned Africans. If that is so, the English language prejudges— that is, it is prejudiced. This short essay by black actor, playwright, and author Ossie Davis is not the first indictment of that implied prejudice, but it is the most succinct and pointed.

A superficial examination of Roget's Thesaurus of the English Language 1 reveals the following facts: the word WHITENESS has 134 synonyms; 44 of which are favorable and pleasing to contemplate, i.e., purity, cleanness, immaculateness, bright, shining, ivory, fair, blonde, stainless, clean, clear, chaste, unblemished, unsullied, innocent, honorable, upright, just, straight-forward, fair, genuine, trustworthy (a white man's colloquialism). Only ten synonyms for WHITENESS appear to me to have negative implications—and these only in the mildest sense: gloss over, whitewash, gray, wan, pale, ashen, etc.

The word BLACKNESS has 120 synonyms, 60 of which are distinctly un- 2 favorable, and none of them even mildly positive. Among the offending 60 were such words as: blot, blotch, smut, smudge, sully, begrime, soot, becloud, obscure, dingy, murky, low-toned, threatening, frowning, foreboding, forbidden, sinister, baneful, dismal, thundery, evil, wicked, malignant, deadly, unclean, dirty, unwashed, foul, etc. . . . not to mention 20 synonyms directly related to race, such as: Negro, Negress, nigger, darky, blackamoor, etc.

When you consider the fact that *thinking* itself is sub-vocal speech—in other 3 words, one must use *words* in order to think at all—you will appreciate the enormous heritage of racial prejudgment that lies in wait for any child born into the English Language. Any teacher good or bad, white or black, Jew or Gentile, who uses the English Language as a medium of communication is forced, willy-nilly, to teach the Negro child 60 ways to despise himself, and the white child 60 ways to aid and abet him in the crime.

Who speaks to me in my Mother Tongue damns me indeed! . . . the En- 4 glish Language—in which I cannot conceive my self as a black man without, at the same time, debasing myself . . . my enemy, with which to survive at all I must continually be at war.

DISCUSSION QUESTIONS

1. If it is true, as Ossie Davis argues, that "black" has all sorts of unfavorable connotations, while "white" has mostly favorable, how can knowing this help us? What do you think Ossie Davis would like us to do about this?

2. Over the centuries black Americans have been labeled "colored," "Afro-Americans," "people of color," "Negroes," and currently "blacks." Each of these terms carries a different connotation with some political ramifications. Try to find a reasonable linguistic explanation for these shifts.

3. Are black people really "black"? Are whites "white"? Can you think of other words that describe the color of the two races more accurately? Why do you think we chose the words "black" and "white" to describe people in the first place? It may be worth noting that when Englishmen first began to arrive in Ireland in the Middle Ages, they were perceived as "yellow" or "sallow" by the apple-cheeked natives, who described themselves as "white."

4. Ours is not the only language to be accused of racial prejudice. There is a group of people in South America called the Djukas, descended from West Africans who escaped from the slave ships during the 1600s. In the Djuka language, black is a color symbolic of happiness, while white is a color for deep mourning. Why do you think this would be so?

5. Not all American writers would agree with the positive associations of "whiteness." One hundred and twenty years ago Herman Melville considered some of the ambiguous implications of whiteness in *Moby Dick*, especially in Chapter XLII. If you have a copy of the book at hand, or in the library, consult it. He suggests that white may also imply the cold, mysterious emptiness of the polar icecaps.

GORDON W. ALLPORT
Linguistic Factors in Prejudice

"Prejudice" means, literally, "prejudgment." While few of us would readily admit we are prejudiced, we may find prejudice easy to detect in others. Rather than being learned formally, most prejudice rests on deep-seated and frequently unconscious attitudes. When those unconscious attitudes cause a speaker to select certain words over others or to load certain words with heavy connotations, he may be trapped in prejudice that no amount of teaching brotherhood or raising consciousness can erase.

The following essay, from a chapter in Allport's *The Nature of Prejudice*, is a landmark in the study of the relation between language and belief. (From *The Nature of Prejudice*, 1954, Addison-Wesley, Reading, Mass.)

Without words we should scarcely be able to form categories at all. A dog   1
perhaps forms rudimentary generalizations, such as small-boys-are-to-be-avoided—but this concept runs its course on the conditioned reflex level, and does not become the object of thought as such. In order to hold a generalization in mind for reflection and recall, for identification and for action, we need to fix it in words. Without words our world would be, as William James said, an "empirical sand-heap."

Nouns That Cut Slices

In the empirical world of human beings there are some two and a half billion   2
grains of sand corresponding to our category "the human race." We cannot
possibly deal with so many separate entities in our thought, nor can we indi-
vidualize even among the hundreds whom we encounter in our daily round. We
must group them, form clusters. We welcome, therefore, the names that help us
to perform the clustering.

The most important property of a noun is that it brings many grains of sand   3
into a single pail, disregarding the fact that the same grains might have fitted just
as appropriately into another pail. To state the matter technically, a noun
abstracts from a concrete reality some one feature and assembles different concrete realities only with respect to this one feature. The very act of classifying
forces us to overlook all other features, many of which might offer a sounder basis
than the rubric we select. Irving Lee gives the following example:

I knew a man who had lost the use of both eyes. He was called a "blind   4
man." He could also be called an expert typist, a conscientious worker, a good
student, a careful listener, a man who wanted a job. But he couldn't get a job in
the department store order room where employees sat and typed orders which
came over the telephone. The personnel man was impatient to get the interview
over. "But you're a blind man," he kept saying, and one could almost feel his
silent assumption that somehow the incapacity in one aspect made the man
incapable in every other. So blinded by the label was the interviewer that he
could not be persuaded to look beyond it.[1]

Some labels, such as "blind man," are exceedingly salient and powerful.   5
They tend to prevent alternative classification, or even cross-classification.
Ethnic labels are often of this type, particularly if they refer to some highly visible
feature, e.g., Negro, Oriental. They resemble the labels that point to some
outstanding incapacity—*feeble-minded, cripple, blind man.* Let us call such
symbols "labels of primary potency." These symbols act like shrieking sirens,
deafening us to all finer discriminations that we might otherwise perceive. Even
though the blindness of one man and the darkness of pigmentation of another
may be defining attributes for some purposes, they are irrelevant and "noisy" for
others.

Most people are unaware of this basic law of language—that every label   6
applied to a given person refers properly only to one aspect of his nature. You
may correctly say that a certain man is *human, a philanthropist, a Chinese, a
physician, an athlete.* A given person may be all of these; but the chances are that
Chinese stands out in your mind as the symbol of primary potency. Yet neither
this nor any other classificatory label can refer to the whole of a man's nature.
(Only his proper name can do so.)

Thus each label we use, especially those of primary potency, distracts our   7
attention from concrete reality. The living, breathing, complex individual—the
ultimate unit of human nature—is lost to sight. As in the figure on p. 91, the

---

[1]I. J. Lee, *How Do You Talk About People? Freedom Pamphlet* (New York: Anti-Defamation
League, 1950), 15.

LABELS OF PRIMARY POTENCY

The effect of linguistic symbols upon perception and thinking about individuals.

label magnifies one attribute out of all proportion to its true significance, and masks other important attributes of the individual.

A category, once formed with the aid of a symbol of primary potency, tends 8 to attract more attributes than it should. The category labeled *Chinese* comes to signify not only ethnic membership but also reticence, impassivity, poverty, treachery. To be sure, there may be genuine ethnic-linked traits, making for a certain *probability* that the member of an ethnic stock may have these attributes. But our cognitive process is not cautious. The labeled category, as we have seen, includes indiscriminately the defining attribute, probable attributes, and wholly fanciful, nonexistent attributes.

Even proper names—which ought to invite us to look at the individual 9 person—may act like symbols of primary potency, especially if they arouse ethnic associations. Mr. Greenberg is a person, but since his name is Jewish, it activates in the hearer his entire category of Jews-as-a-whole. An ingenious experiment performed by Razran shows this point clearly, and at the same time demonstrates how a proper name, acting like an ethnic symbol, may bring it with an avalanche of stereotypes. [2]

Thirty photographs of college girls were shown on a screen to 150 students. 10 The subjects rates the girls on a scale from one to five for *beauty, intelligence, character, ambition, general likability*. Two months later the same subjects were asked to rate the same photographs and fifteen additional ones (introduced to complicate the memory factor). This time five of the original photographs were given Jewish surnames (Cohen, Kantor, etc.), five Italian (Valenti, etc.), and five Irish (O'Brien, etc.); and the remaining girls were given names chosen from the signers of the Declaration of Independence and from the Social Register (Davis, Adams, Clark, etc.).

When Jewish names were attached to photographs there occurred the follow- 11 ing changes in ratings:

decrease in liking
decrease in character
decrease in beauty

---

[2]G. Razran, "Ethnic Dislikes and Stereotypes: A Laboratory Study," *Journal of Abnormal and Social Psychology*, 45(1950), 7–27.

> increase in intelligence
> increase in ambition

For those photographs given Italian names there occurred:

> decrease in liking
> decrease in character
> decrease in beauty
> decrease in intelligence

Thus a mere proper name leads to prejudgments of personal attributes. The individual is fitted to the prejudiced ethnic category, and not judged in his own right.

While the Irish names also brought about depreciated judgment, the depre- 12 ciation was not as great as in the case of the Jews and Italians. The falling of likability of the "Jewish girls" was twice as great as for "Italians" and five times as great as for "Irish." We note, however, that the "Jewish" photographs caused higher ratings in *intelligence* and in *ambition*. Not all stereotypes of out-groups are unfavorable.

The anthropologist, Margaret Mead, has suggested that labels of primary 13 potency lose some of their force when they are changed from nouns into adjectives. To speak of a Negro soldier, a Catholic teacher, or a Jewish artist calls attention to the fact that some other group classifications are just as legitimate as the racial or religious. If George Johnson is spoken of not only as a Negro, but also as a *soldier*, we have at least two attributes to know him by, and two are more accurate than one. To depict him truly as an individual, of course, we should have to name many more attributes. It is a useful suggestion that we designate ethnic and religious membership where possible with *adjectives* rather than with *nouns*.

Emotionally Toned Labels

Many categories have two kinds of labels—one less emotional and one more 14 emotional. Ask yourself how you feel, and what thoughts you have, when you read the words *school teacher*, and then *school marm*. Certainly the second phrase calls up something more strict, more ridiculous, more disagreeable than the former. Here are four innocent letters: m-a-r-m. But they make us shudder a bit, laugh a bit, and scorn a bit. They call up an image of a spare, humorless, irritable old maid. They do not tell us that she is an individual human being with sorrows and troubles of her own. They force her instantly into a rejective category.

In the ethnic sphere even plain labels such as Negro, Italian, Jew, Catholic, 15 Irish-American, French-Canadian may have emotional tone for a reason that we shall soon explain. But they all have their higher key equivalents: nigger, wop, kike, papist, harp, cannuck. When these labels are employed we can be almost certain that the speaker *intends* not only to characterize the person's membership, but also to disparage and reject him.

Quite apart from the insulting intent that lies behind the use of certain labels,   16
there is also an inherent ("physiognomic") handicap in many terms designating
ethnic membership. For example, the proper names characteristic of certain
ethnic memberships strike us as absurd. (We compare them, of course, with
what is familiar and therefore "right.") Chinese names are short and silly; Polish
names intrinsically difficult and outlandish. Unfamiliar dialects strike us as
ludicrous. Foreign dress (which, of course, is a visual ethnic symbol) seems
unnecessarily queer.

But of all these "physiognomic" handicaps the reference to color, clearly   17
implied in certain symbols, is the greatest. The word Negro comes from the
Latin *niger*, meaning black. In point of fact, no Negro has a black complexion,
but by comparison with other blonder stocks, he has come to be known as a
"black man." Unfortunately *black* in the English language is a word having a
preponderance of sinister connotations; the outlook is black, blackball,
blackguard, blackhearted, black death, blacklist, blackmail, Black Hand. In his
novel *Moby Dick*, Herman Melville considers at length the remarkably morbid
connotations of black and the remarkably virtuous connotations of white.

Nor is the ominous flavor of black confined to the English language. A   18
cross-cultural study reveals that the semantic significance of black is more or less
universally the same. Among certain Siberian tribes, members of a privileged
clan call themselves "white bones," and refer to all others as "black bones." Even
among Uganda Negroes there is some evidence for a white god at the apex of the
theocratic hierachy; certain it is that a white cloth, signifying purity, is used to
ward off evil spirits and disease.[3]

There is thus an implied value-judgment in the very concept of *white race*   19
and *black race*. One might also study the numerous unpleasant connotations of
yellow, and their possible bearing on our conception of the people of the Orient.

Such reasoning should not be carried too far, since there are undoubtedly, in   20
various contexts, pleasant associations with both black and yellow. Black velvet is
agreeable, so too are chocolate and coffee. Yellow tulips are well liked; the sun
and the moon are radiantly yellow. Yet it is true that "color" words are used with
chauvinistic overtones more than most people realize. . . . Scores of everyday
phrases are stamped with the flavor or prejudice, whether the user knows it or
not.[4]

We spoke of the fact that even the most proper and sedate labels for minority   21
groups sometimes seem to exude a negative flavor. In many contexts and situations the very terms *French-Canadian*, *Mexican*, or *Jew*, correct and nonmali-
cious though they are, sound a bit opprobrious. The reason is that they are labels
of social deviants. Especially in a culture where uniformity is prized, the name of
any deviant carries with it *ipso facto* a negative value-judgment. Words like
insane, *alcoholic*, *pervert* are presumably neutral designations of a human condi-

---

[3]C. E. Osgood, "The Nature and Measurement of Meaning," *Psychological Bulletin*, 49 (1952),
226.

[4]L. L. Brown, "Words and White Chauvinism" *Masses and Mainstream*, 3 (1950), 3–11. See
also: *Prejudice Won't Hide! A Guide for Developing a Language of Equality* (San Francisco: California Federation for Civic Unity, 1950).

tion, but they are more: they are finger-pointings at deviance. Minority groups are deviants, and for this reason, from the very outset, the most innocent labels in many situations imply a shading of disrepute. When we wish to highlight the deviance and denigrate it still further we use words of a higher emotional key: crackpot, soak, pansy, greaser, Okie, nigger, harp, kike.

Members of minority groups are often understandably sensitive to names given them. Not only do they object to deliberately insulting epithets, but sometimes see evil intent where none exists. Often the word Negro is spelled with a small *n*, occasionally as a studied insult, more often from ignorance. (The term is not cognate with white, which is not capitalized, but rather with Caucasian, which is.) Terms like "mulatto" or "octoroon" cause hard feeling because of the condescension with which they have been used in the past. Sex differentiations are objectionable, since they seem doubly to emphasize ethnic difference: why speak of Jewess and not of Protestantess, or of Negress and not of whitess? Similar overemphasis is implied in terms like Chinaman or Scotchman; why not American man? Grounds for misunderstanding lie in the fact that minority group members are sensitive to such shadings, while majority members may employ them unthinkingly.

DISCUSSION QUESTIONS

1. In several places in this text we have read that language shapes our reality. We might have added "for good or ill." How does this "shaping" relate to the statement that without words our lives would be an "empirical sand-heap" (paragraph 1)? What is an "empirical sand-heap"? Would it be better if we did *not* make discriminations between people and things? Why or why not?

2. What is a "label of primary potency" (paragraph 5)? Does everyone have at least one? If we say that a man is a "Texan," might we allow for the possibility that he is a short elderly man with an East European name—like Leon Jaworsky, who *is* a Texan?

Consider at least five entirely different kinds of people that might be implied by the following terms carrying strong emotional flavoring:

Millionaires
Labor union members
Women drivers
Psychiatrists
Polish people

3. To see how the "label of primary potency" can be misleading, have the class divide into groups of four, which should then form a small circle. From each circle of four a volunteer should tell as much as possible about himself or herself, such as religious or political preferences, ethnic background, major curriculum in college, color of hair, while the others record the items of information, putting the more "potent" at the top of the list and

the less "potent" at the bottom. When you are done, open the discussion to the rest of the class. Without identifying the volunteer, someone (the volunteer or someone *else*) should begin to read off the list from the bottom until the reader has hit upon a label of primary potency that everyone can recognize. For example, you might begin with: "We have here a fan of Fleetwood Mac, a person born in New Brunswick, a left-handed tennis player, a Quaker, a blond, etc." If you are the "volunteer," don't give any information you would rather not share. If you say, for example, that you were once arrested, that may remain your label of primary potency in some people's mind for as long as they know you.

4. The semanticist Alfred Korzybski once said, "Definitions which apply to everyone apply to no one." What did he mean by this? Can you think of some examples of definitions or classifications so broad that they apply to no one? Do they still serve any purpose in the language?

5. In paragraph 3, Allport describes how a noun "brings many grains of sand into a single pail." Do you agree that we are more likely to look for similarities than differences in people, events, objects? If you do agree, then why do you think we do this?

6. What is the significance of the experiment with college girls described in paragraph 10? What does it reveal about language and prejudice?

7. Do you feel any pressures to conform? What people or groups in society demand conformity? Why is conformity so important to us? How important a part does it play in establishing stereotypes?

8. Allport gives several examples of "emotionally toned" words, such as the use of "school marm" for "school teacher" or "nigger" for "Negro." What are some other strongly emotional words we use to label people?

9. Thomas Szasz has said, "The struggle for definition is veritably the struggle for life itself." How does this statement relate to what Allport is saying in paragraphs 6 and 7?

HAIG A. BOSMAJIAN
Defining the "American Indian": A Case Study in the Language of Suppression

Although some of the inherent biases of the English language may have contributed to white discrimination against blacks, as Ossie Davis has argued, the role of our language and the "American Indian" seems altogether different. For one thing, the naming of the "American Indian" originates in the Hispanic languages, and for another, the phrase is based on a double misconception. "America" comes, after all, from

Amerigo Vespucci, the man who did *not* discover America, and "Indian" comes from that place that neither he nor Columbus had reached.

The tendency of our language has been, as Haig Bosmajian points out, to present the native peoples of the Western Hemisphere as something they are not, often for the immediate purpose of misusing them. If we are to perceive the people beneath the label we must first determine something of the implications of those borrowed, misapplied words "American Indian."

One of the first important acts of an oppressor is to redefine the oppressed 1 victims he intends to jail or eradicate so that they will be looked upon as creatures warranting suppression and in some cases separation and annihilation. I say "creatures" because the redefinition usually implies a dehumanization of the individual. The Nazis redefined the Jews as "bacilli," "parasites," "disease," and "demon."[1] The language of white racism has for centuries attempted to "keep the nigger in his place."[2] Our sexist language has allowed men to define who and what a woman is.[3] The labels "traitors," "queers," "pinkoes," "saboteurs," and "obscene degenerates" have all been used to attack students protesting the war in Vietnam and the economic and political injustices in this country.[4] One obviously does not listen to, much less talk to, traitors and outlaws, sensualists and queers. One only punishes them or, as Spiro Agnew suggested in one of his 1970 campaign speeches, indicates that there are some dissenters who should be separated "from our society with no more regret than we should feel over discarding rotten apples from a barrel."[5]

Through the use of the language of suppression the human animal can 2 seemingly justify the unjustifiable, make palatable the unpalatable, and make decent the indecent. Just as our thoughts affect our language, so does our language affect our thoughts and eventually our action and behavior. . . .

The Natural-Religious Redefinition

The "de-civilization," the dehumanization and redefinition of the Indian, 3 began with the arrival of Columbus in the New World. The various peoples in the New World, even though the differences between them were as great as between Italians and Irish or Finns and Portuguese, were all dubbed "Indians,"

---

[1]See Haig A. Bosmajian, "The Magic Word in Nazi Persuasion," *ETC.*, 23 (March 1966), 9–23; Werner Betz, "The National-Socialist Vocabulary," *The Third Reich* (London: Weidenfeld and Nicolson, 1955): Heinz Paechter, *Nazi-Deutsch* (New York: Frederick Ungar, 1944).

[2]See Simon Podair, "Language and Prejudice," *Phylon Review*, 17 (1956), 390–394; Haig A. Bosmajian, "The Language of White Racism," *College English*, 31 (December 1969), 263–272.

[3]See Haig A. Bosmajian, "The Language of Sexism," *ETC.*, 29 (September 1972), 305–313.

[4]See Haig A. Bosmajian, "The Protest Generation and Its Critics." *Discourse: A Review of the Liberal Arts.* 9 (Autumn 1966), 464–469.

[5]*The New York Times*, October 31, 1969. p. 25.

and then "American Indians."[6] Having renamed the inhabitants, the invaders then proceeded to enslave, torture, and kill them, justifying this inhumanity by defining these inhabitants as "savages" and "barbarians." The Europeans' plundering and killing of the Indians in the West Indies outraged a Spanish Dominican missionary, Bartolome de las Casas, who provided the following account of the conquest of the Arawaks and Caribs in his *Brief Relation of the Destruction of the Indies:*

> They [the Spaniards] came with their Horsemen well armed with Sword and Launce, making most cruel havocks and slaughters. . . . Overrunning Cities and Villages, where they spared no sex nor age; neither would their cruelty pity Women with childe, whose bellies they would rip up, taking out the Infant to hew it in pieces. . . . The children they would take by the feet and dash their innocent heads against the rocks, and when they were fallen into the water, with a strange and cruel derision they would call on them to swim. . . . They erected certain Gallowses . . . upon every one of which they would hang thirteen persons, blasphemously affirming that they did it in honor of our Redeemer and his Apostles, and then putting fire under them, they burnt the poor wretches alive. Those whom their pity did think to spare, they would send away with their hands cut off, and so hanging by the skin.[7]

After the arrival of the Spaniards, "whole Arawak villages disappeared through slavery, disease, and warfare, as well as by flight into the mountains. As a result, the native population of Haiti, for example, declined from an estimated 200,000 in 1492 to a mere 29,000 only twenty-two years later."[8]

The Spaniards were followed by the English who brought with them their ideas of their white supremacy. In his *The Indian Heritage in America*, Alvin M. Josephy, Jr., observes that "in the early years of the sixteenth century educated whites, steeped in the theological teaching of Europe, argued learnedly about whether or not Indians were humans with souls, whether they, too, derived from Adam and Eve (and were therefore sinful like the rest of mankind), or whether they were a previously subhuman species."[9] Uncivilized and satanic as the Indian may have been, according to the European invaders, he could be saved; but if he could not be saved then he would be destroyed. As Roy H. Pearce has put it, "Convinced thus of his divine right to Indian lands, the Puritan discovered in the Indians themselves evidence of a Satanic opposition to the very principle of divinity."[10] However, continues Pearce, the Indian "also was a man who had to be brought to the civilized responsibilities of Christian manhood, a wild man to be improved along with wild lands, a creature who had to be made into a Puritan if he was to be saved. Save him, and you saved one of Satan's victims. Destroy him, and you destroyed one of Satan's partisans."[11] Indians who resisted Puritan

---

[6]Peter Farb, *Man's Rise to Civilization as Shown by the Indians of North America from Primeval Times to the Coming of the Industrial State* (New York: E. P. Dutton and Company, 1968), p. xx.

[7]Alvin M. Josephy, Jr., *The Indian Heritage of America* (New York: Bantam Books, Inc., 1969j), p. 286.

[8]Farb, p. 243.

[9]Josephy, p. 4.

[10]*The Savages of America* (Baltimore: The Johns Hopkins Press, 1965), p. 21.

[11] Pearce, pp. 21–22.

invasions of their lands were dubbed "heathens," the "heathen" definition and status in turn justifying the mass killing of Indians who refused to give up their lands to the white invaders: "when the Pequots resisted the migration of settlers into the Connecticut Valley in 1637, a party of Puritans surrounded the Pequot village and set fire to it. . . . Cotton Mather was grateful to the Lord that 'on this day we have sent six hundred heathen souls to hell.' "[12]

The European invaders, having defined themselves as culturally superior to   5
the inhabitants they found in the New World, proceeded to their "manifest destiny" and subsequently to the massive killing of the "savages.". . .

The Political-Cultural Redefinition

If the Indians were not defined as outright "savages" or "barbarians," they   6
were labeled "natives," and as Arnold Toynbee has observed in Volume One of
A Study of History, "when we Westerners call people 'Natives' we implicitly take
the cultural colour out of our perceptions of them. We see them as trees walking,
or as wild animals infesting the country in which we happen to come across
them. In fact, we see them as part of the local flora and fauna, and not as men of
like passions with ourselves; and, seeing them thus as something infrahuman, we
feel entitled to treat them as though they did not possess ordinary human
rights."[13] Once the Indian was labeled "native" by the white invaders, the latter
had in effect established the basis for domesticating or exterminating the former.

In 1787, at the Constitutional Convention, it had to be decided what inhab-   7
itants of the total population in the newly-formed United States should be
counted in determining how many representatives each state would have in
Congress. The Founding Fathers decided: "Representatives and direct taxes shall
be apportioned among the several states . . . according to their respective numbers, which shall be determined by adding to the whole number of free persons,
including those bound to service for a term of years, and excluding Indians not
taxed, three fifths of all other persons." The enslaved black came out three fifths
of a person and the Indian came out a nonentity.

When the Indians had been defined as "savages" with no future, the final   8
result, as Pearce states, "was an image of the Indian out of society and out of
history."[14] Once the Indians were successfully defined as governmental nonen-
tities, no more justification was needed to drive them off their lands and to force
them into migration and eventual death. In the nineteenth century, even the
"civilized Indians" found themselves being systematically deprived of life and
property. The Five Civilized Tribes (Choctaws, Chickasaws, Creeks, Cherokees,
and Seminoles) took on many of the characteristics of the white man's civilization: "Many of them raised stock, tilled large farms, built European style homes,

---

[12]Farb, p. 247.
[13]A Study of History (London: Oxford University Press, 1935), I, p. 152. For further discussion of the connotation of "natives," see Volume II of A Study of History, pp. 574–580.
[14]Pearce, p. 135.

and even owned Negro slaves like their white neighbors. They dressed like white men, learned the whites' methods, skills, and art, started small industries, and became Christians."[15] But they were still Indians, and in the 1820's and 1830's the United States Government forced the Five Civilized Tribes from their lands and homes and sent them "to new homes west of the Mississippi River to present-day Oklahoma, which was then thought to be uninhabitable by white men. Their emigrations were cruel and bitter trials."[16] Fifteen thousand Cherokees who had become "civilized and Christianized" and who resisted the whites' demands that they move west were systematically decimated by the United States Army: "Squads of soldiers descended upon isolated Cherokee farms and at bayonet point marched the families off to what today would be known as concentration camps. Torn from their homes with all the dispatch and efficiency the Nazis displayed under similar circumstances, the families had no time to prepare for the arduous trip ahead of them. No way existed for the Cherokee family to sell its property and possessions and the local Whites fell upon the lands, looting, burning, and finally taking possession."[17]

• • •

While the state and the church as institutions have defined the Indian into   9 subjugation, there has been in operation the use of a suppressive language by society at large which has perpetuated the dehumanization of the Indian. Our language includes various phrases and words which relegate the Indian to an inferior status: "The only good Indian is a dead Indian"; "Give it back to the Indians"; "drunken Indians," "dumb Indians," and "Redskins." Writings and speeches include references to the "Indian problem" in the same manner that references have been made by white Americans to the "Negro problem" and by the Nazis to the "Jewish problem." There was no "Jewish problem" in Germany until the Nazis created the myth; there was no "Negro problem" until white Americans created the myth; similarly, the "Indian problem" has been created in such a way that the oppressed, not the oppressor, evolve as "the problem."

• • •

Just as our thoughts can corrupt our language, so too can our language   10 corrupt our thoughts, and in effect corrupt our behavior. When the Nazis repeated again and again in their propaganda directed to the German masses that the Jews were "bacilli," "parasites," and "disease," the "Final Solution" was made to appear less objectionable. This corrupted use of language made the Nazi oppression of the Jews more palatable to German audiences. Similarly, much of the language used by the Indian's oppressors was used not to define accurately who the Indian was, but to justify the suppression. As Peter Farb has indicated, "cannibalism, torture, scalping, mutilation, adultery, incest, sodomy, rape, filth, drunkenness—such a catalogue of accusations against a people is an indication not so much of the depravity as that their land is up for grabs."[18] The

[15]Josephy, p. 107.
[16]Josephy, p. 108.
[17]Farb, p. 253.
[18]"Indian Corn," *The New York Review*, 17 (December 16, 1971), 36.

language of suppression used to subjugate the Indians for almost five centuries has led to the defense of the indefensible, just as the oppressor intended.

DISCUSSION QUESTIONS

1. After reading this essay, do you think Mohawks, Navajos, Sioux, etc. should object to being called "American Indians"? Why or why not?

2. How old were you when you first realized that the term "Indian" referred also to people from the Asian subcontinent and that the natives of this hemisphere were not the "real" Indians?

3. Although "native" denotes only a link between a person and the place of his/her birth, we recognize that the word carries special flavorful connotations. Consider the old saying "The natives are restless tonight." Why would we be unlikely to use that word for restless Danes or Swedes if we were visiting those countries? How do the comments of Toynbee (paragraph 6) apply to your answer?

4. Do you agree that the ruling of the 1787 Constitutional Convention not to tax Indians made them nonpersons? See paragraph 7. Are you paying any taxes now?

5. Why are so many athletic teams given names that allude to Indian life? Consider for example the Atlanta Braves, the Washington Redskins, the Cleveland Indians, etc. Do these terms imply a favorable or unfavorable depiction of American Indians?

6. We have many phrases in American English that include "Indian" in them, such as "Indian summer," "Indian giver," "Indian club," "Indian bread," etc., and some others that allude to Indian life, "rain-dance," "peace pipe," "war paint," etc. Name as many of these as you can, and then try to generalize from your list. Do most of these support or refute the general direction of Bosmajian's essay?

CLASSROOM EXERCISE

The question of whether language might discriminate against women has been a familiar one in our society for the past few years. Briefly stated, the issue seems to be that many women and at least some men feel that the English language limits the way we can think about women—and that it helps to "keep them in their place." The larger issue of the implications of such words as "woman," "girl," "chick," or for that matter "man" and "boy," are something we shall consider in due time. To seek out the meaning of your own experience before you start to read what others have to say, give yourself the following test. On the left, list all the occupations and roles you would think to be male or only filled by males; some of these may have the suffix "-man" in them. On the right list those for females, including those with the suffix "-woman."

MALE	FEMALE
_____-man	_____-woman
_____-man	_____-woman
_____-man	_____-woman
_____-man	_____-woman
_____-man	_____-woman
_____	_____
_____	_____
_____	_____
_____	_____
_____	_____
_____	_____

Can you generalize from this? What *kinds* of roles and occupations do you feel should be filled by men? And by women?

CASEY MILLER AND KATE SWIFT
Is Language Sexist? One Small Step for Genkind

Although the question of whether language might discriminate against women was first raised only a few years ago, it has, in the interim, become widely discussed. The following essay, first published in *The New York Times Magazine*, is one of the most frequently cited in the continuing argument. Its authors, far from being politicized controversialists, raise a number of practical questions about how language reaffirms—and perhaps shapes—our point of view.

In the view of the authors, our language is so male dominated that even our word for the human race, "mankind," seems either to exclude women or to imply them only as an afterthought. A more impartial word, they suggest, might be "genkind," taking a root from the Latin *genus*, "race," the same root that gives us "generic" and "gender."

A *riddle* is making the rounds that goes like this: A man and his young son   1
were in an automobile accident. The father was killed and the son, who was critically injured, was rushed to a hospital: As attendants wheeled the unconscious boy into the emergency room, the doctor on duty looked down at him and said, "My God, it's my son!" What was the relationship of the doctor to the injured boy?

If the answer doesn't jump to your mind, another riddle that has been around   2
a lot longer might help: The blind beggar had a brother. The blind beggar's

brother died. The brother who died had no brother. What relation was the blind beggar to the blind beggar's brother?

As with all riddles, the answers are obvious once you see them: The doctor 3 was the boy's mother and the beggar was her brother's sister. Then why doesn't everyone solve them immediately? Mainly because our language, like the culture it reflects, is male-oriented. To say that a woman in medicine is an exception is simply to confirm that statement. Thousands of doctors are women, but in order to be seen in the mind's eye, they must be called women doctors.

Except for words that refer to females by definition (mother, actress, con- 4 gresswoman), and words for occupations traditionally held by females (nurse, secretary, prostitute), the English language defines everyone as male. The hypothetical person ("If a man can walk ten miles in two hours . . ."), the average person ("the man in the street"), and the active person ("the man on the move") are male. The assumption is that unless otherwise identified, people in general—including doctors and beggars—are men. It is a semantic mechanism that operates to keep women invisible; man and mankind represent everyone; "he" in generalized use refers to either sex: the "land where our fathers died" is also the land of our mothers—although they go unsung. As the beetle-browed and mustachioed man in a Steig cartoon says to his two male drinking companions, "When I speak of mankind, one thing I don't mean is womankind."

Semantically speaking, woman is not one with the species of man, but a 5 distinct subspecies. "Man," says the 1971 edition of the *Britannica Junior Encyclopaedia*, "is the highest form of life on earth. His superior intelligence, combined with certain physical characteristics, have enabled man to achieve things that are impossible for other animals." (The prose style has something in common with the report of a research team describing its studies on "the development of the uterus in rats, guinea pigs and men.") As though quoting the Steig character, still speaking to his friends in McSorley's, the *Junior Encyclopaedia* continues: "Man must invent most of his behavior, because he lacks the instincts of lower animals. . . . Most of the things he learns have been handed down from his ancestors by language and symbols rather than by biological inheritance."

Considering that for the last five thousand years society has been patriarchal, 6 that statement explains a lot. It explains why Eve was made from Adam's rib instead of the other way around and who invented all those Adam-rib words like female and woman in the first place. It also explains why, when it is necessary to mention woman, the language makes her a lower caste, a class separate from the rest of man; why it works to "keep her in her place."

This inheritance through language and other symbols begins in the home 7 (also called a man's castle) where man and wife (not husband and wife, or man and woman) live for a while with their children. It is reinforced by religious training, the educational system, the press, Government, commerce, and the law.

Consider some of the examples of language and symbols in American his- 8 tory. When schoolchildren learn from their textbooks that the early colonists gained valuable experience in governing themselves, they are not told that the early colonists who were women were denied the privilege of self-government;

when they learn that in the eighteenth century the average man had to manufacture many of the things he and his family needed, they are not told that this "average man" was often a woman who manufactured much of what she and her family needed. Young people learn that intrepid pioneers crossed the country in covered wagons with their wives, children, and cattle; they do not learn that women themselves were intrepid pioneers rather than part of the baggage.

In a paper published in 1972 in Los Angeles as a guide for authors and editors   9
of social-studies textbooks, Elizabeth Burr, Susan Dunn, and Norma Farquhar document unintentional skewings of this kind that occur either because women are not specifically mentioned as affecting or being affected by historical events, or because they are discussed in terms of outdated assumptions. "One never sees a picture of women captioned simply 'farmers' or 'pioneers,' " they point out. The subspecies nomenclature that requires a caption to read "women farmers" or "women pioneers" is extended to impose certain jobs on women by definition. The textbook guide gives as an example the word "housewife," which it says not only "suggests that domestic chores are the exclusive burden of the females," but gives "female students the idea that they were born to keep house and teaches male students that they are automatically entitled to laundry, cooking and housecleaning services from the women in their families."

Sexist language is any language that expresses such stereotyped attitudes and   10
expectations or assumes the inherent superiority of one sex over the other. When a woman says of her husband, who has drawn up plans for a new bedroom wing and left out closets, "Just like a man," her language is as sexist as the man's who says, after his wife has changed her mind about needing the new wing after all, "Just like a woman."

Male and female are not sexist words, but masculine and feminine almost   11
always are. Male and female can be applied objectively to individual people and animals and, by extension, to things. When electricians and plumbers talk about male and female couplings, everyone knows or can figure out what they mean. The terms are graphic and culture free.

Masculine and feminine, however, are as sexist as any words can be, since it   12
is almost impossible to use them without invoking cultural stereotypes. When people construct lists of "masculine" and "feminine" traits they almost always end up making assumptions that have nothing to do with innate differences between the sexes. We have a friend who happens to be going through the process of pinning down this very phenomenon. He is seven years old and his question concerns why his coats and shirts button left over right while his sister's button the other way. He assumes it must have something to do with the differences between boys and girls, but he can't see how.

What our friend has yet to grasp is that the way you button your coat, like   13
most sex-differentiated customs, has nothing to do with real differences but much to do with what society wants you to feel about yourself as a male or female person. Society decrees that it is appropriate for girls to dress differently from boys, to act differently, and to think differently. Boys must be masculine, whatever that means, and girls must be feminine.

Unabridged dictionaries are a good source for finding out what society de-   14 crees to be appropriate, though less by definition than by their choice of associations and illustrations. Words associated with males—"manly," "virile," and "masculine," for example—are defined through a broad range of positive attributes like strength, courage, directness, and independence, and they are illustrated through such examples of contemporary usage as "a manly determination to face what comes," "a virile literary style," "a masculine love of sports." Corresponding words associated with females are defined with fewer attributes (though weakness is often one of them), and the examples given are generally negative if not clearly pejorative: "feminine wiles," "womanish tears," "a woman-like lack of promptness," "convinced that drawing was a waste of time, if not downright womanly."

Male associated words are frequently applied to females to describe some- 15 thing that is either incongruous ("a mannish voice") or presumably commendable ("a masculine mind," "she took it like a man"), but female associated words are unreservedly derogatory when applied to males, and are sometimes abusive to females as well. The opposite of "masculine" is "effeminate," although the opposite of "feminine" is simply "unfeminine."

One dictionary, after defining the word "womanish" as "suitable to or re- 16 sembling a woman," further defines it as "unsuitable to a man or to a strong character of either sex." Words derived from "sister" and "brother" provide another apt example, for whereas "sissy," applied either to a male or female, conveys the message that sisters are expected to be timid and cowardly, "buddy" makes clear that brothers are friends.

The subtle disparagement of females and corresponding approbation of males 17 wrapped up in many English words is painfully illustrated by "tomboy." Here is an instance where a girl who likes sports and the out-of-doors, who is curious about how things work, who is adventurous and bold instead of passive, is defined in terms of something she is not—a boy. By denying that she can be the person she is and still be a girl, the word surreptitiously undermines her sense of identity: it says she is unnatural. A "tomboy," as defined by one dictionary, is a "girl, especially a young girl who behaves like a spirited boy." But who makes the judgment that she is acting like a spirited boy, not a spirited girl? Can it be a coincidence that in the case of the dictionary just quoted the editor, executive editor, managing editor, general manager, all six members of the Board of Linguists, the usage editor, science editor, all six general editors of definitions, and ninety-four out of the 104 distinguished experts consulted on usage—are men?

. . .

Possibly because of the negative images associated with womanish and 18 woman-like, and with expressions like "woman driver" and "woman of the street," the word "woman" dropped out of fashion for a time. The women at the office and the women on the assembly line and the women one first knew in school all became ladies or girls or gals. Now a countermovement, supported by the very term Women's Liberation, is putting back into words like "woman" and "sister" and "sisterhood" the meaning they were losing by default. It is as though, in the nick of time, women had seen that the language itself could destroy them.

Some long-standing conventions of the news media add insult to injury. 19
When a woman or girl makes news, her sex is identified at the beginning of a
story, if possible in the headline or its equivalent. The assumption, apparently, is
that whatever event or action is being reported, a woman's involvement is less
common and therefore more newsworthy than a man's. If the story is about
achievement, the implication is: "Pretty good for a woman." And because people
are assumed to be male unless otherwise identified, the media have developed a
special and extensive vocabulary to avoid the constant repetition of "woman."
The results—"Grandmother Wins Nobel Prize," "Blond Hijacks Airliner,"
"Housewife to Run for Congress"—convey the kind of information that would be
ludicrous in comparable headlines if the subjects were men. Why, if "Unsalaried
Husband to Run for Congress" is acceptable to editors, must women keep explaining that to describe them through external or superficial concerns reflects a
sexist view of women as decorative objects, breeding machines, and extensions of
men, not real people?

Members of the Chicago chapter of the National Organization for Women 20
studied the newspapers in their area and drew up a set of guidelines for the press.
These included cutting out description of the "clothes, physical features, dating
life, and marital status of women where such references would be considered
inappropriate if about men"; using language in such a way as to include women
in copy that refers to homeowners, scientists, and business people where "newspaper descriptions often convey the idea that all such persons are male"; and
displaying the same discretion in printing generalizations about women as would
be shown toward racial, religious, and ethnic groups. "Our concern with what
we are called may seem trivial to some people," the women said, "but we regard
the old usages as symbolic of women's position within this society."

The assumption that an adult woman is flattered by being called a girl is 21
matched by the notion that a woman in a menial or poorly paid job finds
compensation in being called a lady. Ethel Strainchamps has pointed out that
since lady is used as an adjective with nouns designating both high and low
occupations (lady wrestler, lady barber, lady doctor, lady judge), some writers
assume they can use the noun form without betraying value judgments. Not so,
Strainchamps says, rolling the issue into a spitball: "You may write, 'He addressed the Republican ladies,' or 'The Democratic ladies convened' . . . but I
have never seen 'the Communist ladies' or 'the Black Panther ladies' in print."

Thoughtful writers and editors have begun to repudiate some of the old 22
usages. "Divorcée," "grandmother," and "blonde," along with "vivacious,"
"pert," "dimpled," and "cute," were dumped by the Washington Post in the
spring of 1970 by the executive editor, Benjamin Bradlee. In a memo to his staff,
Bradlee wrote, "The meaningful equality and dignity of women is properly under
scrutiny today . . . because this equality has been less than meaningful and the
dignity not always free of stereotype and condescension."

What women have been called in the press—or at least the part that operates 23
above ground—is only a fraction of the infinite variety of alternatives to
"women" used in the subcultures of the English-speaking world. Beyond
"chicks," "dolls," "dames," "babes," "skirts," and "broads" are the words and

Copyright, 1972, G. B. Trudeau/Distributed by Universal Press Syndicate.

phrases in which women are reduced to their sexuality and nothing more. It would be hard to think of another area of language in which the human mind has been so fertile in devising and borrowing abusive terms. In *The Female Eunuch*, Germaine Greer devotes four pages to anatomical terms and words for animals, vegetables, fruits, baked goods, implements, and receptacles, all of which are used to dehumanize the female person. Jean Faust, in an article aptly called "Words That Oppress," suggests that the effort to diminish women through language is rooted in a male fear of sexual inadequacy. "Woman is made to feel guilty for and akin to natural disasters," she writes. "Hurricanes and typhoons are named after her. Any negative or threatening force is given a feminine name. If a man runs into bad luck climbing up the ladder of success (a male-invented game), he refers to the 'bitch goddess' success."

The sexual overtones in the ancient and no doubt honorable custom of 24 calling ships "she" have become more explicit and less honorable in an age of air travel: "I'm Karen. Fly me." Attitudes of ridicule, contempt, and disgust toward female sexuality have spawned a rich glossary of insults and epithets not found in the dictionaries. And the usage in which four-letter words meaning copulate are interchangeable with cheat, attack, and destroy can scarcely be unrelated to the savagery of rape.

In her updating of A *Doll's House*, Clare Boothe Luce has Nora tell her 25 husband she is pregnant—"in the way only men are supposed to get pregnant." "Men pregnant?" he says, and she nods: "With ideas. Pregnancies there (she taps the head) are masculine. And a very superior form of labor. Pregnancies here (taps her tummy) are feminine—a very inferior form of labor."

Public outcry followed a revised translation of the New Testament describing 26 Mary as "pregnant" instead of "great with child." The objections were made in part on esthetic grounds: there is no attractive adjective in modern English for a woman who is about to give birth. A less obvious reason was that replacing the euphemism with a biological term undermined religious teaching. The initiative and generative power in the conception of Jesus are understood to be God's; Mary, the mother, was a vessel only.

Influenced by sexist attitudes, the language of human reproduction lags 27 several centuries behind scientific understanding. The male's contribution to procreation is still described as though it were the entire seed from which a new life grows: the initiative and generative power involved in the process are thought of as masculine, receptivity and nurturance as feminine. "Seminal" remains a synonym for "highly original," and there is no comparable word to describe the female's equivalent contribution.

An entire mythology has grown from this biological misunderstanding and its 28 semantic legacy; its embodiment in laws that for centuries made women nonpersons was a key target of the nineteenth-century feminist movement. Today, more than fifty years after women finally won the basic democratic right to vote, the word "liberation" itself, when applied to women, means something less than when used of other groups of people. An advertisement for the NBC news department listed Women's Liberation along with crime in the streets and the

Vietnam war as "bad news." Asked for his views on Women's Liberation, a highly placed politician was quoted as saying, "Let me make one thing perfectly clear. I wouldn't want to wake up next to a lady pipe-fitter."

. . .

When language oppresses, it does so by any means that disparage and belittle. 29 Until well into the twentieth century, one of the ways English was manipulated to disparage women was through the addition of feminine endings to nonsexual words. Thus a woman who aspired to be a poet was excluded from the company of real poets by the label poetess, and a woman who piloted an airplane was denied full status as an aviator by being called an aviatrix. At about the time poetess, aviatrix, and similar Adam-ribbisms were dropping out of use, H. W. Fowler was urging that they be revived. "With the coming expansion of women's vocations," he wrote in the first edition (1926) of *Modern English Usage*, "feminines for vocation-words are a special need of the future." There can be no doubt he subconsciously recognized the downgrading status implied in the -ess designations. His criticism of a woman who wished to be known as an author rather than an authoress was that she had no need "to raise herself to the level of the male author by asserting her right to his name."

. . .

The demise of most -ess endings came about before the start of the new 30 feminist movement. In the second edition of *Modern English Usage*, published in 1965, Sir Ernest Growers frankly admitted what his predecessors had been up to. "Feminine designations," he wrote, "seem now to be falling into disuse. Perhaps the explanation of this paradox is that it symbolizes the victory of women in their struggle for equal rights."

. . .

Nowhere are women rendered more invisible by language than in politics. 31 The United States Constitution, in describing the qualifications for Representative, Senator, and President refers to each as "he." No wonder Shirley Chisholm, the second woman since 1888 to make a try for the Presidential nomination of a major party [Margaret Chase Smith entered Presidential primaries in 1964], has found it difficult to be taken seriously.

As much as any other factor in our language, the ambiguous meaning of 32 "*man*" serves to deny women recognition as people. In a recent magazine article, we discussed the similar effect on women of the generic pronoun "he," which we proposed to replace by a new common-gender "tey." We were immediately told, by a number of authorities, that we were dabbling in the serious business of linguistics, and the message that reached us from these scholars was loud and clear: It - is - absolutely - impossible - for - anyone - to - introduce - a - new - word - into - the - language - just - because - there - is - a - need - for - it, so - stop - wasting - your - time.

. . .

Without apologies to Freud, the great majority of women do not wish in their 33 hearts that they were men. If having grown up with a language that tells them they are at the same time men and not men raises psychic doubts for women, the doubts are not of their sexual identity but of their human identity Perhaps the present unrest surfacing in the women's movement is part of an evolutionary change in our particular form of life—the one form of all in the animal and plant kingdoms that orders and interprets its reality by symbols. The achievements of the species called man have brought us to the brink of self-destruction. If the species survives into the next century with the expectation of going on, it may only be because we have become part of what science writer Harlow Shapley calls the psychozoic kingdom, where brain overshadows brawn and rationality has replaced superstition.

Searching the roots of Western civilization for a word to call this new species 34 of man and woman, someone might come up with "gen," as in genesis and generic. With such a word, "man" could be used exclusively for males as woman" is used for females, for gen would include both sexes. Like the words "deer" and "bison," gen would be both plural and singular. Gen would express the warmth and generalized sexuality of generous, gentle, and genuine: the specific sexuality of genital and genetic. In the new family of gen, girls and boys would grow to genhood, and to speak of genkind would be to include all the people of the earth.

DISCUSSION QUESTIONS

1. Miller and Swift say that the seeds of male chauvinism are sown in our language. Do you agree? Would changing the language help change social behavior? Why or why not?

2. It is true that the feminine and masculine forms of different words carry different connotations, such as "adventurer" and "adventuress." An "adventurer" is a swashbuckling man who seeks adventure, but an "adventuress" is a woman who uses unscrupulous means to gain favor, usually in the form of money from an older, guileless man. Likewise, "bachelor" and "spinster" both denote an unmarried person, but with distinctly different connotations. How many other examples of this kind can you think of? Are there any examples of masculine and feminine forms of words that do not carry different connotations?

3. In what sense can "female" and "woman" be called "Adam-rib" words? See paragraph 6.

4. What are the different connotations of "mannish" and "womanish"? See paragraphs 14-16. Consult different dictionaries to see if they support the interpretation of Miller and Swift and/or your own feelings. Do "manly" and "womanly" sound better than "mannish" and "womanish"?

5. The authors assert that grown women are demeaned by being called "girl." See paragraph 21. How does this match with your experience? Do older women themselves call each other "girl"? Why?

6. Paragraph 23 mentions Germaine Greer's four-page list of terms used to dehumanize the female person, terms which allude to animals, vegetables, baked goods, implements, etc. How many of these can you think of? Are the ones that you think of insulting? Are there any that are not insulting?

7. From the same paragraph, do you think women are made to feel guilty by having hurricanes named after them? Why do you think the

weather service began to name tropical storms "Alice," "Barbara," "Caroline," etc., instead of "Albert," "Bernard," "Charles"?

8. Paragraph 28 cites a highly placed politician as saying, "I wouldn't want to wake up next to a lady pipe-fitter." How does the use of the word "lady" instead of "woman" affect the tone of the remark? What association do you make with the word "lady" as opposed to "woman" or "girl"?

9. The authors tell us in paragraph 31 that they have been advised not to try to introduce a new word into the language, even though there might be a need for it. Have they succeeded with "genkind" for "mankind"? Have any words from the women's movement become part of the everyday vocabulary of people in North America?

10. Follow your first impulses in making the following word associations:

A. A businessman is _____ (Pick one: aggressive/pushy)
    A business woman is ____

B. She is _____ about details. (picky/careful)
    He is _____ about details.

C. She _____. (is arrogant/exercises authority)
    He _____.

D. He is _____. (a stern taskmaster/hard to
    She is _____.   work for)

E. He _____. (loses his/her temper because
    She _____.   he/she is so busy/is bitchy)

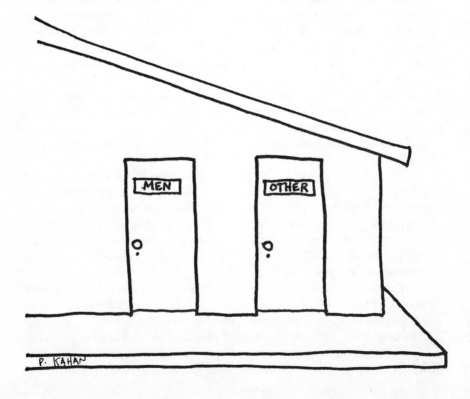

P. KAHAN

LOUIS FOLEY
You Can Overdo Being "A Real *Person*"

Shortly after Miller and Swift's "Genkind" was published, the "person" suffixes, such as "chairperson" and "spokesperson," gained usage. Although such words have had wide acceptance, some people feel they fail in their designated purpose.

Recently I received an advance announcement of a forthcoming national convention to last several days with a number of different programs. Each meeting was to be presided over by a "Chairperson." Apparently this avoidance of the title *Chairman* was intended as recognition of the fact that several of the programs were in charge of women.

Whoever launched this ridiculous expression "Chairperson" evidently did not realize a simple fact about the English (or any other) language. That is the fact that what we may call the "same" word may often have distinctly different meanings in different contexts. Usually the context makes it quite clear which meaning is intended. Really, only visual effect of the spelling makes us aware of the "man" in *chairman*; in modern English pronunciation it subsides into an unrecognizable "mn." But it should make no difference if it were fully pronounced.

The fundamental meaning of *man* is simply "human being" as distinguished from other beings, animals, or things. Only some distance down in the list of definitions, and in special context, as in "man and wife," does it mean a male creature as opposed to female. We read in the Book of Genesis: "So God created man in his own image . . . male and female created he them." The declaration of The Rights of Man means simply the rights of *people*.

"Person" is not a satisfactory substitute. It does not even specifically mean *human*. It can apply to divinity; the Trinity is God in three *persons*. Also we can "personify" animals, things, or abstract ideas. A corporation—about as impersonal as anything one can imagine—is legally a "person." Finally, it is not a term which anyone with a feeling of language would use in a compound word.

We have any number of compounds which show *man* in its basic meaning of "human being" without differentiation as to sex: work*man*ship, sports*man*ship, craft*man*ship, pen*man*ship, and the like. Girls who learn to sail expertly—as many do—may be proud of their sea*man*ship. Would anyone suggest that the celebrated crack-shot Annie Oakley displayed wonderful *markspersonship*?

There are plenty of names which, though ostensibly masculine in form, are commonly applied to people independently of sex. Women make no outcry against having degrees of Bachelor or Master of Arts; no one thinks anything of giving a woman physician the title of Doctor. Some sororities have gone rather far in calling themselves women's *fraternities*, though we hardly imagine they call each other "brothers."

The word *chairman* means the presiding officer of a meeting, a committee, or a board. *Chairwoman* has had some slight usage, but it is unnecessary.

Certainly the vast majority of women who have presided over meetings have been naturally addressed as "Madam Chairman," just as we say "Madam President," and no one has felt any necessity of inventing "Presidentess."

To settle the point once and for all, there is no better example than the word 8 *woman*. It is a corruption of Old English *wifman*, literally a man (human being) who is a female. The word *wif* meant simply female creature without distinction as to whether she was married or not. In fact this meaning persists down to the present in certain expressions such as *housewife*, *fishwife*, or "old wives' tales."

If there be any female chauvinists who have an insuperable intolerance of the 9 word *man* (ignoring its basic meaning) they might logically start by taking the "man" out of woman.

DISCUSSION QUESTIONS

1. Do you agree with Foley that the expression "chairperson" is ridiculous? Why or why not?

2. Although its usage has met with many objections such as this one, the term "chairperson" is in fairly wide use, especially in academic life. Why do you suppose it has been more successful than some other "-person' words such as "markspersonship" (for Annie Oakley), "snowperson"(once used by syndicated columnist Mike Royko), or "personhole cover"?

3. How do you react to some of the other words that have been proposed to eliminate linguistic prejudice? Consider, for example, "genkind" for "mankind," (see the article by Miller and Swift in this chapter), "herstory" for "history," "Ms." for "Miss" or "Mrs.," "himicanes" for "hurricanes," "otto-it" for "ottoman." Are all of these ridiculous? Some of them? None? Explain.

4. What is Foley's attitude toward his subject? What evidence is there of this attitude?

5. Do you agree with Foley's contention in paragraph 3 that the Declaration of the Rights of Man during the French Revolution implied giving rights to all *people*, both male and female? What about the part of our Declaration of Independence that says "All men are created equal?" Discuss.

6. As Foley points out in paragraph 8, "woman" is derived from *wifman*; the Old English *wif*, ancestor of the Modern English "wife," meant simply "female." He concludes, then, that "wife" and "woman" are neutral terms. Do you agree with this conclusion? Why or why not?

7. What are the connotations of "wife" in words like "housewife," "fishwife," and "old wives' tales"?

8. Foley's is not the only attack on the position articulated by Miller and Swift. Women's attempts to change the language in order to eliminate prejudice have met with a good deal of hostility and opposition. To what are the opponents of language change reacting? Does the hostility of the opposition seem justified? Why or why not?

BARBARA LAWRENCE
Four-Letter Words Can Hurt You— If You're a Woman.[1]

> Do you feel that the unwillingness of many newspapers to reprint the half-dozen or so "obscene" words in our language is a sign of publishers' prissy timidity? Or are you angered and offended when you read or see these words? Many contemporary writers of critical standing find these words candid and refreshingly honest. Poet, essayist, and teacher Barbara Lawrence does not. In explaining precisely why she is offended by the "earthy, gut-honest" language often preferred by her students, Lawrence also provides a thoughtful extended definition of "obscenity" itself.

Why should any words be called obscene? Don't they all describe natural human functions? Am I trying to tell them, my students demand, that the "strong, earthy, gut-honest"—or, if they are fans of Norman Mailer, the "rich, liberating, existential"—language they use to describe sexual activity isn't preferable to "phony-sounding, middle-class words like "intercourse' and 'copulate'?" "Cop you Late!" they say with fancy inflections and gagging grimaces. "Now, what is *that* supposed to mean?"

Well, what is it supposed to mean? And why indeed should one group of words describing human functions and human organs be acceptable in ordinary conversation and another, describing presumably the same organs and functions, be tabooed—so much so, in fact, that some of these words still cannot appear in print in many parts of the English-speaking world?

The argument that these taboos exist only because of "sexual hangups" (middle-class, middle-age, feminist), or even that they are a result of class oppression (the contempt of the Norman conquerors for the language of their Anglo-Saxon serfs), ignores a much more likely explanation, it seems to me, and that is the sources and functions of the words themselves.

The best known of the tabooed sexual verbs, for example, comes from the German *ficken* meaning "to strike"; combined, according to Partridge's etymological dictionary *Origins*, with the Latin sexual verb *futuere*; associated in turn with the Latin *fustis*, "a staff or cudgel"; the Celtic *buc*, "a point, hence to pierce"; the Irish *bot*, "the male member"; the Latin *Battuere*, "to beat"; the Gaelic *batair*, "a cudgeller"; the Early Irish *bualaim*, "I strike"; and so forth. It is one of what etymologists sometimes call "the sadistic group of words for the man's part in copulation."

The brutality of this word, then, and its equivalents ("screw," "bang," etc.), is not an illusion of the middle class or a crotchet of Women's Liberation. In their origins and imagery these words carry undeniably painful, if not sadistic, implications, the object of which is almost always female. Consider, for example, what a "screw" actually does to the wood it penetrates; what a painful, even

---

[1]Title original with this publication.

mutilating, activity this kind of analogy suggests. "Screw" is particularly interesting in this context, since the noun, according to Partridge, comes from words meaning "groove," "nut," "ditch," "breeding sow," "skrofula" and "swelling," while the verb, besides its explicit imagery, has antecedent associations to "write on," "scratch," "scarify," and so forth—a revealing fusion of a mechanical or painful action with an obviously denigrated object.

Not all obscene words, of course, are as implicitly sadistic or denigrating to women as these, but all that I know seem to serve a similar purpose: to reduce the human organism (especially the female organism) and human functions (especially sexual and procreative) to their least organic, most mechanical dimension; to substitute a trivializing or deforming resemblance for the complex human reality of what is being described.   6

Tabooed male descriptives, when they are not openly denigrating to women, often serve to divorce a male organ or function from any significant interaction with the female. Take the word "*testes*," for example, suggesting "witnesses" (from the Latin *testis*) to the sexual and procreative strengths of the male organ; and the obscene counterpart of this word, which suggests little more than a mechanical shape. Or compare almost any of the "rich," "liberating" sexual verbs, so fashionable today among male writers, with that much-derided Latin word "copulate" ("to bind or join together") or even that Anglo-Saxon phrase (which seems to have had no trouble surviving the Norman Conquest) "make love."   7

How arrogantly self-involved the tabooed words seem in comparison to either of the other terms, and how contemptuous of the female partner. Understandably so, of course, if she is only a "skirt," a "broad," a "chick," "a pussycat" or a "piece." If she is, in other words, no more than her skirt, or what her skirt conceals; no more than a breeder, or the broadest part of her; no more than a piece of a human being or a "piece of tail."   8

The most severely tabooed of all the female descriptives, incidentally, are those like a "piece of tail," which suggest (either explicitly or through antecedents) that there is no significant difference between the female channel through which we are all conceived and born and the anal outlet common to both sexes—a distinction that pornographers have always enjoyed obscuring.   9

This effort to deny women their biological identity, their individuality, their humanness, is such an important aspect of obscene language that one can only marvel at how seldom, in an era preoccupied with definitions of obscenity, this fact is brought to our attention. One problem, of course, is that many of the people in the best position to do this (critics, teachers, writers) are so reluctant today to admit that they are angered or shocked by obscenity. Bored, maybe, unimpressed, aesthetically displeased, but—no matter how brutal or denigrating the material—never angered, never shocked.   10

And yet how eloquently angered, how piously shocked many of these same people become if denigrating language is used about any minority group other than women; if the obscenities are racial or ethnic, that is, rather than sexual. Words like "coon," "kike," "spic," "wop," after all, deform identity, deny individuality and humanness in almost exactly the same way that sexual vulgarisms and obscenities do.   11

No one that I know, least of all my students, would fail to question the values 12
of a society whose literature and entertainment rested heavily on racial or ethnic
pejoratives. Are the values of a society whose literature and entertainment rest as
heavily as ours on sexual pejoratives any less questionable?

DISCUSSION QUESTIONS

1. Lawrence traces the etymologies of two of the "obscene" synonyms
for sexual intercourse to show that the words imply a violent action toward
women. But most people probably do not know the history of these words.
Does that mean that most people who use these words do not intend to
degrade or demean women?

2. In paragraph 10 Lawrence says that obscene language is part of an
"effort to deny women their biological individuality, their humanness." Do
you agree with this statement? Who or what is behind this "effort"? The
language itself? The people who first used the words this way? The people
who use these words now?

3. William H. Masters and Virginia E. Johnson shocked many reviewers
with the publication, in 1966, of *Human Sexual Response,* the most
thorough, scientific study of what happens to bodies in sexual activity. Although the authors were anything but inhibited prudes, they used clinical
rather then "gut-honest" words to describe parts of the body and sexual
activity. Why would we expect them to avoid the language Lawrence con-
demns?

4. Is there a relationship between obscene language and pornography?
An English writer said recently that a distinction of pornography, as opposed
to eroticism, was a denial of life and a hatred of the human. Could it be that
these are all subjective classifications?

5. Why is the so-called middle class, and its conventions, so often accused of having sexual hangups—and thus all sorts of sex-related taboos?

6. Has Lawrence succeeded in encouraging you to feel resentment and
anger when you hear obscenities? Why or why not?

MURIEL R. SCHULZ
Is The English Language Anybody's Enemy?

As we said earlier in this chapter, the question of language's contribution to discrimination is controversial, not simply because race,
feminism, and sex are hot topics, but more because some people feel
that the English language, as it is inherited from tradition, is not guilty as
charged. One of the most concise defenses of the neutrality of the language is this one.

Ossie Davis started it. In an article, "The English Language Is My Enemy," 1
he complained that in English we equate the word *white* with good things and
black with evil. *White* is associated with pleasant, favorable attributes (pure,
innocent, clean), while *black* is associated with feared, unfavorable ones (foul,
sinister, dismal). Mixed in among the synonyms for *black* are words denoting
race (*Black, Nigger, Darky*), and this association with evil is just one more
burden the Blacks are forced to carry in our society. He suggested that if we were
to compare the connotations of the word *Jew* (unfavorable) with those of the word
Hebrew (neutral), we would understand why he was fighting to stop using the
word *Negro* (unfavorable) and to substitute *Afro-American* (neutral).

We were not very far into the Women's Movement of the Sixties before 2
women, too, discovered the English language to be their enemy. It is contemptuous of them, having a great wealth of derogatory labels like *whore, slut, slat-
tern, hag, bag,* and *witch.* It derides female characteristics by the easy insult,
using feminine terms, such as *sissy, old maidish,* and *effeminate,* as scornful
slurs. It implies that some qualities (*weakness, frivolity, timidity,* and *passivity,*
for example) are appropriate only to women, while others (like *courage, power,
forcefulness,* and *bravery*) are available only to men. It renders women invisible,
by considering masculine to be the norm for such terms as *doctor, professor,
lawyer,* and *worker,* by subsuming women under the cover terms *man* and
mankind, and by using the masculine pronoun whenever sex is unknown or
unspecified (as in "Everyone must have his ticket punched"). Women wonder,
with some justice, just what the effect is upon the female child, who is forming a
sense of her own identity, when she finds herself alternately abused and ignored
by her own language.

But is our language so one-sided? Are Blacks and women dealt with more 3
harshly than men? Have race and sex provided categories subject to a kind of
linguistic abuse that doesn't operate against White Anglo-Saxon males?

Not at all! English is rich in scathing terms for men. Consider, for example, 4
the synonyms for *scoundrel* "a bold, selfish man who has very low ethical standards." We have *cur, dog, hound, mongrel, reptile, viper, serpent, snake, swine,
skunk, polecat, insect, worm, louse,* and *rat* in animal metaphors, as well as
*bounder, knave, rotter, rascal, rogue, villain, blackguard, shyster, heel, stinker,
son of a bitch, bastard,* and many more. Our language enables us to make fine
distinctions in describing villainy, and English attributes this quality to the male.
When the grizzled old prospector curls his lip and snarls, "You dirty, low-down
varmint," we automatically assume that his adversary is a man.

Our terms for people who drink too much are also primarily masculine in 5
reference. Statistics argue that a large percentage of our alcoholics are women,
but English doesn't carry such a message. The synonyms for *inebriate,* whether
happy or obnoxious, habitual or temporary, seem to be coded primarily "male":
for example, *boozer, drunkard, tippler, toper, swiller, tosspot, guzzler, barfly,
drunk, lush, boozehound, souse, tank, stew, rummy,* and *bum.*

In a similar way, our words for law-breakers seem to have masculine 6
reference: *crook, felon, criminal, conspirator, racketeer, gangster, outlaw, con-
vict, jailbird, desperado,* and *bookie* all designate males. And when used figura-

tively, the reference remains masculine. Any man who bests another in a money transaction may earn the epithet of "dirty crook," and when we hear the phrase, we have no doubt of the sex of the person so named.

We are most venomous in characterizing men sexually. Women complain of the richness of vocabulary denoting them as sex objects, but at least many of these are positive, admiring terms. Not so the words which designate a man as a sexual being. Of *rapist, debaucher, despoiler, seducer, rip, betrayer, deceiver, ravisher, ravager, violator, defiler, rake,* and *dirty old man,* perhaps only the last two can be said to have positive connotations. In an article, "Our Sexist Language," Ethel Strainchamps has pointed out an ironic double standard which operate against men in our society: "If a man watches a woman undressing before a window, he can be arrested as a Peeping Tom. If a woman watches a man undressing before a window, the man can be arrested for indecent exposure." *Voyeur* and *exhibitionist* are both masculine terms.

Thus, men come in for a share of abuse in English, too. What we see operating is a natural function of language, one which Stuart Flexner noticed when he was gathering materials for his *Dictionary of American Slang.* There is no rich vocabulary of slang for attractive, chaste women, nor for good amiable wives and mothers, for sober, hardworking men, nor for intelligent, attractive older people. Commenting on these impoverished areas, he remarked, "Slang—and it is frequently true for all language levels—always tends toward degradation rather than elevation." It may not be an admirable quality, but it does appear to be human nature. The chant, "Sticks and stones may break my bones, but names can never hurt me," is acknowledgment that we can use names in an attempt to get at others, to categorize them as Other, to label what we dislike in them (and in ourselves). Language is potentially everyone's enemy, whether he or she is old (*geezer, old fool, codger, fogey, crone*) or young (*squirt, young punk, hippie*), whether a farmer (*yokel, hick, rube, bumpkin, clod*) or a laborer (*menial, flunky, hack, drudge,*) whether a physician (*quack, croaker, pill pusher, butcher*) or an attorney (*shyster, ambulance chaser*).

Can we eliminate this use of language? The slogan, "Black is Beautiful," seems to have succeeded in de-mythicizing the word *Black*, removing from it our associations with evil, as well as removing from it the suggestions it carried when used as a label by a White Southerner in the Fifties. Having neither the euphemistic qualities of *Colored Person* nor the stigma of *Nigger*, it has given us a fairly neutral label, relatively free of the associations and stereotypes of the past. Women have introduced *Ms.* and *chairperson* and have suggested new neutral pronouns as a means of escaping from under the cloak of masculine reference. And they have urged us all to become aware of the unfavorable connotations of many of the words we use denoting women and to avoid abusive terms. But if Whites continue to think of Blacks as Other, and if men continue to think of women as Other, we will find the old associations drifting to the new terminology. As Simone de Beavoir says in *The Second Sex*, "The category of the *Other* is as primordial as consciousness itself. In the most primitive societies, in the most ancient mythologies, one finds the expression of a quality—that of Self and the Other." We should not be surprised to find this opposition expressed in language. Language is nobody's enemy. It is simply used to express the hostility and fear we feel toward others. Whether the difference is one of race, or sex, or religion, or behavior does not matter. The human responds to differences with suspicion and distrust, and those responses are going to be expressed in language.

DISCUSSION QUESTIONS

1. What is Professor Schulz's principal point? How does the evidence support her argument?

2. Professor Schulz points out that our language lacks words for a female who is drunk in public or who breaks the law in any of various ways (see paragraphs 5 and 6). Why is this so? What reason does Professor Schulz give for this lack?

3. How would Miller and Swift, the authors of a previous article, explain the lack of those uncomplimentary terms for women?

4. In paragraph 7 we learn that there is no feminine implication in—and no feminine counterparts for—"voyeur" and "exhibitionist." Does this mean women are incapable of being either voyeurs or exhibitionists?

5. The author says in paragraph 7, "Women complain of the richness of vocabulary denoting them as sex objects, but at least many of these are positive, admiring terms." What are some of these? Does everyone in your class agree they are admiring and positive? Why are there so few counterparts for men? Would most men be happy to be described in terms admiring of their sexuality? Why or why not?

6. Schulz argues that our language merely reflects current social attitudes and that these attitudes cannot change until society itself changes. Do you agree with this? When societal changes occur, will the language change too? Why or why not?

7. Why is our language deficient in slang terms for attractive, chaste women or good, amiable wives and mothers? Why none for sober, hardworking men or for intelligent, attractive older people? (See paragraph 8.)

Student Essay
Don't Call Me a "Wop"!

My great-grandfather, whose surname I bear, was born in Caltanissetta, 1
Sicily. Some of my other ancestors were born in Wales, Austria, and France (by way of Quebec). A few others lived in the new world before any pale or swarthy faces came across the seas from Europe. But when people hear that I have my

great-grandfather's name, they say, "Oh, you're Italian," as though I shouldn't be because I have blond hair and a short nose. I don't think people are trying to be vicious. They just seem to think an Italian name makes you Italian, even though, in my case, I don't know very much about the Italian language and cannot cook any Italian foods. It never occurs to them to call me an Italian-American, but, then again, it's obvious that I am an American, so I suppose the "Italian" is enough to imply the rest. And, if they want to be impolite, there are worse things they could call me—and occasionally they do.

I suppose I ought to say that I am proud to be Italian because Italy has,   2 through the centuries, given so much to the world. I would certainly like to visit Italy some day. I like a lot of Italian food. I would like to learn the Italian language. And I would like to own an Italian sports car. But the truth of the matter is I don't *feel* very Italian, except that some people rile me by attacking my Italian name. If that's all it takes to be Italian, I accept.

Some of the slurs against us are fairly inoffensive, such as "spaghetti-bender"   3 or "meatball." Some others, like "*Paisan*" seem actually affectionate. I don't hear any of these very often. Kids in the neighborhood I grew up used "spaghetti-bender," but never with much poison in their voices. And "*paisan*" is a favorite of my father's cousin Joe, whose face always lights up when he meets us: "Hey, *paisan*, howsa family?" "*Paisan*" translates as "peasant" in English, but when an Italian uses it, the word can mean affection (although my father thinks cousin Joe just wants to sell a car). I don't think a Swede or a Russian could use "*paisan*," though.

But there are three terms I hear from time to time, and they are often used to   4 hurt: "dago," "guinea," and "wop."

Of these three "dago" seems to inflict the least damage. When people call   5 cheap, homemade red wine "dago red," they don't *really* seem to be trying to hurt anybody. According to the *American Heritage Dictionary*, "dago" comes a mispronunciation of "Diego," the Spanish name, which means that the people who started to use this word didn't know the difference between Spaniards and Italians and were not very careful with their pronunciation. Still, I sometimes hear "dago" used with "dumb," making it more potent. Recently the father of a friend of mine was retelling his adventures in World War II, concentrating on his low opinion of Mussolini's army, which he thought cowardly. After he had called them "Dumb dagos" for about the seventh time, he caught my eye and said, "Sorry, Kevin."

I don't hear "guinea" very often, but when I do I can tell it's supposed to hurt.   6 It's usually a modifier, as in "guinea food," guinea football players," or "guinea musician." I associate it with people who are trying to sound tough, probably because of an experience I had in high school. There was an effeminate boy in our high school who had an Italian name, although he was about as Italian as I am. He was always getting picked on by the toughest kid in the school, a boy who must have been the last person in America wearing a greasy DA. The tough kid liked to call the effeminate one "guinea fruitcake," as though each word packed the same amount of violence.

The word that tries to be lethal is "wop," which I was called for the first time   7
last summer while I was working on a construction crew. The foreman was
always on my back because he disliked college kids as much as he disliked wops,
niggers, spics, and kikes. He said, "You know how they make a wop? They throw
a turd (not quite the word he used, but let that pass) against the wall, and it goes
'wop.' " When I told my father about this, he said he had first heard the same
story in 1946. Later, when I checked *The American Heritage Dictionary*, I found
quite a different story. "Wop" comes from the dialect word *guappo*, which means
"dandy" or "fancy dresser." From this I guess that the word was not insulting in
Italian dialect but must have become so when it was heard by Americans who
knew only English. The English word "wop" shows not only ignorance and
hatred but also a resentment of Italian love of refinement and show. Someone
who calls me this not only hates me (for my name) but also resents me. And it
comes in just one syllable—like a club.

When I think about all this, the thing that surprises me most is there don't   8
seem to be any words for any nationality which suggest admiration. Take the
Chinese, for example. If you don't called them Chinese, the only other terms to
use are all insulting: "Chinaman," "Chink," or "slanty-eyes." I wish I could get
all the people together who think in these words and say, "Hey, folks, under that
ethnic label is a real person!"

RHETORICAL ANALYSIS

1. The first five sentences in paragraph 2 all begin, "I . . ." Is this repetition a flaw? Or does it serve an effective purpose?

2. At the beginning of paragraph 3, the narrator switches to the first person plural, breaking the pattern he established in the previous two paragraphs. Can it be justified?

3. Why did he make paragraph 4 so short? Would it have been better if he had developed it more fully?

4. In enumerating the three anti-Italian slurs, the author goes from "dago" to "guinea" to "wop." Was this the best order he could have chosen? What reason was behind it? Can you suggest a better order?

5. How does the student author give us his understanding of the connotations of the different words?

6. No etymology is given for the origin of "guinea" in paragraph 6. Is this a weakness? The author provides dictionary etymologies for "dago" and "wop."

7. Why does the author begin paragraph 7: "The word *that* tries to be lethal is 'wop,' *which* . . . instead of "The word *which* tries to be lethal is 'wop,' *that* . . . '?

8. Is paragraph 8 an effective summary of the whole paper? Or only part? Or does it introduce a new point not raised in the paper?

POINTS OF DEPARTURE

A

It will be argued, of course, that definitions of color and the connotations that   1
go with them are independent of sociological implications. There is no getting
around the fact, it will be said, that whiteness means cleanliness and blackness
means dirtiness. Are we to doctor the dictionary in order to achieve a social good?
What this line of argument misses is that people in Western cultures do not
realize the extent to which their racial attitudes have been conditioned since
early childhood by the power of words to ennoble or condemn, augment or
detract, glorify or demean. Negative language infects the subconscious of most
Western people from the time they first learn to speak. Prejudice is not merely
imparted or superimposed. It is metabolized in the bloodstream of society. What
is needed is not so much a change in language as an awareness of the power of
words to condition attitudes. If we can at least recognize the underpinnings of
prejudice, we may be in a position to deal with the effects.

Norman Cousins "The Environment of Language"

B   After reading Ossie Davis's "The English Language Is My Enemy"
with a group of forty black students at Claflin College in South Carolina,
Professor Louie Crews set out to find more synonyms for "white" and
"black" than are listed in *Roget's Thesaurus*. His resource was not the
Standard (white) English used in the classic reference book but rather the
spoken language of the students. As an exercise he asked the students to
try to say, "White is ugly," without actually using the word "ugly," and
"Black is beautiful," without using "beautiful." As with any language or
dialect, as Professor Crew reports, there are greater resources for hostility than for affirmation; his students had more words of negative connotation for "white" than they had ones of positive connotation for
"black." Here are some of the results from his students' exercise.

Blackness	Whiteness	
	Nouns	
Soul Brothers	Whitey	Crackers
Africans	Bleachy	Southern pale trash
Africanism	Pinky	Buchra
Brother/Sister	Ghost	Honky
Dude	Superghost	Mister Charlie
Night	Pig	Peckerwood
Cat	Maggot	Hunk of funk
Eagle	Cancer	Redneck
Ram	Butcher	Rabbit-ass
Midnight (even	Cream-of-dung	Abominal snowman
"a midnight")	Buzzard	Pale face
Brown sugar	Hookworm	Snowy-faced monkies
Mystery	Dried Butt Meat	Chuck
	Pimpleface	Rice-patties
	(Skinned) Rabbit	

Blackness	Whiteness	
	Adjectives	

Blackness		Whiteness
Together	Puke-faced	Red
Natural	Bald-faced	Colorless
"Bad"	Frosted-faced	Pale-faced
Tanned	Pink	Raw
Radiant	Intestinal	Dead
Blended	Transparent	Salmon-faced
Shaded	Non-Black	Vanilla
Chocolate	Bland	Yellow
Naturally	Flour-faced	
camouflaged		
Tar		
Dark brown		
Brown		
Smooth		
Kinky		
Mystical		
Mysterious		
Delving		

Louie Crews A Black Addendum to Roget

C

A few years ago three Tufts University researchers—Zella Luria, Jeffrey Rubin, and Frank Provenzano—interviewed thirty pairs of first-time parents, fifteen with newborn sons, fifteen with newborn daughters—all within twenty-four hours after delivery.   1

"Is it a boy or girl?" they asked. The replies to that question immediately stimulated a set of adjectives which parents use to describe their newborn.   2

According to the study, published in the *American Journal of Ortho-* psychiatry, "daughters, in contrast to sons, were rated as significantly softer, finer featured, littler, and more inattentive," even though there was no difference in size or weight between the male and female infants.   3

In 1974, researchers Luria and Rubin had 150 Tufts undergraduates look at three slides of a week-old infant named Sandy. When they were told Sandy was a girl they stereotyped the infant as "littler," "weaker," or "cuddlier."   4

When Does Sex Stereotyping Begin? Summarized from the *American Journal of Orthopsychiatry* by
J. J. MacKillop and D. W. Cross

D

When the feminist movement began to raise consciousness in the 1970s, one of their goals became the elimination of names for different jobs that would imply an exclusiveness for one sex or the other. One of the first to go was the title "Girl Friday," a term denoting a general office worker with a heavy allusion to Robinson Crusoe's subservient man of all work. Soon after, newspapers ceased to have separate columns for "Help Wanted—Male" and "Help Wanted—Female." By the middle of the decade, the United States Bureau of the Census agreed to change the terms for 52 of its 441 work categories in an effort to eliminate sex stereotyping. Here are some examples.

OLD	NEW
credit men	credit and collection managers
newsboys	newspaper carriers and vendors
foremen	blue-collar worker supervisors
telephone linemen and splicers	telephone line installers and repairers
furnace men	furnace tenders
motormen	rail vehicle operators
fishermen	fishers
busboys	waiters' assistants
firemen	firefighters
chambermaids	lodging quarters cleaners
charwomen	building interior cleaners
airline stewardesses	flight attendants
laundresses	launderers
maids and servants	private household cleaners

Compiled from news reports by J. J. MacKillop and D. W. Cross

E

In 1974 the McGraw-Hill Book Company issued a comprehensive manual for its authors and editors designed "to show the role language has played in reinforcing inequality; and to indicate positive approaches toward providing fair, accurate, and balanced treatment of both sexes in our publications." The guidelines are intended for use in teaching materials, reference works, and nonfiction works in general. Some of the offending words and phrases are given at the left with their alternatives at the right.

NO	YES
the fair sex; the weaker sex	*women*
the distaff side	*the female side or line*
the girls or the ladies (when adult females are meant)	*the women*
girl, as in: I'll have my *girl* check that.	I'll have my *secretary* (or my *assistant*) check that. (Or use the person's name.)
lady used as a modifier, as in *lady* lawyer.	*lawyer* (A woman may be identified simply through the choice of a pronoun. . . .)

NO	YES
the little woman; the better half; the ball and chain	*wife*
female-gender word forms, such as *authoress, poetess, Jewess*	*author, poet, Jew*
female-gender or diminutive word forms such as *suffragette, usherette, aviatrix*	*suffragist, usher, aviator* (or *pilot*)
libber	*feminist, liberationist*
sweet young thing	*young woman, girl*
co-ed (as a noun)	*student*
housewife	*homemaker*, for a person who works at home, or rephrase with a more precise or more inclusive term

Summarized from " 'Man': Memo from a Publisher" by J. J. MacKillop and D. W. Cross

F

Have you ever noticed how language seems to discriminate against left- 1
handed people? The left-handed sometimes complain that every device from
doorknobs to kitchen sinks is designed for right-handed people. Left-handers
might well object also to the implications of designating the socially inept as
"gauche" ("left" in French), the evil as "sinister" ("left" in Latin), and barbed
flattery as a "left-handed compliment."

On the other hand, the skillful worker is "adroit" (French *à droit*, "to the 2
right") and "dexterous" (from Latin *dexter*, "right" or "right hand"). The boss
depends on the worker who is his "right-hand man." Who ever heard of anyone's
having a "left-hand man"? When Stonewall Jackson was severely wounded,
didn't General Lee say, "He has lost his left arm. I have lost my right arm"?

If a young lady complains after a dance that her partner had "two left feet," 3
she is immediately understood to mean that he was impossibly awkward. Still,
she may try to stay on the "right side" of him, so she will not lack for partners
another time. For popularity many a girl will dance with a "gawky" (original
meaning, "left" or "left-handed") boy occasionally.

Many successful athletes have been both left-handed and extremely well 4
coördinated. No one in his "right mind" would deny that Sandy Koufax was a
great baseball player. Nor has the sports world a corner on famous left-handers.
Other "lefties" were Alexander the Great, Charlemagne, Leonardo da Vinci,
and Holbein.

Yet, undeterred by the facts, we go right on with our canards. When a person 5
becomes very mixed up indeed, we may say that he is "way out in left field," in
contrast to "right-minded" individuals, whom everyone recognizes as "right as
rain."

These aspersions on the one out of twenty—the estimated number of left- 6 handed people in the world—have been cast for too long for there to be much hope of stopping them. It's enough to make a maligned left-hander send the next unsuspecting right-hander he meets to the store for a "left-handed monkey wrench."

From *English Highlights*, Volume 25, Number 3, March-April 1968. "Does Language Libel the Left-Handed?" Copyright © 1968 by Scott, Foresman and Company. Reprinted by permission.

WRITING ASSIGNMENTS

Essays

1. Do you belong to a group which is in any way stigmatized by language? What kind of language is used against you? Who uses the offensive language?

2. The essays by Davis, pp. 88–89, and Miller and Swift, pp. 101–109, are confronted by Muriel Schulz's "Is the English Language Anybody's Enemy?" Who makes the strongest case? What further evidence might either side have included?

3. Review some of the derogatory terms for white people collected from the black English college students by Louie Crews, pp. 121–122. Does this suggest that verbal abuse of one race or the other is a matter of choice or that it is implicit in the language itself? Is it possible for someone speaking standard English not to be a racist? How does the language accommodate this? Explain.

4. Feminists argue that women tend to be invisible in the English language because "man," meaning the human species and the male of the species, does not evoke images of women. It is not the same in all languages In Latin, for example:
vir is "a male" and *homo* is "a member of the human race." With this in mind, reconsider the arguments of Miller and Swift. Do the terms "doctor," "lawyer," "merchant," "chief," "beggar," "senator," "professor," "teacher," "scientist," and "judge" imply women as well as men? Write an essay summarizing your responses to these words and any others you may think of.

5. Consult a dictionary of slang to see which ethnic epithets have been around the longest. Use some of the examples from Allport and in the student essay, and any others you may know of. Which ones carry the most power? Do these words become stronger or weaker as they stay in the language?

6. Check the *Oxford English Dictionary* or a dictionary of etymology on the histories of the words "lady," "woman," "girl," and "female." Do their histories support the arguments of Miller and Swift, or of Schulz?

7. What associations do you think people have with your own name? Do you think people ever prejudge you on the basis of these associations?

Were you ever aware of discrimination because of your name or label of primary potency?

8. Prospective parents usually spend a lot of time trying to come up with names for their new babies. Think of some examples of names (for both boys and girls) that you find very attractive and some you find distasteful. (If you like, put these names in front of your own surname and see how you like that effect.) Write a short essay in which you explain the reasons for your feelings about these names.

9. Are you a member of a racial, religious, social, or national group that has stereotyped characteristics? Write an essay comparing the stereotyped image with the way *you* view the group. What accounts for the differences in the way the group is perceived by members and nonmembers?

JOURNAL KEEPING

1. We acquire knowledge in two ways: through words and through experience. What we learn through words—by reading, listening, asking questions—is called our *verbal* world; what we learn by experience—by actually being there—is called our *experiential* world. The only way you know there was an American Civil War is from reading about it, so the Civil War and your thoughts about it are part of your verbal world. But if you witness a battle between two street gangs, this "war" and your thoughts about it are part of your experiential world. You can also think of this distinction as the difference between "maps" and "territories." The "map" is a report of what is actually out there in the "territory."

We never run into any problem so long as our verbal and experiential worlds correspond fairly closely. That is, as long as there *was* a Civil War and the Union *did* win it, then our "map" is a reliable guide to the "territory." But if our verbal and experiential worlds are not in accord, the consequences can be serious. For example, a child of average abilities who is constantly told by his parents that he is a genius would obviously have trouble adjusting when he goes out into the world and finds that his beliefs do not accurately reflect reality.

Many of our prejudices are based on knowledge picked up from our verbal world, and they do not *necessarily* correspond with our experiential world. It is possible to have a strong prejudice or dislike for black people *without ever having met or spoken with one in your life.* Then your feelings would be based on things you have heard or have been told, *not* on what you have actually found out for yourself.

Begin now to test the validity of some of your beliefs. Complete the following sentences with the first word that comes to mind. (You might, for example, think of the words "crazy" or "money-grubbers" to complete the sentence "Psychiatrists are＿＿＿＿＿＿＿.") If no word comes to mind immediately, then just forget about that sentence and go on to the next.

Truck drivers are_____

Southerners are _____

Republicans are _____

Communists are _____

Black people are _____

White people are _____

Stewardesses are _____

Catholics are _____

Women drivers are_____

Teachers are _____

Italians are _____

Hairdressers are _____

Democrats are_____

Boy scouts are_____

Women's libbers are _____

Polish people are_____

Nurses are _____

People on welfare are_____

Only children are _____

People who smoke marijuana are _____

People who don't smoke marijuana are _____

Russians are_____

Texans are _____

Movie stars are _____

Football players are _____

Each completed sentence reveals one of your attitudes or beliefs. Now, for each completed sentence, write about whatever experiences you have had that justify or explain this attitude. If you have had *no* experiences or even only one or two experiences with this group of people, then you know that your ideas come mostly from your verbal world. Try to write down as many of the sources for your information as you can remember. Where and from what did you get the ideas or attitudes? How much of it is based on experience? How much from reports or hearsay? How accurate or reasonable are your ideas about this?

Try thinking up new sentences to complete and continue to test yourself in this way.

2. Think of further associations of the words "black" and "white." Are some of those in widespread use different from what Ossie Davis says they are? What about "in the black," i.e., making a profit? How about blackboards, blackberry jam, a black belt in karate, blacktop, black-eyed susans, the game of blackjack? Try to keep a record of them as you hear them.

3. Make a list of associations with the word "old." Look over your list and see how many words are favorable, how many unfavorable. Do you see any relationship between these associations and the role of old people in our society? Try the same thing with "yellow." Do you think these associations influence our perception of East Asians?

4. People's names can also have a very strong association that encourages positive or negative attitudes. Recently a man named John Adams was elected to public office from a field of six, even though he never compaigned and was not well known in the community. Accordingly, many celebrities have changed their names to avoid this kind of prejudice. In the following column you will find the actual names of different celebrities followed, in parentheses, with the names under which they have become famous. What kind of associations are suggested by the real names? Write down what you think they might look like if you didn't know what they really were. Try to decide *why* these people decided to change their names. Do you think the new name is an improvement? Why or why not?

Dallas Burrows (Orson Bean)
Aaron Chwatt (Red Buttons)
Issur Danielovitch Demsky (Kirk Douglas)
Rodolfo Gugliemi (Rudolph Valentino)
Frances Gumm (Judy Garland)
Patricia Hrunek (Betsy Palmer)
Amos Jacobs (Danny Thomas)
Allen S. Konigsberg (Woody Allen)
Doris Koppelhoff (Doris Day)
Joseph Levitch (Jerry Lewis)
Marion Michael Morrison (John Wayne)
M. Orowitz (Michael Landon)
William Henry Pratt (Boris Karloff)
Leonard Schneider (Lenny Bruce)
Bernard Schwartz (Tony Curtis)
Larushka Skikne (Laurence Harvey)
Leonard Slye (Roy Rogers)
Robert Zimmerman (Bob Dylan)

5. In the first issue of *Ms. Magazine*, Casey Miller and Kate Swift suggested the introduction of a new pronoun in English to remove sexist bias. The paradigm would be as follows:

| | Singular | | Plural |
	Distinct Gender	Common Gender	Common Gender
Nominative	*he* and *she*	*tey*	*they*
Possessive	*his* and *her*		
	(or hers)	*ter* (or *ters*)	*their* (or *theirs*)
Objective	*him* and *her*	*tem*	*them*

Write a paragraph using the *tey-ter-tem* system wherever appropriate. Do you find the substitution useful and effective? Or uncomfortable? Explain.

4

"I Want to Make One Thing Perfectly Clear"
The Misuse of Language

CLASSROOM EXERCISE

A common misconception among beginning writers is that simple words are somehow a sign of immaturity or lack of class. After all, they feel, if we are supposed to be developing our vocabularies in college, why not use some of the fancier words we are learning? This can lead some writers to say "utilize" when they only mean "use." Other writers, wishing to appear hip, may say "heavy" when they mean "powerful" or "profound." Using an uncommon word for a simple one (or a Latinate one for an Anglo-Saxon one) has to serve a definite purpose, perhaps to give the writing greater precision or variety. When the uncommon vocabulary serves only to advertise the pomposity or self-aggrandizement of the author, then the writing he or she produces is not only unclear, it is irritating as well. The essays in this chapter deal with different kinds of writing that get in the way of clarity and communication—even when they are kinds of writing that some misguided people find attractive.

Before starting the reading, see if you can decipher these examples of writing which are too complicated to communicate anything but the pretensions of their authors. Each will translate to a well-known proverb or saying.

1. Although a substantial plurality of the participants consulted have found that it is within the realm of possibility to escort or conduct any large, hoofed mammal (*viz. Equus caballus*) to a location providing a measurable quantity of a potable mixture of hydrogen and oxygen (not to be consumed in a gaseous or solid state), it is demonstrably affirmative that one cannot coerce the mammal (*Equus caballus*) to imbibe the mixture if it has not expressed a previous desire to do so.

2. We have found that the individual under study should find the most feasible means that will enable him or her, as the case may be, to enter into a rapid repose, facilitating, as soon as possible, an actual somnolent condition along an interface as well as a precocious cessation of the condition and re-entry into a scheduled plan of activities that will maximize salubrious and/or salutary conditions, in addition to factors which favor a rise in profits or, as the circumstances may dictate, greater growth in the level of mental performance and achievement.

3. If your input is counterproductive and your gig is dysfunctional, making you feel hassled so that the whole situation is a bummer, get your head in there and grope for the good vibes as many times as you can.

4. One of the remarkable and characteristic properties currently under intensive laboratory study that are demonstrated by a form of receptacle composed of a metallic alloy is that when the said metallic receptacle is subjected to a careful and continuous scrutiny of a deliberate nature, the mixture which it is the nature and purpose of the said receptacle to contain will not, in point of fact, undergo a phase change and permit entry into a gaseous form at any point of time within the duration of the afore-mentioned scrutiny.

5. In order to reduce the maximum labor utilization, which may run to about three quarters (.75) of a dozen individual movements of a threaded, small, slender sewing instrument, the committee recommends an immediate implementation of a single individual movement of the designated small, slender (but sufficiently large to be threaded) sewing instrument, hopefully, before the crisis situation encumbers us all.

6. The birth-death continuum can elicit responses of the highest measurable aesthetic order from all the participants in its achievement.

STUART CHASE
Gobbledygook

During his long career, economist and semanticist Stuart Chase has been a constant enemy of a special kind of obfuscated language that has come to be known as "gobbledygook." At one time Chase was hired by the federal government in Washington to help bureaucrats write in a language that somebody might understand. Although the gobbledygook beast may have been too great for him to conquer, Stuart Chase tells us how to recognize it so that we might continue the fight.

Said Franklin Roosevelt, in one of his early presidential speeches: "I see   1
one-third of a nation ill-housed, ill-clad, ill-nourished." Translated into standard
bureaucratic prose his statement would read:

It is evident that a substantial number of persons within the Continental bound-   2
aries of the United States have inadequate financial resources with which to purchase

the products of agricultural communities and industrial establishments. It would appear that for a considerable segment of the population, possibly as much as 33·3333* of the total, there are inadequate housing facilities, and an equally significant proportion is deprived of the proper types of clothing and nutriment.

---

*Not carried beyond four places.

This rousing satire on gobbledygook—or talk among the bureaucrats—is adapted from a report[1] prepared by the Federal Security Agency in an attempt to break out of the verbal squirrel cage. "Gobbledygook" was coined by an exasperated Congressman, Maury Maverick of Texas, and means using two, or three, or ten words in the place of one, or using a five-syllable word where a single syllable would suffice. Maverick was censuring the forbidding prose of executive departments in Washington, but the term has now spread to windy and pretentious language in general.

"Gobbledygook" itself is a good example of the way a language grows. There was no word for the event before Maverick's invention; one had to say: "You know, that terrible, involved, polysyllabic language those government people use down in Washington." Now one word takes the place of a dozen.

A British member of Parliament, A. P. Herbert, also exasperated with bureaucratic jargon, translated Nelson's immortal phrase, "England expects every man to do his duty":

> England anticipates that, as regards the current emergency, personnel will face up to the issues, and exercise appropriately the functions allocated to their respective occupational groups.

A New Zealand official made the following report after surveying a plot of ground for an athletic field:[1]

> It is obvious from the difference in elevation with relation to the short depth of the property that the contour is such as to preclude any reasonable developmental potential for active recreation.

Seems the plot was too steep.

An office manager sent this memo to his chief:

> Verbal contact with Mr. Blank regarding the attached notification of promotion has elicited the attached representation intimating that he prefers to decline the assignment.

Seems Mr. Blank didn't want the job.

> A doctor testified at an English trial that one of the parties was suffering from "circumorbital haematoma."

Seems the party had a black eye.

---

[1]Milton Hall, *Getting Your Ideas Across Through Writing* (Washington: Federal Security Agency. Training Manual No. 7, 1950).

[2]This item and the next two are from the piece on gobbledygook by W. E. Farbstein, *The New York Times*, March 29, 1953.

In August 1952 the U.S. Department of Agriculture put out a pamphlet entitled: 12
"Cultural and Pathogenic Variability in Single-Condial and Hyphaltip Isolates of
Hemlin-Thosporium Turcicum Pass."

Seems it was about corn leaf disease.

On reaching the top of the Finsteraarhorn in 1845, M. Dollfus-Ausset, when   13
he got his breath, exclaimed:

The soul communes in the infinite with those icy peaks which seem to have their   14
roots in the bowels of eternity.

Seems he enjoyed the view.

A government department announced: 15

Voucherable expenditures necessary to provide adequate dental treatment re-   16
quired as adjunct to medical treatment being rendered a pay patient in in-patient
status may be incurred as required at the expense of the Public Health Service.

Seems you can charge your dentist bill to the Public Health Service. Or can you?

Legal Talk

Gobbledygook not only flourishes in government bureaus but grows wild and   17
lush in the law, the universities, and sometimes among the literati. Mr.
Micawber was a master of gobbledygook, which he hoped would improve his
fortunes. It is almost always found in offices too big for face-to-face talk.
Gobbledygook can be defined as squandering words, packing a message with
excess baggage and so introducing semantic "noise." Or it can be scrambling
words in a message so that meaning does not come through. The directions on
cans, bottles, and packages for putting the contents to use are often a good
illustration. Gobbledygook must not be confused with double talk, however, for
the intentions of the sender are usually honest.

I offer you a round fruit and say, "Have an orange." Not so an expert in legal   18
phraseology, as parodied by editors of *Labor*:

I hereby give and convey to you, all and singular, my estate and interests, right,   19
title, claim and advantages of and in said orange, together with all rind, juice, pulp
and pits, and all rights and advantages therein . . . anything hereinbefore or hereinaf-
ter or in any other deed or deeds, instrument or instruments of whatever nature or
kind whatsoever, to the contrary, in any wise, notwithstanding.

The state of Ohio, after five years of work, has redrafted its legal code in   20
modern English, eliminating 4,500 sections and doubtless a blizzard of "where-
ases" and "hereinafters." Legal terms of necessity must be closely tied to their
referents, but the early solons tried to do this the hard way, by adding synonyms.
They hoped to trap the physical event in a net of words, but instead they created a
mumbo-jumbo beyond the power of the layman, and even many a lawyer, to
translate. Legal talk is studded with tautologies, such as "cease and desist," "give
and convey," "irrelevant, incompetent, and immaterial." Furthermore, legal
jargon is a dead language; it is not spoken and it is not growing. An official of one

of the big insurance companies calls their branch of it "bafflegab." Here is a sample from his collection:[3]

> One-half to his mother, if living, if not to his father, and one-half to his mother- 21
> in-law, if living, if not to his mother, if living, if not to his father. Thereafter payment
> is to be made in a single sum to his brothers. On the one-half payable to his mother, if
> living, if not to his father, he does not bring in his mother-in-law as the next payee to
> receive, although on the one-half to his mother-in-law, he does bring in the mother
> or father.

You apply for an insurance policy, pass the tests, and instead of a straightfor- 22
ward "here is your policy," you receive something like this:

> This policy is issued in consideration of the application therefor, copy of which 23
> application is attached hereto and made part hereof, and of the payment for said
> insurance on the life of the above-named insured.

Academic Talk

The pedagogues may be less repetitious than the lawyers, but many use even 24
longer words. It is a symbol of their calling to prefer Greek and Latin derivatives
to Anglo-Saxon. Thus instead of saying: "I like short clear words," many a
professor would think it more seemly to say: "I prefer an abbreviated phraseology,
distinguished for its lucidity." Your professor is sometimes right, the longer word
may carry the meaning better—but not because it is long. Allen Upward in his
book *The New Word* warmly advocates Anglo-Saxon English as against what he
calls "Mediterranean" English, with its polysyllables built up like a skyscraper.

Professional pedagogy, still alternating between the middle Ages and modern 25
science, can produce what Henshaw Ward once called the most repellent prose
known to man. It takes an iron will to read as much a page of it. Here is a sample
of what is known in some quarters as "pedageese":

> Realization has grown that the curriculum or the experiences of learners change 26
> and improve only as those who are most directly involved examine their goals,
> improve their understandings and increase their skill in performing the tasks necessary
> to reach newly defined goals. This places the focus upon teacher, lay citizen and
> learner as partners in curricular improvement and as the individuals who must
> change, if there is to be curriculum change.

I think there is an idea concealed here somewhere. I think it means: "If we 27
are going to change the curriculum, teacher, parent, and student must all help."
The reader is invited to get out his semantic decoder and check on my translation. Observe there is no technical language in this gem of pedageese, beyond
possibly the word "curriculum." It is just a simple idea heavily ververbalized.

In another kind of academic talk the author may display his learning to 28
conceal a lack of ideas. A bright instructor, for instance, in need of prestige may

---

[3]Interview with Clifford B. Reeves by Sylvia F. Porter, *The New York Evening Post*, March 14, 1952.

select a common sense proposition for the subject of a learned monograph—say, "Modern cities are hard to live in" and adorn it with imposing polysyllables: "Urban existence in the perpendicular declivities of megalopolis . . . " et cetera. He coins some new terms to transfix the reader—"mega-decibel" or "strato-cosmopolis"—and works them vigorously. He is careful to add a page or two of differential equations to show the "scatter." And then he publishes, with 147 footnotes and a bibliography to knock your eye out. If the authorities are dozing, it can be worth an associate professorship.

While we are on the campus, however, we must not forget that the technical 29 language of the natural sciences and some terms in the social sciences, forbidding as they may sound to the layman, are quite necessary. Without them, specialists could not communicate what they find. Trouble arises when experts expect the uninitiated to understand the words; when they tell the jury, for instance, that the defendant is suffering from "circumorbital haematoma."

Here are two authentic quotations. Which was written by a distinguished 30 modern author, and which by a patient in a mental hospital? You will find the answer at the end of the essay.

> (A) Have just been to supper. Did not knowing what the woodchuck sent me here. How when the blue blue blue on the said anyone can do it that tries. Such is the presidential candidate.
>
> (B) No history of a family to close with those and close. Never shall he be alone to be alone to be alone to be alone to be alone to lend a hand and leave it left and wasted.

Reducing the Gobble

As government and business offices grow larger, the need for doing some- 31 thing about gobbledygook increases. Fortunately the biggest office in the world is working hard to reduce it. The Federal Security Agency in Washington,[4] with nearly 100 million clients on its books, began analyzing its communication lines some years ago, with gratifying results. Surveys find trouble in three main areas: correspondence with clients about their social security problems, office memos, official reports.

Clarity and brevity, as well as common humanity, are urgently needed in this 32 vast establishment which deals with disability, old age, and unemployment. The surveys found instead many cases of long-windedness, foggy meanings, clichés, and singsong phrases, and gross neglect of the reader's point of view. Rather than talking to a real person, the writer was talking to himself. "We often write like a man walking on stilts."

Here is a typical case of long-windedness: 33

> *Gobbledygook as found:* "We are wondering if sufficient time has passed so that 34 you are in a position to indicate whether favorable action may now be taken on our recommendation for the reclassification of Mrs. Blank, junior clerk-stenographer, CAF $_2$, to assistant clerk-stenographer, CAF $_3$?"

---

[4]Now the Department of Health, Education, and Welfare.

Suggested improvement: "Have you been able to act on our recommendation to   35
reclassify Mrs. Blank?"

Another case: 36

Although the Central Efficiency Rating Committee recognizes that there are   37
many desirable changes that could be made in the present efficiency rating system in
order to make it more realistic and more workable than it now is, this committee is of
the opinion that no further change should be made in the present system during the
current year. Because of conditions prevailing throughout the country and the result-
ant turnover in personnel, and difficulty in administering the Federal programs,
further mechanical improvement in the present rating system would require staff
retraining and other administrative expense which would seem best withheld until the
official termination of hostilities, and until restoration of regular operations.

The F.S.A. invites us to squeeze the gobbledygook out of this statement.   38
Here is my attempt:

The Central Efficiency Rating Committee recognizes that desirable changes   39
could be made in the present system. We believe, however, that no change should be
attempted until the war is over.

This cuts the statement from 111 to 30 words, about one-quarter of the   40
original, but perhaps the reader can do still better. What of importance have I left
out?

Sometimes in a book which I am reading for information—not for literary   41
pleasure—I run a pencil through the surplus words. Often I can cut a section to
half its length with an improvement in clarity. Magazines like *The Reader's
Digest* have reduced this process to an art. Are long-windedness and obscurity a
cultural lag from the days when writing was reserved for priests and cloistered
scholars? The more words and the deeper the mystery, the greater their prestige
and the firmer the hold on their jobs. And the better the candidate's chance today
to have his doctoral thesis accepted.

The F.S.A. surveys found that a great deal of writing was obscure although   42
not necessarily prolix. Here is a letter sent to more than 100,000 inquirers, a
classic example of murky prose. To clarify it, one needs to *add* words, not cut
them:

In order to be fully insured, an individual must have earned $50 or more in   43
covered employment for as many quarters of coverage as half the calendar quarters
elapsing between 1936 and the quarter in which he reached age 65 or dies, whichever
first occurs.

Probably no one without the technical jargon of the office could translate this:
nevertheless, it was sent out to drive clients mad for seven years. One poor
fellow wrote back: "I am no longer in covered employment. I have an outside job
now."

Many words and phrases in officialese seem to come out automatically, as if   44
from lower centers of the brain. In this standardized prose people never *get jobs*,
they "secure employment"; *before* and *after* become "prior to" and "subsequent
to"; one does not *do*, one "performs"; nobody *knows* a thing, he is "fully cogni-
zant"; one never *says*, he "indicates." A great favorite at present is "implement."

Some charming boners occur in this talking-in-one's-sleep. For instance: 45

The problem of extending coverage to all employees, regardless of size, is not as 46
simple as surface appearances indicate.

Though the proportions of all males and females in ages 16-45 are essentially the 47
same. . . .

Dairy cattle, usually and commonly embraced in dairying. . . . 48

In its manual to employees, the F.S.A. suggests the following: 49

Instead of	*Use*
give consideration to	consider
make inquiry regarding......................	inquire
is of the opinion..............................	believes
comes into conflict with................................	conflicts
information which is of a confidential nature	confidential information

Professional or office gobbledygook often arises from using the passive rather 50
than the active voice. Instead of looking you in the eye, as it were, and writing
"This act requires . . . " the office worker looks out of the window and writes: "It
is required by this statute that. . . . " When the bureau chief says, "We expect
Congress to cut your budget," the message is only too clear; but usually he says,
"It is expected that the departmental budget estimates will be reduced by Congress."

Gobbled: "All letters prepared for the signature of the Administrator will be single 51
spaced."

Ungobbled: "Single space all letters for the Administrator." (Thus cutting 13 52
words to 7.)

Only People Can Read

The F.S.A. surveys pick up the point that human communication involves a 53
listener as well as a speaker. Only people can read, though a lot of writing seems
to be addressed to beings in outer space. To whom are you talking? The sender of
the officialese message often forgets the chap on the other end of the line.

A woman with two small children wrote the F.S.A. asking what she should 54
do about payments, as her husband had lost his memory. "If he never gets able to
work," she said, "and stays in an institution would I be able to draw any benefits? . . . I don't know how I am going to live and raise my children since he is
disable to work. Please give me some information. . . . "

To this human appeal, she received a shattering blast of gobbledygook, 55
beginning, "State unemployment compensation laws do not provide any benefits
for sick or disabled individuals . . . in order to qualify an individual must have a
certain number of quarters of coverage . . . " et cetera, et cetera. Certainly if the
writer had been thinking about the poor woman he would have not dragged in
unessential material about old-age insurance. If he had pictured a mother without means to care for her children, he would have told her where she might get
help—from the local office which handles aid to dependent children, for instance.

Gobbledygook of this kind would largely evaporate if we thought of our 56 messages as two way—in the above case, if we pictured ourselves talking on the doorstep of a shabby house to a woman with two children tugging at her skirts, who in her distress does not know which way to turn.

. . .

My favorite story of removing the gobble from gobbledygook concerns the 57
Bureau of Standards at Washington. I have told it before but perhaps the reader will forgive the repetition. A New York plumber wrote the Bureau that he had found hydrochloric acid fine for cleaning drains, and was it harmless? Washington replied: "The efficacy of hydrochloric acid is indisputable, but the chlorine residue is incompatible with metallic permanence."

The plumber wrote back that he was mighty glad the Bureau agreed with 58
him. The Bureau replied with a note of alarm: "We cannot assume responsibility for the production of toxic and noxious residues with hydrochloric acid, and suggest that you use an alternate procedure." The plumber was happy to learn that the Bureau still agreed with him.

Whereupon Washington exploded: "Don't use hydrochloric acid; it eats hell 59
out of the pipes!"

Final note: The second quote on page 134 is from *Lucy Church Amiably* by Gertrude Stein (1874-1946).

DISCUSSION QUESTIONS

1. What is a good, one-line definition of "gobbledygook"?
2. What makes people want to write gobbledygook?
3. Why do you think bureaucrats, lawyers, and academicians are the worst practitioners? Are such people, in your experience, capable of speaking plain English? How, for example, might they order a meal in a restaurant?
4. Look again at the examples in paragraphs 34 and 35, 37 and 39. Is Chase correct in claiming that nothing has been lost when the statements have been reduced? Why or why not?
5. Can there ever be a justification for gobbledygook or technical language? Not long ago a scientific writer defended the use of his specialized language, saying that his writing was complicated because his ideas were complicated. If he were to translate his ideas into simpler language, he would lose them. For example, he pointed out that Disney Studios explained a nuclear chain reaction in a well-known film by showing a large floor covered with mousetraps loaded with ping-pong balls. When another ball was thrown at the floor, the traps began to go off in an accelerating sequence until it seemed that all the ping-pong balls were bouncing at once. The public could grasp this idea easily, says the science writer, but it is an inaccurate representation of what nuclear reaction is like. How does this bear on what Chase argues in this essay?
6. Have you heard gobbledygook in professions that Chase has not named? What are they?
7. As many of his allusions show, Chase was most active on this question a few years ago. Do you think things are better or worse since this essay was written? Explain. Cite examples.

MELVIN MADDOCKS
The Limitations of Language

An idea we contemplated in Chapter 2 is that language shapes our thoughts and our understanding of the world. If that is true, as it probably is, what happens to our understanding of the world when our language is so strangled or bloated that we cannot always recognize it for our own? Can any words still have the same meaning for us when we are obliged to read them constantly on billboards or when they are recited to us endlessly in jingles?

If we are suffocating in words we can no longer read or hear, our condition may be described as "semantic aphasia." In the study of diseases, "aphasia" is a disorder of the brain which renders its victim incapable of articulating speech.

In J.M.G. Le Clézio's novel *The Flood*, the anti-hero is a young man suffer- 1 ing from a unique malady. Words—the deluge of daily words—have overloaded his circuits. Even when he is strolling down the street, minding his own business, his poor brain jerks under the impact of instructions (WALK—DON'T WALK), threats (TRESPASSERS WILL BE PROSECUTED), and newsstand alarms (PLANE CRASH AT TEL AVIV). Finally Le Clézio's Everyman goes numb—nature's last defense. Spoken words become mere sounds, a meaningless buzz in the ears. The most urgent printed words—a poem by Baudelaire, a proclamation of war—have no more profound effect than the advice he reads (without really reading) on a book of matches: PLEASE CLOSE COVER BE-FORE STRIKING.

If one must give a name to Le Clézio's disease, perhaps semantic aphasia will 2 do. Semantic aphasia is that numbness of ear, mind and heart—that tone deafness to the very meaning of language—which results from the habitual and prolonged abuse of words. As an isolated phenomenon, it can be amusing if not downright irritating. But when it becomes epidemic, it signals a disastrous decline in the skills of communication, to that mumbling low point where language does almost the opposite of what it was created for. With frightening perversity—the evidence mounts daily—words now seem to cut off and isolate, to cause more misunderstandings than they prevent.

Semantic aphasia is the monstrous insensitivity that allows generals to call 3 war "pacification," union leaders to describe strikes or slowdowns as "job actions," and politicians to applaud even moderately progressive programs as "revolutions." Semantic aphasia is also the near-pathological blitheness that permits three different advertisers in the same women's magazine to call a wig and two dress lines "liberated."

So far, so familiar. Whenever the ravishing of the English language comes 4 up for perfunctory headshaking, politicians, journalists, and ad writers almost invariably get cast as Three Horsemen of the Apocalypse. The perennially identified culprits are guilty as charged, God knows. At their worst—and how often they are!—they seem to address the world through a bad PA system. Does it matter what they actually say? They capture your attention, right? They are word manipulators—the carnival barkers of life who misuse language to pitch and con and make the quick kill.

So let's hear all the old boos, all the dirty sneers. . . . Take the ribbons out of 5 the typewriters of all reporters and rewritemen. Force six packs a day on the guy who wrote "Winston tastes good *like*. . ." Would that the cure for semantic aphasia were that simple.

What about, for example, the asphasics of the counterculture? The ad writer 6 may dingdong catch phrases like Pavlov's bells in order to produce saliva. The Movement propagandist rings his chimes ("Fascist!" "Pig!" "Honky!" "Male chauvinist!") to produce spit. More stammer than grammar, as Dwight Macdonald put it, the counterculture makes inarticulateness an ideal, debasing words into clenched fists ("Right on!") and exclamation points ("Oh, wow!"). Semantic aphasia on the right, semantic aphasia on the left. Between the excesses of square and hip rhetoric the language is in the way of being torn apart.

The semantic aphasia examined so far might be diagnosed as a hysterical 7 compulsion to simplify. Whether pushing fluoride toothpaste or Women's Lib, the rhetoric tends to begin, rather than end, at an extreme. But there is a second, quite different variety of the disease: overcomplication. It damages the language less spectacularly but no less fatally than oversimplification. Its practitioners are commonly known as specialists. Instead of unjustified clarity they offer unjustified obscurity. Whether his discipline is biophysics or medieval Latin, the specialist jealously guards trade secrets by writing and speaking a private jargon that bears only marginal resemblances to English. Cult words encrust his sentences like barnacles, slowing progress, affecting the steering. And the awful truth is that everybody is a specialist at something.

If the oversimplifier fakes being a poet, the overcomplicator fakes being a 8 scientist. Perhaps it is unfair to pick on economists rather than anybody else— except that they are, after all, talking about money. And as often as not it turns out to be our money. Here is a master clarifier-by-smokescreen discussing the recruiting possibilities of a volunteer army if wages, civilian (W_m) are nudged seductively in the direction of wages, civilian (W_c): "However, when one considers that a military aversion factor must be added to W_c or subtracted from W_m, assuming average aversion is positive, and that only a portion of military wages are perceived, the wage ratio is certainly less than unity and our observations could easily lie on the increasing elasticity segment of the supply curve." All clear, everyone?

The ultimate criticism of the overcomplicator is not that he fuzzes but that he 9 fudges. If the cardinal sin of the oversimplifier is to inflate the trivial, the cardinal sin of the overcomplicator is to flatten the magnificent—or just pretend that it is not there. In the vocabulary of the '70s, there is an adequate language for fanaticism, but none for ordinary, quiet conviction. And there are almost no words left to express the concerns of honor, duty or piety.

For the noble idea leveled with a thud, see your nearest Bible. "Vanity of 10 vanities, saith the Preacher. . ." In one new version his words become, "A vapor of vapors! Thinnest of vapors! All is vapor!"—turning the most passionate cry in the literature of nihilism into a spiritual weather report. The new rendition may be a mere literal expression of the Hebrew original, but at what a cost in grace and power.

Who will protect the language from all those oversimplifiers and overcompli- 11 cators who kill meaning with shouts or smother it with cautious mumbles? In theory, certain professions should serve as a sort of palace guard sworn to defend the mother tongue with their lives. Alas, the enemy is within the gates. Educators talk gobbledygook about "non-abrasive systems intervention" and "low structure-low consideration teaching style." Another profession guilty of nondefense is lexicography. With proud humility today's dictionary editor abdicates even as arbiter, refusing to recognize any standards but usage. If enough people misuse "disinterested" as a synonym for "uninterested," Webster's will honor it as a synonym. If enough people say infer when they mean imply, then that becomes its meaning in the eyes of a dictionary editor.

Con Edison can be fined for contaminating the Hudson. Legislation can 11 force Detroit to clean up automobile exhausts. What can one do to punish the semantic aphasics for polluting their native language? None of man's specialties of self-destruction—despoliation of the environment, overpopulation, even war—appear more ingrained than his gift for fouling his mother tongue. Yet nobody dies of semantic aphasia, and by and large it gets complained about with a low-priority tut-tut.

The reason we rate semantic aphasia so low—somewhere between athlete's 12 foot and the common cold on the scale of national perils—is that we don't understand the deeper implications of the disease. In his classic essay "Politics and the English Language," George Orwell pointed out what should be obvious—that sloppy language makes for sloppy thought. Emerson went so far as to suggest that bad rhetoric meant bad men. Semantic aphasia, both men recognized, kills after all. "And the Lord said: 'Go to, let us go down, and there confound their language, that they may not understand one another's speech.' " Is there a more ominous curse in the Bible? It breathes hard upon us at this time of frantic change, when old purposes slip out from under the words that used to cover them, leaving the words like tombstones over empty graves.

How, then, does one rescue language? How are words repaired, put back in 13 shape, restored to accuracy and eloquence, made faithful again to the commands of the mind and the heart? There is, sadly enough, no easy answer. Sincerity is of little help to clichés, even in a suicide note, as Aldous Huxley once remarked. Read, if you can, the Latinized technopieties of most ecologists. Good intentions are not likely to produce another Shakespeare or a Bible translation equivalent to that produced by King James' bench of learned men. They wrote when English was young, vital and untutored. English is an old, overworked language, freshened sporadically only by foreign borrowings or the flickering, vulgar piquancy of slang. All of us—from the admen with their jingles to the tin-eared scholars with their jargon—are victims as well as victimizers of the language we have inherited.

Concerning aphasia, the sole source of optimism is the logic of necessity. No 14 matter how carelessly or how viciously man abuses the language he has inherited, he simply cannot live without it. Even Woodstock Nation cannot survive on an oral diet of grunts and expletives. Mankind craves definition as he craves lost innocence. He simply does not know what his life means until he says it. Until the day he dies he will grapple with mystery by trying to find the word for it. "The limits of my language," Ludwig Wittgenstein observed, "are the limits of my world." Man's purifying motive is that he cannot let go of the Adam urge to name things—and finally, out of his unbearable solitude, to pronounce to others his own identity.

DISCUSSION QUESTIONS

1. Maddocks calls misuse of language "semantic aphasia." Do you think this term is appropriate? Why or why not? How is semantic aphasia comparable to, say, speech aphasia?

2. Do you agree that semantic aphasia presents a real danger to us? How many other people are talking about it? How could it present a danger to you?

3. The phrase "limitations of language" sounds like the idea, discussed in Chapter 2, that the language we speak limits or shapes our reality. Is Maddocks's concept of "limitation of language" similar to that suggested by Whorf, Chase, Kluckhohn, etc.?

4. In paragraph 14, Maddocks says that man "simply does not know what his life means until he says it." What does this statement mean? Do you think this is true?

5. Maddocks says that overcomplicators "flatten the magnificent." How do they do this? What would some examples be? In reverse, how do over-simplifiers "inflate the trivial?"

6. If Ludwig Wittgenstein is correct in asserting that the limits of our language are the limits of our world, then what is actually happening to the limits of our world in the present age?

EDITORS OF *TIME MAGAZINE*
The Euphemism: Telling It Like It Isn't

In a world where courtesy and politeness are rare, one might think that euphemisms, from the Greek for "words of good omen" present ways of blunting jagged truths or smoothing coarse realities. But which truths and realities will be hid from us? And who will disguise them? And

> why? Could it be that those who "shield us from the truth" (a
> euphemism) are really lying to us? A euphemism in the wrong place
> might be anything but a service to us. In the words of *Time* journalist
> Stefan Kanfer, "Euphemisms are to the tongue what novocain is to the
> gums."

Modern American speech, while not always clear or correct or turned with   1
much style, is supposed to be uncommonly frank. Witness the current explosion
of four-letter words and the explicit discussion of sexual topics. In fact,
gobbledygook and nice-Nellyism still extend as far as the ear can hear.
Housewives on television may chat about their sex lives in terms that a decade
ago would have made gynecologists blush; more often than not, these emanci-
pated women still speak about their children's "going to the potty." Government
spokesmen talk about "redeployment" of American troops; they mean withdrawal. When sociologists refer to blacks living in slums, they are likely to
mumble about "nonwhites" in a "culturally deprived environment." The CIA
may never have used the expression "to terminate with extreme prejudice" when
it wanted a spy rubbed out. But in the context of a war in which "pacification of
the enemy infrastructure" is the military mode of reference to blasting the Viet
Cong out of a village, the phrase sounded so plausible that millions readily
accepted it as accurate.

The image of a generation blessed with a swinging, liberated language is   2
largely an illusion. Despite its swaggering sexual candor, much contemporary
speech still hides behind that traditional enemy of plain talk, the euphemism.

From a Greek word meaning "to use words of good omen," euphemism is   3
the substitution of a pleasant term for a blunt one—telling it like it isn't.
Euphemism has probably existed since the beginning of language. As long as
there have been things of which men thought the less said the better, there have
been better ways of saying less. In everyday conversation the euphemism is, at
worst, a necessary evil; at its best, it is a handy verbal tool to avoid making
enemies needlessly, or shocking friends. Language purists and the blunt-spoken
may wince when a young woman at a party coyly asks for direction to "the
powder room," but to most people this kind of familiar euphemism is probably
no more harmful or annoying than, say, a split infinitive.

On a larger scale, though, the persistent growth of euphemism in a language   4
represents a danger to thought and action, since its fundamental intent is to
deceive. As Linguist Benjamin Lee Whorf has pointed out, the structure of a
given language determines, in part, how the society that speaks it views reality. If
"substandard housing" makes rotting slums appear more livable or inevitable to
some people, then their view of American cities has been distorted and their
ability to assess the significance of poverty has been reduced. Perhaps the most
chilling example of euphemism's destructive power took place in Hitler's Germany. The wholesale corruption of the language under Nazism, notes Critic
George Steiner, is symbolized by the phrase *endgültige Lösung* (final solution),
which "came to signify the death of 6,000,000 human beings in gas ovens."

No one could argue that American English is under siege from linguistic   5 falsehood, but euphemisms today have the nagging persistence of a headache. Despite the increasing use of nudity and sexual innuendo in advertising, Madison Avenue is still the great exponent of talking to "the average person of good upbringing"—as one TV executive has euphemistically described the ordinary American—in ways that won't offend him. Although this is like fooling half the people none of the time, it has produced a handsome bouquet of roses by other names. Thus there is "facial-quality tissue" that is not intended for use on faces, and "rinses" or "tints" for women who might be unsettled to think they dye their hair. In the world of deodorants, people never sweat or smell; they simply "offend." False teeth sound truer when known as "dentures."

Admen and packagers, of course, are not the only euphemizers. Almost any   6 way of earning a salary above the level of ditchdigging is known as a profession rather than a job. Janitors for several years have been elevated by image-conscious unions to the status of "custodians"; nowadays, a teen-age rock guitarist with three chords to his credit can class himself with Horowitz as a "recording artist." Cadillac dealers refer to autos as "preowned" rather than "secondhand." Government researchers concerned with old people call them "senior citizens." Ads for bank credit cards and department stores refer to "convenient terms"—meaning 18% annual interest rates payable at the convenience of the creditor.

Jargon, the sublanguage peculiar to any trade, contributes to euphemism   7 when its terms seep into general use. The student New Left, which shares a taste for six-syllable words with Government bureaucracy, has concocted a collection of substitute terms for use in politics. To "liberate," in the context of campus uproars, means to capture and occupy. Four people in agreement form a "coalition." In addition to "participatory democracy," which in practice is often a description of anarchy, the university radicals have half seriously given the world "anticipatory Communism," which means to steal. The New Left, though, still has a long way to go before it can equal the euphemism-creating ability of Government officials. Who else but a Washington economist would invent the phrase "negative saver" to describe someone who spends more money than he makes?

A persistent source of modern euphemisms is the feeling, inspired by the   8 prestige of science, that certain words contain implicit subjective judgments, and thus ought to be replaced with more "objective" terms. To speak of "morals" sounds both superior and arbitrary, as though the speaker were indirectly questioning those of the listener. By substituting "values," the concept is miraculously turned into a condition, like humidity or mass, that can be safely measured from a distance. To call someone "poor," in the modern way of thinking, is to speak pejoratively of his condition, while the substitution of "disadvantaged" or "underprivileged," indicates that poverty wasn't his fault. Indeed, says Linguist Mario Pei, by using "underprivileged," we are "made to feel that it is all our fault." The modern reluctance to judge makes it more offensive than ever before to call a man a liar; thus there is a "credibility gap" instead.

The liberalization of language in regard to sex involves the use of perhaps a   9 dozen words. The fact of their currency in what was once known as polite

From *The New World* (Harper & Row). © Saul Steinberg. Originally in *The New Yorker*.

conversation raises some unanswered linguistic questions. Which, really, is the rose, and which the other name? Are the old forbidden obscenities really the crude bedrock on which softer and shyer expressions have been built? Or are they simply coarser ways of expressing physical actions and parts of the human anatomy that are more accurately described in less explicit terms? It remains to be seen whether the so-called forbidden words will contribute anything to the honesty and openness of sexual discussion. Perhaps their real value lies in the power to shock, which is inevitably diminished by overexposure. Perhaps the Victorians, who preferred these words unspoken and unprinted, will prove to have had a point after all.

For all their prudery, the Victorians were considerably more willing than 10 modern men to discuss ideas—such as social distinctions, morality and death— that have become almost unmentionable. Nineteenth century gentlewomen whose daughters had "limbs" instead of suggestive "legs" did not find it necessary to call their maids "housekeepers," nor did they bridle at referring to "upper" or "lower" classes within society. Rightly or wrongly, the Victorian could talk without embarrassment about "sin," a word that today few but clerics use with frequency or ease. It is even becoming difficult to find a doctor, clergyman or undertaker (known as a "mortician") who will admit that a man has died rather than "expired" or "passed away." Death has not lost its sting; the words for it have.

There is little if any hope that euphemisms will ever be excised from man- 11 kind's endless struggle with words that, as T. S. Eliot lamented, bend, break and crack under pressure. For one thing, certain kinds of everyday euphemisms have proved their psychological necessity. The uncertain morale of an awkward teen-ager may be momentarily buoyed if he thinks of himself being afflicted by facial "blemishes" rather than "pimples." The label "For motion discomfort" that airlines place on paper containers undoubedly helps the squeamish passenger keep control of his stomach in bumpy weather better than if they were called "vomit bags." Other forms of self-deception may not be beneficial, but may still be emotionally necessary. A girl may tolerate herself more readily if she thinks of herself as a "swinger" rather than as "promiscuous." Voyeurs can salve their guilt feelings when they buy tickets for certain "adult entertainments" on the ground that they are implicitly supporting "freedom of artistic expression."

Lexicographer Bergen Evans of Northwestern University believes that 12 euphemisms persist because "lying is an indispensable part of making life tolerable." It is virtuous, but a bit beside the point, to contend that lies are deplorable. So they are; but they cannot be moralized or legislated away, any more than euphemisms can be. Verbal miasma, when it deliberately obscures truth, is an offense to reason. But the inclination to speak of certain things in uncertain terms is a reminder that there will always be areas of life that humanity considers too private or too close to feelings of guilt, to speak about directly. Like stammers or tears, euphemisms will be created whenever men doubt, or fear, or do not know. The instinct is not wholly unhealthy; there is a measure of wisdom in the familiar saying that a man who calls a spade a spade is fit only to use one.

DISCUSSION QUESTIONS

1. Although the word "euphemism" may come from the Greek meaning "words of good omen," it now implies much more. After reading the *Time* essay, how would you define it?

2. To test that you know how to read some current euphemisms, see if you can find "translations" for the following examples taken from actual usage. Not one has been contrived (i.e., faked). The "translations" are at the right, jumbled.

A. Non-retained	(1) Lie
B. Confrontation management	(2) Tax collector
C. Encore telecast	(3) Sweat
D. Occasional irregularity	(4) Fired
E. Nervous wetness	(5) Riot control
F. Internal Revenue Service	(6) Budget cuts
G. Civilian irregular defense soldier	(7) Constipation
H. Terminate with extreme prejudice	(8) Rerun
I. Advance downward adjustments	(9) Mercenary
J. Pre-owned	(10) Execute
K. Inoperative statement	(11) Used

3. In paragraphs 9 and 10, the editors of *Time* compare our use of euphemisms unfavorably with that of the Victorians. Whereas we may speak more freely and honestly of sex, we are squeamish about matters of class and status. Why do most people today want to be thought of as "middle-class"? How many students in the room would readily describe themselves as being

in some other class than the "middle"? What makes them feel they are in a different social class?

4. Think of some other subjects in which euphemisms are regularly used. What are some of the euphemisms used in them? What makes those subjects so ticklish? Why don't we want to face facts about them?

5. Look again at paragraphs 11 and 12. Are there still some areas of "emotional necessity" where all of us will want to use euphemisms? How do these differ from those in which euphemisms are used against us? Are euphemisms dishonest or are they a sign of good manners?

6. Do you agree with Bergen Evans (paragraph 12) that "lying is an indispensable part of making life tolerable"? Why or why not?

Typical Descriptions of a Blind Date for Homecoming (female) (and what they really mean)

Typical Descriptions of a Blind Date for Homecoming (male)

JUDITH KAPLAN
Catch Phrases Don't Communicate

One of the ways in which our language continues to renew itself and to grow is the adoption of new words from the ever-changing but specialized vocabularies of young people. Not all of these words remain current, and some older ones may communicate very little today. For example few people now would use the youth phrase from the 1920s "the cat's pajamas" (outstanding, wonderful, superb), and fewer still would remember the youth-oriented word from the 1940s and 1950s "copacetic" (confidential, between only us). Even when these words and phrases are current, it is questionable whether everyone is defining them in the same way. Such words and phrases may be fashionable or "in," but they may not communicate anything more than *trying* to be "in." The author, Judith Kaplan, knows the subject first-hand. When this essay was first published, she was an 18-year-old college freshman. Reprinted from *Seventeen*® Magazine. Copyright © 1970 by Triangle Communication Inc. All rights reserved.

Recently while gorging on ice cream sundaes with some friends, I overheard 1 a boy saying to his girl, "Baby, there's really a generation gap at our house! My parents just don't dig the whole drug scene. You know, like I really turn them off!"

What was this fellow actually trying to say? Roughly, I translated to myself 2 what might be his situation at home: His dad's probably a businessman, wears his hair short and close-cropped and has always been conservative and traditional. Son has long hair, most likely enjoys rock concerts, has smoked marijuana and is active in the peace movement. He and his parents cannot talk to each other. Why? Because both sides end up shrugging their shoulders and sighing, "I just don't understand you."

This boy persists in belaboring the "generation gap," convinced that he can't 3 communicate with his parents because of some flaw of theirs. Yet his own conversation was so chock-full of catch phrases that it was relatively meaningless.

When people rely on such phrases, real communication is doomed to fail- 4 ure. Words like "swinger," "uptight," "groovy," "super" are overused to such an extent that their meaning and emotional content have been lost. The deep, underlying feelings that may have inspired the thought are simply not reflected in such cursory expressions. True, it's easier to use one word or phrase to cover a complicated thought. But it's certainly less revealing—and aren't you cheating yourself as well as your listeners?

Recently I told a friend that my article was to be published in *Seventeen*. 5 "That's super," she said. Although she sounded enthusiastic, what did she really mean? Did she feel that this was a lucky break for me, or that it was a great magazine, or even that she wished she could do the same? The point is that she didn't say exactly what she meant. Granted, I had a general idea of what she was trying to convey, but nothing definite came through.

Being ambiguous, I think, is just slightly better than saying nothing. Once, I 6 remember, I was wearing a new dress, and a boy I liked came over and told me that I looked "groovy." What a letdown! I know it was a favorable comment, but it would have meant so much more to me if he had said I looked as fresh as a newly cut flower or that the color suited my eyes. "Groovy" left me empty inside—the compliment was over so quickly and seemed so superficial.

And how many times does a young person insist she wants to "do her own 7 thing" without bothering to explain what her "thing" is? Could it be that she hasn't taken the time to analyze herself carefully and truly determine what she does want to do? What about those who talk loftily about "commitment" to such obscure goals as peace, nonviolence, equality? It's not often that they can elaborate on what they would really do if they could. Usually, it's all talk—and relatively little action.

In short, many people use glib catch phrases as an easy way out. But it's sheer   8
laziness not to bother to put meaning and substance behind an utterance. Television watching may be partly responsible for some of this habit: "Sock it to me," after all, is easier to remember than the many phrases for which it is often substituted.

Obviously, then, talking and communicating are not always synonymous. A   9
person can utter a lot of meaningless words or she can communicate with a glance something words wouldn't say as well. Talking transmits only words, but communicating transports thoughts and true feelings between people. To share these emotions with friends is to give part of yourself—as opposed to chatting about the weather with your hairdresser. There really should be a difference in how one speaks about something meaningful—if we don't make that distinction, we have no right to complain that adults don't communicate with us.

I'm not saying that our language should not be breezily informal enough to   10
suit our fast-moving culture, and certainly there are times when only a short exclamatory word will express one's genuine feelings. (Even those rendered "speechless" can usually manage to say "wow!") Generally when someone asks, "How are you?" they don't expect a long discourse on the general state of your health. But expressions that are overworked become totally meaningless, and our generation cannot afford not to be expressive. There are too many important ideas to be expressed well! Language should not be shortcut to hide our feelings.

DISCUSSION QUESTIONS

1. What is a catch phrase? How does it differ from a slang expression or a cliché?

2. Do you agree that the language of your generation is stale? Which expressions currently in use has Kaplan neglected to mention? How about "hassle," "rip-off," and "bummer."? What if anything, do these words communicate?

3. Can you give a precise definition for "groovy" and "uptight"? Do these words carry connotations that cannot be expressed in near synonyms from Standard English?

4. Try to translate the boy's statement in paragraph 1 into Standard English. Is your translation clearer? Did his ideas lose something in the translation? What?

5. Who is harder on the language of today's youth, Kaplan or Maddocks? In his article earlier in this chapter, see his comments about "The Movement" (paragraph 6) and "Woodstock Nation" (paragraph 14).

6. Are there some expressions from the language of the current crop of college students that cannot be translated thoroughly into Standard English? Are there ideas you can put into the catch phrases of youth that just cannot be said in more formal English?

JAMES P. DEGNAN
Masters of Babble:
Turning Language into Stone

Bureaucrats, advertising copywriters, lawyers, and youths are not the only people who mangle the language. We would be hypocritical if we did not also examine the shortcomings of our own profession of college teaching. Professor Degnan castigates not only such familiar targets as sociologists but English teachers and linguists as well.

The babble that we pedagogues master is free from the crude gobbledygook of Washington bureaucrats, free from numbing and dishonest euphemism, free from groovy catch phrases, and free from what usually passes for error (using "like" as a conjunction, etc.). It is instead, as Degnan says, a "stone" language. How many students have been intimidated by it? How many of us, students and teachers alike, have blamed ourselves for not being able to consume such indigestible talk as ". . . contingent upon the derivations of certain multiple correlation coefficients"?

Much of what Professor Degnan says can be used as defense for student word-consumers.

Despite all the current fuss and bother about the extraordinary number of 1 ordinary illiterates who overpopulate our schools, small attention has been given to another kind of illiterate, an illiterate whose plight is, in many ways, more important, becase he is more influential. This illiterate may, as often as not, be a university president, but he is typically a Ph.D., a successful professor and textbook author. The person to whom I refer is the straight-A illiterate, and the following is written in an attempt to give him equal time with his widely publicized counterpart.

The scene is my office, and I am at work, doing what must be done if one is 2 to assist in the cure of a disease that, over the years, I have come to call straight-A illiteracy. I am interrogating, I am cross-examining, I am prying and probing for the meaning of a student's paper. The student is a college senior with a straight-A average, an extremely bright, highly articulate student who has just been awarded a coveted fellowship to one of the nation's outstanding graduate schools. He and I have been at this, have been going over his paper sentence by sentence, word by word, for an hour. "The choice of exogenous variables in relation to multi-colinearity," I hear myself reading from his paper, "is contingent upon the derivations of certain multiple correlations coefficients." I pause to catch my breath. "Now that statement," I address the student—whom I shall call, allegorically, Mr. Bright—"that statement, Mr. Bright—what on earth does it mean?" Mr. Bright, his brow furrowed, tries mightily. Finally, with both of us combining our linguistic and imaginative resources, finally, after what seems another hour, we decode it. We decide exactly what it is that Mr. Bright is trying to say, what he really *wants* to say, which is: "Supply determines demand."

Over the past decade or so, I have known many students like him, many 3 college seniors suffering from Bright's disease. It attacks the best minds, and gradually destroys the critical faculties, making it impossible for the sufferer to detect gibberish in his own writing or in that of others. During the years of higher education it grows worse, reaching its terminal stage, typically, when its victim receives his Ph.D. Obviously, the victim of Bright's disease is no ordinary illiterate. He would never turn in a paper with misspellings or errors in punctuation; he would never use a double negative or the word *irregardless*. Nevertheless, he *is* illiterate, in the worst way: he is incapable of saying, in writing, simply and clearly, what he means. The ordinary illiterate—perhaps providentially protected from college and graduate school—might say: "Them people down at the shop better stock up on what our customers need, or we ain't gonna be in business long." Not our man. Taking his cue from years of higher education, years of reading the textbooks and professional journals that are the major sources of his affliction, he writes: "The focus of concentration must rest upon objectives centered around the knowledge of customer areas so that a sophisticated awareness of those areas can serve as an entrepreneurial filter to screen what is relevant from what is irrelevant to future commitments." For writing such gibberish he is awarded straight As on his papers (both samples quoted above were taken from papers that received As), and the opportunity to move, inexorably, toward his fellowship and eventual Ph.D.

As I have suggested, the major cause of such illiteracy is the stuff—the   4
textbooks and professional journals—the straight-A illiterate is forced to read during his years of higher education. He learns to write gibberish by reading it, and by being taught to admire it as profundity. If he is majoring in sociology, he must grapple with such journals as the *American Sociological Review*, journals bulging with barbarous jargon, such as "ego-integrative action orientation" and "orientation toward improvement of the gratification-deprivation balance of the actor" (the latter of which monstrous phrases represents, to quote Malcolm Cowley, the sociologist's way of saying "the pleasure principle"). In such journals, Mr. Cowley reminds us, two things are never described as being "alike." They are "homologous" or "isomorphic." Nor are things simply "different." They are "allotropic." In such journals writers never "divide" anything. They "dichotomize" or "bifurcate" things.

Sociology has long been notorious for producing illiterates of all kinds, but   5
such supposedly more literate and humane disciplines as philosophy, or even English, turn them out as well. If the potential victim majors in English with emphasis on linguistics, it will be almost impossible for him to emerge with literacy intact. He will habitually read such masters of babble as Dr. Noam Chomsky or Dr. Zellig Harris. From Chomsky's *Syntactic Structures:* "When transformational analysis is properly formulated we find that it is essentially more powerful than description in terms of phrase structure, just as the latter is essentially more powerful than description in terms of finite state Markov processes that generate sentences from left to right." Or from Dr. Harris's renowned text, *Structural Linguistics:* "Another consideration is the availability of simultaneity, in addition to successivity, as a relation among linguistic elements."

If the student's emphasis is on literary criticism, he may browse through   6

Prisms, in which Dr. Albert Cook delivers himself of such major pronouncements as:

> The modern predicament (as rendered by dramatists like Beckett and Ionesco) in   7
> the abstract verbal structures of the stage, is envisioned by means of a procedure that
> implicitly questions those very structures, very much as the extreme literalness of film
> technique in certain directors (Buñuel and Antonioni) pushes the emotions, of a
> geometry visual rather than primarily verbal, into an abstractness that seems unliteral;
> into a realm where terms like "realism" and "surrealism" have been superseded and
> transcended.

If he is majoring in philosophy, the potential victim might read Father   8
Bernard Lonergan's book, the infelicitously titled, 900-page *Insight*. It begins:

> The aim of the present work may be bracketed by a series of disjunctions. In the   9
> first place, the question is not whether knowledge exists, but what precisely is its
> nature. Secondly, while the content of the known cannot be disregarded, still it is to
> be treated only in the schematic and incomplete fashion needed to provide a dis-
> criminant or determinant of cognitive acts. Thirdly, the aim is not to set forth a list of
> the abstract properties of human knowledge but to assist the reader in effecting a
> personal appropriation of the concrete, dynamic structure immanent and recurrently
> operative in his own cognitional activities. Fourthly, such an appropriation can occur
> only gradually, and so there will be offered, not a sudden account of the whole of the
> structure, but a slow assembly of its elements, relations, alternatives, and implica-
> tions. Fifthly, the order of the assembly is governed, not by abstract considerations of
> logical or metaphysical priority, but by concrete motives of pedagogical efficacy.

Such reading reduces the student's mind to gruel. His capacity to think clearly
degenerates, and, with it, his capacity to write readable English.

From time to time, visionaries and radicals of various kinds have tried to do   10
away with straight-A illiteracy (Franklin Roosevelt once hired the semanticist
Stuart Chase to do this in the American Civil Service, but, obviously, to little
effect). The problem with stamping out illiteracy in the schools, whether it is
straight-A or ordinary, is that, while the cure is simple, it could be economically
disastrous for the schools and for the nation. For instance, the cure for the
ordinary illiteracy that flourishes in colleges and graduate schools is simply for
these institutions to stop admitting people who cannot read and write. This
would mean, at the average college, a drop in enrollment of about 75 percent,
and it would be calamitous, not only for the colleges, but, more important in the
eyes of many, for the National Football League, which depends almost entirely
on the colleges for its free system of farm clubs.

As for straight-A illiteracy, the cure is simply for the various academic disci-   11
plines to recognize and reaffirm the homely truth that the one thing they share,
and *must* share if they are to communicate with one another, is a common
language, the English language, a language with conventions and standards
available in such civilized (but, these days, apparently unused) sources as
Fowler's *Modern English Usage* and *Webster's Second New International Dictionary* (*Webster's Third*, obviously the work of straight-A illiterates, is not to be
countenanced).

To recognize the truth that writing well tends to mean writing simply,   12
clearly, vividly, and forcefully, whether such writing is done by a philosopher or
an engineer; to recognize the truth that, having nothing to say, one should
refrain from using thousands of words to say it; to recognize the truth that
pretentious nonsense is not profundity, is painful for many, and, as I have
suggested, perhaps economically disastrous. as one of the many straight-A illiterates I have known once explained, "If I followed your advice, I could never write
the 5,000-word term papers I am regularly assigned; I could never get a fellowship to graduate school, or a contract to do a textbook, or a decent job in business
or government. What you're asking is just too much. Think what it would do in
the universities alone. It would wipe out hundreds of courses and all of the
colleges of education. And think what it would do to the economy, think of the
depression it would cause in the paper and ink and business-machine industries;
think what would happen in the publishing business; think of all the secretaries
who would be out of work. No, I'm sorry, literacy might be okay, but I can't
afford it."

DISCUSSION QUESTIONS

1. How many of your teachers are "masters of babble"? What subjects
do they teach?

2. Are such instructors generally clearer or more obfuscated than the
textbooks they assign? How can you be sure that your difficulty in understanding them comes from their inability to master the language rather than
your inability to grasp the subtlety of their thought?

3. Do you believe that there is such a thing as "straight-A illiteracy"?
Are the people who write this way very bright themselves?

4. Is the kind of writing Degnan cites, as in paragraph 2, a sign of
genuine intelligence? Or is it produced by someone pretending to greater
knowledge and intelligence than he or she actually has?

5. Examine the vocabulary at the end of paragraph 4. How many of
these words do you recognize? How many of these words would you use in
another class (other than this one)? Would your instructor be impressed if
you used such words?

6. Does the example from Bernard Lonergan in paragraph 9 "reduce a
student's mind to gruel?" Or does it challenge the mind, leading it to grasp
finer distinctions?

7. Many of the writers Degnan cites have eminent reputations, Lonergan
and Chomsky especially. What defense might they—or their admirers—give
on their behalf?

8. Do you agree with Degnan's proposal to limit enrollment in college
to students who can genuinely read and write (as he has implicitly defined
those terms)? Would the enactment of such a proposal actually lead to a
drop in enrollment of 75 percent? If not, how big a drop? In which percentage would you find yourself?

RICHARD K. REDFERN
A Brief Lexicon of Jargon: For Those Who Want to Speak and Write Verbosely and Vaguely.

Many of the authors in this chapter have condemned jargon rather offhandedly. Perhaps we should pause to take a closer look at what they are talking about. Our word "jargon" was borrowed from the Old French *jargoun* or *gargon,* meaning "twittering," "jibberish." or "unintelligible language." As it has been used in English the word has acquired three definitions. First, like the French word, "jargon" may mean simply "gibberish"; second, a hybrid language, such as the pidgin English once spoken in Far Eastern ports; and third, most importantly, the technical oi specialized language of a trade, profession, or class, etc. Some jargons— spoken by pop musicians and long-distance truck drivers—have become immensely popular and are thus intelligible to large numbers of people. But most jargon, especially that of bureaucrats, puts a barrier between an idea and a reader—and it bores him.

Through the verbal irony of this "Lexicon," Richard K. Redfern shows us how four otherwise simple words and phrases can add vagueness and verbosity to writing. His last two items of "advice" are more general, but just as effective.

Area

The first rule about using *area* is simple. Put *area* at the start or end of hundreds of words and phrases. *The area of* is often useful when you want to add three words to a sentence without changing its meaning.

Instead of	*Say or write*
civil rights	the area of civil rights
in spelling and pronunciation	in the area of spelling and pronunciation
problems, topics	problem areas, topic areas
major subjects	major subject (*or* subject-matter) areas

Second, particularly in speech, use *area* as an all-purpose synonym. After mentioning scheduled improvements in classrooms and offices, use *area* for later references to this idea. A few minutes later, in talking about the courses to be offered next term, use *area* to refer to required courses, to electives, and to both required and elective courses. Soon you can keep three or four *area*'s going and thus keep your audience alert by making them guess which idea you have in mind, especially if you insert, once or twice, a neatly disguised geographical use of *area*: "Graduate student response in this area is gratifying."

Field

If the temptation arises to say "clothing executive," "publishing executive," 4
and the like, resist it firmly. Say and write "executive in the clothing field" and
"executive in the field of publishing." Note that *the field of* (like *the area of*)
qualifies as jargon because it adds length, usually without changing the meaning,
as in "from the field of literature as a whole" and "prowess in the field of
academic achievement" (which is five words longer than the "academic prowess"
of plain English). With practice you can combine *field* with *area*, *level*, and
other standbys:

> In the sportswear field, this is one area which is growing. (Translation from context: 5
> Ski sweaters are selling well.)
> [The magazine is] a valuable source of continuing information for educators at all
> levels and for everyone concerned with this field. (Plain English: The magazine is a
> valuable source of information for anyone interested in education.)

A master of jargon can produce a sentence so vague that it can be dropped 6
into dozens of other articles and books: "At what levels is coverage of the field
important?" Even in context (a scholarly book about the teaching of English), it
is hard to attach meaning to *that* sentence!

In Terms of

A sure sign of the ability to speak and write jargon is the redundant use of *in* 7
terms of. If you are a beginner, use the phrase instead of prepositions such as *in*
("The faculty has been divided in terms of opinions and attitudes") and *of* ("We
think in terms of elementary, secondary, and higher education"). Then move on
to sentences in which you waste more than two words:

Instead of	*Say or write*	8
The Campus School expects to have three fourth grades.	In terms of the future, the Campus School expects to have three fourth grades. (5 extra words)	
I'm glad that we got the response we wanted.	I'm glad that there was a response to that in terms of what we wanted. (6 extra words)	

Emulate the masters of jargon. They have the courage to abandon the effort 9
to shape a thought clearly:

> A field trip should be defined in terms of where you are.
> They are trying to get under way some small and large construction in terms of
> unemployment.
> When we think in terms of muscles, we don't always think in terms of eyes.

Level

Although *level* should be well known through overuse, unobservant young instructors may need a review of some of its uses, especially if they are anxious to speak and write *on the level of* jargon. (Note the redundancy of the italicized words.) 10

Instead of	*Say or write*	11
She teaches fifth grade.	She teaches on the fifth grade level. (3 extra words)	
Readers will find more than one meaning.	It can be read on more than one level of meaning. (4 extra words).	
My students	The writers on my level of concern. (5 extra words)	

Long Forms

When the shorter of two similar forms is adequate, choose the longer; e.g., say *analyzation* (for *analysis*), orientate (for *orient*), *origination* (for *origin*), *summarization* (for *summary*). Besides using an unnecessary syllable or two, the long form can make your audience peevish when they know the word has not won acceptance or, at least, uneasy ("Is that a new word that I ought to know?"). If someone asks why you use *notate* instead of *note* (as in "Please notate in the space below your preference . . . "), fabricate an elaborate distinction. Not having a dictionary in his pocket, your questioner will be too polite to argue. 12

With practice, you will have the confidence to enter unfamiliar territory. Instead of the standard forms (*confirm, interpret, penalty, register,* and *scrutiny*), try *confirmate, interpretate, penalization, registrate,* and *scrutinization*. 13

Vogue Words

You have little chance of making a name for yourself as a user of jargon unless you sprinkle your speech and writing with vogue words and phrases, both the older fashions (e.g., *aspect, background, field, level, situation*) and the newer (e.g., *escalate, relate to, share with; facility, involvement; limited, minimal*). An old favorite adds the aroma of the cliché, while a newly fashionable term proves that you are up-to-date. Another advantage of vogue words is that some of them are euphemisms. By using *limited*, for example, you show your disdain for the directness and clarity of *small*, as in "a man with a limited education" and "a limited enrollment in a very large room." 14

Unfortunately, some vogue expressions are shorter than standard English, but their obscurity does much to offset the defect of brevity.

Instead of	Say or write	15
The children live in a camp and have both classes and recreation outdoors.	The children live in a camp-type situation.	
She reads, writes, and speaks German and has had four years of Latin.	She has a good foreign-language background.	
Many hospitals now let a man stay with his wife during labor.	The trend is to let the father have more involvement.	

A final word to novices: dozens of words and phrases have been omitted from 16 this brief lexicon, but try to spot them yourselves. Practice steadily, always keeping in mind that the fundamentals of jargon—verbosity and needless vagueness—are best adorned by pretentiousness. Soon, if you feel the impulse to say, for example, that an office has one secretary and some part-time help, you will write "Administrative clerical aids implement the organizational function." Eventually you can produce sentences which mean anything or possibly nothing: "We should leave this aspect of the definition relatively operational" or "This condition is similar in regard to other instances also."

DISCUSSION QUESTIONS

1. What purpose is served here by Professor Redfern's irony? As he clearly does not want to encourage us to write in jargon, why does his article tell us how to go about it?

2. To see if you have gained from Redfern's "advice," recast the following sentences into jargon:

These are the times that try men's souls. (Thomas Paine)
Don't look back. Something may be gaining on you. (Satchel Paige)
The business of America is business. (Calvin Coolidge)
I been poor, and I been rich. Rich is better. (Sophie Tucker)
The secret of being a bore is to tell everything. (Voltaire)

3. On the average, how much longer are your rewrites of the sentences under question 2?

4. Are the sentences translated into jargon in any way clearer? Might somebody who has not read this essay or any of the others in this chapter find the jargonized sentences clearer? Might such a reader find the sentences more impressive?

5. Professor Redfern refers to his "Lexicon" as "brief." How many of the following words might he have wanted to include in a longer essay? Are these also jargon? Or do they lend distinction to writing?

A. Logistical	D. Incremental	G. Contingency	J. Options
B. Functional	E. Interface	H. Reciprocal	K. Systematized
C. Responsive	F. Affirmative	I. Capability	L. Transitional

6. In recent years there has been a fashion for using words taken from computer technology. These include such words as "input" (for "information"), "output" (for "results"), and "throughput" (for "process"), etc. Are such words precise, vivid metaphors or they a new form of jargon?

R. D. ROSEN
Psychobabble

Psychology, once thought an obscure academic pursuit, has now become one of the most popular subjects for a wide range of readers. Many of the nonfiction titles available in any bookstore—or from any paperback bookrack—are some kind of popular pyschology. This large-scale study of psychology, often self-tutored, has had a tremendous effect on the subjects we talk about in everyday conversation and the language we use with those and other subjects.

Initially one might think this change would fit well with the sentiments of many of the authors of this textbook. As Rosen says in this article, one of the characteristics of present-day cultural life is an insistence on preventing failures of communication. Instead of suppressing some of our more intimate feelings, many among us articulate them as freely as we can. And in articulating those feelings we can use the language of psychology; instead of the more generalized "fearful" or "nasty," we have the seemingly precise "paranoid."

Does this free communication, or doesn't it?

While having drinks recently with a young woman I had not seen for some time, I asked how things were going and received this reply: "I've really been getting in touch with myself lately. I've struck some really deep chords." I recoiled slightly at the grandeur of her remarks, but she proceeded, undaunted, to reel out a string of broad psychological insights with an enthusiasm attributable less to her Tequila Sunrises than to the confessional spirit that is sweeping America.

I could not help thinking that I disappointed her with my inability to summon more lyricism and intensity in my own conversation. Now that reticence has gone out of style I sensed an obligation to reciprocate her candor but couldn't bring myself to use the popular catch phrases of revelation. Would she understand if I said that instead of striking deep chords I had merely tickled the ivories of my psychic piano? That getting my head together was not exactly the way in which I wanted to describe what was going on above *my* neck? Surely it wouldn't do any good if I resorted to more precise, but pompously clinical, language and admitted that I was well on my way to resolving my attitude toward my own maternal introject.

Whenever I see you," she said brightly, "it makes me feel very good inside. It's a real high-energy experience." 3

So what was wrong with me that I couldn't feel the full voltage of our 4 meeting. Unable to match her incandescence, I simply agreed, "Yes, it's good to see you, too," then fell silent.

Finally she said, her beatific smile widening, "But I can really dig your 5 silence. If you're bummed out, that's OK."

If anything characterizes the cultural life of the Seventies in America, it is an 6 insistence on preventing failures of communication. Everything must now be spoken. The Kinsey Report, Masters and Johnson, *The Joy of Sex* and its derivatives; The *Playboy* Advisor, the *Penthouse* Forum, *Oui's* Sex Tapes; contraception; Esalen and the human potential movement; the democratization of psychotherapy—all these various oils have helped lubricate the national tongue. It's as if the full bladder of civilization's squeamishness has finally burst. The sexual revolution, this therapeutic age, has culminated in one profuse, steady stream of self-revelation, confessed profligacy and publicized domestic trauma.

It seems that almost everybody belongs to the Cult of Candor these days, and 7 that everyone who does speaks the same dialect. Are you relating? Good. Are you getting in touch with yourself? Fine. Gone through some heavy changes? Doing your own thing? (Or are you, by some mistake, doing someone else's?) Is your head screwed on straight? Are you going to get your act together . . . or just engaging in mental foreplay?

One hears it everywhere, like endless panels of a Feiffer cartoon. In restau- 8 rants distraught lovers lament, "I wish I could get into your head." A man on a bus says to his companion, "I just got back from the coast. What a different headset!" The latest reports from a corrupt Esalen provide us with new punch lines: A group leader there intones that "it's beautiful if you're unhappy. Go with the feeling . . . You gotta be you 'cause you're you and you gotta be, and besides, if you aren't gonna be you who else's gonna be you, honey. . . . This is the Aquarian Age and the time to be oneself, to love one's beauty, to go with one's process."

Are you sufficiently laid back to read this article? Will it be a heavy experi- 9 ence, or merely the mock?

It's time we lend a name to this monotonous patois, this psychological patter, 10 whose concern is to faithfully catalog the ego's condition: Psychobabble. As Psychobabble begins to tyrannize conversations everywhere, it is difficult to avoid, and there is an embarrassment involved in not using it in the presence of other Psychobabblers that is akin to the mild humiliation experienced by American tourists in Paris who cannot speak the native language. It is now spoken by magazine editors, management consultants, sandal makers, tool and die workers and Ph.D.s in clinical psychology alike. What the sociologist Philip Rieff in the mid-Sixties called "Psychological Man," that mid-20th century victim of his own interminable introspection, has become Psychobabbler, the victim of his own inability to describe human behavior with anything but platitudes.

* * *

As one Boston psychoanalyst, who has practiced for over 30 years, says, 11 "After the war, everyone was talking simplistically about the Oedipus complex. It was the rage. Everyone had the idea that knowledge itself would make you free." Now he has to listen to the new Psychobabble. A social worker patient in his 30s, himself a group leader, eagerly responded at the beginning of therapy to each interpretation his analyst made by saying, "I hear you, I hear you."

"I'm sorry," said the doctor, "I didn't know you were a little deaf." 12

"I'm not. I *hear* you. It means I comprehend." 13

"Well, *what* do you comprehend?" 14

The patient paused. "Jesus," he replied, "I don't know." 15

* * *

The Psychobabblers don't even seem to know the terms of Freud, Jung, 16 Adler, or any body of psychological thought. Their language seems to free-float in some linguistic atmosphere, a set of repetitive verbal formalities that kills off the very spontaneity, candor and understanding it pretends to promote. It's an idiom that reduces psychological insight and therapeutic processes to a collection of standardized insights, that provides only a limited lexicon to deal with an infinite variety of problems. "Uptight" is a word now used to describe an individual who is experiencing anything from mild uneasiness to a clinical depression. To ask someone why he or she refers to another as being "hung-up" produces a reply along the line of: "Why? Man, he's just *hung-up*." Oddly, those few psychiatric terms borrowed by Psychobabble are used recklessly. One is no longer fearful: one is *paranoid*. The adjective is applied to the populace with a generosity that must confuse the real clinical paranoiacs. Increasingly, people describe their moody friends as *manic-depressives* and almost anyone you don't like is psychotic, or at least *schizzed-out*.

* * *

If Psychobabble were a question of language alone, the worst one could say 17 about it is that it is just another example of the corrosion and unimaginativeness of spoken English. But the prevalence of Psychobabble reflects more than a mere "loss for words." It indicates that, in an era when the national gaze has turned inward, and in a country that needs therapy perhaps more than any other, Americans still have enormous difficulty in understanding the depth of their psychological problems, perhaps even in understanding that psychological problems *have* depth.

* * *

Psychobabble has insinuated itself into many American art forms, and in 18 most cases this is no surprise. That we can now hear it on *The Bob Newhart Show*, in which Newhart plays a Chicago psychotherapist, seems only fitting for a medium that unerringly reflects mid-cult values. In rock music, the incidence of Psychobabble is high, which is only natural for an art form whose audience does not prize it above all for its ability to elucidate and whose requirements of rhyme and comprehensibility do not encourage the refinement of insights (ideas are normally at the mercy of "love/above," "out tonight/treat her right" couplets). But it is interesting to note that the English progressive rock group Gentle Giant has a song called "Knots," based on R. D. Laing's book, that the American group The Flock has a new cut titled "My O.K. Today," inspired by their reading of *I'm O.K.! You're O.K.!* and that lines like Todd Rundgren's "Get your trip together, be a real man" abound more than ever. But the most eloquent Psychobabbler in rock music today is John Denver, who, fresh from Erhard Seminars Training in California, now sounds like the Fritz Perls posters that adorned the walls of student cells in 1971. From his *Rolling Stone* interview of last May:

> How far out it is to be a bird and fly around the trees. I am what I've always wanted to be and that is the truth. And I think—in fact, it's not what I think, but I observe that if people were to really take a good look at themselves, they are exactly the way that they have always wanted to be. . . . My experience is that if I can tell you the truth, just lay it out there, then I have totally opened up a space for you to be who you are and that it really opens up all the room in the world for us to do whatever we want to do in regard to each other. If I don't like you, I'll tell you. And that's great.

As for contemporary films that deal in Psychobabble (*Alice Doesn't Live Here   19 Anymore, Diary of a Mad Housewife, I Love You, Alice B. Toklas* and others), one is always tempted to praise highly those that capture the essence of Psychobabble dialogues, simply on the basis of verisimilitude. Because film and also rock music are to some extent engaged in *representing* the way people talk, and not in analyzing why, they are easy targets to attack for using Psychobabble. One has to look elsewhere to find a medium that has truly suffered at the hands of Psychobabble.

Such a victim is American publishing (although one might also say it vic-   20 timizes itself). Psychobabble's influence on publishing in this country has been disastrous, and the number of Psychobabble books offered to the public with a solemnity reserved for great works is astounding. Seventeen years ago, Alfred Kazin derided the Myth of Universal Creativity engendered by the Freud craze, "the assumption," as he put it, "that every idle housewife was meant to be a painter and that every sexual deviant is really a poet." The time has never been more propitious than now for ordinary citizens to spill their beans in print. To an older and still mistaken belief that you only had to be neurotic to create has been added the more recent societal sanction—that, according to the Cult of Candor, it is virtuous to reveal to as many people as possible the tragedies and erotic and emotional secrets of one's private life. It seems that all one needs today in order to become a bona fide author is a few months of therapy and an ability to compose grammatical sentences.

Books written in Psychobabble almost always seem "touchingly human," as   21 the phrase goes, but in their simplification of human problems they engage in what Jacoby has called (referring to the neo-Freudians, to whom Psychobabblers are indebted) "the monotonous discovery of common sense." They present revelation uninformed by history, unmediated by ideology; like verbal home movies.

Now this tendency has flowered in the garden of rampant Psychobabble. In 22
the newly released book *Intimate Feedback: A Lover's Guide to Getting in Touch with Each Other* by Barrie and Charlotte Hopson (Simon & Schuster), we are offered these startling insights, quintessentially Psychobabble:

> Who am I? This is a question which has always been central to man's awareness of himself.
>
> Human existence is exemplified by one person trying to communicate with others.
>
> When couples say that they have nothing new to learn about each other, this is due to stereotyped communication patterns, unless they really do not like one another and have no interest in their partner.

· · ·

The publishing industry's enthusiasm for Psychobabble of the above variety 23
as well as of the more explicitly therapeutic strain (*How to Be Your Own Best Friend, How to Be Awake & Alive, When I Say No, I Feel Guilty*)—a story in itself—was foreshadowed during the past five or six years by the success of confessional books. To name but a few, Gestalt Therapy "refounder" Fritz Perls' *In and Out the Garbage Pail* was a lesson in incontinent narcissism ("I am becoming a public figure," he announces on page 1); R. D. Laing's *Knots* made relationships seem irresistibly complex; Nancy Friday gave women's sexual fantasies a good name with *My Secret Garden* and *Forbidden Flowers*; Erica Jong aired her own fantasies in her too-touted *Fear of Flying*; and an equally overrated book, Nigel Nicolson's tribute to his famous parents, Harold Nicolson and Vita Sackville-West, in *Portrait of a Marriage*, endowed the polymorphous perverse with historical dignity.

· · ·

The popularity of Psychobabble has eclipsed the public taste for literature, in 24
which there are surely more compelling answers to human problems than there are to be found in the books I've mentioned and those like them. Novelists are slowly going out of business while small-town gurus appear on talk shows to exchange insights with Joey Bishop.

Please! No more books by unhappy housewives crying, "I've just got to be 25
me!" No more 33-year-old ad agency executives telling me how they make men want to get into their pants at the singles bar! No more divorced men screaming for justice! No more daydreams of Great Danes with searching tongues! Enough!

This very week in the bookstores, one can find on the hard-cover nonfiction 26
shelf *Your Inner Conflicts–How to Solve Them; How to Give and Receive Advice; How to Live With Another Person; Free to Love; Creating and Sustaining Intimacy in Marriage; Stand Up, Speak Out, Talk Back* and countless others. The field of self-help and confession is becoming so specialized that before long we might well have Psychobabble books written on the thinnest pretexts: *How to Grocery Shop Without Having an Anxiety Attack, How to Achieve Transference in Elevators, You CAN Marry Your Mother, The Promiscuous Coleus.*

Words themselves do not "cure" a person, and words themselves, even the 27
most virulent Psychobabble, cannot make one "sick." However, in the absence of more profound understandings of what we feel and why we feel it,

Psychobabble deludes many people into thinking they need not examine themselves with anything but its dull instruments. The danger of Psychobabble is that it anesthetizes curiosity, numbs the desire to know. And, in that state, emotional growth is eventually stunted, no matter how many times one repeats, "I've just got to go with my feelings." Knowledge itself may not free anyone, but the lack of it only reinforces the chains.

Language may, in the end, prove too inadequate to systematically describe   28 wants, desires and emotional states in general. Even the borders delineated by clinical terminology blur badly in the face of actual human behavior. The best one can do now is challenge Psychobabble by declining courteously to accept its usage, as did a young man I know who grew up in a suburb with a group of peers who were "morbidly sensitive to each other's feelings, you know the kind. They'd get into these psychosensitive moods." He dated a girl from the group who one day asked him point-blank if he was getting his head together.

"Yes," he replied. "I can feel it congealing."   29

DISCUSSION QUESTIONS

1. Can you define "Psychobabble"? Does the word include only language? Language and ideas? Language and attitudes? Give examples. Be precise.

2. The author ends the essay by recommending that certain kinds of discussion cease. What are they? What kind of talk annoys him most? Is it Psychobabble?

3. What is the cult of candor? See paragraph 7. Have you experienced this among the college students you know.

4. Can you translate paragraph 9 into Standard English? Is something gained or lost in the translation?

5. Do you object to Psychobabble when it is used by pop musicians such as Todd Rundgren or Bob Denver? See paragraph 18. Does Psychobabble help the singers' popularity? Are other singers more or less popular because they do not use it?

6. Do you agree with the sentiment expressed in paragraph 21 that popular psychology is eclipsing the public taste for literature? Take this poll of your class: have each member name the title of the last book he or she has read. Was it "literature"? That is, was it a novel, a collection of poems or short stories, a drama, or a filmscript? Or was it a work of psychology? Popular or academic?

7. If you are presently taking a course in psychology, ask your instructor how he or she feels about the popular use of specialized vocabulary. Are there many terms misdefined in popular use?

8. Why do people use Psychobabble? Do you think they are more attracted to the denotations or the connotations of specialized psychological vocabulary?

FRANCINE HARDAWAY
Foul Play: Sports Metaphors as Public Doublespeak

Are games a parody of "real life"? Or is life but an extension of many games? The paradoxical relation of games to life has given rise to thousands of figures of speech, some as old as Shakespeare's "The game is up" (Cymbeline, c. 1610).

The suggestion that games are like life is an analogy, and like all analogies, it is at least partially false. A political campaign may be like a horse race, but that does not mean the candidates are ridden by diminutive characters in satin suits. Thus it may be, as Hardaway asserts, that the more often we portray different activities in sports metaphors, the less clearly we perceive them.

Nobody would argue the place of sports in American life; they are big business. And they are big business because they fit philosophically with the widely accepted American dream of open competition in a free market economy. Americans believe in competition, foster it, and encourage it. They live by its rules. No wonder the language of athletic competition has found its way as metaphor into every aspect of American life. If we are at a disadvantage, we say we've "got two strikes against us," things have "taken a bad bounce," or we're "on the ropes." If we are being aggressive, we "take the ball and run with it," "take the bull by the horns," "come out swinging," or "make a sweep." If the fates still conspire against us, we "take it on the chin," "throw in the towel," or "roll with the punches" until we're "saved by the bell." 1

It's worth taking some time to think about how these sports metaphors, so ubiquitous and so ignored until Watergate brought them to our attention, describe the quality of life in America. 2

The purpose of such metaphors is to explain unfamiliar or difficult concepts in terms of familiar images. But recently there have been some changes in our national self-concept and these changes are duly reflected in sports metaphors. We seem to have changed drastically from a society in which "it isn't whether you win or lose, but how you play the game," to one in which, to use Vince Lombardi's words, "winning isn't everything, it's the only thing." And our sports metaphors have changed with us. "The good fight" and "the old college try" have given way to the more sophisticated "game plans," "play-calling," and quarterbacking rhetoric of Vietnam and Watergate. Sports metaphors now often function as public doublespeak: language meant to manipulate its audience unconsciously. Analyzing sports doublespeak reveals some scary truths about how we Americans look at life. In John Mitchell's words, "when the going gets tough, the tough get going," and we turn out to be a society in which "nice guys finish last," and everybody wants to "be on the winning side." 3

The rhetoric of the playing field appears in advertising, business, and government. Let's take an obvious example first. President Ford, in publicizing his 4 economic strategies when he first took office, devised the W.I.N. button. An offshoot of Ford's other unfortunate sports metaphor, the promise to "hold the line" on inflation, the W.I.N. button was meant to appeal by familiarity to the sports-minded American who will "get up for the game," and "tackle the job" if the coach just tells him what to do. Ford hoped that the "win" mentality was so strongly ingrained in America that the very word would alter attitudes and behavior.

With the W.I.N. button, Ford hoped to make use of a sports metaphor the way advertising does. He wanted to make the analogy from athletic success to success in other fields. We all expect to be manipulated by advertising, so it is no surprise to see professional athletes advertising hair tonic, shaving cream, even frozen pizza or panty hose. The doublespeak is implicit: use this product, and you will enjoy the same success as Frank Gifford, Arthur Ashe, Joe Namath. Associating the athlete with the product, however, makes another claim for the athlete: it extends his expertise beyond the playing field. Ad agencies hope we will take the advice of these "pros" about shaving cream, hair tonic, frozen pizza, or panty hose; after all, the pro wouldn't make a wrong choice about these products any more than he would throw the ball away at a crucial moment of the game. So the athlete is an expert, as well as a hero. His ability to "score" carries over into financial and the sexual arenas as well; there is even a product named "Score."

Since it has been established by advertising that the athlete is both hero and expert, sports metaphors are used more subtly to sell products. In the MGB ad that reads "MGB. Think of it as a well-coordinated athlete," we can see how much athletic ability is admired. No longer do we compare the good athlete or the good team to a well-oiled machine: now we're comparing the machine to the good athlete. Like a well-coordinated athlete, you'll "score" in your MGB.

But advertising is an easy target for doublespeak analysis. More complex by far is the way sports metaphors function in business, where their analysis leads to crucial revelations about American ethics. Business has always been fond of the football analogy, as William H. Whyte, Jr. points out:

> No figure of speech is a tenth as seductive to the businessman. Just why this should be—baseball curiously is much less used—is generally explained by its adaptability to all sorts of situations. Furthermore, the football analogy is *satisfying*. It is bounded by two goal lines and is thus finite. There is always a solution. And that is what makes it so often treacherous.[1]

Business uses the team philosophy, says Whyte, to hedge on moral issues. By making analogies to sports, business convinces the outside world that its decisions aren't truly consequential: they are "games" executed by good "team players." The fact that dollars and human lives may also be involved is not included when the sports metaphor is used, for the sports metaphor imposes automatic limits on the way business activity is seen.

[1]William H. Whyte, Jr., "The Language of Business," in *Technological and Professional Writing*, ed. Herman A. Estrin (New York: Harcourt, Brace & World, 1963), p. 83. In this part of the paper, I am indebted to an unpublished paper on "Sports Metaphors in Business" by John Driscoll.

The goal of sports activity is always unambiguous and non-controversial; participants do not come together to discuss or debate the ends for which the activity has been established, but rather take this end for granted and apply themselves in a single-minded fashion to the task of developing the most efficient means to achieve the predetermined unchanging and non-controversial end: winning.[2]

So the sports metaphor precludes thought; it operates on unconscious and irrational levels, manipulating its users as well as its audiences. Perhaps its use in business, where the idea of competition in the free marketplace still carries moral force, has something to do with man's aggressive nature; what sports and business have in common that allows the sports metaphor to be drawn so often and so successfully by American businessmen is aggressiveness. Sports are an acceptable form of releasing aggressive impulses; if business uses the sports metaphor, isn't the aggressiveness of business automatically acceptable?

. . . [the] same aggressive impulse which can lead to strife and violence also underlies man's urge to independence and achievement. Just as a child could not possibly grow up into an independent adult if it were not aggressive, so an adult must needs continue to express at least part of his aggressive potential if he is to maintain his own autonomy.[3]

No wonder the Duke of Wellington was able to observe that "the battle of Waterloo was won on the playing fields of Eton." The skills learned on the playing field by the child are translated into the battles of the adult.

But there is also a certain cynicism associated with the use of the sports metaphor by business:

What happens to some guys is—well, I'll draw the analogy to sports again. Baseball has its hot players and the next year the hot players cool off, and what happens is that their salaries drop and they get optioned out to Toledo.[4]

In Jerry Della Femina's description of what happens to advertising men who don't produce, the sports metaphor obscures the human position of the advertising executive, the man who has a good year followed by a bad year and suddenly finds himself nursing an ulcer and out of a job. Like most sports metaphors, this one permits the reader to ignore the ethical implications of cut-throat competition among advertising agencies for top talent.

But business still isn't the "Big Game"—that's government. And, as we might now expect, the bigger the game, the more prevalent the sports metaphor as doublespeak. Watergate revealed the wholesale use of the sports lexicon by politicians, but Watergate was neither the beginning nor the end of the sports metaphor. As William Safire points out in his excellent book *The New Language*

---

[2]Ike Balbus, "Politics as Sports: The Political Ascendancy of the Sports Metaphor in America," *Monthly Review*, March 1975, p. 30.

[3]Anthony Storr, *Human Aggression* (New York: Atheneum, 1970), p. 59.

[4]Jerry Della Femina, *From Those Wonderful Folks Who Brought You Pearl Harbor* (New York: Simon & Shuster, 1971), p. 124.

of Politics,[5] Shakespeare may have been the first to use these comparisons. King Henry V told his troops before Harfleur, "I see you stand like greyhounds in the slips, straining upon the start. The game's afoot . . ." But Safire also notes that Shakespeare wasn't the last; the section on "Sports Metaphors" in *The New Language of Politics* is a wonderful compendium of quotations from past political greats beginning with Woodrow Wilson's "I have always in my own thought summed up individual liberty, and business liberty, and every other kind of liberty, in the phrase that is common in the sporting world, 'A free field and no favor,' " and stopping at JFK's "Politics is like football. If you see daylight, go through the hole."

Amusingly enough, politics doesn't content itself only with the football [10] metaphor so favored by business. Instead, it inadvertently reveals its seamier side by the frequent use of the horse race analogy. There are front-runners and dark horses, long shots and shoo-ins. The winner takes the reins of government, while the loser is an also-ran who was "nosed out." Harry Truman said, "I am trying to do in politics what Citation has done in the horse races. I propose at the finish line on November 2 to come out ahead. . . ." It seems that in politics, more than in advertising or in business, the use of the sports metaphor reveals more than gamesmanship, competition, or vicarious aggression; it also reveals an affinity with gambling.

But Safire's compendium, while amusing and instructive, is pre-Watergate [11] and he therefore views the sports metaphor as innocuous. He says,

> Sports metaphors relate closely to many people, which is why politicians spend the time to create them; at other times they are tossed off without thinking because they are already a part of the language. After a Kennedy aide appeared on Lawrence Spivak's television panel show *Meet the Press*, the President called to say "They never laid a glove on you." It is the classic remark of a trainer to a prize fighter who has been belted all over the ring. (pp. 421-22)

Since Watergate, we have become more attuned to the way sports metaphors are often used to make big decisions involving all our lives seem trivial and inconsequential.

> Nixon's "jocko'macho" talk (as Nicholas von Hoffman called it) was amply demonstrated; the limited supply of tough-guy metaphors, akin to verbal locker room swaggering of muscle-flexing *machismo* at the beach: . . . Years earlier, some critics had felt that Nixon's overt enthusiasm for spectator sports (shaking hands with athletes, telegrams and phone calls to coaches) was simply a calculated ploy ("a grandstand play") to win the favor of certain voters, to create the illusion that he was "just one of the guys." It was no illusion. Nixon was not the first politician to use the imagery of athletics. . . but the transcripts reveal that the traditional emphasis on "fair play," "following the rules," and "good sportsmanship" had been replaced by a "win at all costs" mentality.[6]

---

[5]New York: Random House, 1968, p. 421.
[6]Hugh Rank, "Watergate and the Language," in *Language and Public Policy*, ed. Hugh Rank (Urbana, Ill.: NCTE, 1974), pp. 8-9.

One need hardly comment further on what Watergate did to the language; its only good effect was to alert many Americans to the way language does both form and corrupt thinking. For that, we should probably be grateful.

Unfortunately, the effects of Watergate aren't longlasting. In the midst of the 12 recent New York City financial crisis, the *Wall Street Journal* carried the following story:

> After a seven-month game of political brinkmanship, the Ford administration has browbeaten New York City into "fiscal responsibility" and the city has pressured Washington into limited federal help.
>
> But the path to that outcome proved to be far different than either side had expected, and the ultimate results happier than either would have predicted just a short time ago. There seems to be no clear winner in the long struggle—just losers of varying degrees. . . .
>
> The reconstruction of these events leading up to the Wednesday statement discloses basic miscalculations by every player in the game. . . .
>
> The city's fiscal crisis, surfacing last May, rapidly developed into a high-level game of political chess—played out in Washington and New York and Albany, full of bluff and bombast, maneuver and surprise.[7]

Only the name of the game has changed; the article goes on to discuss how New York's crisis developed into a standoff between Ford and the city, in which participants in the negotiations between New York and Washington felt that "it was hardball both ways, and nothing was spared." The "hardball season" of negotiations ran from September through November, when Ford and New York City finally reached a compromise.

This story illustrates very well the dangers of relying too heavily on sports 13 metaphors. Here a genuine crisis has been reduced for readers to a game in which participants are trying to out-bluff and out-maneuver each other while New York and perhaps the rest of the nation await the consequences. And the crisis is portrayed as a strategy problem, rather than a human problem or a problem in responsible government.

What is the lesson to be learned from looking at our culture's continuing use 14 of sports metaphors to render important situations innocuous in advertising, in business, and in government? If it is true, as Walker Gibson said to the NCTE[8] Convention in 1973, that "learning to read is learning to infer dramatic character from linguistic evidence," then examining the metaphors used in popular culture provides good insight into our character as a nation. And if it is also true, as Orwell remarked in *Politics and the English Language*, that "language can corrupt thought," then sports metaphors become not merely ways of revealing our adolescent preoccupation with aggressiveness, with winning, with games, but also ways of perpetuating those concerns, of glorifying them, of passing them on unexamined to our children through our national culture. It is at least worth a few minutes of our time to wrestle (there it is again) with the decision of whether we really want to see ourselves forever as a nation of teamplayers and sports fans.

---

[7]November 28, 1975.
[8]National Council of Teachers of English.

DISCUSSION QUESTIONS

1. How many students agree that "Nobody would argue the place of sports in American life"? Are spectator sports genuinely popular? Or popular only with certain people? If your college has an intercollegiate sports program, do most of the students attend the games? Or do people who are not students attend? How does your attitude toward sports affect your attitude to sports metaphors?

2. Winning may be the most important thing in the playing of a game, but what does "winning" mean in life? See paragraph 4. Does it mean driving your opponents off the field?

3. Why are football metaphors so attractive to businessmen? Is there some reason that racing metaphors are used more often in politics?

4. Can you think of some other games that have contributed metaphors to common speech? Start with "gambit" and "joker." Is there something in a game or a sport that makes it especially valuable as a source of metaphors?

5. Comment on the validity of these quotations from the text: From paragraph 7: "So the sports metaphor precludes thought; it operates on unconscious and irrational levels, manipulating its users as well as its audiences." From paragraph 8: "Like most sports metaphors, this one permits the reader to ignore the ethical implications of cut-throat competition among advertising agencies for top talent."

6. Do you agree with Hardaway's charge that sports metaphors fail to portray different situations in human terms? See paragraphs 12-13.

Student Essay
Truckers—Keep on Truckin',
Away from Me

"Double nickels," "chicken coop," "negatory," and "ten-four." This, as   1
everyone in the country must know by now, is truckers' talk. Sometime after
Christmas, 1975, several million Middle Americans began to want to sound like
truck drivers. Who could have predicted it? Who wants it? What do the words
mean? How can we stop it? These are some of the questions that came into my
mind, because I think I must be one of the few people in America who is turned
off by the whole thing and wishes it would all go away.

I know that truckers' talk began as a mass movement around Christmas,   2
1975, because that is when the discount house where I work found it could
barely keep citizens' band radios in stock. I say "citizens' band" because I am not
a fan, but if you are a fan you should say "CB" radio, the way a tourist fresh back
from California says "LA" for "Los Angeles." Anyway, we couldn't keep the
radios on the shelf. People came swarming into the store—perfectly middle-

class, suburban-looking people—and would take the radios out of the stockboy's hands before we could put them on the shelves. The radios were for listening to the truckers on the highways. The truckers talk to each other because they're bored, but people are driving out to the highways just to listen to the truckers as they cruise by. This little pleasure costs the people at least $39.95 plus tax, not to mention gasoline, occasional tolls, and wear and tear on their cars.

What did the truckers ever do to win this glamor? Is there anything necessarily heroic about piloting one of those big rigs? Not as far as I can see. I have been sharing the road with truckers ever since I have been old enough to drive. My family moved here from western Pennsylvania when I started high school, and since that time I have made many trips along Interstate 80 where about 70% of the traffic is made up of cross country trucks. Most of them drive as though they wish the "pleasure cars" would stay off their roads. But they're not as bad on the roads as they are in the restaurants. There the choice areas are cordoned off for the truckers. As we sit on our stools we can look over and see them swagger into their padded booths and sneer back at us. Funny, even though their license plates say New York, Ontario, Maryland, or Wisconsin, they all seem to talk as though they come from Arkansas. Maybe sounding as though they come from Arkansas makes them all, the truckers and the trucker-lovers, think they're cowboys.

The people who love truckers' talk seem to think it's clever, but most of the time it seems rather stale. I think the cleverest CB expression I ever heard is "Tijuana Taxi" for a police car with a flashing light. That's a step up from what we used to call them in high school, "Gum Ball Machines." The cleverness of some of the other terms is strictly a matter of personal taste. Maybe calling a weighing station a "chicken coop" sounds clever once or twice, but it isn't an expression that can be repeated indefinitely. And some of the expressions sound as though they were copied from not-so-bright kids. "Negatory," for example, sounds like a kid trying to say "negative," but not quite making it. Saying that a return trip is a "flipside" sounds like a borrowing from bubble gum music. Does a grown-up person call a big truck an "eighteen-wheeler" and a smaller one a "four-wheeler"? When these big kids are done with a job they say, "We gone."

The secret of the American love affair with truckers and truckers' talk is probably the national speed limit of 55 miles per hour. Everybody knows that the truckers help each other to spot the police and so evade the law. There's no missing the hatred the truckers feel for the law; they call it "double nickels." And their names for the police are probably the most famous examples of truckers' talk: "Smokey the bear," "smokies," "and just "bears." The few times I have listened to the truckers, in friends' cars, that's all they have talked about. "You seen any bears?" "No, there ain't no bears around here," and so on. Perhaps I should admit that my being in the police science curriculum has something to do with the way I feel. Truckers' talk makes the police sound as though they are dumb, heavy-handed authority figures who are just trying to stop people from having fun. Most state policemen don't like the 55 mile an hour speed limit either. But if it helps save lives and gasoline, why shouldn't they enforce it?

No fad can last for very long. Pretty soon there ought to be more people who think that "ten-four" for "OK" sounds dumb. Part of the attraction in truckers' talk is that not everybody knows it. When everybody knows it, perhaps it will go away. I was encouraged to think this by talking with my uncle. He told me that when he was in high school in the fifties, everyone wanted to talk like George Gobel, the old comedian. By the time he graduated nobody wanted to talk like George Gobel anymore.

RHETORICAL ANALYSIS

1. The essay begins with four examples of truckers' talk in an elliptical sentence. Was this an effective beginning? Or would the author have done better to begin with a complete sentence?

2. The introductory paragraph includes four successive questions beginning with "Who could have predicted it?" etc. Does the author answer all of these questions? Are all of the questions *answerable*? Is there any worth in asking an unanswerable question?

3. In paragraph 3 the author tries to explain how truckers gained their contemporary glamor by citing personal experience and by asserting that they all speak with the same accent. Do these two analyses belong in the same paragraph? Why or why not?

4. Excluding paragraph 1 (the introduction) and paragraph 6 (the conclusion), the body of the paper seems to be ordered thus:

> Paragraph 2 gives the historical background of the popularity of CB radios.
> Paragraph 3 tries to explain the glamor and appeal of truckers.
> Paragraph 4 considers examples of truckers' talk and finds them stale.
> Paragraph 5 explains the appeal of truckers' talk as part of resistance to the national speed limit.

If you accept this as the outline of the paper, can you justify the order of the paragraphs? Do they come in the right order? Or would you suggest a different order for the paragraphs?

5. Is the assertion that the fad for truckers' talk cannot last appropriate in the conclusion, paragraph 6?

6. The author attempts to analyze the fad for truckers' talk and speak against it in one paper. Do you think this is too much to try to say in one paper? Would he have been better off with just an analysis in one paper and a denunciation in another? Or does his argumentative point of view sharpen his analysis?

POINTS OF DEPARTURE

A

The great enemy of clear language is insincerity. When there is a gap between one's real and one's declared aims, one turns instinctively to long words and exhausted idioms, like a cuttlefish squirting out ink. . . . Politics . . . is a mass of lies, evasions, folly, hatred and schizophrenia. When the general atmosphere is bad, the language must suffer. . . .

In our time, political speech and writing are largely the defense of the 2 indefensible. . . .

. . . Political language—and with variations this is true of all political parties, from Conservatives to Anarchists—is designed to make lies sound truthful and murder respectable, and to give the appearance of solidity to pure wind.

George Orwell, from "Politics and the English Language"

B

There is one sports announcer who does not go where the former athletes 1 lead him. That is Howard Cosell. Cosell is a phenomenon, or as some have it, phenomena. Nothing can shake him away from his own bromides, of which the supply is unquenchable. Cosell can range from a relative paucity ("Despite the relative paucity of scoring . . .") to a veritable plethora (Let's continue on this point of this veritable plethora of field goals") without drawing a breath, and there is every reason to believe that when he says "relative paucity" and "veritable plethora" he is not kidding; he means it.

Only Cosell would have described the mood of the crowd at the Bobby 2 Riggs–Billie Jean King match as "an admixture" or remarked that for Riggs "It has not been a comedic night." Only Cosell would speak of a football team "procuring a first down," or say that a fighter was "plagued by minutiae," or that the cards of the referee and judges, made public after each round in a fight in Quebec, "vivified" the problem facing the fighter who was behind. During a Monday night football game nobody else would say, "The Redskins have had two scoring opportunities and failed to avail themselves both times," or that "The mist is drifting over the stadium like a description in a Thomas Hardy novel." At any rate, we may hope that nobody else would say it.

Edwin Newman, "On Howard Cosell," from *Strictly Speaking*

C

No one would ever argue that euphemisms and circumlocutions should never be used in verbal communication. They are our best resources when tact and courtesy are required instead of bluntness. Any person dealing with the public is called upon to use verbal tact at intervals, not only when the subject turns to taste, social differences, and death. In the face of the recurrent problem of talking about disruptive children, a faculty committee in a New York City junior high school compiled a list of phrases by which teachers could convey their complaints about pupil's parents without causing offense:

Awkward and clumsy	Appears to have difficulty with motor control and muscular coordination
Does all right if pushed	Accomplishes tasks when interest is frequently stimulated

Too free with fists	Resorts to physical means of winning his point or attracting attention
Could stand more baths, is dirty, has bad odor	Needs guidance in development of good habits of hygiene
Lies	Shows difficulty in distinguishing between imaginary and factual material
Steals	Needs help in learning to respect the property rights of others

J. J. MacKillop and Cross, "How to Tell Mommy Her Child Is. . . . "

D

Physicians have long used medical jargon to impress gullible laymen. As far ¹ back as the 13th century, the medieval physician Arnold of Villanova urged colleagues to seek refuge behind impressive-sounding language when they could not explain a patient's ailment. "Say that he has an obstruction of the liver," Arnold wrote, "and particularly use the word obstruction because [patients] do not understand what it means." Such deceptions may still occasionally be practiced on patients, but this does not account for the impenetrable prose in contemporary medical journals, which are read mostly by doctors.

To unravel that alphabet soup, Author-Physician Michael Crichton (*The* ² *Great Train Robbery, The Andromeda Strain*) recently looked over some back issues of the *New England Journal of Medicine*. Crichton, who wrote novels even during his days at Harvard Medical School (class of 1969), was appalled by what he read. The style, he reported in the *Journal*, was "as dense, impressive and forbidding as possible." Examples:

Redundancy: The most common form is paired words, for example, "interest ³ and concern," when one would serve nicely.

Wrong words: "purely" for "only." ⁴

Too many abstractions: "Improvement in health care is based, to an impor- ⁵ tant extent, on the viability of the biomedical research enterprise, whose success, in turn, depends. . ."

Ambiguity: "Corticosteroids, antimalarial drugs and other agents may im- ⁶ pede degranulation, because of their ability to prevent granule membranes from rupturing, to inhibit ingestion or to interfere with the degranulation mechanism per se."

Unnecessary qualifications: "Many, *but not all*, of the agents also have ⁷ valuable analgesic effects." "It is usually wise, *unless there is good reason to the contrary*. . ."

Even as late as the 19th century, Crichton says, physicians were writing with ⁸ strength and conviction. Now, however, "voices are passive, modifiers are abstract and qualifying clauses abound. The general tone is one of utmost timidity, going far beyond sensible caution." Crichton finds it all very puzzling. "An eminent surgeon strides purposefully into the operating room each day," he says, "but to read his papers, you wonder how he finds the courage to get out of bed in the morning." Crichton has a theory about the use of obfuscating medical language. In explaining it, however, he unwittingly demonstrates that jargon is highly contagious: "Medical obscurity may now serve an *intra-group recognition function*, rather like a secret fraternal handshake. In any event it is a game, and everybody plays it. Indeed, I suspect one refuses to play at one's professional peril."

Editors of Time Magazine, "Doctor's Jargon"

E

More than 3,500 sociologists have gathered in Washington for the 71st 1
American Sociological Association to discuss . . . well, as one of them might say:

"We are a heterogeneous population with divergent opinions on histori- 2
cism, longitudinal research and theoretical orientation of symbolic interactionism."

More than 700 papers will be presented before the convention's end. Gen- 3
erously sprinkled with the adjective clusters such as "atypical-hypothetical" and "politico-economic-academic," the papers range in subject matter from underdevelopment in South Africa to underemployment in New Zealand.

One report listed in the 234-page booklet of titles and abstracts bears the 4
ambitious heading, "On Social Meaning."

Another is more specific: "A Model for Examination of Multi-Cultural 5
Stresses Experienced by Latin Population in a Pluralistic Context."

The Syracuse Herald Journal, "A Language of Their Own"

F

Another comparatively recent arrival in the scientific field is space, with its 1
language and its slang. In a comprehensive article in the *Los Angeles Times*, Nicholas C. Chriss offers an extended sampling. Some of the words pre-existed the Apollos: for instance, "reticle" (literally, small net; in use since 1731 to describe a network of wires or threads used in the sights of a telescope) and "hypergolic" (self-igniting; from Greek *hyper*, "over," and *ergon*, "strength"). We suspect that "unsymmetrical dimethyl hydrazine" (a component of rocket fuel) belongs to this category though the dictionaries only give the component parts.

Others are recombinations of old words, but with new meanings pertinent to 2
space: "aeropause," the level above the earth's surface where the atmosphere becomes ineffective for human functions and fades off into space (it appears in the more recent Random House and American Heritage, but not in the older Webster Third or Oxford); "aerothermodynamic border," where the atmosphere becomes too thin to generate much heat; "aerothermodynamic" appears in the older Webster Third, but not in the newer American Heritage; "anomalistic period," the time between a space craft's arrival at perigee in one orbit and

perigee on the next; and "specific impulse," an expression of the performance limit of rocket propellants arrived at by dividing the thrust in pounds by the weight flow rate in pounds per second. If this sounds a bit confusing to you, take comfort; it sounds that way to us, too.

There are, as one might expect, plenty of acronymic abbreviations: "RGA" 3 for "rate gyro assembly"; "ROM" for "rough order of magnitude"; "PSI" for "pound per square inch"; "POO" for "program zero-zero"; "BURP" for "backup rate of pitch"; "ACE" for "attitude control electronics." There are a few initial-syllable abbreviations of the more conventional type: "sep" for "separation," "rev" for "revolution." There are a few German expressions (after all, the Germans were the first to develop the rocket as an instrument of warfare): *Gegen-schein* (literally, "against-light," for faint light area in the sky) and *Brennschluss* (literally, "burn-end," for the end of rocket firing).

In space talk, a rocket engine doesn't fire; it "burns." An "afterbody" is a 4 comparison body that trails a spacecraft in orbit (anything from a discarded clamp ring to a spent launch vehicle stage, Mr. Chriss explains). You don't say something is going right; you say it's "nominal." If it's going wrong, you call it an "anomaly." You don't don your spacesuit; you put on a "pressure garment assembly." You don't follow someone; you "configure" him.

Anything weasely about this type of language? Hardly. But it certainly qual- 5 ifies as professional jargon, which mixes up the layman albeit unintentionally.

Mario Pei, "Scientese," from *Doublespeak in America*

G

Mr. Alan Greenspan, Chairman of President Ford's Council of Economic 1 Advisors, explained the problem of dealing with inflation and recession at the same time with the following statement:

"It is a very tricky policy problem to find the particular calibration and timing 2 that would be appropriate to stem the acceleration in risk premiums created by falling incomes without prematurely aborting the decline in the inflation-generated risk premiums." (as quoted in an editorial in the Philadelphia *Inquirer*, December 25, 1974, p.12-A)

The next is from an interview with Yasir Arafat, leader of the Palestinian 3 Liberation Organization, by *Newsweek* senior editor Arnaud de Borchgrave:

Q: "The Israelis say this means you want to destroy their state over the long 4 term instead of the short term."

A: "They are wrong. We do not want to destroy any people. It is precisely 5 because we have been advocating coexistence that we have shed so much blood."

Secretary of the Interior Rogers C. Morton explained President Ford's opposi- 6 tion to a gasoline tax with the following statement:

"I think he foreclosed himself on the basis that it was not a doable thing in 7 Congress." (as quoted by Herb Caen in the San Francisco *Chronicle*, November 20, 1974, p.41)

And then there is this bit of Bicentennial revisionism: 8

Commenting on Washington's defeat at White Plains, New York, on Octo- 9 ber, 28, 1776, Stephen Holden, co-chairman of the Bicentennial Committee of the City of White Plains, said, "Yes, we got thrown off the hill, but we stood our ground." And commenting on Lafayette's humiliating rout by British troops at Conshocken, Pennsylvania, Col. Oran K. Henderson of the Bicentennial Commission of Pennsylvania said that "that was a tactical withdrawal. They did a lot of that during the Revolution." As the New York *Times* wryly observes, it's "almost as though a 200th anniversary were a natural occasion for doublespeak."

"Doublespeak or the Forked Tongue," from an occasional column in *College Composition and Communication* by William D. Lutz, who seeks further examples of this kind of language misuse.
Department of English, Rutgers University, Camden, New Jersey 08102.

WRITING ASSIGNMENTS

Essays

1. Most of us belong to some sublanguage group or other which uses a kind of jargon that excludes outsiders. Almost anyone who has ever worked in a restaurant, for example, knows a handful of words for standard items on the menu—"Adam and Eve on a raft," etc. Although such language communicates little when used in Standard English, it frequently has a richness and color of its own. Describe and analyze a language of this kind that you know.

2. Consider the validity of the frequently cited quotation from George Orwell to the effect that corrupt language corrupts thought. Can people who use gobbledygook, euphemisms, catch phrases, sports metaphors, or even truckers' talk actually think clearly? Think of examples you know from your own experience, although not necessarily yourself.

3. In the "Points of Departure" section we quote a passage from Edwin Newman, himself a television announcer, attacking the language of sports announcer Howard Cosell. Many people find Cosell's language elegant and impressive; how do you feel? Write an essay in which you examine the meaning of what Newman says about Cosell. Listen to a broadcast of Cosell speaking; is this the way he really talks? Check the meaning of the words he uses in a good dictionary; do the words mean what they seem to mean in the context in which he uses them?

4. Write an essay examining the use of language by another familiar figure, perhaps Archie Bunker of *All in the Family*. How many of Archie's problems come from his misunderstanding or misuse of a word at a key moment?

5. Write an essay about how euphemisms are used in one profession or industry. Distinguish between euphemisms and professional jargon. Consult the section on "Doctor's Jargon" in the Points of Departure section. Would it be possible to run a funeral home successfully without using many euphemisms?

6. Consider some of the ironies implicit in Stefan Kanfer's definition of

euphemisms as novocain for the tongue (page 142). Is the use of euphemisms a sophisticated form of lying? Are euphemisms necessary to maintain painless relations between people in a difficult age? Give examples.

7. Defend or attack Francine Hardaway's position on sports metaphors. Do they add a vividness that communicates to an audience? Or do they reduce complex phenomena to a kind of game?

8. Defend or attack R. D. Rosen's position on "Psychobabble." If you oppose him, you are going to need a more favorably inclined word to describe the phenomenon. Is Rosen a snob who dislikes seeing nonspecialists reading about psychology? Or do the books he attacks present misinformation in a pandering way?

9. Apropos of Maddocks's description of "semantic aphasia," try to describe the words which bombard you in a limited period of time. For example, if you are a commuting student, you might try to review all the words which hit you—from billboards, from the car radio, from a passenger's conversations—on part of the route. Do the words wear you down or make life interesting? Contrast this with the feeling of being away from words, such as in a small boat in the middle of a lake, backpacking, or otherwise removed from the noise of modern society.

10. Write an analysis of the textbook you are now reading that is most difficult to read. Is the author guilty of one of the problems described in this chapter? Is she or he a "master/mistress of babble"? A "Pyschobabbler"? Is any of your difficulty in reading the book your fault?

JOURNAL KEEPING

1. Collect some examples of gobbledygook. As Chase suggests, you are likely to find the best ones in government publications, but you can also find them in textbooks and in legal documents. Try to translate them as best you can, using a dictionary if need be. How many words do you need to summarize the gobbledygook? That is, how many of your words per 100 of gobbledygook?

2. Are there some occasions which call for euphemisms out of psychological necessity? What words would you use if you had to deliver some of the following messages? Write you answers in your journal, and try to come up with more.

A. Your foot is too fat for the shoes you are trying on.
B. You have just flunked out of school.
C. Everyone in the room seems to have noticed that your T-shirt has a foul odor.
D. Your face and figure are not attractive enough to allow you to qualify as a contestant in the Miss Middleville contest.
E. Your mother just died.

3. Following the models from the Classroom Exercise at the beginning of this chapter, try to turn some of the following proverbs into gobbledygook, euphemisms, catch phrases, etc.

A. A rolling stone gathers no moss.

B. A bird in the hand is worth two in the bush.

C. Spare the rod and spoil the child.

D. To err is human.

E. People who live in glass houses should not throw stones.

Once you have done these, look over the results. How much longer have you made them? Are the meanings changed slightly when you rewrite the sentences? Are the implications of the sentences made clearer?

4. Listen to examples of your fellow students' language in informal situations. Do they use either catch phrases or Psychobabble? Does Judith Kaplan's article give a fair assessment of their speech? Do they use phrases like "psyched out" to mean something specific or only as pretentious ways of saying "impressed" or "frightened"?

5. Try to collect examples of doublespeak along the lines of the examples given by William D. Lutz. If you find some especially good ones, send them to him at the address given with his article, page 174-175.

5 "That's What I Think Too—Isn't It?"
The Analysis of Propaganda

Propaganda pervades our daily lives, from the moment the radio alarm goes off in the morning to the time we switch off the TV set at night. We hear it from our elected officials and candidates for office; we see it on billboards and the walls of buses and subway stations; we read it in newspapers and on department-store tags and supermarket signs. Many of us persist in thinking that we are somehow immune from the influence of propaganda, that we are not "taken in" by "all that garbage." Yet advertising companies and political candidates spend millions of dollars a year on research in human psychology and motivation because they are convinced that propaganda *does* work.

Test your own "immunity quotient" with the following speech by a fictional senator, Al Yakalot. As you will see, his statements are often exaggerated, even ludicrous, so the propaganda should be fairly easy to detect. (In real life, of course, propaganda is much more subtle and deceptive.) Try not only to identify propaganda in his speech, but to explain what it is that makes some statements unfair or unreasonable. And remember—any propaganda devices that you may miss, *you've* been suckered by!

Speech by Senator Yakalot to His Constituents

My dear friends and fellow countrymen in this great and beautiful town of Gulliville, I stand before you today as your candidate for state senator. And before I say anything else, I want to thank you wonderful people, you hard-working, right-living citizens that make our country great, for coming here today to hear me speak. Now, I'm at a disadvantage here because I

1

don't have the gift of gab that a big-city fella like my opponent has—I'm just a small-town boy like you fine people—but I'm going to try, in my own simple way, to tell you why you should re-elect me, Al Yakalot, next election day.

Now, my opponent may appear to you to be a pretty nice guy, but I'm 2 here today to tell you that his reckless and radical policies represent a dire threat to all that we hold dear. He would tear down all that is great and good in America and substitute instead his own brand of creeping socialism.

For that's just what his ridiculous scheme to set up a hot-meal program 3 for the elderly in this town amounts to—socialism. Sure, he says our local citizens have expressed their willingness to donate some of their time and money to a so-called senior citizens' kitchen. But this kind of supposed "volunteer" work only undermines our local restaurants—in effect, our private-enterprise system. The way I see it, in this world a man's either for private enterprise or he's for socialism. Mr. Stu Pott, one of the leading strategists of the hot-meal campaign (a man who, by the way, sports a Fidel Castro beard) has said the program would be called the "Community Food Service." Well, just remember that the words "Community" and "Communism" look an awful lot alike!

After all, my friends, our forefathers who made this country great never 4 had any free hot-meal handouts. And look what they did for our country! That's why I'm against the hot-meal program. Hot meals will only make our senior citizens soft, useless, and dependent.

And that's not all you should know about my opponent, my fellow 5 citizens. My pinko opponent has been hopping around the state in his little puddle-jumper, whining about the size of cars that most Americans have chosen to drive. He says that if he is elected he will force all government employees out of regular-sized cars and squeeze them into those little gas-driven sewing machines. Now you and I know those little things are unsafe. In fact, a recent study shows that in 1959, when more Americans were driving full-sized cars, there were fewer accidents. Obviously, driving full-sized cars means a better car safety record on our American roads today.

My opponent claims that his vicious attack on full-size cars is just an 6 attempt to preserve the beauty of the American countryside. He is supported in this crackbrain crusade to "save the butterflies" by none other than Congresswoman Doris Schlepp, who is sure no beauty symbol herself! And for this, my opponent wants to jam red-blooded Americans into a bunch of mobile canopeners (many of which are made in Japan and Germany, countries we licked in the last war), rather than allow them the comfort of full-sized cars, which have always been as American as Mom's apple pie or a Sunday drive in the country. Why, full-sized cars have been praised by great Americans like John Wayne and Jack Jones, as well as by leading experts on car safety and comfort.

What's more, full-sized cars are good for working men and women of 7 this country, too. My opponent has tried to sell you the old bill of goods that small cars will save some of our material resources, like chrome, rubber, plastic, and glass. But when manufacturers need greater amounts of these materials to build full-sized cars that means more jobs for these industries right here in the good old U.S. of A. And when our great American chrome industry suffers, then the men and women working in our chrome factories suffer.

My fellow taxpayers, I'm here to tell you today that if we don't use these God-given resources we are going to be a part of a heartless plot to drive working men and women right out of their jobs. My opponent's plan to cram those unsafe motorized baby buggies down the throats of the American people just won't work—because it is unworkable. Trying to take Americans out of the kind of cars they love is as undemocratic as trying to deprive them of the right to vote. And with the help of the American people I am going to put a stop to it. 8

I'm mighty grateful to all you wonderful folks for letting me speak what is in my heart. I know you for what you are—the decent, law-abiding citizens that are the great pulsing heart and the lifeblood of this, our beloved country. I stand for all that is good in America, for our American way and our American birthright. More and more citizens are rallying to my cause every day. Won't you join them—and me—in our fight for America? 9

Thank you and may God bless you all. 10

D. W. CROSS
Propaganda:
How Not to Be Bamboozled

Propaganda. If an opinion poll were taken tomorrow, we can be sure that nearly everyone would be against it because it *sounds* so bad. When we say, "Oh, that's just propaganda," it means, to most people, "That's a pack of lies." But really, propaganda is simply a means of persuasion and so it can be put to work for good causes as well as bad—to persuade people to give to charity, for example, or to love their neighbors, or to stop polluting the environment. 1

For good or evil, propaganda pervades our daily lives, helping to shape our attitudes on a thousand subjects. Propaganda probably determines the brand of toothpaste you use, the movies you see, the candidates you elect when you get to fact: propaganda works best with an uncritical audience. Joseph Goebbels, Propaganda Minister in Nazi Germany, once defined his work as "the conquest of the masses." The masses would not have been conquered, however, if they had known how to challenge and to question, how to make distinctions between propaganda and reasonable argument. 2

People are bamboozled mainly because they don't recognize propaganda when they see it. They need to be informed about the various devices that can be 3 used to mislead and deceive—about the propagandist's overflowing bag of tricks. The following, then, are some common pitfalls for the unwary.

1. Name-Calling

As its title suggests, this device consists of labeling people or ideas with words   4
of bad connotation, literally, "calling them names." Here the propagandist tries to arouse our contempt so we will dismiss the "bad name" person or idea without examining its merits.

Bad names have played a tremendously important role in the history of the   5
world. They have ruined reputations and ended lives, sent people to prison and to war, and just generally made us mad at each other for centuries.

Name-calling can be used against policies, practices, beliefs and ideals, as   5
well as against individuals, groups, races, nations. Name-calling is at work when we hear a candidate for office described as a "foolish idealist" or a "two-faced liar" or when an incumbent's policies are denounced as "reckless," "reactionary," or just plain "stupid." Some of the most effective names a public figure can be called are ones that may not denote anything specific: "Congresswoman Jane Doe is a *bleeding heart!*" (Did she vote for funds to help paraplegics?) or "The Senator is a *tool of Washington!*" (Did he happen to agree with the President?) Senator Yakalot uses name-calling when he denounces his opponent's "radical policies" and calls them (and him) "socialist," "pinko," and part of a "heartless plot." He also uses it when he calls small cars "puddle-jumpers," "canopeners," and "motorized baby buggies."

The point here is that when the propagandist uses name-calling, he doesn't   6
want us to think—merely to react, blindly, unquestioningly. So the best defense against being taken in by name-calling is to stop and ask, "Forgetting the bad name attached to it, what are the merits of the idea itself? What does this name really mean, anyway?"

2. Glittering Generalities

Glittering generalities are really name-calling in reverse. Name-calling uses   7
words with bad connotations; glittering generalities are words with good connotations—"virtue words," as the Institute for Propaganda Analysis has called them. The Institute explains that while name-calling tries to get us to *reject* and *condemn* someone or something without examining the evidence, glittering generalities try to get us to *accept* and *agree* without examining the evidence.

We believe in, fight for, live by "virtue words" which we feel deeply about: 8
"justice," "motherhood," "the American way," "our Constitutional rights," "our Christian heritage." These sound good, but when we examine them closely, they turn out to have no specific, definable meaning. They just make us feel good. Senator Yakalot uses glittering generalities when he says, "I stand for all that is good in America, for our American way and our American birthright." But what

exactly *is* "good for America?" How can we define our "American birthright?" Just what parts of the American society and culture does "our American way" refer to?

We often make the mistake of assuming we are personally unaffected by   9 glittering generalities. The next time you find yourself assuming that, listen to a political candidate's speech on TV and see how often the use of glittering generalities elicits cheers and applause. That's the danger of propaganda: it *works*. Once again, our defense against it is to ask questions: Forgetting the virtue words attached to it, what are the merits of the idea itself? What does "Americanism" (or "freedom" or "truth") really *mean* here?

• • •

Both name-calling and glittering generalities work by stirring our emotions in   10 the hope that this will cloud our thinking. Another approach that propaganda uses is to create a distraction, a "red herring," that will make people forget or ignore the real issues. There are several different kinds of "red herrings" that can be used to distract attention.

3. Plain Folks Appeal

"Plain folks" is the device by which a speaker tries to win our confidence and   11 support by appearing to be a person like ourselves—"just one of the plain folks." The plain-folks appeal is at work when candidates go around shaking hands with factory workers, kissing babies in supermarkets, and sampling pasta with Italians, fried chicken with Southerners, bagels and blintzes with Jews. "Now I'm a businessman like yourselves" is a plain-folks appeal, as is "I've been a farm boy all my life." Senator Yakalot tries the plain-folks appeal when he says, "I'm just a small-town boy like you fine people." The use of such expressions once prompted Lyndon Johnson to quip, "Whenever I hear someone say, 'I'm just an old country lawyer,' the first thing I reach for is my wallet to make sure it's still there."

The irrelevancy of the plain-folks appeal is obvious: even if the man *is* "one of   12 us" (which may not be true at all), that doesn't mean that his ideas and programs are sound—or even that he honestly has our best interests at heart. As with glittering generalities, the danger here is that we may mistakenly assume we are immune to this appeal. But propagandists wouldn't use it unless it had been proved to work. You can protect yourself by asking, "Aside from his 'nice guy next door' image, what does this man stand for? Are his ideas and his past record really supportive of my best interests?"

4. Argumentum ad Populum (Stroking)

Argumentum ad populum means "argument to the people" or "telling the   13 people what they want to hear." The colloquial term from the Watergate era is "stroking," which conjures up pictures of small animals or children being stroked or soothed with compliments until they come to like the person doing the complimenting—and, by extension, his or her ideas.

We all like to hear nice things about ourselves and the group we belong 14 to—we like to be liked—so it stands to reason that we will respond warmly to a person who tells us we are "hard-working taxpayers" or "the most generous, free-spirited nation in the world." Politicians tell farmers they are the "backbone of the American economy" and college students that they are the "leaders and policy makers of tomorrow." Commercial advertisers use stroking more insidiously by asking a question which invites a flattering answer: "What kind of a man reads *Playboy*?" (Does he really drive a Porsche and own $10,000 worth of sound equipment?) Senator Yakalot is stroking his audience when he calls them the "decent law-abiding citizens that are the great pulsing heart and the life blood of this, our beloved country," and when he repeatedly refers to them as "you fine people," "you wonderful folks."

Obviously, the intent here is to sidetrack us from thinking critically about the 15 man and his ideas. Our own good qualities have nothing to do with the issue at hand. Ask yourself, "Apart from the nice things he has to say about me (and my church, my nation, my ethnic group, my neighbors), what does the candidate stand for? Are his or her ideas in my best interests?"

5. Argumentum ad Hominem

Argumentum ad hominem means "argument to the man" and that's exactly 16 what it is. When a propagandist uses *argumentum ad hominem*, he wants to distract our attention from the issue under consideration with personal attacks on the people involved. For example, when Lincoln issued the Emancipation Proclamation, some people responded by calling him the "baboon." But Lincoln's long arms and awkward carriage had nothing to do with the merits of the Proclamation or the question of whether or not slavery should be abolished.

Today *argumentum ad hominem* is still widely used and very effective. You 17 may or may not support the Equal Rights Amendment, but you should be sure your judgment is based on the merits of the idea itself, and not the result of someone's denunciation of the people who support the ERA as "fanatics" or "lesbians" or "frustrated old maids." Senator Yakalot is using *argumentum ad hominem* when he dismisses the idea of using smaller automobiles with a reference to the personal appearance of one of its supporters, Congresswoman Doris Schlepp. Refuse to be waylaid by *argumentum ad hominem* and ask, "Do the personal qualities of the person being discussed have anything to do with the issue at hand? Leaving him or her aside, how good is the idea itself?"

6. Transfer (Guilt or Glory by Association)

In *argumentum ad hominem*, an attempt is made to associate negative aspects 18 of a person's character or personal appearance with an issue or idea he supports.

The transfer device uses this same process of association to make us accept or condemn a given person or idea.

A better name for the transfer device is guilt (or glory) by association. In glory 19 by association, the propagandist tries to transfer the positive feelings of something we love and respect to the group or idea he wants us to accept. "This bill for a new dam is in the best tradition of this country, the land of Lincoln, Jefferson, and Washington," is glory by association at work. Lincoln, Jefferson, and Washington were great leaders that most of us revere and respect, but they have no logical connection to the proposal under consideration—the bill to build a new dam. Senator Yakalot uses glory by association when he says full-sized cars "have always been as American as Mom's apple pie or a Sunday drive in the country."

The process works equally well in reverse, when guilt by association is used to 20 transfer our dislike or disapproval of one idea or group to some other idea or group that the propagandist wants us to reject and condemn. "John Doe says we need to make some changes in the way our government operates; well, that's exactly what the Ku Klux Klan has said, so there's a meeting of great minds!" That's guilt by association for you; there's no logical connection between John Doe and the Ku Klux Klan apart from the one the propagandist is trying to create in our minds. He wants to distract our attention from John Doe and get us thinking (and worrying) about the Ku Klux Klan and its politics of violence. (Of course, there are sometimes legitimate associations between the two things; if John Doe had been a *member* of the Ku Klux Klan, it would be reasonable and fair to draw a connection between the man and his group.) Senator Yakalot tries to trick his audience with guilt by association when he remarks that "the words 'Community' and 'Communism' look an awful lot alike!" He does it again when he mentions that Mr. Stu Pott "sports a Fidel Castro beard."

How can we learn to spot the transfer device and distinguish between fair 21 and unfair associations? We can teach ourselves to *suspend judgment* until we have answered these questions: "Is there any legitimate connection between the idea under discussion and the thing it is associated with? Leaving the transfer device out of the picture, what are the merits of the idea by itself?

7. Bandwagon

Ever hear of the small, ratlike animal called the lemming? Lemmings are 22 arctic rodents with a very odd habit: periodically, for reasons no one entirely knows, they mass together in a large herd and commit suicide by rushing into deep water and drowning themselves. They all run in together, blindly, and not one of them ever seems to stop and ask, "Why am I doing this? Is this really what I want to do?" and thus save itself from destruction. Obviously, lemmings are driven to perform their strange mass suicide rites by common instinct. People choose to "follow the herd" for more complex reasons, yet we are still all too often the unwitting victims of the bandwagon appeal.

Essentially, the bandwagon urges us to support an action or an opinion 23 because it is popular—because "everyone else is doing it." This call to "get on the bandwagon" appeals to the strong desire in most of us to be one of the crowd, not to be left out or alone. Advertising makes extensive use of the bandwagon appeal ("join the Pepsi people"), but so do politicians ("Let us join together in this great cause"). Senator Yakalot uses the bandwagon appeal when he says that "More and more citizens are rallying to my cause every day," and asks his audience to "join them—and me—in our fight for America."

One of the ways we can see the bandwagon appeal at work is in the over- 24 whelming success of various fashions and trends which capture the interest (and the money) of thousands of people for a short time, then disappear suddenly and completely. For a year or two in the fifties, every child in North America wanted a coonskin cap so they could be like Davy Crockett; no one wanted to left out. After that there was the hula-hoop craze that helped to dislocate the hips of thousands of Americans. More recently, what made millions of people rush out to buy their very own "pet rocks"?

The problem here is obvious: just because everyone's doing it doesn't mean 25 that *we* should too. Group approval does not prove that something is true or is worth doing. Large numbers of people have supported actions we now condemn. Just a generation ago, Hitler and Mussolini rose to absolute and catastrophically repressive rule in two of the most sophisticated and cultured countries of Europe. When they came into power they were welled up by massive popular support from millions of people who didn't want to be "left out" at a great historical moment.

Once the mass begins to move—on the bandwagon—it becomes harder and 26 harder to perceive the leader *riding* the bandwagon. So don't be a lemming, rushing blindly on to destruction because "everyone else is doing it." Stop and ask, "Where is this bandwagon headed? Never mind about everybody else, is this what is best for *me?*"

• • •

As we have seen, propaganda can appeal to us by arousing our emotions or 27 distracting our attention from the real issues at hand. But there's a third way that propaganda can be put to work against us—by the use of faulty logic. This approach is really more insidious than the other two because it gives the appearance of reasonable, fair argument. It is only when we look more closely that the holes in the logical fiber show up. The following are some of the devices that make use of faulty logic to distort and mislead.

8. Faulty Cause and Effect

As the name suggests, this device sets up a cause-and-effect relationship that 28 may not be true. The Latin name for this logical fallecy is *post hoc ergo propter hoc*, which means "after this, therefore because of this." But just because one thing happened after another doesn't mean that one *caused* the other.

An example of false cause-and-effect reasoning is offered by the story (proba- 29 bly invented) of the woman aboard the ship *Titanic*. She woke up from a nap and, feeling seasick, looked around for a call button to summon the steward to bring her some medication. She finally located a small red button on one of the walls of her cabin and pushed it. A split second later, the *Titanic* grazed an iceberg in the terrible crash that was to send the entire ship to its destruction. The woman screamed and said, "Oh, God, what have I done? What have I done?" The humor of that anecdote comes from the absurdity of the woman's assumption that pushing the small red button resulted in the destruction of a ship weighing several hundred tons: "It happened after I pushed it, therefore it must be *because* I pushed it"—*post hoc ergo propter hoc* reasoning. There is, of course, no cause-and-effect relationship there.

The false-cause-and-effect fallacy is used very often by political candidates. 30 "After I came to office, the rate of inflation dropped to 6 percent." But did the person do anything to cause the lower rate of inflation or was it the result of other conditions? Would the rate of inflation have dropped anyway, even if he hadn't come to office? Senator Yakalot uses false cause and effect when he says "our forefathers who made this country great never had free hot meal handouts! And look what they did for our country!" He does it again when he concludes that "driving full-sized cars means a better car safety record on our American roads today."

False-cause-and-effect reasoning is terribly persuasive because it seems so 31 logical. Its appeal is apparently to experience. We swallowed X product—and the headache went away. We elected Y official and unemployment went down. Many people think, "There *must* be a connection." But causality is an immensely complex phenomenon; you need a good deal of evidence to prove that an event that follows another in time was "therefore" caused by the first event.

Don't be taken in by false cause and effect; be sure to ask, "Is there enough 32 evidence to prove that this cause led to that effect? Could there have been any *other* causes?"

10. False Analogy *(used to explain not prove)*

An analogy is a comparison between two ideas, events, or things. But com- 33 parisons can be fairly made only when the things being compared are alike in significant ways. When they are not, false analogy is the result.

A famous example of this is the old proverb "Don't change horses in the 34 middle of a stream," often used as an analogy to convince voters not to change administrations in the middle of a war or other crisis. But the analogy is misleading because there are so many differences between the things compared. In what ways is a war or political crisis like a stream?" Is the President or head of state really very much like a horse? And is a nation of millions of people comparable to a man trying to get across a stream? Analogy is false and unfair when it compares two things that have little in common and assumes that they are identical. Senator Yakalot tries to hoodwink his listeners with false analogy when he says, "Trying to take Americans out of the kind of cars they love is as undemocratic as trying to deprive them of the right to vote."

Of course, analogies can be drawn that are reasonable and fair. It would be 35 reasonable, for example, to compare the results of busing in one small Southern city with the possible results in another, *if* the towns have the same kind of history, population, and school policy. We can decide for ourselves whether an analogy is false or fair by asking, "Are the things being compared truly alike in significant ways? Do the differences between them affect the comparison?"

11. Begging the Question

Actually, the name of this device is rather misleading, because it does not 36 appear in the form of a question. Begging the question occurs when, in discussing a questionable or debatable point, a person assumes as already established the very point that he is trying to prove. For example, "No thinking citizen could approve such a completely unacceptable policy as this one." But isn't the question of whether or not the policy *is* acceptable the very point to be established? Senator Yakalot begs the questions when he announces that his opponent's plan won't work "because it is unworkable."

We can protect ourselves against this kind of faulty logic by asking, "What is 37 assumed in this statement? Is the assumption reasonable, or does it need more proof?"

12. The Two Extremes Fallacy (False Dilemma)

Linguists have long noted that the English language tends to view reality in 38 sets of two extremes or polar opposites. In English, things are either black or white, tall or short, up or down, front or back, left or right, good or bad, guilty or not guilty. We can ask for a "straightforward yes-or-no answer" to a question, the understanding being that we will not accept or consider anything inbetween. In fact, reality cannot always be dissected along such strict lines. There may be (usually are) *more* than just two possibilities or extremes to consider. We are often told to "listen to both sides of the argument." But who's to say that every argument has only two sides? Can't there be a third—even a fourth or fifth— point of view?

The two-extremes fallacy is at work in this statement by Lenin, the great 40 Marxist leader: "You cannot eliminate *one* basic assumption, one substantial part of this philosophy of Marxism (it is as if it were a block of steel), without abandoning truth, without falling into the arms of bourgeois-reactionary false-hood." In other words, if we don't agree 100 percent with every premise of Marxism, we must be placed at the opposite end of the political-economic spectrum—for Lenin, "bourgeois-reactionary falsehood." If we are not entirely *with* him, we must be against him; those are the only two possibilities open to us. Of course, this is a logical fallacy; in real life there are any number of political positions one can maintain *between* the two extremes of Marxism and capitalism. Senator Yakalot uses the two-extremes fallacy in the same way as Lenin when he tells his audience that "in this world a man's either for private enterprise or he's for socialism."

One of the most famous examples of the two-extremes fallacy in recent 41
history is the slogan, "America: Love it or leave it," with its implicit suggestion
that we either accept everything just as it is in America today without
complaint—or get out. Again, it should be obvious that there is a whole range of
action and belief between those two extremes.

Don't be duped; stop and ask, "Are those really the only two options I can 42
choose from? Are there other alternatives not mentioned that deserve consideration?"

13. Card Stacking

Some questions are so multifaceted and complex that no one can make an 43
intelligent decision about them without considering a wide variety of evidence.
One selection of facts could make us feel one way and another selection could
make us feel just the opposite. Card stacking is a device of propaganda which
selects only the facts that support the propagandist's point of view, and ignores all
the others. For example, a candidate could be made to look like a legislative
dynamo if you say, "Representative McNerd introduced more new bills than any
other member of the Congress," and neglect to mention that most of them were
so preposterous that they were laughed off the floor.

Senator Yakalot engages in card stacking when he talks about the proposal to 44
use smaller cars. He talks only about jobs without mentioning the cost to the
taxpayers or the very real—though still denied—threat of depletion of resources.
He says he wants to help his countrymen keep their jobs, but doesn't mention
that the corporations that offer the jobs will also make large profits. He praises the
"American chrome industry," overlooking the fact that most chrome is imported. And so on.

The best protection against card stacking is to take the "Yes, but . . . " 45
attitude. This device of propaganda is not untrue, but then again it is not the
whole truth. So ask yourself, "Is this person leaving something out that I should
know about? Is there some other information that should be brought to bear on
this question?

• • •

So far, we have considered three approaches that the propagandist can use to 46
influence our thinking: appealing to our emotions, distracting our attention, and
misleading us with logic that may appear to be reasonable but is in fact faulty and
deceiving. But there is a fourth approach that is probably the most common
propaganda trick of them all.

14. Testimonial

The testimonial device consists in having some loved or respected person give 47
a statement of support (testimonial) for a given product or idea. The problem is
that the person being quoted may *not* be an expert in the field; in fact, he may

know nothing at all about it. Using the name of a man who is skilled and famous in one field to give a testimonial for something in another field is unfair and unreasonable.

Senator Yakalot tries to mislead his audience with testimonial when he tells 48 them that "full-sized cars have been praised by great Americans like John Wayne and Jack Jones, as well as by leading experts on car safety and comfort."

Testimonial is used extensively in TV ads, where it often appears in such 49 bizarre forms as Joe Namath's endorsement of a pantyhose brand. Here, of course, the "authority" giving the testimonial not only is no expert about pantyhose, but obviously stands to gain something (money!) by making the testimonial.

When celebrities endorse a political candidate, they may not be making 50 money by doing so, but we should still question whether they are in any better position to judge than we ourselves. Too often we are willing to let others we like or respect make our decisions *for us*, while we follow along acquiescently. And this is the purpose of testimonial—to get us to agree and accept *without* stopping to think. Be sure to ask, "Is there any reason to believe that this person (or organization or publication or whatever) has any more knowledge or information than I do on this subject? What does the idea amount to on its own merits, without the benefit of testimonial?"

The cornerstone of democratic society is reliance upon an informed and 51 educated electorate. To be fully effective citizens we need to be able to challenge and to question wisely. A dangerous feeling of indifference toward our political processes exists today. We often abandon our right, our duty, to criticize and evaluate by dismissing *all* politicians as "crooked," *all* new bills and proposals as "just more government bureaucracy." But there are important distinctions to be made, and this kind of apathy can be fatal to democracy.

If we are to be led, let us not be led blindly, but critically, intelligently, with 52 our eyes open. If we are to continue to be a government "by the people," let us become informed about the methods and purposes of propaganda, so we can be the masters, not the slaves of our destiny.

DISCUSSION QUESTIONS

1. How susceptible do you think you have been to propaganda? What factors determine an individual's receptivity to propaganda, anyway? Are people who live in small communities more likely to be influenced by propaganda than people who live in big cities?

2. Think about your own interests and activities. Does any organization you belong to use propaganda?—to attract new membership, increase subscriptions, obtain public support? Does the propaganda include the use of misleading statements? As a member of the organization, do you feel you are responsible for its propaganda?

3. In paragraph 1, D. W. Cross says that "propaganda can be put to

work for good causes as well as bad." Do you agree with this statement? Can you think of any examples where propaganda is used to gain sympathy and support for a "good" cause? How do we decide whether a cause is "good" or not?

4. What do you think of Joseph Goebbels's definition of propaganda (paragraph 2) as "the conquest of the masses"? Can you think of a better definition? Has your definition changed as a result of reading this article?

5. Do you go along with the author's repeated assertions that the best defense against propaganda is to ask questions? What other ways are there to protect yourself against propaganda?

6. Look at some pieces of political and commercial propaganda for examples of direct emotional appeals. Is the appeal to people's hopes and desires? Desire for what? Or is the appeal to things people fear? What things?

7. In paragraph 4, the author says that "bad names . . . have ruined reputations and ended lives, sent people to prison and to war, and just generally made us mad at each other for centuries." What are some of the "bad names" that have moved men in the past?

8. What things might a politician say to you if he wanted to win your support with the *argumentum ad populum* (stroking)? Have you ever responded to this propaganda device? When? Does an understanding of the technique prevent you from responding to it?

9. In paragraph 19, glory by association is defined as a transfer of "the positive feelings of something we love and respect to the group or idea [the propagandist] wants us to accept." For example, the American flag has often been invoked by politicians to transfer positive feelings toward a specific proposal or policy of their own. what are some of the other symbols commonly used to bring out positive feelings? What symbols are often used to bring out negative feelings?

10. Pain-reliever advertisements make extensive use of cause-and-effect statements. Discuss some of these advertisements and decide if the cause-and-effect relationships are false or fair.

11. Think of some people who have given testimonials for a given product or political candidate. Should these people be accepted as valid authorities on the subject? Why or why not?

RICHARD M. NIXON
The Checkers Speech

In 1952, Dwight D. Eisenhower was the Republican candidate for President. He was enormously popular at the time, a war hero with a reputation for the highest integrity. Victory for the Republican ticket seemed assured. But then, two months before the election, Eisenhower's running mate, Richard M. Nixon, was accused of graft. The charge was that he had accepted $18,000 in personal gifts from interested parties.

With his career under a cloud, Nixon decided to go on TV and appeal to the American people. Eisenhower, who at that point regarded Nixon as a political liability and was considering dropping him from the ticket, approved of the plan. It was clear that the question of whether or not Richard Nixon would remain the Vice Presidential candidate would depend on the public reaction to his speech. And so, on September 23, 1952, with his entire career at stake and most of America watching, Richard Nixon went on the air. The following, only slightly edited, is a transcript of what he said.

My Fellow Americans: 1

I come before you tonight as a candidate for the Vice Presidency and as a   2
man whose honesty and integrity have been questioned.

The usual political thing to do when charges are made against you is to either   3
ignore them or to deny them without giving details.

I believe we've had enough of that in the United States, particularly with the   4
present Administration in Washington, D.C. To me the office of the Vice Presidency of the United States is a great office, and I feel that the people have got to have confidence in the integrity of the men who ran for that office and who might obtain it.

I have a theory, too, that the best and only answer to a smear or to an honest   5
misunderstanding of the facts is to tell the truth. And that's why I'm here tonight. I want to tell you my side of the case.

I am sure that you have read the charge and you've heard it that I, Senator   6
Nixon, took $18,000 from a group of my supporters.

Now, was that wrong? And let me say that it was wrong—I'm saying, inciden-   7
tally, that it was wrong and not just illegal. Because it isn't a question whether it was legal or illegal, that isn't enough. The question is, was it morally wrong?

I say that it was morally wrong if any of that $18,000 went to Senator Nixon   8
for my personal use. I say that it was morally wrong if it was secretly given and secretly handled. And I say that it was morally wrong if any of the contributors got special favors for the contributions that they made.

And now to answer those questions let me say this: 9

Not one cent of the $18,000 or any other money of that type ever went to me   10
for my personal use. Every penny of it was used to pay for political expenses that I did not think should be charged to the taxpayers of the United States.

It was not a secret fund. As a matter of fact, when I was on "Meet the Press,"   11
some of you may have seen it last Sunday—Peter Edson came up to me after the program and said, "Dick, what about this fund we hear about?" And I said, Well, there's no secret about it. Go out and see Dana Smith, who was the administrator of the fund. And I gave him his address, and I said that you will find that the purpose of the fund simply was to defray political expenses that I did not feel should be charged to the Government.

And third, let me point out, and I want to make this particularly clear, that   12
no contributor to this fund, no contributor to any of my campaign, has ever

received any consideration that he would not have received as an ordinary constituent.

I just don't believe in that and I can say that never, while I have been in the 13 Senate of the United States, as far as the people that contributed to this fund are concerned, have I made a telephone call for them to an agency, or have I gone down to an agency in their behalf. And the record will show that, the records which are in the hands of the Administration.

• • •

But then I realize that there are still some who may say, and rightly so, and 14 let me say that I recognize that some will continue to smear regardless of what the truth may be, but that there has been understandably some honest, misunderstanding on this matter, and there's some that will say: "Well, maybe you were able, Senator, to fake this thing. How can we believe what you say? After all, is there a possibility that maybe you got some sums in cash? Is there a possibility thay you may have feathered your own nest?"

And so now what I am going to do—and incidentally this is unprecedented in 15 the history of American politics—I am going at this time to give to this television and radio audience a complete financial history; everything I've earned; everything I've spent; everything I owe. And I want you to know the facts. I'll have to start early.

I was born in 1913. Our family was one of modest circumstances and most of 16 my early life was spent in a store out in East Whittier. It was a grocery store—one of those family enterprises. The only reason we were able to make it go was because my mother and dad had five boys and we all worked in the store.

I worked my way through college and to a great extent through law school. 17 And then, in 1940, probably the best thing that ever happened to me happened. I married Pat—sitting over here. We had a rather difficult time after we were married, like so many of the young couples who may be listening to us. I practiced law; she continued to teach school. I went into the service.

Let me say that my service record was not a particularly unusual one. I went 18 to the South Pacific. I guess I'm entitled to a couple of battle stars. I got a couple of letters of commendation but I was just there when the bombs were falling and then I returned. I returned to the United States and in 1946 I ran for the Congress.

When we came out of the war, Pat and I—Pat during the war had worked as a 19 stenographer and in a bank and as an economist for a Government agency—and when we came out the total of our savings from both my law practice, her teaching and all the time that I was in the war—the total for that entire period was just a little less than $10,000. Every cent of that, incidentally, was in Government bonds.

Well that's where we start when I go into politics. Now what have I earned 20 since I went into politics? Well here it is—I jotted it down, let me read the notes. First of all I've had my salary as a Congressman and as a Senator. Second, I have received a total in this past six years of $1,600 from estates which were in my law firm at the time that I severed my connection with it.

And, incidentally, as I said before, I have not engaged in any legal practice 21 and have not accepted any fees from business that came into the firm after I went into politics. I have made an average of approximately $1,500 a year from non-political speaking engagements and lectures. And then, fortunately, we've inherited a little money. Pat sold her interest in her father's estate for $3,000 and I inherited $1,500 from my grandfather.

We live rather modestly. For four years we lived in an apartment in Park 22 Fairfax, in Alexandria, Va. The rent was $80 a month. And we saved for the time that we could buy a house.

Now, that was what we took in. What did we do with this money? What do 23 we have today to show for it? This will surprise you, because it is so little, I suppose, as standards generally go, of people in public life. First of all, we've got a house in Washington which cost $41,000 and on which we owe $20,000.

We have a house in Whittier, Calif., which cost $13,000 and on which we 24 owe $3,000. My folks are living there at the present time.

I have just $4,000 in life insurance, plus my G.I. policy which I've never 25 been able to convert and which will run out in two years. I have no life insurance whatever on Pat. I have no life insurance on our two youngsters, Patricia and Julie. I own a 1950 Oldsmobile car. We have our furniture. We have no stocks and bonds of any type. We have no interest of any kind, direct or indirect, in any business.

Now, that's what we have. What do we owe? Well, in addition to the 26 mortgage, the $20,000 mortgage on the house in Washington, the $10,000 one on the house in Whittier, I owe $4,500 to the Riggs Bank in Washington, D.C., with interest 4½ per cent.

I owe $3,500 to my parents and the interest on that loan which I pay 27 regularly, because it's the part of the savings they made through the years they were working so hard. I pay regularly 4 per cent interest. And then I have a $500 loan which I have on my life insurance.

Well, that's about it. That's what we have and that's what we owe. It isn't very 28 much but Pat and I have the satisfaction that every dime that we've got is honestly ours. I should say this—that Pat doesn't have mink coat. But she does have a respectable Republican cloth coat. And I always tell her that she'd look good in anything.

One other thing I probably should tell you, because if I don't they'll probably 29 be saying this about me too, we did get something—a gift—after the election. A man down in Texas heard Pat on the radio mention the fact that our two youngsters would like to have a dog. And, believe it or not, the day before we left on this campaign trip we got a message from Union Station in Baltimore saying they had a package for us. We went down to get it. You know what it was?

It was a little cocker spaniel dog in a crate that he sent all the way from Texas. 30 Black and white spotted. And our little girl—Trisha, the 6-year-old—named it Checkers. And you know the kids love the dog and I just want to say this right now, that regardless of what they say about it, we're gonna keep it.

It isn't easy to come before a nation-wide audience and air your life as I've 31 done. But I want to say some things before I conclude that I think most of you will agree on. Mr. Mitchell, the chairman of the Democratic National Committee, made the statement that if a man couldn't afford to be in the United States Senate he shouldn't run for the Senate.

And I just want to make my position clear. I don't agree with Mr. Mitchell 32 when he says that only a rich man should serve his Government in the United States Senate or in the Congress.

I don't believe that represents the thinking of the Democratic party, and I 33 know that it doesn't represent the thinking of the Republican party.

I believe that it's fine that a man like Governor Stevenson who inherited a 34 fortune from his father can run for President. But I also feel that it's essential in this country of ours that a man of modest means can also run for President. Because, you know, remember Abraham Lincoln, you remember what he said: "God must have loved the common people—he made so many of them."

• • •

Now, let me say this: I know that this is not the last of the smears. In spite of 35 my explanation tonight other smears will be made; others have been made in the past. And the purpose of the smears, I know, is this—to silence me, to make me let up.

• • •

. . . [But] I intend to continue the fight. 36

Why do I feel so deeply? Why do I feel that in spite of the smears, the 37 misunderstandings, the necessities for a man to come up here and bare his soul as I have? Why is it necessary for me to continue this fight?

And I want to tell you why. Because, you see, I love my country. And I think 38 my country is in danger. And I think that the only man that can save America at this time is the man that's running for President on my ticket—Dwight Eisenhower.

. . . I say that the only man who can lead us in the fight to rid the Govern- 39 ment of both those who are Communists and those who have corrupted this Government is Eisenhower, because Eisenhower, you can be sure, recognizes the problem and he knows how to deal with it.

Now let me say that, finally, this evening I want to read to you just briefly 40 excerpts from a letter which I received, a letter which, after all this is over, no one can take away from me. It reads as follows:

Dear Senator Nixon,
    Since I'm only 19 years of age I can't vote in this Presidential election but believe me if I could you and General Eisenhower would certainly get my vote. My husband is in the Fleet Marines in Korea. He's a corpsman on the front lines and we have a two-month-old son he's never seen. And I feel confident that with great Americans like you and General Eisenhower in the White House, lonely Americans like myself will be united with their loved ones now in Korea.
    I only pray to God that you won't be too late. Enclosed is a small check to help you in your campaign. Living on $85 a month it is all I can afford at present. But let me know what else I can do.

Folks, it's a check for $10, and it's one that I will never cash. 41

And just let me say this. We hear a lot about prosperity these days but I say, 42 why can't we have prosperity built on peace rather than prosperity built on war?

Why can't we have prosperity and an honest government in Washington, D.C., at the same time? Believe me, we can. And Eisenhower is the man that can lead this crusade to bring us that kind of prosperity.

And, now, finally, I know that you wonder whether or not I am going to stay 43 on the Republican ticket or resign.

Let me say this: I don't believe that I ought to quit because I'm not a quitter. 44 And, incidentally, Pat's not a quitter. After all, her name was Patricia Ryan and she was born on St. Patrick's Day, and you know the Irish never quit.

But the decision, my friends, is not mine. I would do nothing that would 45 harm the possibilities of Dwight Eisenhower to become President of the United States. And for that reason I am submitting to the Republican National Committee tonight through this television broadcast the decision which it is theirs to make.

Let them decide whether my position on the ticket will help or hurt. And I 46 am going to ask you to help them decide. Wire and write the Republican National Committee whether you think I should stay on or whether I should get off. And whatever their decision is, I will abide by it.

But just let me say this last word. Regardless of what happens I'm going to 47 continue this fight. I'm going to campaign up and down America until we drive the crooks and the Communists and those that defend them out of Washington. And remember, folks, Eisenhower is a great man. Believe me. He's a great man. And a vote for Eisenhower is a vote for what's good for America.

DISCUSSION QUESTIONS

1. Public response to "The Checkers Speech" was overwhelmingly favorable. Telegrams poured into the Republican National Committee expressing support of Nixon and urging that he be kept on the ticket. If you had been watching Nixon's speech that night, how would you have reacted to it? Would your reaction have been based on reason or emotion? On the evidence, or on your feelings about the man? Explain.

2. Do you think that his speech qualifies as propaganda? All of it? Some of it? Why or why not?

3. Although Nixon never gave this speech a title, it has long been known as "The Checkers Speech." How does this title reflect on what is said in the speech? Why do you think it came to be remembered this way? Can you think of any other titles that would be appropriate?

4. In the speech, does Mr. Nixon ever attempt to "stir your emotions" so as to "befog your thinking"? Does he use name-calling or glittering generalities? Cite examples.

5. Do you see any "red herrings" or devices to distract your attention from the main issue? Does Mr. Nixon ever use plain folks, stroking, transfer, or *argumentum ad hominem*? Where? Are these devices effective? Why or why not?

6. Does Mr. Nixon use faulty logic? Where? Is it one of the kinds of

faulty logic identified by D. W. Cross (faulty cause and effect, false analogy, begging the question, two-extremes fallacy) or is there something else the matter with the reasoning? Explain.

7. Do you think that the question of whether or not Mr. Nixon took graft is satisfactorily answered in this speech? Why or why not?

JAMES E. (JIMMY) CARTER
In Changing Times, Eternal Values
(Inaugural Address, January 20, 1977)[1]

Because the Carter presidency is of such recent history, it scarcely needs much retelling here. When he began campaigning, two years before the inauguration, he was one of the least-known candidates in either party, yet he went on to take the nomination of his party on the first ballot—even though he has never demonstrated himself to be an outstanding orator.

When Carter assumed the presidency in January 1977, he was still an enigma to most of the North American public, even to many of the people who had supported him. He seemed to elude most of the principal political labels, even as he articulated his positions. His task in the speech reprinted here was to placate an uneasy electorate, to rally his supporters, to give the rudiments of his political philosphy, as well as to give a preview of some of the directions his administration might take.

For myself and for my nation, I want to thank my predecessor for all he has 1 done to heal our land. In this outward and physical ceremony we attest once again to the inner and spiritual strength of our nation.

As my high school teacher, Miss Julia Coleman, used to say, "We must 2 adjust to changing times and still hold to unchanging principles."

Here before me is the Bible used in the inauguration of our first president in 3 1789, and I have just taken the oath of office on the Bible my mother gave me just a few years ago, opened to a timeless admonition from the ancient prophet Micah:

"He hath showed thee, O man, what is good; and what doth the Lord require of thee, but to do justly, and to love mercy, and to walk humbly with thy God." (Micah 6:8)

This inauguration ceremony marks a new beginning, a new dedication 4 within our Government, and a new spirit among us all. A President may sense and proclaim that new spirit, but only people can provide it.

Two centuries ago our nation's birth was a milestone in the long quest for 5 freedom, but the bold and brilliant dream which excited the founders of our

[1]From the text appearing in *The New York Times*, January 21, 1977.

nation still awaits its consummation. I have no new dream to set forth today, but rather urge a fresh faith in the old dream.

Ours was the first society openly to define itself both in terms of spirituality 6 and human liberty. It is that unique self-definition which has given us an exceptional appeal—but it also imposes on us a special obligation, to take on those moral duties which, when assumed, seem invariably to be in our own best interests.

You have given me a great responsibility—to stay close to you, to be worthy 7 of you and to exemplify what you are. Let us create together a new national spirit of unity and trust. Your strength can compensate for my weakness, and your wisdom can help minimize my mistakes.

Let us learn together and laugh together and work together and pray together, 8 confident that in the end we will triumph together in the right.

The American dream endures. We must once again have faith in our 9 country—and in one another. I believe America can be better. We can be even stronger than before.

Let our recent mistakes bring a resurgent commitment to the basic principles 10 of our nation, for we know that if we despise our own Government we have no future. We recall in special times when we have stood briefly, but magnificently, united; in those times no prize was beyond our grasp.

But we cannot dwell upon remembered glory. We cannot afford to drift. We 11 reject the prospect of failure and mediocrity or an inferior quality of life for any person.

Our government must at the same time be both competent and compassion- 12 ate.

We have already found a high degree of personal liberty, and we are now 13 struggling to enhance the equality of opportunity. Our commitment to human rights must be absolute, our laws fair, our natural beauty preserved; the powerful must not persecute the weak, and human dignity must be enhanced.

We have learned that "more" is not necessarily "better," that even our great 14 nation has its recognized limits and that we can neither answer all questions nor solve all problems. We cannot afford to do everything, nor can we lack boldness as we meet the future. So together, in a spirit of individual sacrifice for the common good, we must simply do our best.

Our nation can be strong abroad only if it is strong at home, and we know 15 that the best way to enhance freedom in other lands is to demonstrate here that our democratic system is worthy of emulation.

To be true to ourselves, we must be true to others. We will not behave in 16 foreign places so as to violate our rules and standards here at home, for we know that this trust which our nation earns is essential to our strength.

The world itself is now dominated by a new spirit. Peoples more numerous 17 and more politically aware are craving and now demanding their place in the sun—not just for the benefit of their own physical condition, but for basic human rights.

The passion for freedom is on the rise. Tapping this new spirit, there can be 18 no nobler nor more ambitious task for America to undertake on this day of a new beginning than to help shape a just and peaceful world that is truly humane.

We are a strong nation and we will maintain strength so sufficient that it need 19 not be proven in combat—a quiet strength based not merely on the size of an aresenal, but on the nobility of ideas.

We will be ever vigilant and never vulnerable, and we will fight our wars 20 against poverty, ignorance and injustice, for those are the enemies against which our forces can be honorably marshaled.

We are a proudly idealistic nation, but let no one confuse our idealism with 21 weakness.

Because we are free we can never be indifferent to the fate of freedom 22 elsewhere. Our moral sense dictates a clearcut preference for those societies which share with us an abiding respect for individual human rights. We do not seek to intimidate, but it is clear that a world which others can dominate with impunity would be inhospitable to decency and a threat to the well-being of all people.

The world is still engaged in a massive armaments race designed to insure 23 continuing equivalent strength among potential adversaries. We pledge persever- ance and wisdom in our efforts to limit the world's armaments to those necessary for each nation's own domestic safety. We will move this year a step toward our ultimate goal—the elimination of all nuclear weapons from this earth.

We urge all other people to join us, for success can mean life instead of 24 death.

Within us, the people of the United States, there is evident a serious and 25 purposeful rekindling of confidence, and I join in the hope that when my time as your President has ended, people might say about our nation:

That we had remembered the words of Micah and renewed our search for 26 humility, mercy, and justice; that we had torn down the barriers that separated those of different race and region and religion, and where there had been mis- trust, built unity, with a respect for diversity; that we had found productive work for those able to perform it; that we had strengthened the American family, which is the basis of our society; that we had insured respect for the law, and equal treatment under the law, for the weak and the powerful, for the rich and the poor; and that we had enabled our people to be proud of their own Govern- ment once again.

I would hope that nations of the world might say that we had a built a lasting 27 peace, based not on weapons of war but on international policies which reflect our own most precious values.

These are not just my goals. And they will not be my accomplishments, but 28 the affirmation of our nation's continuing moral strength and our belief in an undiminished, ever-expanding American dream.

DISCUSSION QUESTIONS

1. Compare President Carter's speech with "The Checkers Speech" just preceding it. Which of the two do you think is more effective? Which makes more use of propaganda? What differences do you see in the way the two men express themselves?

2. Both the Checkers speech and the Inaugural address try to appeal to the listener's emotions. Which one is more successful at doing this ? Why?

3. Before the Inauguration, Carter and his aides tried to think of an effective catch phrase that he could use in this speech, one that might come to be identified with his administration, as "New Deal" is with Roosevelt's and "New Frontier" is with Kennedy's. They decided on "New Spirit." The word "spirit" appears four times in the speech, in paragraphs 4, 7, 14, and 17. What does the phrase "New Spirit" denote, specifically? Is the meaning of the word "spirit" the same in all four contexts, or does it change? Explain.

4. What do words like "unity" "strength," "morality," and "wisdom" mean? As you look at them in context in the speech, do they seem to be glittering generalities? Why or why not?

5. Does President Carter use any "red herrings" to distract the listener's attention from the main issue? What *is* the main issue of this speech?

6. Do you detect any faulty logic in this speech? Where? What is wrong with the reasoning?

ALDOUS HUXLEY
Propaganda in a Democratic Society

Aldous Huxley is probably best-known today for *Brave New World*, a satiric fantasy intended to apply to the present as much as to the remote future. In the "world" of the novel, the search for contentment, pleasure, security, and mindless diversion, aided by technology and politics, has obliterated any interest in justice, truth, or anything that lies beyond the self. Although the novel was by no means prophecy, many readers have felt that the world is drawing closer to the anti-utopia of *Brave New World* rather than moving away from it.

In the following essay, from a collection titled *Brave New World Revisited*, Huxley shows us how modern propaganda helps to drive us toward the "world" he described. This is not simply the propaganda which urges us to vote or buy in certain prescribed steps but more the mass of information thrust upon us that helps to insulate us from the realities that surround us.

There are two kinds of propaganda—rational propaganda in favor of action   1
that is consonant with the enlightened self-interest of those who make it and those to whom it is addressed, and non-rational propaganda that is not consonant with anybody's enlightened self-interest, but is dictated by, and appeals to, passion. . . . Propaganda in favor of action that is consonant with enlightened self-interest appeals to reason by means of logical arguments based upon the best available evidence fully and honestly set forth. Propaganda in favor of action dictated by the impulses that are below self-interest offers false, garbled or incomplete evidence, avoids logical argument and seeks to influence its victims by

the mere repetition of catchwords, by the furious denunciation of foreign or domestic scapegoats, and by cunningly associating the lowest passions with the highest ideals, so that atrocities come to be perpetrated in the name of God and the most cynical kind of *Realpolitik* is treated as a matter of religious principle and patriotic duty.

· · ·

The power to respond to reason and truth exists in all of us. But so, unfortunately, does the tendency to respond to unreason and falsehood—particularly in those cases where the falsehood evokes some enjoyable emotion, or where the appeal to unreason strikes some answering chord in the primitive, subhuman depths of our being. In certain fields of activity men have learned to respond to reason and truth pretty consistently. The authors of learned articles do not appeal to the passions of their fellow scientists and technologists. They set forth what, to the best of their knowledge, is the truth about some particular aspect of reality, they use reason to explain the facts they have observed and they support their point of view with arguments that appeal to reason in other people. All this is fairly easy in the fields of physical science and technology. It is much more difficult in the fields of politics and religion and ethnics. Here the relevant facts often elude us. As for the meaning of the facts, that of course depends upon the particular system of ideas, in terms of which you choose to interpret them. And these are not the only difficulties that confront the rational truth-seeker. In public and in private life, it often happens that there is simply no time to collect the relevant facts or to weigh their significance. We are forced to act on insufficient evidence and by a light considerably less steady than that of logic. With the best will in the world, we cannot always be completely truthful or consistently rational. All that is in our power is to be as truthful and rational as circumstances permit us to be, and to respond as well as we can to the limited truth and imperfect reasonings offered for our consideration by others.

"If a nation expects to be ignorant and free," said Jefferson, "it expects what never was and never will be. . . . The people cannot be safe without information. Where the press is free, and every man able to read, all is safe." . . . Once more we hear the note of eighteen-century optimism. Jefferson, it is true, was a realist as well as an optimist. He knew by bitter experience that the freedom of the press can be shamefully abused. "Nothing," he declared, "can now be believed which is seen in a newspaper." And yet, he insisted (and we can only agree with him), "within the pale of truth, the press is a noble institution, equally the friend of science and civil liberty." Mass communication, in a word, is neither good nor bad; it is simply a force and, like any other force, it can be used either well or ill. Used in one way, the press, the radio and the cinema are indispensable to the survival of democracy. Used in another way, they are among the most powerful weapons in the dictator's armory. In the field of mass communications as in almost every other field of enterprise, technological progress has hurt the Little Man and helped the Big Man. As lately as fifty years ago, every democratic country could boast of a great number of small journals and local newspapers. Thousands of country editors expressed thousands of independent opinions. Somewhere or other almost anybody could get almost anything printed. Today the press is still legally free; but most of the little papers have

disappeared. The cost of woodpulp, of modern printing machinery and of syndicated news is too high for the Little Man. In the totalitarian East there is political
censorship, and the media of mass communication are controlled by the State.
In the democratic West there is economic censorship and the media of mass
communication are controlled by members of the Power Elite. Censorship by
rising costs and the concentration of communication power in the hands of a few
big concerns is less objectionable than State ownership and government propaganda; but certainly it is not something of which a Jeffersonian democrat could
possibly approve.

In regard to propaganda the early advocates of universal literacy and a free   4
press envisaged only two possibilities: the propaganda might be true, or it might
be false. They did not foresee what in fact has happened, above all in our
Western capitalist democracies—the development of a vast mass communications industry, concerned in the main neither with the true nor the false, but
with the unreal, the more or less totally irrelevant. In a word, they failed to take
into account man's almost infinite appetite for distractions.

In the past most people never got a chance of fully satisfying this appetite.   5
They might long for distractions, but the distractions were not provided. Christmas came but once a year, feasts were "solemn and rare," there were few readers
and very little to read, and the nearest approach to a neighborhood movie theater
was the parish church, where the performances, though frequent, were somewhat monotonous. For conditions even remotely comparable to those now prevailing we must return to imperial Rome, where the populace was kept in good
humor by frequent, gratuitous doses of many kinds of entertainment—from
poetical dramas to gladiatorial fights, from recitations of Virgil to all-out boxing,
from concerts to military reviews and public executions. But even in Rome there
was nothing like the non-stop distraction now provided by newspapers and magazines, by radio, television and the cinema. In *Brave New World* non-stop distractions of the most fascinating nature (the feelies, orgy-porgy, centrifugal bumble-
puppy) are deliberately used as instruments of policy, for the purpose of preventing people from paying too much attention to the realities of the social and
political situation. The other world of religion is different from the other world of
entertainment; but they resemble one another in being most decidedly "not of
this world." Both are distractions and, if lived in too continuously, both can
become, in Marx's phrase, "the opium of the people" and so a threat to freedom.
Only the vigilant can maintain their liberties, and only those who are constantly
and intelligently on the spot can hope to govern themselves effectively by democratic procedures. A society, most of whose members spend a great part of their
time, not on the spot, not here and now in the calculable future, but somewhere
else, in the irrelevant other worlds of sport and soap opera, of mythology and
metaphysical fantasy, will find it hard to resist the encroachments of those who
would manipulate and control it.

In their propaganda today's dictators rely for the most part on repetition,   6
suppression and rationalization—the repetition of catchwords which they wish to
be accepted as true, the suppression of facts which they wish to be ignored, the
arousal and rationalization of passions which many be used in the interests of the
Party or the State. As the art and science of manipulation come to be better

understood, the dictators of the future will doubtless learn to combine these techniques with the non-stop distractions which, in the West, are now threatening to drown in a sea of irrelevance the rational propaganda essential to the maintenance of individual liberty and the survival of democratic institutions.

DISCUSSION QUESTIONS

1. Huxley calls the first of the two kinds of propaganda (see paragraph 1) "rational." How else might that kind of propaganda be defined? What do you understand it to be?

2. What is the second, "irrational," kind of propaganda? What kind of things does Huxley imply by it? Are you used to calling this kind of material "propaganda"? Why or why not?

3. Do you agree that the cost of publishing little newspapers in modern culture (see paragraph 3) serves as a kind of censorship? Can "economic censorship" be equated with the censorship of ideas in a totalitarian state?

4. Do you agree with the judgment in paragraph 4 that modern newspapers are concerned "with the unreal, the more or less totally irrelevant"? As a test, do you think you are most likely to read (a) the sports pages, (b) an astrology column, (c) the "front page," or (d) the editorial page of your local paper? Which would you not read at all? Which is real and relevant?

5. In paragraph 5 Huxley argues that much of radio, television, and films is a kind of "opium of the people." What is an "opium of the people"? Does it relieve pain or make us thoughtless and lethargic? Is an "opium of the people" a threat to freedom in a democracy? Why or why not?

6. What happens when a news event such as an important Presidential announcement interrupts a football game or a soap opera on television? How would you characterize public reaction? How does public reaction to such an event relate to what Huxley is talking about here?

7. Do you think that a "sea of irrelevance" threatens the future of freedom in our democracy?

WILLIAM SAFIRE
Political Labels: Conservative, Liberal, Democrat, Republican

Each year the average citizen of this country faces a thousand political choices, everything from "Should a local sewer be built?" to "Should we support country X with foreign aid?" When we deal with people who hold strong positions on these questions we tend to categorize them with any of a thousand political labels, from some very old ones like "mugwump" to more contemporary ones like "hawk" or "dove." After a while we may use one of these labels as a kind of shorthand for what might be a complex and well-considered position. In the United States, four labels are used more often than any of the others, even though there is sometimes a question whether we are all defining the terms the same way. As a means of approaching these labels, the following article employs sections of five different entries from Mr. Safire's *The New Language of Politics,* an informal dictionary of political language.

Labels

oversimplified identification of ideological position; widely used and universally   1
rejected by politicians unwilling to be pigeonholed.

· · ·

Party labels are readily accepted by political figures in those areas where that   2
party's registration dominates, but it has become popular in recent years to denounce ideological labels. . . . More Americans consider themselves "liberal" than "conservative," and the Republicans are more closely identified with conservatism, often placing them in an electoral bind. Thomas E. Dewey was frank to admit it: "One of the standard weapons of party conflict both between conventions and during campaigns is the effort to pin labels on individuals or movements, attractive or sinister, depending upon the point of view. On the whole, the Democratic party in recent years has been the more successful in this use of semantics."

Lyndon Johnson adopted a few labels and rejected labeling in a 1958 state-   3
ment of his political philosophy:

I am a free man, an American, a United States Senator, and a Democrat, in that   4
order.

I am also a liberal, a conservative, a Texan, a taxpayer, a rancher, a businessman,   5
a consumer, a parent, a voter, and not as young as I used to be nor as old as I expect to be—and I am all these things in no fixed order.

I am unaware of any descriptive word in the second paragraph which qualifies,   6
modifies, amends, or is related by hyphenation to the terms listed in the first paragraph. In consequence, I am not able—nor even the least interested in trying—to define my political philosophy by the choice of a one-word or two-word label.

The reasons for political squirming when it comes to ideological labeling are   7
these: (1) a label excludes more voters than it includes, and no politician wants to say "I am not one of you" to a large portion of the electorate. (2) although in one area one label may predominate, politicians are ambitious; acceptance of a label may preclude advancement. . . . (3) A label is simplistic, and thoughtful men reject its rigidity.

Conservative

a defender of the status quo who, when change becomes necessary in tested   8
institutions or practices, prefers that it come slowly, and in moderation.

In modern U.S. politics, as in the past, "conservative" is a term of oppro- 9
brium to some, and of veneration to others. Edmund Burke, the early defender
and articulator of the conservative philosophy, argued that the only way to
preserve political stability was by carefully controlling change and seeking a slow,
careful integration of new forces into venerable institutions. . . . Abraham
Lincoln called it "adherence to the old and tried, against the new and untried."

Today, the more rigid conservative generally opposes virtually all gov- 10
ernmental regulation of the economy. He favors local and state action over
federal action, and emphasizes fiscal responsibility, most notably in the form of
balanced budgets. William Allen White, the Kansas editor, described this type of
conservative when he wrote of Charles Evans Hughes as "a businessman's candidate, hovering around the status quo like a sick kitten around a hot brick."

But there exists a less doctrinaire conservative who admits the need for 11
broad-gauged government action in many fields and for steady change in many
areas. Instead of fighting a rear-guard action, he seeks to achieve such change
within the framework of existing institutions, occasionally changing the institutions when they show need of it.

Liberal

currently, one who believes in more government action to meet individual 12
needs; originally, one who resisted government encroachment on individual
liberties.

In the original sense the word described those of the emerging middle classes 13
in France and Great Britain who wanted to throw off the rules the dominant
aristocracy had made to cement its own control.

During the 1920's the meaning changed to describe those who believed a 14
certain amount of governmental action was necessary to protect the peoples'
"real" freedoms as opposed to their purely legal—and not necessarily existent—
freedoms.

This philosophical about-face led former New York Goverer Thomas 15
Dewey to say, after using the original definition, "Two hundred years later, the
transmutation of the word, as the alchemist would say, has become one of the
wonders of our time."

In the U.S. politics, the word was used by George Washington to indicate a 16
person of generosity or broad-mindedness, as he expressed distaste for those who
would deprive Catholics and Jews of their rights.

In its present usage, the word acquired significance during the presidency of 17
Franklin D. Roosevelt, who defined it this way during the campaign for the first
term: ". . . say that civilization is a tree which, as it grows, continually produces
rot and dead wood. The radical says: 'Cut it down.' The conservative says: 'Don't
touch it.' The liberal compromises: 'Let's prune, so that we lose neither the old
trunk nor the new branches.

Sometimes liberals cannot avoid the temptation to assault the term. Adlai 18
Stevenson, quoting an uncertain source, once described a liberal as "one who

has both feet firmly planted in the air." And columnist Heywood Broun, who came to consider himself a radical, wrote: "A liberal is a man who leaves a room when a fight begins," a definition since adopted by an apostle of Negro militancy, Saul Alinsky.

The more radical wing of the civil-rights movement is the latest to use the 19 word in a spirit of contempt, in the phrase "white liberal." This is designed to describe whites who talk about racial equality but are not prepared to fight for it in what militants deem a sufficiently dedicated manner, and who are therefore suspect.

Liberals are variously described as high-minded, double-domed, screaming, 20 knee-jerk, professional, "bleeding heart."

Democrat

a member of one of the two major U.S. political parties, or "democrat with a 21 small 'd' ": one who favors strong governmental action for the welfare of the many.

It was under Andrew Jackson that the Democratic party, founded in 1828, 22 began using its present name, but "democrat" was current long before that. "Washington," wrote John Adams scornfully toward the end of the eighteenth century, "appointed a multitude of democrats and jacobins of the deepest dye. I have been more cautious in this respect."

In 1955, Leonard Hall, a former Republican National Chairman, began 23 referring to the "Democrat' rather than the "Democratic" party, a habit begun by Thomas E. Dewey. Hall dropped the "ic," he said because "I think their claims that they represent the great mass of the people, and we don't, is just a lot of bunk."

Some Democrats suggested retaliating by shortening Republican to Publican, 24 but the National Committee overruled them, explaining that Republican "is the name by which our opponents' product is known and mistrusted."

Probably the best-known modern quote involving the word comes from Will 25 Rogers: "I belong to no organized party. I am a Democrat."

Republican

advocates of a democratic form of government, as their Democratic opponents 26 are advocates of a republican form of government.

John Adams worried about the word in 1790: ". . . all good government is 27 and must be republican. But, at the same time, you can or will agree with me, that there is not in lexicography a more fraudulent word. . . . Are we not, my friend, in danger of rendering the word republican unpopular in this country by an indiscreet, indeterminate, and equivocal use of it?"

Thomas Jefferson, who used the word as an antonym for "monarchic" all his 28 life, disagreed in 1816: ". . . of the import of the term republic, instead of saying, as has been said, 'that it may mean anything or nothing,' we may say with truth and meaning, that governments are more or less republican as they have more or less of the element of popular election and control in their composition. . . ."

Stricly speaking, a *republic* is a form of government in which the people 29 exercise their power through elected representatives, while a *democracy* is a government where the people exercise their powers directly *or* through elected representatives. In current usage, the two terms are interchangable, which is why the definition above is not as flippant as it seems.

DISCUSSION QUESTIONS

1. How many of these four political labels would you apply to yourself? Are they so elastic that all of them might apply to one person?

2. How many of these apply to your friends? College? Community? Local newspaper? On what basis would you apply these labels?

3. If you feel at least one of these labels applies to you, do you agree with Mr. Safire's definition of it? For example, if you are a "conservative" do you have specific ideas about the role of "free enterprise" or "big business"? How do you feel about "national defense" or "the arms race"? Might a liberal ever hold the same positions?

4. If you call yourself a liberal, (see paragraph 13), do you feel this implies a position about education? They women's movement? How about "affirmative action" or "racial and sexual quotas"?

5. Some critics have argued that the terms "Democrat" and "Republican" count for more than "liberal" and "conservative" in the long run because they refer to organized parties which raise money and get out the vote. Despite this, Mr. Safire seems to have more difficulty in defining them. Why do you think this is so?

6. What connotative advantage did Leonard Hall hope to gain in changing the name of his rivals from "Democratic" to "Democrat"? Why does one sound better or worse than the other if they both refer to the same thing?

7. After considering the definitions of these four political labels, do you think it is possible for a politician to change them? Can you believe a politician who is a liberal or a Republican in one year and a conservative or a Democrat in another?

8. Would you read Mr. Safire's definitions differently if you applied some of these labels to him? For example, he now lives in New York City, which often votes Democratic. For several years he held a post in the Nixon administration, and he wrote several speeches for Vice President Agnew. In recent years he has been a conservative columnist for *The New York Times*, which is often portrayed as a liberal newspaper.

BILL GARVIN
Mad's Guaranteed Effective All-Occasion Non-Slanderous Political Smear Speech

One dictionary of American slang[1] defines "to smear" as "to destroy" . . . the good reputation of another, especially by making false or exaggerated accusations. . . . " It would be unfair and untrue to say that all politicians smear their opponents; for one thing it is dangerous: the opponents might sue. This makes the best kind of smear a legal—that is, a non-slanderous—one. But how to find just the right words? Ah, leave it to the editors of the irrepressible *Mad Magazine* to tell us how to do it. Charge your enemies with committing "a piscatorial act." Tell all the world that your opponent is a "flagrant heterosexual." Win the votes and the lawsuits too.

My fellow citizens, it is an honor and a pleasure to be here today. My opponent has openly admitted he feels an affinity toward your city, but I happen to *like* this area. It might be a salubrious place to him, but to me it is one of the nation's most delightful garden spots.   1

When I embarked upon this political campaign I hoped that it could be conducted on a high level and that my opponent would be willing to stick to the issues. Unfortunately, he has decided to be tractable instead—to indulge in unequivocal language, to eschew the use of outright lies in his speeches, and even to make repeated veracious statements about me.   2

At first I tried to ignore these scrupulous, unvarnished fidelities. Now I do so no longer. *If my opponent wants a fight, he's going to get one!*   3

It might be instructive to start with his background. My friends, have you ever accidentally dislodged a rock on the ground and seen what was underneath? Well, exploring my opponent's background is dissimilar. All the slime and filth and corruption you can possibly imagine, even in your wildest dreams, are glaringly nonexistent in this man's life. And even during his childhood!   4

Let us take a very quick look at that childhood: It is a known fact that, on a number of occasions, he emulated older boys at a certain playground. It is also known that his parents not only permitted him to masticate excessively in their presence, but even urged him to do so. Most explicable of all, this man who poses as a paragon of virtue exacerbated his own sister when they were both teenagers!   5

I ask you, my fellow Americans: is this the kind of person we want in public office to set an example for our youth?   6

---

[1] H. Wentworth and S. B. Flexner, *Dictionary of American Slang* (New York: Crowell, 1960), 492.

Of course, it's not surprising that he should have such a typically pristine   7
background—no, not when you consider the other members of his family:

His female relatives put on a constant pose of purity and innocence, and   8
claim they are inscrutable, yet every one of them has taken part in hortatory
activities.

The men in the family are likewise completely amenable to moral suasion.   9

My opponent's second cousin is a Mormon.   10

His uncle was a flagrant hetrosexual.   11

His sister, who has always been obsessed by sects, once worked as a proselyte   12
outside a church.

His father was secretly chagrined at least a dozen times by matters of a   13
pecuniary nature.

His youngest brother wrote an essay extolling the virtues of being a homo   14
sapiens.

His great-aunt expired from a degenerative disease.   15

His nephew subscribes to a phonographic magazine.   16

His wife was a thespian before their marriage and even performed the act in   17
front of paying customers.

And his own mother had to resign from a women's organization in her later   18
years because she was an admitted sexagenarian.

Now what shall we say of the man himself?   19

I can tell you in solemn truth that he is the very antithesis of political   20
radicalism, economic irresponsibility and personal depravity. His own record
proves that he has frequently discountenanced treasonable, un-American
philosophies and has perpetrated many overt acts as well.

He perambulated his infant son on the street.   21

He practiced nepotism with his uncle and first cousin.   22

He attempted to interest a 13-year-old girl in philately.   23

He participated in a seance at a private residence where, among other odd   24
goings-on, there was incense.

He has declared himself in favor of more homogeneity on college campuses.   25

He has advocated social intercourse in mixed company—and has taken part   26
in such gatherings himself.

He has been deliberately averse to crime in our streets.   27

He has urged our Protestant and Jewish citizens to develop more catholic   28
tastes.

Last summer he committed a piscatorial act on a boat that was flying the   29
American flag.

Finally, at a time when we must be on our guard against all foreign isms, he   30
has cooly announced his belief in altruism—and his fervent hope that some day
this entire nation will be altruistic!

I beg you, my friends, to oppose this man whose life and work and ideas are   31
so openly and avowedly compatible with our American way of life. A vote for
him would be a vote for the perpetuation of everything we hold dear.

The facts are clear; the record speaks for itself.   32

Do your duty.   33

DISCUSSION QUESTIONS

1. Almost every sentence in this essay contains an illustration of a technique of propaganda. Starting with paragraph 1, sentence 1, how many of them can you name?

2. Most of the gags in this essay rely on a kind of punning called "mala-propism," named for a character in R. B. Sheridan's play, *The Rivals*. Mrs. Malaprop made a pretentious fool of herself by falling into them, but the author of this essay, Bill Garvin, writes them purposefully. For example, what was the implied intention of "salubrious" in paragraph 1, sentence 3?

3. What is the general suggestion in the misuse of words like "to masti-cate" and "exacerbate" (paragraph 5), "hortatory activities" (paragraph 8), "degenerative disease" (paragraph 15), and "sexagenarian" (paragraph 18)?

4. Can you use these words in another context in which their implication would be unmistakably positive?

5. How many people in the general public would know what is meant by "catholic tastes" (paragraph 28) without consulting a dictionary?

6. Do you think that any portions of this essay, read with the proper tone of voice, could fool an inattentive listener? Which sections are they?

7. What is the point of view of the pretended speaker of this essay?

MORRIS K. UDALL
Affective Language in Political Propaganda: "Federal Spending"

"Affective language" is a general name for the kind of language that carries a stronger connotation than denotation—that evokes strong reac-tions from people, even when they are not sure just what the language means. Many of the propagandistic devices described by D. W. Cross in the first essay in this chapter—"name calling," "glittering generalities," etc.—would fall in the general category of "affective language."

One specific phrase that might be classed as affective language is "federal spending," something that many politicians seem to be cam-paigning against. When some of his constituents wrote to complain about federal spending, Congressman Udall of Arizona wrote (but did not mail) the following response. He is for some "federal spending" and against some other; it all depends on where and what the money is spent.

If, when you say "federal spending," you mean the billions of dollars wasted   1
on outmoded naval shipyards and surplus airbases in Georgia, Texas and New York; if you mean the billions of dollars lavished at Cape Kennedy and Houston

on a "moondoggle" our nation cannot afford it; if, sir, you mean the $2 billion wasted each year in wheat and corn price supports which rob Midwestern farmers of their freedoms and saddle taxpayers with outrageous costs of storage in already bulging warehouses; if you mean the $4 billion spent every year to operate veterans hospitals in other states in order to provide 20 million able-bodied veterans with care for civilian illness; if you mean such socialistic and pork-barrel projects as urban renewal, public housing and TVA which cynically seek votes while robbing our taxpayers and weakening the moral fiber of millions of citizens in our Eastern states; if you mean the bloated federal aid to education schemes calculated to press federal educational controls down upon every student in this nation; if you mean the $2 billion misused annually by our Public Health Service and National Institutes of Health on activities designed to prostitute the medical profession and foist socialized medicine on every American; if, sir, you mean all these ill-advised, unnecessary federal activities which have destroyed state's rights, created a vast, ever-growing, empire-building bureaucracy regimenting a once free people by the illusory bait of cradle-to-grave security, and which indeed have taken us so far down the road to socialism that it may be, even at this hour, too late to retreat—then I am unyielding, bitter, and four square in my opposition, regardless of the personal or political consequences.

But, on the other hand, if when you say "federal spending" you mean those funds which maintain Davis-Monthan Air Force Base, Fort Huachuca and other Arizona defense installations so vital to our nation's security, and which every year pour hundreds of millions of dollars into our state's economy; if you mean the Truman-Eisenhower-Kennedy-Johnson mutual security program which bolsters our allies along the periphery of the Iron Curtain, enabling them to resist the diabolical onslaught of a Godless Communism and maintain their independence; if you mean those funds to send our brave astronauts voyaging, even as Columbus, into the unknown, in order to guarantee that no aggressor will ever threaten these great United States by nuclear blackmail from outer space; if you mean those sound farm programs which insure our hardy Arizona cotton farmers a fair price for their fiber, protect the sanctity of the family farm, ensure reasonable prices for consumers, and put to work for all the people of the world the miracle of American agricultural abundance; if you mean those VA programs which pay pensions to our brave soldiers crippled in mortal combat and discharge our debt of honor to their widows and orphans and which provide employment for thousands of Arizonans in our fine VA hospitals in Tucson, Phoenix and Prescott; if, sir, you refer to such federal programs as the Central Arizona Reclamation project which will, while repaying 95 percent of its cost with interest, provide our resourceful people with water to insure the growth and prosperity of our state; if you mean the federal education funds which build desperately needed college classrooms and dormitories for our local universities, provide little children in our Arizona schools with hot lunches (often their only decent meal of the day), furnish vocational training for our high school youth, and pay $10 million in impact funds to relieve the hard-pressed Arizona school property taxpayers from the impossible demands created by the presence of large federal installations; if you mean the federal medical and health programs which have eradicated the curse of malaria, small-pox, scarlet fever and polio from our country, and which even now enable dedicated teams of scientists to close in mercilessly on man's old age enemies of cancer, heart disease, muscular dystrophy, multiple sclerosis, and mental retardation that afflict our little children, senior citizens and men and women in the prime years of life; if you mean all these federal activities by which a free people in the spirit of Jefferson, Lincoln, Teddy Roosevelt, Wilson and FDR, through a fair and progressive income tax, preserve domestic tranquillity and promote the general welfare while preserving all our cherished freedoms and our self-reliant national character, then I shall support them with all the vigor at my command.

DISCUSSION QUESTIONS

1. Now that you have read some of Congressman Udall's examples, try to give an informal definition of "affective language." How does it relate to any of the materials in Chapter 2?

2. Representative Udall gives many more examples of affective language than "federal spending." Starting with the first sentence of the first paragraph, point out some of the slanted words he uses: " . . . billions of dollars *wasted* on *outmoded* naval shipyards and *surplus* airbases in Georgia, Texas, and New York . . . "

3. This effect of this short piece is to satirize two different points of view. Briefly summarized, what two points of view are they? Does Representative Udall actually hold either of these points of view? How can you tell?

4. Was Representative Udall correct about the ambiguity of "federal spending"? Take a poll of the students in your room. How many would still say they were against "federal spending" without knowing specifically what it meant?

5. Ask five people who did not read the Udall letter or have not participated in your classroom discussion: would they want to vote for a politician who agreed to increase federal spending by 10 percent?

6. A good example of affective language now used in the United States is "Americanism." It means different things to different people. For example, not long age the Independent Grocer's Association (IGA) ran an ad campaign whose catch line was " . . . in the good old American way." The implication was that small, independently run grocery stores were in the "good old American" tradition. Would this not imply that large chain stores—A&P, Safeway, Grand Union, Kroger's, etc.—are somehow "un-American"? On the other hand, small, independently owned grocery stores are common in many West European countries, such as Belgium and France, where large supermarket chains are known as "American stores." Can you resolve this? Does "Americanism" have other definitions? Give some other examples.

7. What are some other words whose strong connotations sometimes overshadow their denotations? What does "natural" mean in reference to "natural cereals" such as Heartland and Nature Valley? What do words like "unity," "progress," or "leadership" mean in a political campaign?

DAVID OGILVY
How to Write Potent Copy

In "The Limits of Language," Melvin Maddocks describes the deluge of words that pours upon us each day. Many of the words are a part of some kind of advertising, often in the form of a headline. But though the language of advertising may be everywhere, it is carefully chosen—more calculated and crafted than almost anything else written today. In the following essay, master advertising copywriter David Ogilvy gives us ten points to help us write—or at least understand—effective advertising headlines.

I. Headlines

The headline is the most important element in most advertisements. It is the telegram which decides the reader whether to read the copy. 1

On the average, five times as many people read the headline as read the body copy. When you have written your headline, you have spent eighty cents out of your dollar. 2

If you haven't done some selling in your headline, you have wasted 80 per cent of your client's money. The wickedest of all sins is to run an advertisement *without* a headline. Such headless wonders are still to be found; I don't envy the copywriter who submits one to me. 3

A change of headline can make a difference of ten to one in sales. I never write fewer than sixteen headlines for a single advertisement, and I observe certain guides in writing them: 4

(1) The headline is the "ticket on the meat." Use it to flag down the readers who are prospects for the kind of product you are advertising. If you are selling a remedy for bladder weakness, display the words BLADDER WEAKNESS in your headline; they catch the eye of everyone who suffers from this inconvenience. If you want *mothers* to read your advertisement, display MOTHERS in your headline. And so on. 5

Conversely, do not say anything in your headline which is likely to *exclude* any readers who might be prospects for your product. Thus, if you are advertising a product which can be used equally well by men and women, don't slant your headline at women alone; it would frighten men away. 6

(2) Every headline should appeal to the reader's *self-interest*. It should promise her a benefit, as in my headline for Helena Rubinstein's Hormone Cream: HOW WOMEN OVER 35 CAN LOOK YOUNGER. 7

(3) Always try to inject *news* into your headlines, because the consumer is always on the lookout for new products, or new ways to use an old product, or new improvements in an old product. 8

The two most powerful words you can use in a headline are FREE and NEW. You can seldom use FREE, but you can almost always use NEW—if you try hard enough. 9

(4) Other words and phrases which work wonders are HOW TO, SUDDENLY, 10
NOW, ANNOUNCING, INTRODUCING, IT'S HERE, JUST ARRIVED, IMPORTANT DEVEL-
OPMENT, IMPROVEMENT, AMAZING, SENSATIONAL, REMARKABLE, REVOLUTIONARY,
STARTLING, MIRACLE, MAGIC, OFFER, QUICK, EASY, WANTED, CHALLENGE, ADVICE
TO, THE TRUTH ABOUT, COMPARE, BARGAIN, HURRY, LAST CHANCE.

Don't turn up your nose at these clichés. They may be shopworn, but they 11
work. That is why you see them turn up so often in the headlines of mail-order
advertisers and others who can measure the results of their advertisements.

Headlines can be strengthened by the inclusion of *emotional* words, like 12
DARLING, LOVE, FEAR, PROUD, FRIEND, and BABY. One of the most provocative
advertisements which has come out of our agency showed a girl in a bathtub,
talking to her lover on the telephone. The headline: *Darling, I'm having the most
extraordinary experience . . . I'm head over heels in* DOVE.

(5) Five times as many people read the headline as read the body copy, so it is 13
important that these glancers should at least be told what brand is being advertised. That is why you should always include the brand name in your headlines.

(6) Include your selling promise in your headline. This requires long head- 14
lines. When the New York University School of Retailing ran headline tests with
the cooperation of a big department store, they found that headlines of ten words
or longer, containing news and information, consistently sold more merchandise
than short headlines.

Headlines containing six to twelve words pull more coupon returns than 15
short headlines, and there is no significant difference between the readership of
twelve-word headlines and the readership of three-word headlines. The best
headline I ever wrote contained *eighteen* words: *At Sixty Miles an Hour the
Loudest Noise in the New Rolls-Royce comes from the electric clock.* [1]

People are more likely to read your body copy if your headline arouses their 16
curiosity; so you should end your headline with a lure to read on.

(8) Some copywriters write *tricky* headlines—puns, literary allusions, and 17
other obscurities. This is a sin.

In the average newspaper your headline has to compete for attention with 350 18
others. Research has shown that readers travel so fast through this jungle that
they don't stop to decipher the meaning of obscure headlines. Your headline
must *telegraph* what you want to say, and it must telegraph it in plain language.
Don't play games with the reader.
                                   •   •   •

(9) Research shows that it is dangerous to use *negatives* in headlines. If, for 19
example, you write OUR SALT CONTAINS NO ARSENIC, many readers will miss the
negative and go away with the impression that you wrote OUR SALT CONTAINS
ARSENIC.

(10) Avoid *blind* headlines—the kind which mean nothing unless you read 20
the body copy underneath them; most people don't.

---

[1] When the chief engineer at the Rolls-Royce factory read this, he shook his head sadly and said,
"It is time we did something about the damned clock."

DISCUSSION QUESTIONS

1. In the previous article, David Ogilvy was concerned with creating headlines for the printed page. Do TV and radio advertising use any of the techniques for selling that Ogilvy mentions? Which ones?

2. What differences can you find between printed advertisement and other kinds of advertisement? Do TV and radio use any appeals that do *not* appear in printed advertisement—newspapers, magazines, billboards? What are they?

3. Select three different headlines for newpaper or magazine ads and analyze them according to Ogilvy's principles. How closely do the headlines follow Ogilvy's suggestions? Do you think they are effective? Why or why not?

4. Think up some ad headlines for the following products:

A. A fifteen-speed bicycle.
B. A soap that smells like apricots.
C. A frozen beef stew dinner.
D. Kitty litter with multi-colored granules.
E. A herbicide that selectively kills weeds but not grass.

5. In another chapter of the same book that this article came from, David Ogilvy defends advertising, saying that it is "a force for sustaining standards of quality and service." He goes on to state the following example:

> When we started advertising KLM Royal Dutch airlines as "punctual" and "reliable," their top management sent out an encyclical, reminding their operations staff to live up to the promise of our advertising.
>
> It may be said that a good advertising agency represents the consumer's interest in the councils of industry.

Do you see any contradiction between these remarks and Ogilvy's suggestions in paragraphs 8 to 12 in his article? How do you think Ogilvy would explain his position? Discuss.

CARL P. WRIGHTER,[1]
Weasel Words: God's Little Helpers

As the previous article by David Ogilvy revealed, admen have made quite an art out of the business of commercial selling. Still, many of us feel we are immune to the adman's tricks. In the next selection, Carl Wrighter, himself an adman, argues that we are all "suckered" by adver-

---

[1]Published originally under ths pseudonym "Paul Stevens."

tising, whether we know it or not, and he identifies one of the sneakiest forms of deception known to man—the weasel word.

The article is taken from Wrighter's book *I Can Sell You Anything*.

Like everyone else in this country, you are an advertising expert. Why not? You have been brought up with advertising. The first words you ever read were probably written on a billboard or the front of a box of cereal. The first sounds you ever heard were probably emanating from a radio or a television set. Before you knew who daddy was, you knew that Wheaties was the breakfast of champions. Before you could tell a Republican from a Democrat, you could tell a Bufferin from a plain aspirin. Naturally, you're an advertising expert, and as such you know two things for sure.

First, you know what you like and what you don't like. You know which commercials make you laugh, which ones make you giggle, which ones raise a lump in your throat, and which ones bore you to tears. In short, you react emotionally to each of them, and are able instantly to identify these emotions. Indeed, advertising is the art form of the common man, making just about all of us react just about the same way, just about all the time. Preplanned? You bet it is. We know what will make you feel happy or sad or calm or mad. And we elicit those emotions from you through the highly skilled use of this art form called advertising. Yet, they are your emotions, your reactions, and you do know how you feel. And that makes you an expert.

The second thing you think you know for sure is the conscious decisions you make concerning products you see advertised. The chances are that you have never made a deliberate decision to buy a product based on an ad you have seen. As a matter of fact, I have heard only quotes to the contrary, ranging from "I would never buy a product that I have seen advertised" to the more basic "Come on, who do they think they're kidding?" Well, we're not kidding anyone. It's you who are kidding yourself. Because every day, in hundreds of ways, we are selling you products on a logical, intellectual, factual basis. And you are being persuaded. You may never have jumped up, after watching a pen shot through a brick wall, and said, "By God, that makes sense, I'm going right out to buy that product!" But you are being convinced—slowly, carefully, logically convinced to make a conscious decision to alter or change your buying habits. You are being taught to buy false eyelashes, order automatic transmissions, vote for candidates, invest in mutual funds. There is a great mythology in America that advertising has, at best, a negligible influence on you. Nothing could be further from the truth. Today's advertising industry is the most potent and powerful mass marketing and merchandising instrument ever devised by man.

• • •

Advertising has power, all right. And advertising works, all right. And what it really boils down to is that advertising works because you believe it. You're the one who believes Josephine the Plumber really knows about stains. You're the one who believes Winston tastes good like a cigarette should. You're the one who believes Plymouth is coming through. The real question is, why do you believe all these things? And the answer is, because you don't yet understand how advertising makes you believe. You don't understand what to believe, or even how to believe advertising. Well, if you're ready to learn how to separate the wheat from the chaff, if you're ready to learn how to make advertising work *for* you, if you're ready to learn how to stop being a sucker, then you're ready to go to work.

Weasel Words: God's Little Helpers

First of all, you know what a weasel is, right? It's a small, slimy animal that eats small birds and other animals, and is especially fond of devouring vermin. Now, consider for a moment the kind of winning personality he must have. I mean, what kind of a guy would get his jollies eating rats and mice? Would you invite him to a party? Take him home to meet your mother? This is one of the slyest and most cunning of all creatures; sneaky, slippery, and thoroughly obnoxious. And so it is with great and warm personal regard for these attributes that we humby award this King of All Devious the honor of bestowing his name upon our golden sword: the weasel word.

A weasel word is "a word used in order to evade or retreat from a direct or forthright statement or position" (Webster). In other words, if we can't say it, we'll weasel it. And, in fact, a weasel word has become more than just an evasion or retreat. We've trained our weasels. They can do anything. They can make you hear things that aren't being said, accept as truths things that have only been implied, and believe things that have only been suggested. Come to think of it, not only do we have our weasels trained, but they, in turn, have got you trained. When *you* hear a weasel word, you automatically hear the implication. Not the real meaning, but the meaning *it* wants *you* to hear. So if you're ready for a little re-education, let's take a good look under a strong light at the two kinds of weasel words.

1. Words That Mean Things They Really Don't Mean

Help

That's it. "Help." It means "aid" or "assist." Nothing more. Yet, "help" is the one single word which, in all the annals of advertising, has done the most to say something that couldn't be said. Because "help" is the great qualifier; once you say it, you can say almost anything after it. In short, "help" has helped help us the most.

Helps keep you young
Helps prevent cavities
Helps keep your house germ-free

"Help" qualifies everything. You've never heard anyone say, "This product will keep you young," or "This toothpaste will positively prevent cavities for all time." Obviously, we can't say anything like that, because there aren't any products like that made. But by adding that one little word, "help," in front, we can use the strongest language possible afterward. And the most fascinating part of it is, you are immune to the word. You literally don't hear the word "help." You only hear what comes after it. And why not? That's strong language, and likely to be much more important to you than the silly little word at the front end.

I would guess that 75 percent of all advertising uses the word "help." Think, 9 for a minute, about how many times each day you hear these phrases:

Helps stop . . .
Helps prevent . . .
Helps fight . . .
Helps overcome . . .
Helps you feel . . .
Helps you look . . .

I could go on and on, but so could you. Just as a simple exercise, call it homework if you wish, tonight when you plop down in front of the boob tube for your customary three and a half hours of violence and/or situation comedies, take a pad and pencil, and keep score. See if you can count how many times the word "help" comes up during the commercials. Instead of going to the bathroom during the pause before Marcus Welby operates, or raiding the refrigerator prior to witnessing the Mob Squad wipe out a nest of dope pushers, stick with it. Count the "helps," and discover just how dirty a four-letter word can be.

Like

Coming in second, but only losing out by a nose, is the word "like," used in 10 comparison. Watch:

It's like getting one bar free
Cleans like a white tornado
It's like taking a trip to Portugal

Okay. "Like" is a qualifier, and is used in much the same way as "help." But 11 "like" is also a comparative element, with a very specific purpose; we use "like" to get you to stop thinking about the product per se, and to get you thinking about something that is bigger or better or different from the product we're selling. In other words, we can make you believe that the product is more than it is by likening it to something else.

Take a look at that first phrase, straight out of recent Ivory Soap advertising. 12 On the surface of it, they tell you that four bars of Ivory cost about the same as three bars of most other soaps. So, if you're going to spend a certain amount of money on soap, you can buy four bars instead of three. Therefore, it's like getting one bar free. Now, the question you have to ask yourself is, "Why the weasel? Why do they say 'like'? Why don't they just come out and say, 'You get one bar free'?" The answer is, of course, that for one reason or another, you really don't. Here are two possible reasons. One: sure, you get four bars, but in terms of the actual amount of soap that you get, it may very well be the same as in three bars of another brand. Remember, Ivory has a lot of air in it—that's what makes it float. And air takes up room. Room that could otherwise be occupied by more soap. So, in terms of pure product, the amount of actual soap in four bars of Ivory may be only as much as the actual amount of soap in three bars of most others. That's why we can't—or won't—come out with a straightforward declaration such as, "You get 25 percent more soap," or "Buy three bars, and get the fourth one free."

Reason number two: the actual cost and value of the product. Did it ever 13 occur to you that Ivory may simply be a cheaper soap to make and, therefore, a cheaper soap to sell? After all, it doesn't have any perfume, or hexachlorophene, or other additives that can raise the cost of manufacturing. It's plain, simple, cheap soap, and so it can be sold for less money while still maintaining a profit margin as great as more expensive soaps. By way of illustrating this, suppose you were trying to decide whether to buy a Mercedes-Benz or a Ford. Let's say the Mercedes cost $7,000, and the Ford $3,500. Now the Ford salesman comes up to you with this deal: as long as you're considering spending $7,000 on a car, buy my Ford for $7,000 and I'll give you a second Ford, free! Well, the same principle can apply to Ivory: as long as you're considering spending 35 cents on soap, buy my cheaper soap, and I'll give you more of it.

I'm sure there are other reasons why Ivory uses the weasel "like." Perhaps 14 you've thought of one or two yourself. That's good. You're starting to think.

Now, what about the wonderful white tornado? Ajax pulled that one out of 15 the hat some eight years ago, and you're still buying it. It's a classic example of the use of the word "like" in which we can force you to think, not about the product itself, but about something bigger, more exciting, certainly more powerful than a bottle of fancy ammonia. The word "like" is used here as a transfer word, which gets you away from the obvious—the odious job of getting down on your hands and knees and scrubbing your kitchen floor—and into the world of fanstasy, where we can imply that this little bottle of miracles will supply all the elbow grease you need. Isn't that the name of the game? The whirlwind activity of the tornado replacing the whirlwind motion of your arm? Think about the swirling of the tornado, and all the work it will save you. Think about the power of that devastating windstorm; able to lift houses, overturn cars, and now, pick the dirt up off your floor. And we get the license to do it simply by using the word "like."

It's a copywriter's dream, because we don't have to substantiate anything. 16 When we compare our product to "another leading brand," we'd better be able to prove what we say. But how can you compare ammonia to a windstorm? It's ludicrous. It can't be done. The whole statement is so ridiculous it couldn't be challenged by the government or the networks. So it went on the air, and it worked. Because the little word "like" let us take you out of the world of reality, and into your own fantasies.

Speaking of fantasies, how about that trip to Portugal? Mateus Rosé is ac- 17 tually trying to tell you that you will be transported clear across the Atlantic Ocean merely by sipping their wine. "Oh, come on," you say. "You don't expect me to believe that." Actually, we don't expect you to believe it. But we do expect you to get our meaning. This is called "romancing the product," and it is made possible by the dear little "like." In this case, we deliberately bring attention to the word, and we ask you to join us in setting reality aside for a moment. We take your hand and gently lead you down the path of moonlit nights, graceful dancers, and mysterious women. Are we saying that these things are all contained inside our wine? Of course not. But what we mean is, our wine is part of all this, and with a little help from "like," we'll get you to feel that way, too. So don't think of us as a bunch of peasants squashing a bunch of grapes. As a matter of fact, don't think of us at all. Feel with us.

"Like" is a virus that kills. You'd better get immune to it.   18

Other Weasels

"Help" and "like" are the two weasels so powerful that they can stand on their   19 own. There are countless other words, not quite so potent, but equally effective when used in conjunction with our two basic weasels, or with each other. Let me show you a few.

Virtual or Virtually

How many times have you responded to an ad that said: 20

Virtually trouble-free. . . .
Virtually foolproof . . .
Virtually never needs service . . .

Ever remember what "virtual" means? It means "in essence or effect, but not in fact." Important—"but not in fact." Yet today the word "virtually" is interpreted by you as meaning, "almost or just about the same as. . . ." Well, gang, it just isn't true. "Not," in fact, means not, in fact. I was scanning, rather longingly I must confess, through the brochure Chevrolet publishes for its Corvette, and I came to this phrase: "The seats in the . . . Corvette are virtually handmade." They had me, for a minute. I almost took the bait of that lovely little weasel. I almost decided that those seats were just about completely handmade. And then I remembered. Those seats were not, *in fact*, handmade. Remember, "virtually" means "not, in fact," or you will, in fact, get sold down the river.

Acts or Works

These two action words are rarely used alone, and are generally accompanied   21 by "like." They need help to work, mostly because they are verbs, but their implied meaning is deadly, nonetheless. Here are the key phrases:

Acts like . . .
Acts against . . .
Works like . . .
Works against . . .
Works to prevent (or help prevent) . . .

You see what happens? "Acts" or "works" brings an action to the product that might not otherwise be there. When we say that a certain cough syrup "acts on the cough control center," the implication is that the syrup goes to this mysterious organ and immediately makes it better. But the implication here far exceeds what the truthful promise should be. An act is simply a deed. So the claim "acts on" simply means it performs a deed on. What that deed is, we may never know.

The rule of thumb is this: if we can't say "cures" or "fixes" or use any other 22 positive word, we'll nail you with "acts like" or "works against," and get you thinking about something else. Don't.

Miscellaneous Weasels

Can Be

This is for comparison, and what we do is to find an announcer who can 23 really make it sound positive. But keep your ears open. "Crest can be of significant value when used in . . . ," etc., is indicative of an ideal situation, and most of us don't live in ideal situations.

Up To

Here's another way of expressing an ideal situation. Remember the cigarette 24 that said it was aged, or "cured for up to eight long, lazy weeks"? Well, that could, and should, be interpreted as meaning that the tobaccos used were cured anywhere from one hour to eight weeks. We like to glamorize the ideal situation; it's up to you to bring it back to reality.

As Much As

More of the same. "As much as 20 percent greater mileage" with our gasoline 25 again promises the ideal, but qualifies it.

Refreshes, Comforts, Tackles, Fights, Comes On

Just a handful of the same action weasels, in the same category as "acts" and 26 "works," though not as frequently used. The way to complete the thought here is to ask the simple question, "How?" Usually, you won't get an answer. That's because, usually, the weasel will run and hide.

Feel or the Feel of

This is the first of our subjective weasels. When we deal with a subjective 27 word, it is simply a matter of opinion. In our opinion, Naugahyde has the feel of real leather. So we can say it. And, indeed, if you were to touch leather, and then touch Naugahyde, you may very well agree with us. But that doesn't mean it is real leather, only that it feels the same. The best way to handle subjective weasels is to complete the thought yourself, by simply saying, "But it isn't." At least that way you can remain grounded in reality.

The Look of or Looks Like

"Look" is the same as "feel," our subjective opinion. Did you ever walk into a 28 Woolworth's and see those $29.95 masterpieces hanging in their "Art Gallery"?

"The look of a real oil painting," it will say. "But it isn't," you will now reply. And probably be $29.95 richer for it.

2. Words That Have No Specific Meaning

If you have kids, then you have all kinds of breakfast cereals in the house. 29 When I was a kid, it was Rice Krispies, the breakfast cereal that went snap, crackle, and pop. (One hell of a claim for a product that is supposed to offer nutritional benefits.) Or Wheaties, the breakfast of champions, whatever that means. Nowadays, we're forced to a confrontation with Quisp, Quake, Lucky Stars, Cocoa-Puffs, Clunkers, Blooies, Snarkles and Razzmatazz. And they all have one thing in common: they're all "fortified." Some are simply "fortified with vitamins," while others are specifically "fortified with vitamin D," or some other letter. But what does it all mean?

"Fortified" means "added on to." But "fortified," like so many other weasel 30 words of indefinite meaning, simply doesn't tell us enough. If, for instance, a cereal were to contain one unit of vitamin D, and the manufacturers added some chemical which would produce two units of vitamin D, they could then claim that the cereal was "fortified with twice as much vitamin D." So what? It would still be about as nutritional as sawdust.

That point is, weasel words with no specific meaning don't tell us enough, 31 but we have come to accept them as factual statements closely associated with something good that has been done to the product. Here's another example.

Flavor and Taste

These are two totally subjective words that allow us to claim marvelous things 32 about products that are edible. Every cigarette in the world has claimed the best taste. Every supermarket has advertised the most flavorful meat. And let's not forget "aroma," a subdivision of this category. Wouldn't you like to have a nickel for every time a room freshener (a weasel in itself) told you it would make your home "smell fresh as all outdoors"? Well, they can say it, because smell, like taste and flavor, is a subjective thing. And, incidentally, there are no less than three weasels in that phrase. "Smell" is the first. Then, there's "as" (a substitute for the ever-popular "like"), and, finally, "fresh," which, in context, is a subjective comparison, rather than the primary definition of "new."

Now we can use an unlimited number of combinations of these weasels for 33 added impact. "Fresher-smelling clothes." "Fresher-tasting tobacco." "Tastes like grandma used to make." Unfortunately, there's no sure way of bringing these weasels down to size, simply because you can't define them accurately. Trying to ascertain the meaning of "taste" in any context is like trying to push a rope up a hill. All you can do is be aware that these words are subjective, and represent only one opinion—usually that of the manufacturer.

Style and Good Looks

Anyone for buying a new car? Okay, which is the one with the good looks? 34 The smart new styling? What's that you say? All of them? Well, you're right.

Because this is another group of subjective opinions. And it is the subjective and collective opinion of both Detroit and Madison Avenue that the following cars have "bold new styling": Buick Riviera, Plymouth Satellite, Dodge Monaco, Mercury Brougham, and you can fill in the spaces for the rest. Subjectively, you have to decide on which bold new styling is, indeed, bold new styling. Then, you might spend a minute or two trying to determine what's going on under that styling. The rest I leave to Ralph Nader.

Different, Special, and Exclusive

To be different, you have to be not the same as. Here, you must rely on your 35 own good judgment and common sense. Exclusive formulas and special combinations of ingredients are coming at you every day, in every way. You must constantly assure yourself that, basically, all products in any given category are the same. So when you hear "special," "exclusive," or "different," you have to establish two things: on what basis are they different, and is that difference an important one? Let me give you a hypothetical example.

All so-called "permanent" antifreeze is basically the same. It is made from a 36 liquid known as ethylene glycol, which has two amazing properties: It has a lower freezing point than water, and a higher boiling point than water. It does not break down (lose its properties), nor will it boil away. And every permanent antifreeze starts with it as a base. Also, just about every antifreeze has now got antileak ingredients, as well as antirust and anticorrosion ingredients. Now, let's suppose that, in formulating the product, one of the companies comes up with a solution that is pink in color, as opposed to all the others, which are blue. Presto—an exclusivity claim. "Nothing else looks like it, nothing else performs like it." Or, how about, "Look at ours, and look at anyone else's. You can see the difference our exclusive formula makes." Granted, I'm exaggerating. But did I prove a point?

SUMMARY

A weasel word is a word that's used to imply a meaning that cannot be 37 truthfully stated. Some weasels imply meanings that are not the same as their actual definition, such as "help," "like," or "fortified." They can act as qualifiers and/or comparatives. Other weasels, such as "taste" and "flavor," have no definite meanings, and are simply subjective opinions offered by the manufacturer. A weasel of omission is one that implies a claim so strongly that it forces you to supply the bogus fact. Adjectives are weasels used to convey feelings and emotions to a greater extent than the product itself can.

In dealing with weasels, you must strip away the innuendos and try to 38 ascertain the facts, if any. To do this, you need to ask questions such as: How? Why? How many? How much? Stick to basic definitions of words. Look them up if you have to. Then, apply the strict definition to the text of the advertisement or commercial. "Like" means similar to, but not the same as. "Virtually" means the same in essence, but not in fact.

Above all, never underestimate the devious qualities of a weasel. Weasels 39 twist and turn and hide in the dark shadows. You must come to grips with them, or advertising will rule you forever.

My advice to you is: Beware of weasels. They are nasty and untrainable, and 40 they attack pocketbooks.

DISCUSSION QUESTIONS

1. What differences do you see between advertising propaganda and political propaganda? Is one more difficult to detect than the other? Why or why not?

2. In paragraph 3, Wrighter says that "there is a great mythology in America today that advertising has, at best, a negligible influence on you." What accounts for the prevalence of this attitude? Wrighter obviously feels that this idea is naive. What do *you* think?

3. Think of some popular advertising slogans, like "Coca-Cola: It's the real thing!" or "That's what Campbell's soups are—mm-mm good!" Do these slogans use any weasel words? Which ones? What accounts for the fact that these slogans have become so well known?

4. Wrighter says the word "like" is used by admen to "force you to think, not about the product, but about something bigger, more exciting, more powerful." In what ways is the use of the word "like in advertising similar to glory by association? In what ways is it different?

5. See if you can detect the "weasel" in the following statements:

   A. Three out of four doctors recommend the major ingredient in Anacin for the relief of headache pain.
   B. Lowest sticker price in America.
   C. Arrid is 1½ times as effective as any other leading deodorant tested.
   D. Prices reduced as much as 25 percent.
   E. Our paint roller holds paint like no brush can!
   F. If Nescafé can please the whole wide world, we can sure please you.
   G. Imagine feeling so good in the morning when you had that headache last night.
   H. Dentu-grip holds up to 40 percent stronger after seven hours.

6. The next time you are in a restaurant, look at the way the different foods are described in the menu. Do you see any weasel words? Which ones? Any other appeals which could correctly be called "propaganda"?

7. Weasel words are not the only things admen use to appeal to the consumer. Consider the effectiveness of the following advertising devices: a picture of a beautiful girl or good-looking young man, a picture of the product, a pretty or attention-getting picture *not* connected with the product, the use of color, the use of large or small typeface. Bring in examples of these visual appeals and comment on their usefulness as propaganda.

JOHN D. LOFTON, JR.
Does the Consumer Really Care?

In the two previous selections we have read that advertisers can use language—weasel words and legalisms—to sell you anything, if they put their minds to it. The two essays might be classed as kinds of consumer protection in that they caution buyers to beware of deceptive language.

Syndicated columnist John D. Lofton, Jr., is not so sure about that. Although he has no intention of defending either weasel words or legalisms, he does argue that the consumer is *not*, in fact, the easy target he or she is made out to be. The question he raises deals with another kind of advertising language, labeling. Do or do not most consumers know there is no real Sara Lee, Aunt Jemima, or Chef Boy-ar-dee? Lofton thinks the answer is right at hand.

You've all heard the advertising jingle "Everybody doesn't like something but   1
nobody doesn't like Sara Lee"—right?

Well, forget it. There is somebody who doesn't like Sara Lee and his name is   2
Sen. James Abourezk.

Now, it isn't just Sara Lee who bugs Sen. Abourezk, he's also down on the   3
folks at Pepperidge Farm, Wonder Bread, Dad's Root Beer, Mama Celeste's
Pizza, Minute Maid, and Madria-Madria Sangria, among others.

The reason? Well, the South Dakota Democrat thinks that consumers are   4
being tricked because these businesses "deceptively advertise themselves as small
business or family-owned business" when they are not.

He says that people often have a strong preference for buying things from
small business because they feel they get better quality items, more personal
service and prompt attention on warranty claims.

Sen. Abourezk emphasizes: "Better labeling is not the answer to this prob-   6
lem. Fine print on a product does not have the impact on consumers that mass
media advertising does.

"People should know that Minute Maid orange juice is made by Coca Cola,   7
that Madria-Madria Sangria is made by Gallo and that Wonder Bread is made by
ITT. This type of knowledge is healthy for the marketplace because consumers
can reward a socially responsible company for its positive contributions or avoid
the products of a corporation they feel is not acting in the public interests."

So, Sen. Abourezk has petitioned the Federal Trade Commission (FTC) to   8
require advertisers to disclose the name of any corporation of which they are a
division or subsidiary.

But my question is: Why? So what? Who in the real world—which I define as   9
that area outside of Washington, D.C.—honestly cares about such trivia? The
answer, as far as I've been able to determine, is: nobody.

Chuck Ludlam, the Abourezk aide who thought up this brilliant idea, tells   10
me that he knows of no survey or study showing that consumers who bought
products they thought were made by small businesses considered themselves
deceived when they later found out big business had made what they bought.

Ludlam, who—wouldn't you know it—used to work in the national advertis- 11
ing division of the FTC, says he knows of no one who has ever complained
because Dad's Root Beer doesn't say it is a product of the Illinois Central Railroad.

A spokeman for the National Federation of Independent Business, which 12
represents over 400,000 small businesses, tells me he has heard no gripes from
their members as regards this subject.

Ditto a spokeswoman at the Small Business Administration, which is gen- 13
erally familiar with the concerns of the over 9,000,000 small businessmen in
America. She says this subject is "not exactly a burning issue."

Just think about it a minute. How dumb does Sen. Abourezk think the 14
American consumer is? Does he really believe that those people who buy Pepperidge Farm products think they are actually made in that small, snow-covered
farm shown on the label?

Does he really believe that consumers believe that someone's dad makes all 15
that root beer, or that Chef Boy-ar-dee, that kindly-looking, mustachioed old
gentleman in the white hat, really cooks all that spaghetti? Or that Aunt Jemima
sweats over a hot stove all day making that pancake mix?

And what about White House applesauce? Is the senator really worrying that 16
some unsuspecting consumer may buy this product because he or she thinks it's
made in the basement at 1600 Pennsylvania Avenue?

And Kiwi shoe polish. Does anyone buy it because they believe it is manufac- 17
tured by the little, wingless bird on the can?

C'mon, senator. Give us consumers a little credit for having some intelli- 18
gence.

The reason why American business is drowning in an ocean of governmental 19
red tape is precisely because of busybodies like Sen. Abourezk, who spend their
waking hours dreaming up solutions for which there are no problems.

The Federal Trade Commission should send Sen. Abourezk's petition back 20
to him unopened, and refuse to act on it until he can prove a deceptive trade
practice by coming up with a real, live consumer who says he's been deceived.

DISCUSSION QUESTIONS

1. Do you know why you buy the brand of toothpaste (or deodorant or
detergent) that you do? Could it be because of propaganda? Why or why
not?

2. In paragraph 14, Lofton implies that people who buy Pepperidge
Farm products don't believe they are really made "in that small, snow-
covered farm shown on the label." If this is so, then why do people buy
Pepperidge Farm products? What do you consider to be a "good" reason for
purchasing a particular product brand? A "bad" reason?

3. Does knowing that Wonder Bread is made by ITT change your feeling
about the product? Do you think that knowing the truth about who really

makes the products we buy would change many consumer's buying habits? Why or why not?

4. In paragraph 7, Lofton quotes Senator Abourezk as saying that "consumers can reward a socially responsible company for its positive contributions or avoid the products of a corporation they feel is not acting in the public interests." Do you think this would be a good idea? Why or why not? Do you think many consumers would change their buying habits to conform to their social and political beliefs? Why or why not?

5. Earlier in paragraph 14 Lofton asks, "How dumb does Sen. Abourezk think the American consumer is?" Do you think Abourezk actually does think the American consumer is "dumb"? Does Lofton make a strong case against the Senator here? Is the Senator's labeling law frivolous?

6. Can the claims against consumer protection made here be extended to larger issues? Is consumer protection really only harassment of manufacturers and merchants? Is the public prepared to deal with the weasel words and legalisms that protect advertisers? Give examples.

DAWN ANN KURTH
Bugs Bunny Says They're Yummy

In the previous selection, John D. Lofton, Jr., argued that people do not take commercial advertising seriously and so they are not in danger of being deceived or misled. But what about children? Do TV commercials take unfair—and even dangerous—advantage of children's trust and inexperience?

Dawn Ann Durth was a surprise witness at a Senate subcommittee hearing in Washington on the effects of TV advertising. She was 11 years old at the time of her testimony, and her parents and her teacher insist that she received no help in preparing the following statement to the committee.

Mr. Chairman:

My name is Dawn Ann Kurth. I am 11 years old and in the fifth grade at   1
Meadowlane Elementary School in Melbourne, Florida. This year I was one of the 36 students chosen by the teachers out of 20,000 5th-through-8th graders, to do a project in the Talented Student Program in Brevard County. We were allowed to choose a project in any field we wanted. It was difficult to decide. There seem to be so many problems in the world today. What could I do?

A small family crisis solved my problem. My sister Martha, who is 7, had   2
asked my mother to buy a box of Post Raisin Bran so that she could get the free record that was on the back of the box. It had been advertised several times on

Saturday morning cartoon shows. My mother bought the cereal, and we all (there are four children in our family) helped Martha eat it so she could get the record. It was after the cereal was eaten and she had the record that the crisis occurred. There was no way the record would work.

Martha was very upset and began crying and I was angry too. It just didn't 3 seem right to me that something could be shown on TV that worked fine and people were listening and dancing to the record and when you bought the cereal, instead of laughing and dancing, we were crying and angry. Then I realized that perhaps here was a problem I could do something about or, if I couldn't change things, at least I could make others aware of deceptive advertising practices to children.

To begin my project I decided to keep a record of the number of commercials 4 shown on typical Saturday morning TV shows. There were 25 commercial messages during one hour, from 8 to 9 A.M., not counting ads for shows coming up or public service ads. I found there were only 10 to 12 commercials during shows my parents like to watch. For the first time, I really began to think about what the commercials were saying. I had always listened before and many times asked my mother to buy certain products I had seen advertised, but now I was listening and really thinking about what was being said. Millions of kids are being told:

"Make friends with Kool-aid. Kool-aid makes good friends." 5

"People who love kids have to buy Fritos." 6

"Hershey chocolate makes milk taste like a chocolate bar." Why should milk 7 taste like a chocolate bar anyway?

"Cheerios make you feel groovy all day long." I eat them sometimes and I 8 don't feel any different.

"Libby frozen dinners have fun in them." Nothing is said about the food in 9 them.

"Cocoa Krispies taste like a chocolate milk shake only they are crunchy." 10

"Lucky Charms are magically delicious with sweet surprises inside." Those 11 sweet surprises are marshmallow candy.

I think the commercials I just mentioned are examples of deceptive advertis- 12 ing practices.

Another type of commercial advertises a free bonus gift if you buy a certain 13 product. The whole commercial tells about the bonus gift and says nothing about the product they want you to buy. Many times, as in the case of the record, the bonus gift appears to be worthless junk or isn't in the package. I wrote to the TV networks and found it costs about $4,000 for a 30-second commercial. Many of those ads appeared four times in each hour. I wonder why any company would spend $15,000 or $20,000 an hour to advertise worthless junk.

The ads that I have mentioned I consider deceptive. However, I've found 14 others I feel are dangerous.

Bugs Bunny vitamin ads say their vitamins "taste yummy" and taste good. 15

Chocolate Zestabs says their product is "delicious" and compare taking it 16 with eating a chocolate cookie.

If my mother were to buy those vitamins, and my little sister got to the   17
bottles, I'm sure she would eat them just as if they were candy.

I do not know a lot about nutrition, but I do know that my mother tries to   18
keep our family from eating so many sweets. She says they are bad for our teeth.
Our dentist says so too. If they are bad, why are companies allowed to make
children want them by advertising on TV? Almost all of the ads I have seen
during children's programs are for candy, or sugar-coated cereal, or even sugar-
coated cereal with candy in it.

I know people who make these commercials are not bad. I know the com-   19
mercials pay for TV shows and I like to watch TV. I just think that it would be as
easy to produce a good commercial as a bad one. If there is nothing good that can
be said about a product that is the truth, perhaps the product should not be sold
to kids on TV in the first place.

I do not know all the ways to write a good commercial, but I think commer-   20
cials would be good if they taught kids something that was true. They could teach
about good health, and also about where food is grown. If my 3-year-old sister
can learn to sing, "It takes two hands to handle a whopper 'cause the burgers are
better at Burger King," from a commercial, couldn't a commercial also teach her
to recognize the letters of the alphabet, numbers, and colors? I am sure that
people who write commercials are much smarter than I and they should be able
to think of many ways to write a commercial that tells the truth about a product
without telling kids they should eat because it is sweeter or "shaped like fun"
(what shape *is* fun, anyway?) or because Tony Tiger says so.

I also think kids should not be bribed to buy a product by commercials telling   21
of the wonderful free bonus gift inside.

I think kids should not be told to eat a certain product because a well-known   22
hero does. If this is a reason to eat something, then, when a well-known person
uses drugs, should kids try drugs for the same reason?

Last of all, I think vitamin companies should never, never be allowed to   23
advertise their product as being delicious, yummy, or in any way make children
think they are candy. Perhaps these commercials could teach children the dangers of taking drugs or teach children that, if they do find a bottle of pills, or if the
medicine closet is open, they should run and tell a grown-up, and never, never
eat the medicine.

I want to thank the Committee for letting me appear. When I leave   24
Washington, the thing that I will remember for the rest of my life is that some
people *do* care what kids think. I know I could have led a protest about commercials through our shopping center and people would have laughed at me or
thought I needed a good spanking or wondered what kind of parents I had that
would let me run around in the streets protesting. I decided to gather my information and write letters to anyone I thought would listen. Many of them didn't
listen, but some did. That is why I am here today. Because some people cared
about what I thought. I hope now that I can tell every kid in America that when
they see a wrong, they shouldn't just try to forget about it and hope it will go
away. They should begin to do what they can to change it.

People will listen. I know, because you're here listening to me.   25

DISCUSSION QUESTIONS

1. Dawn Ann Kurth discusses advertisements aimed at one particular kind of consumer group—children. What other consumer groups do ads appeal to? Can you think of any ads that specialize their appeals in this way?

2. What kind of consumer group might you belong to? Do you find that ads directed at your consumer group influence you more than others? Why or why not?

3. Do commercials for children use the same kind of appeals as commercials for adults? What are they? Are there any appeals used in children's commercials that would *not* work with adults?

4. Have you ever bought anything because of an offer of a "free gift"? Was the "free gift" really worth anything? What is the appeal of "free gift offers"?

5. In paragraphs 5 through 11, Dawn Ann Kurth gives a list of children's commercials that she considers deceptive. Do you agree that these statements are misleading? Why or why not? Discuss each one, commenting on the appeals used.

6. In paragraph 4, Dawn Ann Kurth mentions that she counted twenty-five commercial messages on a typical one-hour children's show, as compared to ten to twelve commercials during programs for adults. Can you think of any explanation for this?

Student Essay
What Is Avon Calling to Me?

When I was first given the assignment to analyze the propaganda of advertising I thought I would search out the ways in which advertising insulted women. Remembering the "No Comment" section of *Ms. Magazine*, I started to look for oversexed, incompetent, or dumb women in ads from television and magazines. I found relatively few examples, perhaps because I did not have the time to watch daytime television. What I found instead was that many ads insult women while outwardly pretending to flatter us. And most often this insult came from the unmistakable suggestions that we could not resist flattery and were incapable of following logic.

After four days of watching television ads with notebook in hand, I found that I had about ten examples of this kind of advertising, but the one I saw most was an Avon commercial that begins with a chic, highcheekboned model (barely stifling a giggle) saying, "I sell Avon, and I never felt so good." (What makes her feel so good? Meeting people? The commissions she makes?) After we hear the trademarked doorbell, the camera shows us a fashionably dressed housewife and her cutesy-poo daughter. Instead of dialogue, we hear a chorus, dominated by male voices, crooning, "Yoooouuuuu, you never looked so good." The saleslady helps the customer try on some make-up. Then the camera cuts to another highcheekboned model's face, this time a black one. She's happy and beautiful too as she tries on some make-up. The chorus is still insisting, "Yoooouuuuu, you never looked so good." And before the sequence is over, the cutesy-poo daughter has come up behind the chic-model-saleslady and put her hands over her eyes—careful not to muss her hair, which looks as though it has been freshly done by Mr. Kenneth. Everyone laughs; it's the end of the ad.

What was the ad *trying* to tell us? The argument seems to run something like this. The women who sell Avon are chic, sweet-tempered ladies who will be fun to have in your house. They come to help you look as beautiful as they are, not to take your money (selling cosmetics that run a bit higher than comparable items in department stores). And without actually saying it, they also seem to mean that people will be saying to you after you use Avon cosmetics, "Yoooouuuuu, you never looked so good." 3

How well does the ad match with our experience? Avon is sold door-to-door, and most people hate door-to-door salespersons; thus at least part of the ad is directed toward helping us overcome our distaste for the salespeople. And Avon is probably the most successful of all the companies selling door-to-door, apparently because the company uses women from the neighborhood instead of men from God knows where. That's why my mother buys Avon products: she wants to help out Mrs. Baldwin, a neighbor whose husband left her with three children and hasn't heard from in several years. Mrs. Baldwin would never be the model for anything except the "Before" panels in Ayds ads. And I don't think she feels especially good; she is usually popping Gelusils when she comes to visit my mother. And neither does my mother look or feel especially good after Mrs. Baldwin leaves because she has usually bought some expensive cosmetics she doesn't really need. 4

But the improbability of this ad is not what bothers me about it. Instead, I am really annoyed by the use of two old tricks of propaganda: flattery and ill-logic. 5

The flattery is the crude, "Yoooouuuuu, you never looked so good." Technically, this is called *argumentum ad populum* or "stroking." Much of the ad is devoted to telling us women we are beautiful. Are we beautiful because we're us or because we use Avon? Cosmetics, skillfully applied, can do a lot for most women, but they can't perform miracles. And they don't do anything for those of us who prefer the natural look. But even for those women who want to pay for the whole treatment, no cosmetics can make up for what nature failed to give them. I wonder if ads like these make them unhappier with the faces they already have. Now they also have the increased desire for a face they can't have, a face that wins compliments. 6

Finally, there are two problems in logic, both of them *non sequitors*. The first is the model's statement, "I sell Avon, and I never felt so good." What is the relationship between the two clauses in the sentence? "And" does not mean "because." In fact, there is not any necessary connection between selling Avon and feeling good, but the ad tries hard to insinuate it. We see a woman who sells 7

Avon and she's happy—as well as beautiful, self-confident, and prosperous—at least prosperous enough to buy fine clothes. The second *non sequitur* is subtler: it encourages us to think that we can be all those things if we use Avon too. Without actually stating it, the ad implies that if we will only buy some Avon products the whole world will be singing to us, "Yoooouuuuu, you never looked so good."

I have nothing against Avon products, but I don't believe their advertising. 8

RHETORICAL ANALYSIS

1. Did the author make a wise choice in beginning on a personal note, "When I was first given the assignment to analyze . . . "? Is her comment about searching out ads which insult women germaine to the introduction?

2. Is the author's use of "highcheekboned" (paragraph 2) as one word a kind of propaganda? What would she have lost if she had written the standard "high-cheekboned"? What is she trying to imply about cheekbones?

3. Paragraphs 3 and 4 ask rhetorical questions about the effect of Avon advertisement. Has the author given adequate answers to the questions she raises?

4. Does the author use any propagandistic devices in describing the Avon saleslady, Mrs. Baldwin? Can you assume what she looks like? How might she want to describe herself?

5. Is the author justified in keeping paragraph 5 so short? Would it be more effective if it were developed more?

6. Is this essay written in a conversational tone? Could it be read aloud or said? Are there any sentences which by their very construction show that the author composed them in quiet, working them out phrase by phrase? How would you characterize the author's sense of sentence variety?

POINTS OF DEPARTURE: A Propaganda Sampler.

A

An American journalist noted for his use of name calling is William Loeb, publisher of The Manchester (New Hampshire) Union Leader. Here is a sample of names and other invective he has applied to some prominent figures.

BELLA S. ABZUG, Congresswoman from New York: "A Prize Jerk," "The pot-bellied, porcine-featured Congresswomen."

JAMES B. CONANT, former president of Harvard University: "An educated ignoramus."

JOHN FOSTER DULLES, former U.S. Secretary of State: "Dulles, Duller, Dullest."

DWIGHT D. EISENHOWER, former President of the U.S.: "Dopey Dwight," "That stinking hypocrite," "As much backbone and substance as a ribbon of toothpaste," "Fatuous—fat-headed," "A slick general on the political make."

BETTY B. FORD, former First Lady of the U.S.: "A disgrace to the White House," "Babblin' Betty."

GERALD R. FORD, former President of the U.S.: "Jerry the Jerk," "Jerry IS a Jerk."

SEYMOUR HERSH, reporter for *The New York Times*: "The ineffable ass."

LYNDON B. JOHNSON, former President of the U.S.: "Snake oil Lyndon."

JACQUELINE B. KENNEDY, former First Lady of the U.S.: "Unspeakable—uneatable."

JOHN F. KENNEDY, former President of the U.S.: "Calamity Jack," "No. 1 Liar in the U.S.A."

HENRY M. KISSENGER, former U.S. Secretary of State: "Kissinger the Kike?"

ROBERT McNAMARA, former U.S. Secretary of Defense: "Blubbering Bob."

EDMUND S. MUSKIE, U.S. Senator from Maine: "Flip-flop Muskie," "Moscow Muskie."

NELSON A. ROCKEFELLER, former Vice President of the U.S.: "Wife swapper," "Home wrecker," "Kennedy's alter ego, errand boy and all-around flunky," "Nelson the Knife."

MARGARET CHASE SMITH, former U.S. Senator from Maine: "Moscow Maggie," "State of Maine's liability."

BARBARA WALTERS, TV newscaster: "A shameless huckster," "A hussy."

Collected by Kevin Cash, from Who The Hell Is William Loeb?

B

Astrological Research News Bulletin

Newest Discovery by ————May be the Biggest in the History of Astrology ("Interview" with "Lady Luck," Cary Franks)

Question: What did you find out as a result of your investigation of fortunate people?

Answer: We confirmed what we had already suspected—that most fortunate people got that way by using astrology. Professional astrologers will tell you that nearly all rich and famous people past and present, use astrologers. Even present and historic world leaders use or have used astrology. . . .

Question: I understand you have combined astrology with numerology (a related field to astrology) as a result of your research. That's a first, isn't it?

Answer: Yes. We found that numerology is a very useful tool in producing good luck.

For example, the letters in the alphabet have assigned numbers. Singer Dionne Warwicke took the advice from her numerologist and added an "e" to the end of her name. Her numerologist told her this would bring about the correct, fortunate combination.

She immediately skyrocketed to fame. . . .

I'm not exaggerating when I say that we were able to turn people into winners who had never won anything in their lives. . . . We were able to increase the good luck in over 95% of our research subjects. In other words, I will go out on the limb and say that although some people are luckier than others, there is a 95% chance that their luck horoscope will guarantee that they get all the potential luck that they have coming.

From a newspaper advertisement

C.

Dear Mr.————,

Frankly, you're someone magazines such as *Harper's, They New Yorker, and* 1 Time most want as a subscriber. Judging from the neighborhood you live in, you're far above average in means, intellect and influence among all those who live in————and nearby areas.

Thus,————magazine wants to offer you worthwhile benefits not nor- 2 mally given by magazines. To be sure, there is a moneysaving basic subscription rate, just 50¢ an issue, rather than $1.00 at newsstands. *You save half.*

• • •

Here—in just an hour or two a week—is the most respected source for a busy, 3 intelligent person like yourself to keep informed on the events and ideas that affect our lives.

• • •

To order, use the form already typed in your name. Simply fill in the number 4 of weeks you want————magazine and mail in the postage-free envelope today. Hurry! To receive the————correspondents' "Little Black Book of the Best" free, your order must be postmarked by October 15."

From a magazine subscription appeal

D

We hold the future of peace in the world and our own future in our hands. 1

Let us reject, therefore, the policies of those who whine and whimper about 2 our frustrations and call on us to turn inward. Let us not turn away from greatness. . . .

[In] the cemetery in Leningrad I visited . . . I saw the picture of a 12-year- 3 old girl. She was a beautiful child. Her name was Tanya. I read her diary. It tells the terrible story of war. In the simple words of a child, she wrote of the deaths of the members of her family—Senya in December, Granny in January, then Yenka, then Uncle Basha, then Uncle Leosha, then Mama in May.

And finally these were the last words in her diary: "All are dead, only Tanya is 4 left."

Let us think of Tanya and of the other Tanyas and their brothers and sisters 5 everywhere in Russia and in China and in America as we proudly meet our reponsibilities for leadership in the world in a way worthy of a great people. . . .

From a speech by a Presidential candidate accepting the party nomination.

E

Sex education is, of course, the most pertinent case in point, with some   1
educators claiming it is sound practice to teach "the facts of life" as biology alone
(indispensable enlightenment for our times); what's more, they loudly protest
there is no relationship between their methods and promiscuity.

Yet, the facts are disheartening, to say the least.   2

At a time when youngsters know more about sex than any preceding genera-   3
tion, we have more venereal disease, more teen-age pregnancies, more teen-age
prostitution, more rape and generally, more sex-related problems than at any
other time in history. If the advocates of sex education as now taught consider
this an endorsement of their approach, then I think they're more in need of
"instruction" than their childish charges.

From a columnist in a local U.S. newspaper

F

OUR CIGARETTE IS MORE.

Compare your cigarette to ours and you'll find that ours is More . . .

Long, lean and burnished brown, More has more style. It has more flavor. It
has more . . .

They smoke slower and draw easy for more enjoyment . . .

They're More.

From a cigarette advertisement

G

Well, it may take a constitutional amendment after all. The Senate spent   1
nine months wrangling over proposals to curtail or to prohibit racial-balance
busing, and at the end of nine days the result is very nearly zero. The language
adopted is as toothless as a newborn babe.

The Senators opposed to racial-balance busing never could muster enough   2
vote to strike directly at the source of the evil. The source is the federal ju-
diciary. . . .

Given a few more votes in opposition to this pernicious practice, Sen. Jesse   3
Helms of North Carolina might have made an assault that would have stopped
racial-balance busing in its tracks. . . .

And where is the black child this morning?   4

Why sir, he is being bused past a school half a mile from his home because   5
he is black. The identical lunacy sweeps up the white child as well. In cities
across the land, little children stand in the gray light of dawn waiting for buses
that will take them to schools where they will take other buses. And this is solely
because of their race. The architects of apartheid in Johannesburg and Capetown
must look across the seas with positive admiration in their eyes. . . .

From a newspaper editorial on busing

H

... protests over public-school textbooks are surfacing in every corner of   1
America. . . .

Parents have been asked to pay and pay, but are told to leave the education of   2
their children "to the experts." The question should not be how good are the
experts but what kind of an education parents want their children to have. Adolf
Hitler had his experts, often brilliant scholars with impressive degrees after their
names, who prescribed curricula and textbooks designed to fashion the Nazi
mind. In Moscow there is a Ministry of Education composed of equally brilliant
experts whose job it is to manipulate the minds of Soviet youth. The point is that
there are always experts willing to carry out the wishes of those in power. . . .

Kanawha County was told that it must buy books larded with "inter-ethnic   3
and inter-cultural" concepts. . . . What this meant . . . was introduction into
the schools of "authors" like Communist rapist Eldridge Cleaver; pimp, drug
addict, and racist demagogue Malcolm X; and the work of Communist Angela
Davis's erstwhile "lover," George Jackson.

Fortunately, the collectivists did not count on the perseverance of Mrs. Alice   4
Moore. . . . When the texts were approved, this wife of a Christian pastor,
herself the mother of four children, launched a campaign to rescind the decision
and rid the schools of the radical books. . . .

As the textbook controversy continues to rage, "Liberals" are arguing that
fanatics are seeking "censorship." But it is hardly censorship to prefer one book to
another. . . .

From an article in a magazine of political opinion

I

Why are there no negro violinists, classic toe dancers, champion gymnasts,   1
skiers, swimmers, skaters, trapeze performers, chess, billiard or bridge players,
symphony orchestras? White patronage of negro pugilists and most negro "enter-
tainers" is a national disgrace. The negro entertainer would starve to death if he
had to depend on negro patronage.

With the building of the Central Pacific Railroad in the far West after the   2
Civil War, about 15,000 Chinese were imported for cheap labor. They were paid
$1 a day, about half of what a white man would have received. Around the turn
of the century, the Orientals, who are a thrifty, intelligent and industrious race,
began buying farms and establishing their own businesses in California,
Washington and Oregon. Whites began raising the cry of "YELLOW PERIL!"
The Chinese Exclusion Act was passed. It was California Attorney General Earl
Warren who prosecuted and was instrumental in the removal of American-born
Orientals to interior concentration camps and expropriation of their property, in
1942.

Now the Westerners, headed by Earl Warren, Senator Kuchel of California,
and Senator Morse of Oregon, are heartily embracing the BLACK PERIL,

which is many times worse an evil than the yellow peril ever was, or ever could be. If Westerners have a Yellow Chinese Exclusion Act, why shouldn't the South have a Black Negro Exclusion Act? Warren, Kuchel and Morse have the unmitigated gall to accuse the South of RACE DISCRIMINATION!

From a privately published pamphlet on race relations

J

Buffalo Bill, the famous Indian scout, said there were over 300 treaties made   1
with the Indians, and added: "NO INDIAN EVER BROKE A TREATY, AND NO WHITE MAN EVER KEPT ONE."

When we see negroes here jumping up and down, clapping hands, staging   2
restaurant sit-ins, chanting "freedom" and "rights," robbing, raping and murdering white women, rioting and looting, we cannot help but wonder what would have happened to the Indians if they had employed such tactics against the white man 100 to 200 years ago. Furthermore, where would this nation be today if our ancestors had the mentality and backbone of our presentday leadership, and been soft on such utter nonsense.

What a strange quirk of history and fate that the white race, who took the   3
Indian's land by bloody force, and almost exterminated the red race as brutally as any aggression in history, is now trying to destroy his own race by integrating with the black race whom he brought here as his slave!

From a privately published pamphlet on race relations.

K

WANTED FOR CONSPIRACY TO MURDER! County Executive   1
_____ _____! If all goes according to plan, this smiling man will soon become one of the biggest drug pushers in the country, and one of the biggest murderers! _____is part of a nationwide apparatus directed by the psychotic Rockefeller family, presently pushing for nuclear confrontation with the Soviet Union, and the creation of police states in the USA and Europe through CIA agencies. . . . The hysteria created by the collapse of their dollar empire is driving these madmen to use every terror tactic in the book. . . . The use of brainwashed zombies to attempt the assassination of President Ford, or methadone addicts to rape your daughter are all fair play for Rocky. . . .

If you don't move now to organize with the _____Party to destroy this   2
hideous apparatus you are condemning your children to a 1984 world of fascist oppression and ecological holocaust. . . .

From a political-party handout

WRITING ASSIGNMENTS

Essays

1. Write a political speech on a controversial issue (such as busing, abortion, legalizing marijuana, etc.), using as many propaganda devices as you can. *Don't* try to be reasonable or fair. Play dirty: appeal to emotion rather than reason; use faulty logic instead of reasoned argument; use false authority but provide no valid support for your statements. Try to distract the reader's attention from the real issues. (It might be interesting to have everyone read these speeches to the class and see how much of the propaganda the other class members can detect.)

2. Advertising is a big and influential business, as several of the selections in this chapter have shown. Write a paper discussing the impact of advertising on our economic, cultural, and social habits and beliefs.

3. Think of any recent changes you may have had in your own habits and desires. Were any of these due to propaganda? Explain.

4. Write an analysis of a piece of political propaganda, especially something lengthy, such as a handbill or pamphlet. Identify slanted language and biased selection of details as well as specific propaganda devices. (You may find rereading Birk and Birk's article *"Selection, Slanting and Charged Language"* in Chapter 2 helpful for this assignment.)

5. Many people are angered to the point of violence by commercial interruptions of TV programs. But a few people insist that they *like* TV commercials and find them entertaining. Write a paper considering the value of TV ads as entertainment. You many want to include a discussion of ads as fantasy and wish fulfillment.

6. Following the example of the student essay on Avon advertising, keep a notebook in hand as you watch television advertising. If you have a cassette recorder, you might try taping it. How much of its appeal is classifiable under the D. W. Cross article on propaganda? Is any part of its appeal harder to classify?

7. Try to get a copy of Aldous Huxley's *Brave New World,* which is still available in paperback and also in most libraries. Are the people in the book heavily under the sway of any kind of propaganda? Do you feel they are in any way like the people in our society? Explain.

8. Consult back issues of the magazine called *Vital Speeches*, which is available in most college and public libraries. Compare other speeches by Richard Nixon and Jimmy Carter. Do they always talk the way they do in the speeches reprinted in this book?

9. While looking through *Vital Speeches*, look into the oratory of some other figures, especially those you might be inclined to dislike and thus read more critically. What propaganda devices do you find in their speeches? Do they use more or fewer than Nixon and Carter?

10. Write your own definition, with examples, of one of the political terms discussed by Safire in his article.

JOURNAL KEEPING

1. Glittering generalities are also known as "blah words" because they are so vague and indefinite as to be almost meaningless (discussion of glittering generalities is on pages 181–182). Listen to a political speech or advertisement and jot down a few sentences that you think contain glittering generalities. Then rewrite the sentences, substituting "blah" for each word that seems to have no firm meaning. Example:

> In order to preserve justice and our great democratic system, I pledge to institute a campaign against the permissiveness that threatens to destroy our intellectual and spiritual freedom.

This could translate to:

> In order to preserve blah and our blah blah blah, I pledge to institute a blah against the blah that threatens to destroy our blah and blah blah.

How much meaning is left when you have finished?

2. Make a "blah" dictionary of glittering generalities that are used often or particularly effectively. Try to definite what the "blah" word means in the context of one particular speech or advertisement. See if you can find other contexts where the same word seems to be used to mean something completely different. Do you think one meaning is more valid than the other?

3. Cut out advertisements, newspaper articles, and texts of political speeches and paste them in your journal. Comment on the propaganda devices that are used.

4. In paragraph 9 of his article on "weasel words," Carl P. Wrighter challenges you to "plop down in front of the boob tube . . . and keep score" of weasels. Take up the challenge and make a list of all the weasels you can detect in commercials during an hour of TV time. Ask a friend to watch the same program and take note also. Afterward, compare your notes. What weasels did you miss? Why do you think you missed them?

5. Get a copy of Shakespeare's *Julius Caesar* from the library and study the famous speech by Marc Antony in Act III, scene 1. What propaganda devices does Antony use? Is his appeal mostly to emotion or to reason through the use of faulty logic? You might also want to analyze some of Lady Macbeth's speeches for examples of effective use of propaganda.

6 "How Can I Look It Up If I Don't Know How to Spell?" Dictionaries—Etymology, Levels of Usage, and the Fluctuating Meanings of Words

CLASSROOM EXERCISE

Although every college freshman has used a dictionary at some time or another, most do not know how to find all the information a dictionary provides. Once they look further into "*the* dictionary," students are dismayed to find that not all of them say the same thing. To see how widely dictionaries differ, have the members of the class check the works below in their dictionaries. If you cannot find the kind of information asked for, consult the figure on pages 240–241, to make sure you are reading the dictionary carefully. If your dictionary does not provide the kind of information asked for, it is probably inadequate for your needs in college.

1. Which spellings of the following words does your dictionary prefer? It may give both or more, but it has to give first preference to one.
A. Theater/theatre B. Judgment/judgement C. Catsup/ketchup D. Gages/gauges E. Catty-cornered/kitty-cornered F. Catalog/catalogue.

2. From which languages do the following words derive?
A. Buccaneer B. Penguin C. Jumbo D. Slob E. Goober F. Sauna G. Coach H. Bedlam I. Gerrymander

3. What is the preferred pronunciation of the following words? (Many dictionaries give the guide to pronunciation symbols at the bottom of each page.)
A. Harass B. Caribbean C. Comparable D. Lamentable E. Don Quixote

4. What are the regional or subject labels of the following words? Some words mean what they mean only in certain parts of the English-speaking world or in certain professions.
A. Lagniappe B. Censer C. Oxter D. Spanner E. Defense mechanism F. Xylan

deep | defense mechanism

345

(annotation labels: order of definitions · usage label · pronunciation · part of speech · derived terms · inflected forms · reference to further etymology)

deep (dēp) adj. **deeper, deepest. 1.** Extending to or located at: **a.** An unspecified distance below a surface. **b.** A specified distance below a surface. **2.** Extending from front to rear, or inward from the outside, for: **a.** An unspecified distance. **b.** A specified distance. **3.** Arising from or penetrating to a depth. **4.** Far distant. **5. a.** Difficult to fathom or understand; obscure. **b.** Learned; understanding; wise. **c.** Cunning; crafty; sly. **6. a.** Profound; intense; extreme. **b.** Profoundly absorbed or immersed. **7.** Dark rather than pale in shade. See color. **8.** Low in pitch; resonant. —**go off the deep end.** Informal. To act recklessly or hysterically. —**in deep water.** In trouble. —n. **1.** Any deep place on land or in a body of water, especially in the ocean and over 3,000 fathoms in depth: the Mindanao Deep. **2.** The most intense or extreme part. **3.** A distance estimated in fathoms between successive marks on a sounding line: by the deep, 11. —**the deep.** Poetic. The ocean. —adv. **1.** Deeply; profoundly. **2.** Well on in time; late: worked deep into the night. —**in deep.** Informal. Completely committed. [Middle English dep, Old English dēop. See dheu-¹ in Appendix.*] —**deep'ly** adv. —**deep'ness** n.

deep-dyed (dēp'dīd') adj. Unmitigated; absolute.

deep-en (dē'pən) v. **-ened, -ening, -ens.** —tr. To make deep or deeper. —intr. To become deep or deeper. —**deep'en-er** n.

Deep-freeze (dēp'frēz') n. **1.** A trademark for a refrigerator designed to freeze and store food for long periods. **2.** Often small d. Informal. Storage in, or as if in, a Deepfreeze.

deep-fry (dēp'frī') tr.v. **-fried, -frying, -fries.** To fry by immersing in a deep pan of fat or oil.

deep-root-ed (dēp'rōō'tĭd, -rŏŏt'ĭd) adj. Firmly implanted.

deep-sea (dēp'sē') adj. Pertaining to deep parts of the sea.

deep-seat-ed (dēp'sē'tĭd) adj. Deeply rooted; ingrained.

Deep South. Also **deep South.** The southeasternmost part of the United States; especially, the Confederate heartland of South Carolina, Georgia, Alabama, and Mississippi.

deep space. The regions beyond the moon, encompassing interplanetary, interstellar, and intergalactic space.

deer (dîr) n., pl. **deer** or **deers. 1.** Any of various hoofed ruminant mammals of the family Cervidae, characteristically having deciduous antlers borne only by the males. **2.** Any of various smaller deerlike mammals, such as the mouse deer. [Middle English der, animal, beast, deer, Old English dēor. See dheu-¹ in Appendix.*]

deer fly. Any of various blood-sucking flies of the genus Chrysops, having dark bars or spots on the wings.

deer grass. A plant, the meadow beauty (see).

deer-hound (dîr'hound') n. A dog of a breed developed in Scotland, resembling a greyhound but larger and having a wiry coat. Also called "Scottish deerhound."

deer mouse. Any of various New World mice of the genus Peromyscus, having large ears, white feet and underparts, and a

de-fea-sance (dĭ-fē'zəns) n. **1.** An annulment or rendering void. **2.** The voiding of a contract or deed. **3.** A clause within a contract or deed providing for annulment. [Middle English defesance, from Old French desfesance, from desfaire, present participle of desfaire, to destroy, DEFEAT.]

de-fea-si-ble (dĭ-fē'zə-bəl) adj. Of that which may be annulled or terminated. —**de-fea'si-bil'i-ty, de-fea'si-ble-ness** n.

de-feat (dĭ-fēt') tr.v. **-feated, -feating, -feats. 1.** To win victory over; vanquish. **2.** To prevent the success of; thwart. **3.** Law. To annul or make void. —n. **1.** The act of defeating or state of being defeated. **2.** Failure to win; overthrow. **3.** A coming to naught; frustration. **4.** Law. A making null and void. [Middle English defeten, from Old French desfaire (past participle desfait), from Medieval Latin disfacere, to undo, destroy : Latin dis- (reversal) + facere, to do, make (see dhē-¹ in Appendix*).] —**de-feat'er** n.

Synonyms: defeat, conquer, vanquish, beat, rout, subdue, subjugate, overcome. These verbs mean to get the better of an adversary. Defeat, the most general, does not necessarily imply finality of outcome. Conquer suggests decisive wide-scale victory. Vanquish emphasizes total and final mastery. Beat, less formal, is often the equivalent of defeat, though beat may convey greater emphasis. Rout implies not only complete victory but also putting an adversary to flight. Subdue suggests mastery and control by suppression or taming. Subjugate more strongly implies making an opponent subservient. Overcome stresses the importance of the conquest to the victor's well-being and often implies courage and perseverance.

de-feat-ism (dĭ-fē'tĭz'əm) n. Acceptance of, or resignation to, the prospect of defeat. —**de-feat'ist** n.

def-e-cate (dĕf'ə-kāt') v. **-cated, -cating, -cates.** —intr. To void feces from the bowels. —tr. To clarify (a chemical solution). [Latin dēfaecāre : dē- (removal) + faex, dregs, FECES.] —**def'e-ca'tion** n. —**def'e-ca'tor** (-kā'tər) n.

de-fect (dē'fĕkt', dĭ-fĕkt') n. **1.** The lack of something necessary or desirable; deficiency. **2.** An imperfection; a failing; fault. —intr.v. (dĭ-fĕkt') **defected. -fect-ing. -fects.** To leave, without consent or permission, an allegiance which one had espoused or acknowledged. [Middle English, from Old French, from Latin dēfectus, deficiency, lack, from the past participle of dēficere, to remove from, desert, fail, be wanting : dē-, away from + facere, to do, set (see dhē-¹ in Appendix*).] —**de-fec'tion** n. —**de-fec'tor** (-fĕk'tər) n.

de-fec-tive (dĭ-fĕk'tĭv) adj. Abbr. **def. 1.** Lacking perfection; having a defect; faulty. See Usage note below. **2.** Grammar. Lacking one or more of the inflected forms normal for a particular category of word. In English, may is a defective verb. **3.** Of subnormal intelligence. —n. **1.** Something imperfect or damaged. **2.** Someone mentally incapacitated. —**de-fec'tive-ly** adv. —**de-fec'tive-ness** n.

deer·skin (dîr'skin') *n.* **1.** Leather made from the hide of a deer. **2.** A garment made from such leather.

deer's-tongue (dîrz'tŭng') *n.* A tall plant, *Frasera speciosa*, of western North America, having whorls of greenish flowers.

deer·weed (dîr'wēd') *n.* Any of several bushlike, yellow-flowered plants of the genus *Lotus*, of southwestern North America, sometimes used as forage in arid regions.

de·es·ca·late (dē'ĕs'kə-lāt') *tr.v.* **-lated, -lating, -lates.** To decrease the scope or intensity of (a war). —**de·es·ca·la'tion** *n.*

def. **1.** defective. **2.** defendant. **3.** defense. **4.** deferred. **5.** definite. **6.** definition.

de·face (di-fās') *tr.v.* **-faced, -facing, -faces. 1.** To spoil or mar the surface or appearance of; disfigure. **2.** To impair the usefulness, value, or influence of. **3.** To efface or obliterate. [Middle English *defacen*, from Old French *desfacier* : *des-*, from Latin *dē-* (undoing, ruin) + *face*, FACE.] —**de·face'ment** *n.* —**de·fac'er** *n.*

de fac·to (dē fǎk'tō). **1.** In reality or fact; actually. **2. a.** Actual. **b.** Actually exercising power. Compare **de jure.** [Latin, "from the fact."]

de·fal·cate (di-fǎl'kāt', di-fôl'kāt', dĕf'əl-kāt') *intr.v.* **-cated, -cating, -cates.** To misuse funds; embezzle. [Medieval Latin *dēfalcāre*, to cut off : Latin *dē-*, off + *falx* (stem *falc-*), sickle (see **falcate**).] —**de·fal·ca'tion** *n.* —**de·fal'ca'tor** *n.*

def·a·ma·tion (dĕf'ə-mā'shən) *n.* Calumny; slander or libel. —**de·fam'a·to·ry** (-tôr'ē, -tōr'ē) *adj.*

de·fame (di-fām') *tr.v.* **-famed, -faming, -fames.** To attack the good name of by slander or libel. —See Synonyms at **malign.** [Middle English *diffamen, defamen*, from Old French *diffamer, defamer*, from Latin *diffāmāre* : *dis-* (undoing, ruin) + *fāma*, report, fame (see **bha-²** in Appendix*).] —**de·fam'er** *n.*

de·fault (di-fôlt') *n.* **1.** A failure to perform a task or fulfill an obligation; especially, failure to meet a financial obligation. **2.** Failure to make a required appearance in court. **3.** The failure of one or more competitors or teams to participate in a contest: *win by default.* —Through the failure, absence, or lack of. —*v.* **defaulted, -faulting, -faults.** —*intr.* **1.** To fail to do that which is required. **2.** To fail to pay money when it is due. **3.** *Law.* **a.** To fail to appear in a court when summoned. **b.** To lose a case by not appearing. **4.** *Sports.* To fail to compete in or complete a scheduled contest. —*tr.* **1.** To fail to perform or pay. **2.** To fail to take part in or complete, as a contest. **3.** *Law.* To lose (a case) by failing to take part in it. [Middle English *defaute*, from Old French *defaute*, from Vulgar Latin *dēfallita* (unattested), from *dēfallire* (unattested), from *dē-* (intensive) + *fallire* (unattested), variant of Latin *fallere*, to fail (see **fail**).] —**de·fault'er** *n.*

Usage: *Defective* applies especially to what has a discernible fault and is therefore primarily concerned with quality. *Deficient* refers to insufficiency or incompleteness and is therefore basically a quantitative term associated with *deficit*.

de·fend (di-fĕnd') *v.* **-fended, -fending, -fends.** —*tr.* **1.** To protect from danger, attack, or harm; to shield; guard. **2.** To support or maintain, as by argument or action; justify. **3.** *Law.* **a.** To represent (the defendant) in a civil or criminal case. **b.** To contest (a legal action or claim). —*intr.* To make a defense. [Middle English *defenden*, from Old French *defendre*, from Latin *dēfendere*, to ward off. See **gwhen-¹** in Appendix.*] —**de·fend'a·ble** *adj.* —**de·fend'er** *n.*

Synonyms: *defend, protect, guard, preserve, shield, safeguard.* These verbs mean to make safe from danger or attack. *Defend* implies use of countermeasures in repelling an actual attack. *Protect* suggests providing a cover to repel discomfort, injury, or attack. *Guard* suggests keeping watch over a person or thing. *Preserve* implies protective measures to maintain something as it is for an extended period. *Shield* suggests protection in the form of something or someone placed between the threat and the threatened. *Safeguard* stresses protection against potential or less imminent danger, often by preventive action.

de·fen·dant (di-fĕn'dənt) *n.* *Abbr.* **def.** *Law.* A person against whom an action is brought. Compare **plaintiff.**

Defender of the Faith. *Abbr.* **D.F.** A title of English sovereigns, originally conferred upon Henry VIII by Pope Leo X (1521).

de·fen·es·tra·tion (dē-fĕn'ə-strā'shən) *n.* An act of throwing something or someone out of a window. [DE- + FENESTRA.]

de·fense (di-fĕns') *n.* Also chiefly British **de·fence.** *Abbr.* **def.** **1.** The act of defending against attack, danger, or injury; protection. **2.** Anything that defends or protects. **3.** *Psychoanalysis.* An unconsciously acquired, involuntarily operating mental attribute, mechanism, or dynamism, such as regression, repression, reaction-formation, or projection, that protects the individual from shame, anxiety, or loss of self-esteem. **4.** An argument in support or justification of something. **5.** *Law.* **a.** The action of the defendant in opposition to complaints against him. **b.** The defendant and his legal counsel. The science or art of defending oneself; self-defense. **7.** *Sports.* The team or those players on the team attempting to stop the opposition from scoring. —*tr.v.* **defensed, -fensing, -fenses.** *Football.* To act as defense: *defense a play.* [Middle English *defense*, from Old French, from Latin *dēfensa*, from the feminine past participle of *dēfendere*, DEFEND.] —**de·fense'less** *adj.* —**de·fense'less·ly** *adv.* —**de·fense'less·ness** *n.*

defense mechanism. **1.** *Biology.* Any reaction of an organism used in self-defense, as against germs. **2.** *Psychoanalysis.* Loosely, a defense; especially, the psychic structure or mechanism underlying a defense.

Labels (marginal annotations): usage note · synonyms · standard abbreviation · alternate British spellings · subject labels · syllabification · etymology · pronunciation guide

5. What are the usage labels for the following words? Does your dictionary also include any additional information in a usage note?
A. Ain't B. Irregardless C. Alright D. Transmogrify E. Yclept F. Rubberneck

6. Finally, what about the definitions of the following words? Many people find them ambiguous. What does your dictionary do to clarify the ambiguity about them?
A. Aggravate B. Disinterested C. Sensuous/sensual D. Fulsome

As you will find when you try to do this exercise, only a few of the dictionaries calling themselves "college dictionaries" are worthy of the name. You should also know that "Webster's" is not a copywritten name, and thus any dictionary produced in the United States can use the name "Webster's" if it so chooses. The editors of this text do not recommend one dictionary over another, but we have included a list of the dictionaries most often recommended by college English teachers. As their official titles are long and sometimes similar, dictionaries are often referred to by their standardized initials.

ACD	*The American College Dictionary.* New York: Random House, 1947, 1964.
AHD	*The American Heritage Dictionary of the English Language.* Boston: Houghton Mifflin, 1969, 1970, 1971, 1973, 1975, 1976.
RHD	*The Random House College Dictionary.* New York: Random House, 1968, 1969, 1972, 1973, 1975.
SCD	*The Standard College Dictionary.* New York: Harcourt, Brace, Jovanovich, 1963. Earlier editions of this dictionary were published by Funk and Wagnalls. It is also sold under the title *The Reader's Digest Dictionary*.
SOD	*The Shorter Oxford Dictionary on Historical Principles.* Oxford: Oxford University Press, 1944. Not really a college dictionary, but the handiest abridgement of the great *Oxford English Dictionary*; it employs British spellings, and therefore is a preferred dictionary in the British Isles, Canada, and the Commonwealth.
WNCD	*Webster's New Collegiate Dictionary*, eighth edition. Springfield, Mass.: G. & C. Merriam Co., 1973. Based on *Webster's New International Dictionary, Third Edition*.
WNWD	*Webster's New World Dictionary of the American Language, College Edition*, revised. Cleveland: Collins-World Publishing Co., 1971. This dictionary also appears under the title *Collier's Encyclopedia Dictionary*.

The dictionary page we have reprinted as Fig. 18 is from *The American Heritage Dictionary*, and although each dictionary differs from its rivals in many subtle ways, this page is fairly representative of all college dictionaries. There are, despite this, some features individual to the AHD. One of the most important is the least noticeable: the order of definitions for words with multiple meanings, as under the entry for "deep." The AHD editors did not follow an order of most frequent usage or chronological order (which would list the oldest meaning of the word first); instead, they give the different definitions of words in what they term "psychologically meaningful order, with one subgroup leading to another."

Two other features of the AHD are its concern for usage and etymology. The four-line usage note after "defective" is not paralleled in other dictionaries. Similarly, the ADH includes a lengthy appendix tracing word roots to Indo-European sources. The notations for *dheu*[1] under "deer" and *dhe-*[1] under "defeat" are references to that index.

PAUL ROBERTS
How to Find Fault with a Dictionary

Because of the complexities of our language, a dictionary is a necessity in an English-speaking household. For the same reason, many colleges require their students to own a good dictionary when they start classes. Thus it becomes easy to take a dictionary for granted, as though it were a telephone directory with pictures. The following essay should help you dispel that illusion. Not only are dictionaries quite various, as we established in the Classroom Exercise for this chapter, but they are constantly expanding and reshaping themselves. For these and other reasons, the aware student has an advantage in finding fault with a dictionary.

Dictionary Worship

It is probably fair to say that most present-day Americans show rather more respect for the dictionary than they do for the Bible. It is significant that we speak of "the dictionary" rather than "a dictionary," as if there were only one. When we say, "The dictionary says so," we feel that we have settled the matter once and for all, that we have carried the appeal to the final authority. The popular feeling seems to be that the dictionary editor visits heaven every few years to receive the material for the next edition.

Well, modern dictionaries are good, but they're not that good. It is true that they are generally more sophisticated linguistically than the people that use them; that they are prepared with great care at considerable expense by squads of experts; that keen competition for a large market keeps them up to date, well presented, and generally sharp. But it is also true that they are prepared by men and women liable, like all men and women, to error. It is further true that the nature of their subject—the word units of a vast, boiling, constantly changing language—makes it impossible, or at least economically unfeasible, for them to be prepared by what could be called scientific methods.

It is the intent of this [essay] to look at dictionaries in perspective, to trace their growth briefly, and to see what they offer their modern users.

The Evolution of the Modern Dictionary

It has been said wisely that nobody ever begins anything. Look behind every   4
bright idea and you find some earlier bright idea that contains its kernel. This is
so at least with the English dictionary. It is hard to say which the first one was
because we find word lists of one kind or another going deep into the Middle
Ages. But these early lists were two-language dictionaries—e.g., Latin words
with English translations. The first English-English word list was published in
1603, and this is usually called the first English dictionary.

Interestingly enough, it was not called a dictionary. Its title was A *Table*   5
Alphabeticall and its author a man named Robert Cawdrey. Cawdrey's dictionary contained about 2500 words. They were all "hard words," words that
readers, or at least inexperienced readers, might be expected to stumble over.
The definitions were fairly primitive—synonyms usually, and not always accurate.

Cawdrey did not pick his 2500 words out of the air. For the most part he got   6
them by copying from an earlier Latin word list. Thus at the very beginning was
born that splendid tradition of plagiarism in dictionary-making that has lasted
nearly to the present day. Plagiarism in dictionary-making is next to inevitable.
Suppose you wanted to produce a dictionary. How could you, how could anyone, arrive at all the words except by looking in dictionaries already in existence?
Presumably you would have your own contribution to make, but you would be a
plain fool if you didn't check your competitors' books to make sure you hadn't
overlooked something important. There is, as it happens, one other way of going
about it, but it is fearfully toilsome, and it has been undertaken only once, as we
shall see.

Anyway, Cawdrey copied from his predecessors, and his successors copied   7
from him. But each lexicographer produced not only his predecessor's word list
but also more words that he had dredged up by himself, and as the seventeenth
century wore on, dictionaries, as they had come to be called, grew larger and
larger. By the end of the century they were crowding 25,000 words.

They were getting better as well as bigger. Generally they copied not only one   8
another's word lists but one another's definitions as well; nevertheless, there was
steady improvement in the definitions. Being much worked over, they grew more
accurate, more elaborate, and more refined.

In the second half of the seventeenth century an important addition to the   9
dictionary was made: etymologies. The etymology is that part of the dictionary
entry which explains the history of the word. It is now an essential part of
dictionaries and is most carefully and accurately done. In the beginning the
etymologies were slipshod and primitive. Usually they consisted of a single
letter—F or L or G—to indicate whether the word was borrowed from French,
Latin, or Greek. Many words were not labeled at all. But once somebody
thought of putting in etymologies, all his successors had to include them too or
risk losing the market; and, like the definitions, the etymologies, worked over
decade after decade, became better and better. Thus free enterprise triumphed
again.

The dictionaries of the seventeenth century were all hard-word dictionaries. 10
Nobody made any attempt to include all the words of the language, but only
those likely to give a reader trouble. However, shortly after 1700 a man named
John Kersey took the step of including common words too. His purpose
presumably was to provide a complete spelling list, but he didn't shrink from the
difficult task of providing definitions for the common words. These are sufficiently crude. The word *an*, for instance, is given thus "An: as, *an* apron." This
may make us smile until we try to define it ourselves. Ultimately the only
important thing we can do with words like *an, of, with, some, the*, is to show how
they are used.

• • •

Dr. Johnson

But the great figure of lexicography in the eighteenth century was Dr. 11
Samuel Johnson, the king of literary London in the time of George the Third.
Johnson made his reputation with his dictionary, published in 1755 after seven
years of labor. It was originally intended . . . to regulate the English language. It
didn't do that, of course, but it did contribute much to the growth of lexicography and indeed exerted considerable influence on English writing.

Students of literature are likely to pass rapidly over the dictionary and con- 12
cern themselves with Johnson's literary works and with Boswell's great biography
of Johnson. They note the dictionary only as the subject of a famous letter to
Lord Chesterfield in which Johnson repudiates help offered too late, or as a book
containing occasionally waspish definitions:

> PENSION: An allowance made to anyone without an equivalent. In England it is
> generally understood to mean pay given to a state hireling for treason to his
> country.
> LEXICOGRAPHER: a writer of dictionaries; a harmless drudge.

But Johnson's dictionary, as his contemporaries well knew, was not a collection
of amusing definitions but a serious and important work.

Johnson had, first of all, a rare ability for definition, a greater one, possibly, 13
than anyone before or after him. His definitions, sometimes overcomplicated,
are mostly strong and clear. He also made a couple of lexicographical innova-
tions. One was the practice of separating and numbering word meanings, thus:

> MAN: 1. Human being. 2. Not a woman. 3. Not a boy. 4. A servant; an attendant; a
> dependent. 5. A word of familiarity bordering on contempt. 6. It is used in loose
> signification like the French *on*, one, any one.

This is now of course standard procedure in dictionaries.

Another, even more important innovation was the citing of contexts to show 14
word meanings or particular usages. As he worked on the dictionary, Johnson
read widely in earlier literature and marked passages for secretaries to copy out,
and many of these passages found their way into the dictionary. Definition-by-
context is not carried through in anything like a complete or systematic way.

But in a great many entries, the reader is given not only Johnson's definition but a sentence to show how the word was used by Shakespeare or Milton or Addison or Swift.[1]

Johnson's dictionary went through four editions in his lifetime and more after   15 his death. In the early nineteenth century it was revised by Todd, and in one form or another it continued to be "The Dictionary" in England much as Noah Webster's became "The Dictionary" in America.

Others, however, we making their contributions to lexicography. In the late   16 eighteenth century synonymies were added to entries in dictionaries. These are lists of close synonyms. Thus after *courage* one might find *bravery, boldness, valor, heroism, fortitude,* etc. In the course of time lexicographers undertook to define the shades of meaning between such synonyms. This is not only an integral part of modern dictionaries but has been expanded outside the dictionary proper. We now have "dictionaries of synonyms" such as *Roget's Thesaurus* or *Webster's Dictionary of Synonyms*, devoted entirely to the listing and explication of synonymous words.

Also in the second half of the eighteenth century, dictionaries began to   17 include guides to pronunciation. A pioneer in this department was Thomas Sheridan, the father of the playwright Richard Brinsley Sheridan. The elder Sheridan was also connected with the theatre, as were other people experimenting with pronunciation guides. They of course set down as "correct pronunciation" the pronunciation current in their own theatrical circles. This had a considerable effect on how people thought they ought to pronounce words, if not on how they actually did pronounce them. Probably its effect is still going on.

The Oxford English Dictionary

The greatest lexicographical effort in England in the nineteenth century—   18 perhaps the greatest of any century anywhere—was the *Oxford English Dictionary*. This has gone under various names in its long career. It is sometimes called the *Oxford Dictionary*, the *Historical English Dictionary*, and the *New English Dictionary*, and it is variously abbreviated the OED, the OD, the HED, and the NED. It is usually bound in ten or twelve or twenty volumes, and it costs in the neighborhood of 250 dollars.

The idea for the *Oxford English Dictionary* was born and nurtured in the   19 Philological Society in England. In the year 1857 one of its members read a paper criticizing existing dictionaries. He pointed out that the best of them were hit-and-miss affairs, unscientifically produced, impressionistic. He suggested that the Society undertake a new dictionary to be planned along quite different lines. The Society agreed enthusiastically, not knowing that none of them would live long enough to see the project completed.

The idea was that the dictionary would draw its data from English writing and   20 would not only give word meanings but would systematically cite contextual

---

[1]Or other early writers. [eds.].

evidence to verify the meanings given. The dictionary would include all words in use between the year 1100 and the date of publication. It was intended to cite the first occurrence of each word in English writing and the last occurrence if the word had dropped out of use, together with other citations across the centuries to show developments in meaning. It was decided that all extant English writing dating from before 1500 should be read and as much of the later writing as possible. In the end, practically all of English literature was covered, together with great quantities of cookbooks, religious tracts, trade manuals, newspapers, and the like.

The reading was done by thousands of volunteers. If you volunteered to read 21 for the dictionary, you would be assigned, say, the works of Jane Austen. You would be told to read the novels carefully, looking for any unusual word, any word unusually used, and words that struck you as new or old or in any way remarkable. When you came on such a word, you wrote it on a slip together with the sentence in which it occurred, noting the page or chapter number and the edition. You were also instructed to excerpt as many ordinary words and their contexts as time permitted. In the end some five million quotations were gathered of which about a million and a half appeared in the dictionary.

As the slips came in, they were sorted and filed in storehouses and eventually 22 studied by the editors and their assistants. When an editor came to write the entry for the word *buxom*, for example, he began by assembling all the slips on *buxom*. He then deduced its meaning and its changes of meaning from those slips. It didn't matter what he thought it meant or ought to mean or what other dictionaries said about it. He was bound by the slips. They gave him all the variant spellings and different usages and displayed the whole history of the word. Everything he had to say about *buxom* came out of those slips, and in the finished article, he included quotations to demonstrate the meanings given.

In the first quarter of a century, progress on the dictionary was spasmodic. 23 The Philological Society found the undertaking vaster than it had imagined; financial troubles arose; editors died; interest flagged. But in the 1880's a man named James Murray was hired as editor, and the work picked up again. Murray got out the first volume, A to Ant, in 1884. About this time Henry Bradley, a young philologist, was hired as coeditor, and the pace was doubled. After the turn of the century, two more editors, William Craigie and Charles Talbot Onions, were added to the staff. These last were the only ones who saw the work completed in 1928. Murray and Craigie were knighted for their work on the dictionary.[2]

Anyone with any curiosity at all about words should make the acquaintance 24 of the *Oxford English Dictionary*. It is to be found in the reference room of any

---

[2]The Last volume of the OED, Vol. X, Part II, V-Z, was published in 1928. A supplement appeared in 1933 to deal with new words and meanings and also to correct and modify entries already in print. The Supplement should be distinguished from the *Shorter Oxford Dictionary*, a selection from the whole work, which has appeared in both one- and two-volume editions. Further, the entire work was issued in a two-volume microprint edition in 1973. Although it can barely be read without a magnifying glass, it was so popular as to be offered as a premium by book clubs. In 1972 editors issued the first volume of a three-volume supplement to deal with words that have appeared in the language since the original was completed; it will replace the 1933 Supplement.

college library, along with its abridgement, the two-volume *Shorter Oxford*. You may find it rather a maze at first. The entry on the word *set*, the longest entry in the dictionary, runs to some twenty-three small-type, triple-columned pages; there is a good deal to say about *set* if you say everything. But brief acquaintance will quickly make the plan and possibilities clear. You will find there everything known about most English words and, through the words, the key to much in the development of English culture. The *Oxford* has contributed to thousands of scholarly studies that would have been altogether impossible without it. The *Oxford* is itself one of scholarship's greatest triumphs and a monument to the thousands of men and women who contributed their leisure hours for years and decades, for neither money nor fame but only for the satisfaction of extending human knowledge.

Dictionaries in America

In America the great pioneer in lexicography was of course Noah Webster, 25 whose name came to be closely linked with lexicography in this country as Johnson's was in England. Webster was a Connecticut school teacher, a graduate of Yale. He early became a producer of spelling books and an advocate of spelling reform and his interest led him into the making of dictionaries. His *Compendious Dictionary*, published in 1806, included such spellings as *fether* (feather), *hed* (head), *masheen* (machine), *bilt* (built), *leen* (lean), *thum* (thumb), *magic* (for *magick*), *color* (for *colour*), *center* (for centre). Most of these sensible suggestions were rejected by the writing public, and it could not be said that Webster was greatly effective in simplifying English spelling. On the other hand, he was more effective than anyone else had been.

But Webster is famous not as a spelling reformer but as the Webster of 26 Webster's dictionary. Webster brought out his last and greatest effort in lexicography in 1828 under the title *An American Dictionary of the English Language*. This work is in a sense the American counterpart of Johnson's dictionary. Neither is scientifically controlled in the sense that the *Oxford* was to be. . . .

Webster's book was revised once in his lifetime. In 1843 the rights were 27 purchased by Charles and George Merriam, and the Merriam firm continued, and continues, to bring out editions of all sizes, all bearing the Webster name. This name quickly acquired enormous commercial value, and one of the problems of the Merriam Company was how to keep it as their very own. Other publishers would, for example, hire somebody named Joseph Webster and publish a "Webster's Dictionary," neglecting to mention that the Webster involved was Joe and not Noah. The consequence was a series of court battles decided now one way and now another. . . .

In the late nineteenth and early twentieth centuries Merriam's chief competi- 28 tion came from Funk and Wagnalls, publishers of the *Standard Dictionary*. This competition produced, from edition to edition, added features in both dictionaries: improved synonymies, illustrations, biographical and geographical lists, improved methods in presentation, more research. It also produced more words. It was quickly apparent that the customer eyed with favor that dictionary which contained most words, and the result was that editors bringing out a new edition would make sure that it contained everything the other company's had and then dredge up a few thousand more. Under this stimulus the number of entries in the "unabridged" versions rose to around 600,000. They stopped there, not because the editors ran out of words but because the dictionaries are advertised as portable, and 600,000 words seems to be as many as one can carry from one room to another.

The dictionary popularly called "Webster's Unabridged" has more exactly 29 the title *Webster's New International Dictionary*, second edition. It was published in 1934. It seems to be the intention of the Merriam Company to publish revisions of the big book about every twenty-five years. The *New International* is not comparable to the *Oxford*. Its editors did not enjoy the resources available to the editors of the *Oxford*, and they labored under certain commercial limitations, principally that of space. . . . The Merriam Company keeps a staff of editors and assistants and special experts at work to keep its file up to date and to prepare for the next edition.[3]

College Dictionaries

Almost from the beginning of lexicography there has been a market for 30 dictionaries smaller than possible: college dictionaries, high school dictionaries, pocket dictionaries, office dictionaries. The Merriam Company for a long time enjoyed an advantage in the college field as well as in the unabridged class. Until the end of the Second World War, the outstanding dictionary in the college field was the *Webster Collegiate*, fifth edition, published in 1936. A whole generation of college students carried the *Collegiate* from class to class, blissfully unaware that any other dictionaries existed. . . . Few good ones did in America at that time.

. . .

At any rate, shortly after the end of the Second World War, the Merriam 31 monopoly was vigorously challenged. In 1947 Random House and Harper & Brothers jointly brought out *The American College Dictionary* (ACD). In 1949, Merriam answered with a revision of the *Collegiate* under the title *Webster's New Collegiate Dictionary* (WNCD). A few years later the World Publishing Company put the *Webster New World Dictionary* (WNWD) into the ring. The editor of the ACD, Clarence Barnhart, produced the *Thorndike-Barnhart Dictionary* for Scott Foresman. This is similar to the ACD in many features, but of smaller scope.

---

[3]*Webster's New International Dictionary, Third Edition* appeared in 1961. It employed the analyses and methods of modern linguistic science and thus made a sharp departure from the authoritarianism some had criticized in the second edition. Although the third edition pleased many linguists, it was vehemently attacked in such opinion-making journals as *The New York Times* and *Atlantic Monthly*. One of the most trenchant and influential of those reviews is Dwight Macdonald's "The String Untuned," the next essay in this chapter.

It should be said first of all that all of these postwar dictionaries are good 32
books. The college student who owns either the WNCD, the ACD, or the
WNWD owns a dictionary that is adequate for his normal needs, that is rea-
sonably accurate and up to date, and that is sufficiently easy to use. Whichever
one you buy, you buy a lot of scholarship for five or six dollars. . . .

• • •

The college dictionaries contain all the words the student is likely to look up 33
in ordinary work. It is only if your interest is quite special—as when you are
working in very specialized science or dialects or old literature—that the college
dictionary will fail you. Then you will have to turn to the *Oxford* or the *New
International* or a special dictionary for your subject.[4]

Grammatical Designations

Right after the word in the alphabetical list, the dictionary will give an 34
abbreviated designation of its "part of speech"—as *n.*, *v.*, *prep.*, for *noun*, *verb*,
preposition, respectively. The grammatical system used is the traditional
one. . . . It should be remembered that in this as in other matters the dictionary
can give only ordinary usage, not all possible usage. It may, for example, list
horse only as a noun, though it obviously occurs also as a verb as in "Don't horse
around."

If the word occurs in two or more grammatical categories, the dictionary will 35
give the definitions for each. For example, the word *face* will be given as *face*, *n.*,
followed by definitions of *face* as a noun. Then, in the main entry, you will find
the abbreviation *v.t.*, followed by definitions of *face* as a verb. *T.* here means
transitive, and that means that the verb occurs in the pattern N-V-N; *v.i.*, means
verb intransitive, which means that the verb occurs in the pattern N-V. *Face* is
v.t. because we ordinarily say "He faced something" and not just "He faced."[5]
You will find these and other abbreviations explained in the front or back of your
dictionary, usually on the cover. Abbreviations very frequently used are explained at the bottom of each page.

Definitions

Since Johnson's time dictionaries have recognized that words have multiple 36
meanings and have undertaken to separate and number them. A word in a

---

[4]Since the publication of this material, three more desk dictionaries have appeared, each taking a
large slice of the market away from the *Collegiate*. They are: *The Standard College Dictionary*
(Harcourt, Brace, Jovanovich, 1963); *The Random House Dictionary of the English Language* (1966,
1967, 1975); and *The American Heritage Dictionary of the English Language* (Houghton Mifflin,
1970, 1975). Patrick Kilburn's essay, later in this chapter, is a review of *The American Heritage
Dictionary*. [eds.].

[5]N-V-N means noun-verb-noun and refers to the sentence structure-verb-object, as in "She loves
me." Here *loves* is a *v.t.* because it takes an object. N-V means noun-verb and refers to the
subject-verb structure, as in "She loves." Here *loves* is a *v.i.* because it has no object.[eds.].

college dictionary may have fifteen or more numbered meanings. The careless student looking up a word is likely to settle for the definition at the top of the list, which may not be what he's after at all. Often you have to search around a bit.

Note also that dictionaries differ in the way in which they arrange the differ- 37 ent meanings. The Merriam-Webster dictionaries, like the *Oxford*, list the meanings in historical order. The oldest meaning that the word has had in English is given first, then the one that developed next, and so on. The ACD and the WNWD try to give the meanings in the order of current frequency. Both methods have advantages and disadvantages. The order in the WNCD gives you something of the history of the word; its semantic development unfolds as you read the definitions. On the other hand, the definition your eye first lights on is likely to be obsolete and useless to your present purposes.

Etymologies and Synonymies

All modern college dictionaries contain two features which can be of much 38 service to you in strengthening and sharpening your vocabulary. These are the etymologies and the synonymies. The etymology is a very brief explanation of the history of the word, the route by which it has come into English, the elements of which it is made, and so on. The etymology is given in square brackets. In the WNCD and the WNWD it appears at the head of the entry, just after the pronunciation. In the ACD it follows the definitions.

Etymologies are very highly abbreviated in order to conserve space. The 39 abbreviation key is given on the cover of the dictionary, common symbols at the bottom of the page. Thus, in the ACD the etymology of *diminutive* is [ME, t. ML; m.s. *diminutivus*, der. L. *di-*, *deminutis*, pp., *lessened*]. Reference to the symbols will allow you to translate this as "This word, which occurs in Middle English, was taken from Medieval Latin; it is a modification of the stem of *diminutivus*, which derives from Latin *diminutis* or *deminutis*, a past participle meaning 'lessened.' " A very little practice will make the symbols readily familiar to you. . .

Do get in the habit of glancing at the etymology when you look up a word. 40 You will begin to see patterns in word-building that will help you retain words in your vocabulary. You will also make your way into a field most interesting in itself.[6]

The synonymies are also interesting and sometimes helpful. Lists of 41 synonyms are given mostly for abstract words, like *courage, pride, cleverness*. The synonymy will be given only once for one group of synonyms. For example, if you look up *arrogance*, you may be directed to *pride* for the synonymy. there you will find not only the list of synonyms—*pride, arrogance, haughtiness*, etc.—but also an attempt to explain the shades of difference between each word.

---

[6]For a more thorough treatment of etymology, see Chisholm's essay later in this chapter.

Status Designations

Words which are in anything less than general respectable use are marked in 42
the dictionary by such designations as *slang, colloquial, provincial, dialectal,
vulgar, archaic, obsolete.* These are generally abbreviated, as *obs.* for *obsolete* or
col. for *colloquial.* Words or meanings pertaining to special fields are so labeled,
as *Law, Med.* (medicine), *Telg.* (telegraphy). Geographical limitations are also
given: *U.S.* (United States), *Brit.* (British). Words for which there are no status
designations are presumably in current, general, polite use.

It should be said that in applying status designations dictionaries do not walk 43
on very firm ground. . . . The lines between slang and colloquial and between
colloquial and elegant are not sharp lines, and there is really no controllable
procedure by which the lexicographer can decide whether to pin on the label
slang or *colloquial* or to let the word slip by unreproached. Presumably he often
studies all the available evidence and then flips a coin. Here as elsewhere the
student will do well to use his own ears and eyes. They may prove the dictionary
wrong. . . .

Pronunciation

All modern dictionaries indicate a pronunciation of each word, usually in 44
parentheses right after the entry. For all dictionaries this remains one of the
weakest features, though the lexicographers are not obviously to blame for the
shortcomings. . . . In practice, dictionaries include a lot of nonsense about
"short vowels" and "long vowels," and often festoon the vowels with various
squiggles called "diacritical marks." From all this one can, with application, get
a rough notion of how the editor wants the word to be pronounced, but the
procedure could scarcely be called efficient. . . .

There has been much improvement in the last [decade]. The editors of the 45
ACD adopted the symbol called *schwa*: ə. This represents the so-called neutral
vowel which is very common in syllables that do not have primary or secondary
stress. It is for most speakers the first vowel in *event* and *above*, the last two in
sensible. By adopting *schwa*, the dictionary was able to get rid of a whole host of
diacritical marks. The same practice is followed by the WNWD, by the
Thorndike-Barnhart Dictionary, and by others. The Merriam dictionaries cling
to the old system with its confusion of diacritical marks, but they are not likely to
do so forever.[7]

• • •

There is a widespread notion that every word has one and only one correct 46
pronunciation, and that this is inscribed in phonetic symbols on a scroll in
heaven or perhaps carved on the wall of Plato's Cave. One feels that there is some
principle somewhere, some rules or set of rules, which the dictionary-maker

---

[7]The last two Merriam college dictionaries—*Webster's Seventh New Collegiate Dictionary* and
the eighth edition, called *Webster's New Collegiate Dictionary*, 1973—both employ the *schwa*. [eds.]

applies to determine which pronunciation is correct. Actually, the only arbiter of pronunciation is usage. There is no other. None whatsoever. If a pronunciation is correct it is so because people, or more likely those particular people whom one admires and wishes to emulate, pronounce the word that way, and for no other reason.

It seems to be very hard to grasp this. The writer recalls a speech teacher who 47 liked to begin his course with a demonstration of the ignorance of the students. He would write a word on the blackboard—say, *illustrate*—and ask each student to pronounce it in turn. Like as not each one would put the stress on the first syllable: *illustrate*. "You see," the teacher would say triumphantly, "not one of your knows how to pronounce it. The correct pronunciation is *illústrate*." But observe the flaw. The students were themselves members of the educated class. Many of them were sons and daughters of educated people and moved in circles where the English spoken was good and decent and admired and admirable. If they had not encountered the pronunciation *illústrate*, this was substantial evidence that the pronunciation was not current in educated circles. All the teacher succeeded in proving was that he didn't know how to pronounce the word.

• • •

Modern dictionaries do much better than this. To be sure, they do not 48 publicize the methods by which they decide what pronunciations to favor. Perhaps they send around questionnaires, or perhaps the editor just asks his secretary what he thinks he should put down. But in general they try to list pronunciations that are current and common and not just traditional. Often they will give two or more pronunciations for a word, listing them in the order of frequency.

• • •

You and the Dictionary

It has been said that when an educated American has a word problem he 49 tends to consult the dictionary; when an educated Englishman has a word problem he tends to consult his memory, to recall how the word is used or pronounced by his friends and relatives. The latter is certainly the more reasonable approach, though of course it won't always work. The proper procedure is to solve the problem on the basis of your experience if it lies within your experience; if it does not, you consult the dictionary.

Observe, however, that the dictionary is a more reliable guide in some areas 50 than in others. If the question is one of spelling, you can depend on the dictionary absolutely; all you have to be sure of here is that you are using an American dictionary and not a British one. In etymologies also you can take the dictionary's pronouncements as nearly gospel. . . .

Definitions are a somewhat different matter. As we have seen, the ultimate 51 definer is the context. All the editor can do is make a generalization or a series of generalizations from contexts available to him. It may be that these will not apply exactly to the context you are concerned with. Here you use the dictionary to fill out and clarify what you learn from the passage itself.

In word status and pronunciation you are even more on your own. The only 52 real teacher here is observation of what goes on in the circle you belong to or in the one to which you aspire. The dictionary gives you a more or less informed opinion, but it cannot override the facts that confront you. Don't start correcting your betters if they pronounce a word one way and the dictionary suggests another.

Above all, remember that the dictionary does not make laws. It reports usage, 53 usually accurately, sometimes not. It reports mostly the usage of educated people, therefore of the class to which you belong or into which you are moving. It reports, in some degree, your usage. . . . You're a member of the educated class or at least hovering on its outskirts. You're going to college, aren't you?

DISCUSSION QUESTIONS

1. To what extent do people still think of dictionaries only in their original function as "hard-word lists"?

2. In paragraph 17 Roberts tells us that the first guide to pronunciation originated in theatrical circles. Why was this more important to actors than the general run of people? What do you suppose people (including actors) did about pronunciation before dictionaries attempted to establish a standard pronunciation?

3. Only a few of Noah Webster's spelling reforms, e.g. "color" for "colour," have been adopted, although many of his others, such as "masheen" for "machine" and "hed" for "head," are certainly phonetic. In the present century The Chicago Tribune has promoted many other reforms, such as "frate" for "freight." Why do you suppose these reforms have been unsuccessful?

4. Many early dictionary makers, including Dr. Johnson, hoped to fix—hold steady—the everchanging English language. On one point they did; most spellings have been constant for about 200 years. But in other aspects they failed; simple words keep acquiring new meanings, new words are added, and once-fashionable words cease to be used. Why can't a dictionary hold the language in place?

5. To what degree has reading Roberts's article caused you to find fault with your dictionary? Does one fault shake your confidence? How will you react in the future when you hear someone try to argue, "But the dictionary says . . . "?

6. Why do you suppose so many people have unquestioning confidence in dictionaries? Why do they want to believe there is a final answer to questions which have actually remained unsettled?

7. Most people will use some dictionary or other at some time in their lives, whether or not they go to college. But only a few people will learn how to use the other information the dictionary gives? Why do so many remain ignorant of information that is directly at hand?

8. What use can a college student make of such information as

synonomies, etymologies, status designations, etc.? It has been included in the dictionary because *somebody* thought we needed it. What importance does it have to the kind of writing you have to do?

9. If your college has a copy of Samuel Johnson's *Dictionary* (1755), look up his entries for some of these words: "network," "patron," "cough," "pension," "dry," "oats," "Tory," "Whig," "excise," "patriotism," "willow," "transpire."

DWIGHT MACDONALD
The String Untuned

Webster's New International Dictionary, Third Edition often referred to as *Webster's Unabridged* or *Webster's Third*, sits in a place of honor in almost every library—high school, college, and public—in North America. Most students think of it as the big dictionary they use when they can't find what they're looking for in a smaller one. Although criticizing it might look like an assault on Mount Rushmore, that is just what happened when it appeared in 1961. Some of the denunciations were so impassioned that linguist James Sledd collected them for analysis in a book, *Dictionaries and THAT Dictionary*.[1] *One of the reviews continues to be reprinted, not only because it is about the dictionary, but more because it is a challenge to the philosophy which produced it. We reprint it here, somewhat abridged and amended.* [Paragraphs 3 to 6 did not appear in the original version and have been added at Mr. Macdonald's request. They are taken from his essay "The Decline and Fall of English," *Life International* (April 9, 1962), and reprinted in *Against the American Grain* (New York: Random House, 1962), in which "The String Untuned" is also reprinted.]

The third edition of Webster's New International Dictionary (Unabridged), 1
which was published last fall by the G. & C. Merriam Co., of Springfield, Massachusetts, tells us a good deal about the changes in our cultural climate since the second edition appeared, in 1934. The most important difference between Webster's Second (hereafter called 2) and Webster's Third (or 3) is that 3 has accepted as standard English a great many words and expressions to which 2 attached warning labels: *slang, colloquial, erroneous, incorrect, illiterate.* My impression is that most of the words so labelled in the 1934 edition are accepted in the 1961 edition as perfectly normal, honest, respectable citizens. Between these dates in this country a revolution has taken place in the study of English grammar and usage, a revolution that probably represents an advance in scientific method but that certainly has had an unfortunate effect on such nonscientific activities as the teaching of English and the making of dictionaries—at least

_____

[1]With Wilma R. Ebbitt (Chicago: Scott, Foresman, 1962). Sledd's rebuttal of Macdonald appears on pages 268-274.

on the making of this particular dictionary. This scientific revolution has meshed gears with a trend toward permissiveness, in the name of democracy, that is debasing our language by rendering it less precise and thus less effective as literature and less efficient as communication. It is felt that it is snobbish to insist on making discriminations—the very word has acquired a Jim Crow flavor— about usage. And it is assumed that true democracy means that the majority is right. This feeling seems to me sentimental and this assumption unfounded.

• • •

The editor of 2. Dr. William A. Neilson, president of Smith College, fol- 2 lowed lexical practice that had obtained since Dr. Johnson's day and assumed there was such a thing as correct English and that it was his job to decide what it was. When he felt he had to include a sub-standard word because of its common use, he put it in, but with a warning label: *Slang, Dial.*, or even bluntly *Illit.* His approach was normative and his dictionary was an authority that pronounced on which words were standard English and which were not. Bets were decided by "looking it up in the dictionary." It would be hard to decide bets by appealing to 3. whose editor of fifteen years' standing, Dr. Philip Gove, while as dedicated a scholar as Dr. Neilson, has a quite different approach. A dictionary, he writes, "should have no traffic with . . . artificial notions of correctness or superiority. It must be descriptive and not prescriptive." Dr. Gove and the other makers of 3 are sympathetic to the school of language study that has become dominant since 1934. It is sometimes called Structural Linguistics and sometimes, rather magnificently, just Modern Linguistic Science. Its basic principles are defined as follows in *The English Language Arts*, a book published in 1952 by the Commission on the English Curriculum of the National Council of Teachers of English:

1. Language changes constantly.
2. Change is normal.
3. Spoken language is the language.
4. Correctness rests on usage.
5. All usage is relative.

At first glance, these principles seem unexceptionable, indeed almost 3 truisms. But a closer look reveals that the last three are half-truths, the most dangerous of formulations; half a truth is *not* better than no truth at all.

It may be natural for the Structural Linguists, who have devoted most of their 4 attention to primitive languages, to assume that the "real" language is the spoken one and not the written one, but this has not always been true: many of the words coined from Latin and Greek in the Elizabethan period, words we still use, were introduced by scholars or poets in their writings. Today, what with far greater literacy and the proliferation of printed matter, the written word would seem to be even more important than in the past.

"Correctness rests upon usage" is more nearly true, but the Structural 5 Linguists underestimate the influence of purists, grammarians and schoolmarms. It is true that Swift, an arch-conservative, objected to such eighteenth century neologisms as *mob, bully, sham, bubble* and *banter,* all of which have since become standard English. But he also objected, and successfully, to contractions like *disturb'd,* to *phiz* for *face, hyp* for *hypochondriac,* and *pozz* for *positive*. The purists have won at least two major victories: they have made the double negative, often used by Shakespeare and a perfectly legitimate means of emphasis, a stigma of illiteracy, and they have crusaded so effectively against *ain't* that, though Webster's Third alleges differently, it can't be used any more even as a contraction of *am not* without danger of cultural excommunication. One may deplore these victories, as I do, but we cannot deny they have taken place, as the Structural Linguists sometimes seem to do.

"All usage is relative" is either a truism (different classes and localities speak 6 differently) or else misleading. "The contemporary linguist does not employ the terms 'good English' and 'bad English' except in a purely relative sense," *The English Language Arts* explains. "He recognizes the fact that language is governed by the situation in which it occurs." But this principle leads to an undemocratic freezing of status, since "irregardless" and "he knowed" are standard usage in certain circles, and those not the richest or best educated. So the Horatio Alger of today, bemused by teachers well grounded in Structural Linguistics, will keep on massacring the king's English because his follow newsboys do ("language is governed by the situation in which it occurs") and the philanthropic merchant will be so appalled by Horatio's double negatives that he will not give him The Job. In their *Modern American Grammar and Usage* (1956), J. N. Hook and E. G. Mathews, writing in the orthodox canon, observe apropos of what they delicately call "sub-standard English"; "We must reemphasize that this language is not wrong; it is merely not in harmony with the usages generally found in books . . . or heard in the conversations of those persons with a strong consciousness of language." They then give an example of substandard English: "Bein's he uz a'ready late, he done decide not to pay her no mind." If this is not wrong, it seems hardly worth the bother to teach English at all.

While one must sympathize with the counterattack the Structural Linguists 7 have led against the tyranny of the schoolmarms and the purists, who have caused unnecessary suffering to generations of schoolchildren over such matters as *shall* v. *will* and the *who-whom* syndrome—someone has observed that the chief result of the long crusade against "It's me" is that most Americans now say "Between you and I"—it is remarkable what strange effects have been produced in 3 by following Dr. Gove's five little precepts, reasonable as each seems taken separately. Dr. Gove conceives of his dictionary as a recording instrument rather than as an authority; in fact, the whole idea of authority or correctness is repulsive to him as a lexical scientist. The question is, however, whether a purely scientific approach to dictionary-making may not result in greater evils than those it seeks to cure.

When one compares 2 and 3, the first difference that strikes one is that 2 is a 8 work of traditional scholarship and hence oriented toward the past, while 3—though in many ways more scholarly, or at least more academic, than 2—exhales the breezy air of the present. This is hardly surprising, since the new school of linguistics is non-historical, if not anti-historical. Henry Luce's *Time* rather than Joseph Addison's *Spectator* was the hunting ground for 3's illustrative quotations.

· · ·

In seeking out and including all the commonly used words, especially slang   9
ones, the compilers of 3 have been admirably diligent. Their definitions, in the
case of meanings that have arisen since 1900 or so, are usually superior (though,
because of the tiny amount of a dictionary it is possible to read before vertigo sets
in, all generalizations must be understood to be strictly impressionistic). They
have also provided many more quotations (this is connected with the linguistic
revolution), perhaps, indeed, too many more. It is quite true, as the promotional
material for 3 claims, that this edition goes far beyond what is generally understood by the term "revision" and may honestly be termed a new dictionary. But I
should advise the possessors of the 1931 edition to think carefully before they
turn it in for the new model. Although the publishers have not yet destroyed the
plates of 2, they do not plan to keep it in print, which is a pity. There are reasons,
which will presently appear, that buyers should be given a choice between 2 and
3, and that, in the case of libraries and schools, 3 should be regarded as an
up-to-date supplement to 2 rather than a replacement of it.

• • •

The editors of 3 have labored heroically on pronunciation, since one of the   10
basic principles of the new linguistic doctrine is that Language is Speech. Too
heroically, indeed. For here, as in other aspects of their labors, the editors have
displayed more valor than discretion. Sometimes they appear to be lacking in
common sense. The editors of 2 found it necessary to give only two pronunciations for *berserk* and two for *lingerie,* but 3 seems to give twenty-five for the first
and twenty-six for the second. (This is a rough estimate; the system of notation is
very complex. Dr. Gove's pronunciation editor thinks there are approximately
that number but says that he is unable to take the time to be entirely certain.)
Granted that 2 may have shirked its duty, one may still find something compul-
sive in the amplitude with which 3 has fulfilled its obligations. Does anybody
except a Structural Linguist need to know that much? And what use is such
plethora to a reader who wants to know how to pronounce a word?

• • •

One of the most painful decisions unabridgers face is what to do about those   11
obscene words that used to be wholly confined to informal discourse but that of
late, after a series of favorable court decisions, have been cropping up in respectable print. The editors of 2, being gentlemen and scholars, simply omitted them.
The editors of 3, being scientists, were more conscientious. All the chief four-
and five-letter words are here, with the exception of perhaps the most important
one. They defend this omission not on lexical grounds but on the practical and, I
think, reasonable ground that its inclusion would have stimulated denunciations
and boycotts. There are, after all, almost half a million other words in their
dictionary—not to mention an investment of three and a half million dollars—
and they reluctantly decided not to imperil the whole enterprise by insisting on
that word.

• • •

Dr. Gove met the problem of *ain't* head on in the best traditions of Structural   12
Linguistics, labelling it—reluctantly, one imagines—*substandard* for *have not*
and *has not,* but giving it, unlabelled, as a contraction of *am not, are not,* and *is*

not, adding "though disapproved by many and more common in less educated speech, used orally in most parts of the U.S. by many cultivated speakers esp. in the phrase ain't I." This was courageous indeed; when Dr. C. C. Fries, the dean of Structural Linguists today, said, at a meeting of the Modern Language Association several years ago, that *ain't* was not wholly disreputable, a teapot tempest boiled up in the press. When Dr. Gove included a reference to the entry on *ain't* in the press announcement of 3, the newspapers seethed again, from the Houston *Press* ("It Ain't Uncouth To Say Ain't Now") to the San Francisco *Examiner* ("Ain't Bad at All—In Newest Revised Dictionary") and the *World-Telegram* ("It Just Ain't True That Ain't Ain't in the Dictionary"). But moral courage is not the only quality a good lexicographer needs. Once the matter of education and culture is raised, we are right back at the non-scientific business of deciding what is correct—*standard* is the modern euphemism—and this is more a matter of a feeling for language (what the trade calls *Sprachgefühl*) than of the statistics on which Dr. Gove and his colleagues seem to have chiefly relied. For what Geiger counter will decide who is in fact educated or cultivated? And what adding machine will discriminate between *ain't* used because the speaker thinks it is standard English and *ain't* used because he wants to get a special effect? "Survival must have quality, or it ain't worth a bean," Thornton Wilder recently observed. It doesn't take much *Sprachgefühl* to recognize that Mr. Wilder is here being a mite folksy and that his effect would be lost if *ain't* were indeed "used orally in most parts of the U.S. by many cultivated speakers." Though I regret that the nineteenth-century schoolteachers without justification deprived us of *ain't* for *am not*, the deed was done, and I think the *Dial.* or *Illit.* with which 2 labels all uses of the word comes closer to linguistic fact today.

The pejorative labels in 2 are forthright: *colloquial, erroneous, incorrect,* 13 *illiterate.* 3 replaces these self-explanatory terms with two that are both fuzzier and more scientific-sounding: *nonstandard* and *substandard.* The first "indicates status conforming to a pattern of linguistic usage that exists throughout the American language community but differs in choice of word or form from that of the prestige group in that community," which is academese for "Not used by educated people." *Hisself* and *drownded* are labelled *substand.*, which sounds better than *erron.*—more democratic. *Nonstandard* "is used for a very small number of words that can hardly stand without some status label but are too widely current in reputable context to be labeled *substand.*" *Irregardless* is given as an example, which for me again raises doubts about the compilers' notion of a reputable context. I think 2's label for the word, *erron. or humorous,* more accurate.

· · ·

Each such confusion makes the language less efficient, and it is a dictionary's 14 job to *define* words, which means, literally, to set limits to them. 3 still distinguishes *capital* from *capitol* and *principle* from *prinicipal*, but how many more language-community members must join the present sizable band that habitually confuses these words before they go down the drain with the others? Perhaps nothing much is lost if almost everybody calls Frankenstein the monster rather than the man who made the monster, even though Mrs. Shelley wrote it the other way, but how is one to deal with the *bimonthly* problem? 2 defines it as "once in two months," which is correct. 3 gives this as the first meaning and then adds, gritting its teeth, "*sometimes*: twice a month." (It defines *biweekly* as "every two weeks" and adds "2: twice a week.") It does seem a little awkward to have a word that can mean every two weeks *or* every eight weeks, and it would have been convenient if 3 had compromised with scientific integrity enough to replace its perfectly accurate *sometimes* with a firm *erroneous*. But this would have implied authority, and authority is the last thing 3's modest recorders want. ("Let this cup pass from me."—*New Testament*.)

The objection is not to recording the facts of actual usage. It is to failing to 15 give the information that would enable the reader to decide which usage he wants to adopt. If he prefers to use *deprecate* and *depreciate* interchangeably, no dictionary can prevent him, but at least he should be warned.

· · ·

In dealing with words that might be considered slang, 2 uses the label wher- 16 ever there is doubt, while 3 leans the other way. The first procedure seems to me more sensible, since no great harm is done if a word is labelled slang until its pretensions to being standard have been thoroughly tested (as long as it is admitted into the dictionary), while damage may be done if it is prematurely accepted as standard. Thus both 2 and 3 list such women's-magazine locutions as *galore*, *scads*, *scrumptious*, and *too-too*, but only 2 labels them slang. (Fowler's note on *galore* applies to them all: "Chiefly resorted to by those who are reduced to relieving the dullness of the matter by oddity of expression.") Thus *rummy*, *spang* (in the middle of), and *nobby* are in both, but only 2 calls them slang.

· · ·

Admittedly, the question is most difficult. Many words begin as slang and 17 then rise in the world. Some slang words have survived for centuries without bettering themselves, like the Jukes and the Kallikaks. *Dukes* (fists) and *duds* (clothes) are still slang, although they go back to the eighteenth and the sixteenth century, respectively.

The definition of *slang* in 3 is "characterized primarily by connotations of 18 extreme informality . . . coinages or arbitrarily changed words, clipped or shortened forms, extravagant, forced, or facetious figures of speech or verbal novelties usu. experiencing quick popularity and relatively rapid decline into disuse." A good definition (Dr. Gove has added that slang is "linguistically self-conscious"), but it seems to have been forgotten in making up 3, most of whose discriminations about slang strike me as arbitrary. According to 3, *scram* is not slang, but *vamoose* is. "*Goof* 1" (to make a mistake or blunder") is not slang, but "*goof* 2" ("to spend time idly or foolishly") is, and the confusion is compounded when one finds that Ethel Merman is cited for the non-slang *goof* and James T. Farrell for the slang *goof*. "*Floozy* 1" ("an attractive young woman of loose morals") is standard, but "*floozy* 2" ("a dissolute and sometimes slovenly woman") is slang. Can even a Structural Linguist make such fine distinctions about such a word? The many synonyms for *drunk* raise the same question. Why are *oiled*, *pickled*, and *boiled* labelled slang if *soused* and *spifilcated* are not? Perhaps cooking terms for *drunk* are automatically slang, but why?

· · ·

. . . I see only two logical alternatives: to label all doubtful words slang, as 2   19
does, or to drop the label entirely, as I suspect Dr. Gove would have liked to do.
Using the label sparingly, if it is not to produce bizarre effects, takes a lot more
Sprachgefühl[1] than the editors of 3 seem to have possessed. Thus *horse* as a verb
("to engage in horseplay") they accept as standard. The citations are from Norman Mailer ("I never horse around much with the women") and J. D. Salinger
("I horse around quite a lot, just to keep from getting bored"). I doubt whether
either Mr. Mailer or Mr. Salinger would use *horse* straight; in these cites, I
venture, it is either put in the mouth of a first-person narrator or used deliberately
to get a colloquial effect. Slang is concise and vivid—*jalopy* has advantages over
dilapidated automobile—and a few slang terms salted in a formal paragraph bring
out the flavor. But the user must know he *is* using slang, he must be aware of
having introduced a slight discord into his harmonics, or else he coarsens and
blurs his expressions. . . .

. . .

In 1947 the G. & C. Merriam Co. published a little book entitled "Noah's   20
Ark"—in reference to Noah Webster, who began it all—celebrating its first
hundred years as the publisher of Webster dictionaries. Toward the end, the
author, Robert Keith Leavitt, rises to heights of eloquence which have a tinny
round now that "Webster" means not 2 but 3:

> This responsibility to the user is no light matter. It has, indeed, grown heavier with
> every year of increasing acceptance of Webster. Courts, from the United States
> Supreme Court down, rely on the *New International's* definitions as a sort of com-
> mon law: many a costly suit has hinged on a Webster definition, and many a citizen
> has gone behind prison bars or walked out onto the streets a free man, according to
> the light Webster put upon his doings. The statute law itself is not infrequently
> phrased by legislators in terms straight out of Webster. Most daily newspapers and
> magazines, and nearly all the books that come off the press, are edited and printed in
> accordance with Websterian usage. Colleges and schools make the *New International*
> their standard, and, for nearly half a century, students have dug their way through
> pedantic obscurity with the aid of the *Collegiate*. In business offices the secretary
> corrects her boss out of Webster and the boss holds customers and contractors alike in
> line by citing how Webster says it shall be done. In thousands upon thousands of
> homes, youngsters lying sprawled under the table happily absorb from Webster
> information which teachers have striven in vain to teach them from textbooks. Clear
> through, indeed, to the everyday American's most trivial and jocose of doings, Web-
> ster is the unquestioned authority.

While this picture is a bit idyllic—Clarence Barnhart's American College Dictionary, put out by Random House, is considered by many to be at least as good
as the Webster Collegiate—it had some reality up to 1961. But as of today, courts
that Look It Up InWebster will often find themselves little the wiser, since 3
claims no authority and merely records, mostly deadpan, what in fact every
Tom, Dick, and Harry is now doing—in all innocence—to the language. That
freedom or imprisonment should depend on 3 is an alarming idea. The secretary

---

1. "Feeling for the language"; see paragraph 12.

correcting her boss, if he is a magazine publisher, will collide with the unre-solved *bimonthly* and *biweekly* problem, and the youngsters sprawled under the table will happily absorb from 3 the information that *jerk* is standard for "a stupid, foolish, naïve, or unconventional person." One imagines the themes: "Dr. Johnson admired Goldsmith's literary talent although he considered him a jerk." The editors of the New Webster's Vest Pocket Dictionary, thirty-nine cents at any cigar store, label *jerk* as *coll*. But then they aren't Structural Linguists.

The reviews of 3 in the lay press have not been enthusiastic. *Life* and the 21 *Times* have both attacked it editorially as a "say-as-you-go" dictionary that reflects "the permissive school" in language study. The usually solemn editorialists of the *Times* were goaded to unprecedented wit:

> A passel of double-domes at the G. & C. Merriam Company joint in Springfield, Mass. [the editorial began], have been confabbing and yakking for twenty-seven years—which is not intended to infer that they have not been doing plenty work—and now they have finalized Webster's Third New International Dictionary, Unabridged, a new edition of that swell and esteemed word book.
>
> Those who regard the foregoing paragraph as acceptable English prose will find that the new Webster's is just the dictionary for them.

But the lay press doesn't always prevail. The irreverent may call 3 "Gove's 22 Goof," but Dr. Gove and his editors are part of the dominant movement in the professional study of language—one that has in the last few years established strong beachheads in the National Council of Teachers of English and the College English Association. One may grant that for the scientific study of language the Structural Linguistic approach is superior to that of the old grammarians, who overestimated the importance of logic and Latin, but one may still object to its transfer directly to the teaching of English and the making of dictionaries. As a scientific discipline, Structural Linguistics can have no truck with values or standards. Its job is to deal only with The Facts. But in matters of usage, the evaluation of The Facts is important, too, and this requires a certain amount of general culture, not to mention common sense—commodities that many scientists have done brilliantly without but that teachers and lexicographers need in their work.

• • •

There are several reasons that it is important to maintain standards in the use 23 of a language. English, like other languages, is beautiful when properly used, and beauty can be achieved only by attention to form, which means setting limits, or de-fining, or dis-criminating. Language expresses the special, dis-tinctive quality of a people, and a people, like an individual, is to a large extent defined by its past—its traditions—whether it is conscious of this or not. If the language is allowed to shift too rapidly, without challenge from teachers and lexicographers, then the special character of the American people is blurred, since it tends to lose its past. In the same way a city loses its character if too much of it is torn down and rebuilt too quickly. "Languages are the pedigrees of nations," said Dr. Johnson.

The effect on the individual is also unfortunate. The kind of permissiveness 24 that permeates 3 (the kind that a decade or two ago was more common in progressive schools than it is now) results, oddly, in less rather than more individuality, since the only way an individual can "express himself" is in relation to a social norm—in the case of language, to standard usage. James Joyce's creative distortions of words were possible only because he had a perfect ear for orthodox English. But if the very idea of form, or standards, is lacking, then how can one violate it? It's no fun to use *knowed* for *known* if everybody thinks you're just trying to be standard.

Counting cite slips is simply not the way to go about the delicate business of 25 deciding these matters. If nine-tenths of the citizens of the United States, including a recent President, were to use *inviduous*, the one-tenth who clung to *invidious* would still be right, and they would be doing a favor to the majority if they continued to maintain the point. It is perhaps not democratic, according to some recent users, or abusers, of the word, to insist on this, and the question comes up of who is to decide at what point change—for language does indeed change, as the Structural Linguists insist—has evolved from *slang, dial., erron.,* or *substand.* to *standard.* The decision, I think, must be left to the teachers, the professional writers, and the lexicographers, and they might look up Ulysses' famous defense of conservatism in Shakespeare's "Troilus and Cressida":

> The heavens themselves, the planets and this centre
> Observe degree, priority and place,
> Insisture, course, proportion, season, form,
> Office and custom in all line of order. . . .
> Take but degree away, untune that string,
> And, hark, what discord follows! Each thing meets
> In mere oppugnancy. The bounded waters
> Should lift their bosoms higher than the shores
> And make a sop of all this solid globe.
> Strength should be lord of imbecility
> And the rude son should strike his father dead.
> Force should be right, or rather right and wrong
> (Between whose endless jar justice resides)
> Should lose their names, and so should justice too.
> Then every thing includes itself in power,
> Power into will, will into appetite
> And appetite, a universal wolf,
> So doubly seconded with will and power,
> Must make perforce a universal prey
> And, last, eat up himself. . . .

Dr. Johnson, a dictionary-maker of the old school, defined *lexicographer* as 26 'a harmless drudge." Things have changed. Lexicographers may still be drudges, but they are certainly not harmless. They have untuned the string, made a sop of the solid structure of English, and encouraged the language to eat up himself.

DISCUSSION QUESTIONS

1. Macdonald describes "standard" as a modern euphemism for "correct." Is the difference between "correct English" and "standard English" merely one of connotation, or do they denote different things? Look up "correct" and "standard" in your dictionary. Why do linguists and lexicographers prefer "standard" to "correct"?

2. Where do usage labels come from? Does usage itself—that is, the people who use a word of expression—determine the status of a word, which the dictionary then records? Or does the dictionary apply the label, with the people following its advice? How can this question be distinguished from the one about the chicken and the egg that is never resolved?

3. Macdonald begins the essay with a sentence which charges structural linguistics with being a " . . . scientific revolution [which has] meshed gears with a trend toward permissiveness, in the name of democracy." To what extent can the argument over *Webster's Third* be seen in political terms? Macdonald identifies himself with linguistic conservatism toward the end of the essay, yet as a journalist he has been associated with the political left. *Webster's Third* also got bad reviews in the left-wing *Nation* and the right-wing *National Review*.

4. How is the shift from "erroneous," "illiterate," and "slang" to "substandard" and "nonstandard" more democratic? See paragraph 15.

5. Macdonald characterized Dr. Gove, head lexicographer of *Webster's Third*, as hesitant to label "ain't" as substandard. Why would Gove feel this way? Why would Macdonald wish to characterize him as hesitant?

6. Toward the end of paragraph 20, Macdonald comments on the possible formality of the word "jerk." Could you write a sentence in a theme for this class like "Dr. Johnson admired Goldsmith's literary talent although he considered him a jerk"? What role has any dictionary played in your decision?

7. Do you think it is significant that most of the people who objected to *Webster's Third* were professional writers, especially journalists, while the people who both produced and later defended it were professors of English, often at universities in the interior of the country (Northwestern, Syracuse, Ohio State, University of Texas, etc.)? How does this pairing off compare with the disputants in Chapter 1? Then it was the editors of *Newsweek* against a committee from the Conference on College Composition and Communication.

8. Would you still like to own a copy of *Webster's Third*? Why?

PATRICK E. KILBURN
The Gentlemen's Guide
to Linguistic Etiquette

The American Heritage Dictionary, first published in 1969, was produced, in part, as a response to *Webster's Third* and to its critical recep-
tion. Disposing of the statistical measurements used by G. & C. Merriam
& Co., the editors of the AHD employed a usage panel, made up primarily of professional writers, to determine the status of different words; the
labels they used include "slang." In the instances of words whose usage
was in doubt, the AHD reported the panel's decision in percentages: 20
percent for slang, 30 percent for colloquial, 40 percent for standard
usage, etc. In 1975 AHD editor William Morris employed the same
procedure with *The Harper Dictionary of Contemporary Usage*, including the written responses of the usage panel. A selection from the usage
panel's judgments may be found later in this chapter on pages 299–300.

The late Professor Patrick Kilburn was a defender of *Webster's Third*
and thus was in frequent contention with Dwight Macdonald. More to
the immediate point, he found that some aspects of the AHD presented
him with a ready prey.

Until a few years ago, even among those who commonly dismiss the Bible as   1
a collection of quaintly poetic ancient myths, there still reigned a species of Holy
Writ: the dictionary. Sophisticates knew that there were dictionaries and then
there were dictionaries, but no one questioned the Merriam-Webster product of
Springfield, Mass.—*Webster's Unabridged*. That work packed such scholarly
might that it occupied a quasi-legal status: its definitions were cited in court
opinions as the final word on words.

Practically speaking, this situation still obtains in all but the most linguis-   2
tically sophisticated of circles. Discusses of word meaning or usage are settled by
looking it up in "the dictionary" (translate: the dictionary at hand, of whatever
age, publisher, or editorial respectability); "the dictionary" settles the issues and
satisfies all parties. As if there were no differences among dictionaries. As if all
dictionaries were alike.

Dictionaries, of course, have never been alike, any more than cars have been   3
alike: they are similar in gross outline but differ widely to the critical eye; they are
more scholarly and independent or less so; more reliable or less so; and so on.
Even though "Webster's dictionaries" are as ephemeral as the mayfly in their
brief lives on drug- and dime-store shelves (the current *Books in Print* lists 28
"Webster's" dictionaries from 10 publishers), the innocence of belief in "the
dictionary" reigned nearly unchallenged in the general mind until the sixties.
Then, all quietly, with relatively little fanfare, the third edition in this century of
Webster's Unabridged appeared in 1961.

Although the official publication date was not until Sept. 28, the *New York*   4
Times, the *Chicago Tribune*, and the *Chicago Sun-Times* on Sept. 7 carried

greetings whose tone is indicated by the title of the *Tribune* piece: "Saying Ain't Ain't Wrong: See Webster." Through September the hubbub mounted and in the months that followed became a very hullabaloo, culminating in an eruption by Wilson Follett in the *Atlantic* for January 1962, called "Sabotage in Springfield," and a long and determined attack by Dwight Macdonald in *The New Yorker* for March 10, 1962, called "The String Untuned." The substance of this anvil chorus of dispraise was that the new dictionary was unsatisfactory on three counts: 1) it dropped "colloquial" from its list of monitory labesl; 2) it was too "scientific" in its definitions—*scientific* in this dispute became anathema as denoting qualities alien to persons of good sense, taste, and feeling; and 3) it paid too much attention to current usage. It had thereby, it was charged, opened the gates to the barbarians, who, being given sanction by the very bastion of power, would sweep in and do whatever hordes of barbarians are supposed to do. Occasional demurrers to the general outcry appeared, but they were lost in the uproar. The battle was joined largely between denouncing journalists on the one hand and defending academics on the other.

In the midst of it all, James Parton of *American Heritage* called the new 5 dictionary "an affront to scholarship" and announced a move to buy up Merriam-Webster stock, presumably to take over the company in order to produce a dictionary for people of taste, culture, and learning. The move failed since "leading stockholders and officers of Merriam . . . advised the management that they were 'not interested' in the offer." Then Parton, down but not out, set up his own organization, and, under the joint sponsorship of *American Heritage* and the Houghton-Mifflin Company, published amidst a blizzard of advertising *The American Heritage Dictionary of the English Language* (the AHD). The sponsorship of AHD suggests that this is the dictionary Parton would have produced if he had succeeded in taking over G. & C. Merriam. Perhaps it is fair to look at it in that light to see if the publishers' claim of advances in lexicography have been made good.

The advertising enters on one gimmick, the Usage Panel, which deserves 6 special comment. This Panel is really the only thing that distinguishes this dictionary from nearly a dozen college dictionaries on the market today, but the hoopla had echoed so loudly that one ought to examine the principle to determine whether it is the great advance in dictionary making it is claimed to be.

The publishers 7

> asked a panel of 100 outstanding speakers and writers a wide range of questions about how the language is used today, especially with regard to dubious or controversial locutions. After careful tabulation and analysis of their replies . . . [they] . . . prepared several hundred usage notes to guide readers to effectiveness in speech and writing. As a consequence, this Dictionary can claim to be more precisely descriptive, in terms of current usage levels, than any heretofore published—especially in offering the reader the lexical opinions of a large group of highly sophisticated fellow citizens.

This procedure represents a major departure from the usual methods of 8 lexicography. From Dr. Johnson's *Dictionary* of 1755 on down, lexicographers recruited teams of readers, not writers, who collected quotations (called "cites" in the trade) illustrating usage of words *in context*, from which a definer would write a definition, oftentimes quoting the word as it appeared in the cites as illustration. Dr. Johnson himself did the whole job of defining, as did Noah Webster, whose *Dictionary* of 1828 was the last major one-man effort. Since that time even the college dictionaries have mushroomed in size beyond the powers of a single man and are now produced by a swarm of scholars presided over by an editor-in-chief who lays down policy. The essential difference is that previous dictionaries have relied upon research for their findings; the AHD places its faith in a process of introspection by a panel of pundits who ruled upon the credentials of a word or usage deemed scruffy in its lineage.

In fact, they came to think of themselves as Academy of linguistic dictators to   9 rule, dispose, and order the mighty flow of the English language, ridiculous as that may seem. For example, the advertising quotes—even, apparently, takes pride in—Dwight Macdonald's cry regarding *enthuse*: "By God, let's hold the line on this one!"

Gad, what a scene! The whole thing rises before me like a vision: a lonely   10 embattled little band, threatened by a horde of bloodthristy savages, unseen, menacing, bent on destruction of All That We Hold Dear—theme music from *Beau Geste*, punctuated by a ghostly drum beat—and through the dusty air rasps the hoarse voice of Dauntless Dwight Macdonald, "By God, let's hold the line on this one!" One swallows a lump and brushes a tear from his eye, murmuring over and over the spunky line, which could, in time, become as hallowed as "Let's win one for the Gipper."

If I seem to be poking fun, it is because I am only following the wisdom of   11 Dr. Johnson in this matter. Johnson, who individually wielded more linguistic influence than the whole of AHD's instant Academy, "flattered" himself at the outset of his project, he said, that he might "put a stop to those alteratons which time and chance have hitherto been suffered to make in [the language] without opposition." But he mournfully concluded that "with . . . justice may the lexicographer be derided, who . . . shall imagine that his dictionary can embalm his language, and secure it from corruption and decay." AHD raises a great hue and cry over *enthuse* but lists *reminisce* and *grovel* without comment, and yet all three words are of a piece: all are backformations made by people who did not know that *enthusiasm* and *reminiscence* and *groveling* did not come from shorter verb forms. So, while the insignificant barricade is raised at *enthuse*, the tide of the language goes around both ends and finally inundates the whole. The notion that the vaporings of a hundred, even a thousand self-appointed sages might affect the flow of language perceptibly is ludicrous in the extreme.

In his *New Yorker* article, Macdonald showed that he knew the principles of   12 language, but he is a man who knows more than he is willing to understand. Intellectually, he knows—as I am sure that many on the Usage Panel must have known—that his rallying cry of "Hold the line" is preposterous; he is a man hoist on his own metaphor. He knows that usage is never settled finally, that meaning derives from usage, that the language is more like a mighty river than a battle between opposing forces, a river which, as long as the language is spoken by native speakers and thus is still a living language, is quite undammable, quite irreversible in its movement, constantly flowing, ever changing, into which, like the river of Heraclitus, one cannot step twice, for in the interim between steps it has become a different river. Macdonald knows this, but in his heart of hearts, he believes that these are really matters that God has ordained; that God said, "Let there be light," and there was the English language (to be precise, the American language).

Since Johnson's time, lexicographers have been humbler creatures, who 13 recognized the inevitable and accepted the universe. They have sought only to describe the practice of writers, knowing that in a spinning world, full of uncertainty, it is folly to believe men's professions. It is safe only to believe that men say what they actually record in print. It seemed obvious to them, as it should seem obvious to even the most obtuse, that preaching does not match practice, even among the gurus of the Usage Panel. This point, too, seems to have been lost on the AHD's editors.

The Usage Panel is only a gimmick, a linguistic guide to pinky-pointing, for 14 what it comes down to in actuality is that each of the pundits is asked, in essence, "Do you use this word or expression? Are you offended when you hear the expression or read it in print?" And then, God save the mark, since there was unanimity on only one usage ("in disfavor of *simultaneous* as an adverb"), the results are reported in percentages, which must represent the absolute triumph of useless information reported in numbers. (Are you in favor of adultery, Mrs. O'Leary? Ninety-six per cent of the time I am against it.) And then, to compound confusion thrice confounded, they ignore the advice of their own Usage Panel in writing notes: 42 per cent of the panel would restrict *alternative* "to a choice involving only two." But their Usage note at *so-called* tweaks the noses of the 42 per cent: ". . . *these so-called friends.* An alternative construction is *these* '*friends.' So called* (without a hyphen) may be used in still another alternative: *these friends, so called.*" This is like the grammar book that advised, "A preposition is a bad thing to end a sentence with." Therefore, the claim that this dictionary is "more precisely descriptive . . . than any heretofore published" is sheer balderdash; the Usage Notes are "precisely descriptive" of nothing but the state of the pundits' navels.

And a sagging bunch of navels they are, too, to report on the state of the 15 living language of 1970. I have not been able to ascertain the birth dates of all of the panel, but 28 were born in the nineteenth century—are seventy or more years old; 32 are in their sixties, 29 are in their fifties, and out of 95 whose ages I have not been able to discover, only *six* are under fifty years old![1] I have nothing against age—I have a substantial amount of it myself—but the old are as rigid in their language as they are in their joints. Sixty out of the ninety could tell me much, perhaps, about the language of Flaming Youth and bathtub gin, but what could such a huddle of arthritic ancients tell me about the language of 1970— beyond, that is, displaying an understandable touchiness about such terms as "senior citizen" (a locution condemned by over half of the panel as "a

---

[1]Twelve members were added to the panel in 1972, many of whom were then under fifty. [eds.]

euphemism associated with the worlds of politics and advertising." This pronouncement, as well as anything that could be cited, displays in a merciless intensity, the silliness of the method. What, for sweet reason's sake, has the fact that it is a euphemism to do with usage? It may be trite, it may be a euphemism, one may prefer "old man" to "senior citizen," but when has purging the language of euphemisms ever been any part of a dictionary's task? Was there no one on the panel with a saving ounce of logic to protest that classifying euphemisms was not a proper matter for a dictionary?).

In the blizzard of advertising surrounding the appearance of this book, one of 16 the items assured the public that on the day of its publication, AHD had rendered obsolete no less than "61 million" other dictionaries. Perhaps one should not stick at the febrile fancies of a publisher's flack, but that 61 million is a bit much, unless the reader can swallow half the story, in which case I will manfully try to swallow my half of it. Otherwise, the case seems not proved. AHD is an adequate college dictionary, not notably different from a number of others already on the market. The touted Usage Panel is only a gimmick, and a poor one at that.

The best advice would be, don't throw out your old *Webster's Third*. It's not 17 really obsolete. If your dictionary is obsolete, the passage of time made it so, not the AHD.

DISCUSSION QUESTIONS

1. What are the implications of Kilburn's title? What is the difference between "usage," "good usage," and "linguistic etiquette"? Is there something wrong with a "Gentlemen's Guide" to anything in today's world? Would a student who wears jeans to class want to use a "Gentlemen's Guide"?

2. Kilburn characterizes the usage panel as a "gimmick" (paragraph 6, etc.), "a major departure" (paragraph 7), and an "instant academy" (paragraph 10). Do you think he is fair in these semantic judgments? Might not the usage panel also be called an "imaginative innovation"?

3. Most of the members of the AHD usage panel appear to be members of the 10 percent of the populaton who still say "invidious" instead of "inviduous." Do you think the usage panel would have been better help for you (provided that you own the AHD) if it were democratized to include an auto worker from Detroit, a welfare mother from St. Louis, a Hollywood press reporter, and a wheat farmer from Saskatchewan? After all, aren't you more likely to talk to one of these people than to a journalist in New York City?

4. The editors of *Webster's Third* wanted to avoid the authoritarianism of the old dictionaries that appeared to dictate as from a cloud-borne throne. The editors of AHD wanted to avoid the apparent abandonment of standards that came with statistical measurement. Which do you think is more authoritarian or democratic? A small committee or single lexicographer who

measures the body politic and determines the most common usage (as with *Webster's Third*)? Or a large panel of professional writers who take a vote? There has to be a difference between the two, as they usually come up with different answers to questions.

5. Have you ever heard anyone use such "back formations" as "enthuse," "reminisce," and "grovel"? (Back formations are verbs formed by shortening nouns.) If you have heard them, what of people used them? Would you happily imitate other aspects of their behavior?

6. After having read Kilburn's comments, would you be more or less willing to buy a copy of *The American Heritage Dictionary* ? If you received one as a gift would you be satisfied or would you want to exchange it for another?

B. ISAAC CHISHOLM
The Background of Words: A Short Guide to Etymology

The history of the English language and of the different words in it is not a remote or obscure study but rather one that affects what we say and write each day. Each word we use, even each word on this page, has a history which colors its usage. Knowing at least the patterns of word and language history can give us an extra measure of power over what we say and write.

Many students are surprised to learn that words have histories at all, histories   1 often quite apart from what the words name or describe. But knowing something about the origin of any word is a way of understanding its meaning, which is why any good dictionary includes a short etymology as part of the entry for the word. The etymology tells us not only where the word "came from," but also something about the way the original perception of the word evolved. For example, our word "muscle" comes from the Latin *musculus*, "little mouse," apparently a survival from the time when Roman legionnaires tried to impress the girls near the barracks by flexing their biceps to make the "little mouse" appear.

Words and the things or ideas they represent do not always come from the   2 same place. Tigers are native to several regions in south Asia, but our word "tiger" can be traced back to Middle English, Old French, Latin, and Greek— but *not* to Hindi, the language of India. Similarly, our word "lagoon," which we associate with the South Pacific, comes from the Italian word *laguna*; it seems that the eighteenth century sailors who first saw what we call "lagoons" were reminded of Venice. This is not to say that words and ideas can never be related, as can be seen with oranges; both the citrus fruit and the word "orange" come from the Middle East. But even here the word has developed an additional history, not closely related to the fruit or the color; the royal family of the

Family Tree of the Indo-European Languages

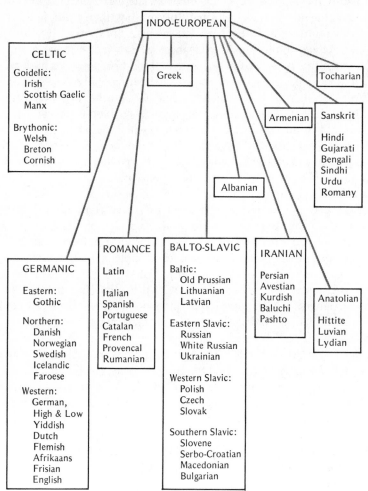

Legend: the names of the families of languages are in capitals, e. g. IRANIAN, CELTIC, etc. Names of the branches within families, e. g. Goidelic, Western Slavic, etc., are followed by colons. Names in lower case without annotation are of actual languages.

Netherlands is the "House of Orange," and an organization of Protestants in Northern Ireland is the "Orange Lodge."

The words we use in the English language come from almost everywhere. In the past 150 years with the expansion of first British and then American power and influence in the world, the English language has absorbed words from all the languages of Europe and from dozens of languages, large and small, from all the other parts of the earth. Keeping track of all these words is one of the reasons we all need to have at least a college or "desk" size dictionary; there are just more words than we are ever going to be able to know.

Most of the words we use every day in conversation have been in the language for a long time. Their ancestors were very likely in Middle English (c. 1150 to 1500 A.D.), and some of *their* ancestors were in Old English (c, 500 to 1100 A.D.). But where are the ancestors of the Old English words? Where did

Old English (or Anglo-Saxon) come from? No language called English existed in any form at the time of the Greeks and Romans, but, then again, it didn't spring out of a vacuum either. Like most of the languages of Europe, English finds its roots in a remote and long-extinct language we call Indo-European.

Although we have no written records in Indo-European, we have no doubt 5 that it once existed. People spoke it from perhaps as early as 5000 B.C. until possibly as late as 2000 B.C., when the different branches of it were developing into the families of languages we recognize today. Indo-European is nowhere near as old as human habitation of Europe, which began many thousands of years before. And not everyone in early Europe spoke it. As best we can tell, the speakers of Indo-European succeeded in getting other people to speak their language, perhaps by military conquest or persuasive influence. Language and genes are not related, after all, and many of the people who came to speak Indo-European and its descendants could well have come from diverse racial stocks, just as today not everyone who speaks English is of English descent. And not everyone who lives in Europe speaks an Indo-European language, even today. Hungarian is not Indo-European, for example, although there is no doubt that Hungarians *are* Europeans. Similarly, Finnish is not Indo-European, and neither is Estonian, a language closely related to Finnish. Another non-Indo-European language is Basque, spoken in the Pyrenees Mountains along the French and Spanish borders. Basque is so different from its neighbors that a Spanish proverb describes it as a language only the devil can learn.

One of the ways we can tell if a language is Indo-European is the way it puts 6 itself together, by its structure, and the common stock of words that appear to be related to words in other Indo-European languages. Travellers had noticed the similarities in many of the languages of Europe from earliest times, but it was not until the British began to arrive in India in large numbers in the eighteenth century that scholars began to work out the family relationships between the languages in a coherent way. The breakthrough came with the discovery that Sanskrit, the ancient language of India, bears a strong relationship to the older languages of Europe, such as Latin, Greek, Gothic, Old Irish, etc. Sanskrit was not identical with Indo-European itself, as some careless scholars hastily assumed, but rather an early descendant of it. When selected Sanskrit words were compared with some from the major European languages, the parallels were unmistakable. One key example is in the words for family relationships, such as "brother" and "sister."

LANGUAGE	"BROTHER"	"SISTER"
English	brother	sister
Sanskrit	bhrātar	svasar
Latin	frater	soror
Italian	fratello	sorella
Russian	brat	sestra
Polish	brat	szestra (siostra)
French	frère	soeur
German	bruder	schwester
Irish	brathir	siur

The spellings of the words in different languages was not by any means identical, but, with study, the differences began to fall into patterns. For example, the root for "sister appears to be "s____s-" as in "sister," "svasar," etc., but in Latin it becomes "sor——," with "r" taking the place of "s" just as in the English verbs "was" and "were."

When we put all these together, along with parallel examples from all the rest of the Indo-European languages, we can make some assumptions about what the original must have been like. The calculations of scholars are: 7

    Indo-European   brater-   swesor-

These parallel forms of words, like "brother" and *bhrātar*, are called *cog-* 8 *nates*. In the case of the different words for "brother" the cognates mean virtually the same thing in each language, but this is not always the case. As anyone who has studied a foreign language knows, one of the worst mistakes one can make in translation is to assume that cognates have identical meaning. To take an oft-cited example, the English "alley" and the German *Allee* obviously come from a common source, but the German *Allee* denotes something grand, more like the English "avenue."

The common stock of cognates in the Indo-European languages suggests that 9 the first speakers lived in a northerly climate. Archaeologists have not succeeded in locating the original Indo-Europeans, although some ambitious scholars have not hesitated to suggest a number of physically identifiable people. The problem is to associate a language, probably unwritten, with a method of making pottery, building a hut, digging a barrow, etc. The Kurgan people who roamed the steppes north of the Black Sea before 2500 B.C. are often suggested. Other speculation focuses on an area south and east of the Baltic in what is today Lithuania. Indo-European languages have many common words for snow and winter but not for summer or autumn. Similarly, our languages have common words for the animals of a northerly climate, such as "bear" and "wolf," but not for animals of warmer regions, such as "camel" or "horse." The early Indo-Europeans were probably herders and nomads rather than settled farmers as we can see in the widespread cognates for "cow" and "honey" and the lack of them for "farmer," "crops," and "tillage."

When the speakers of Indo-European languages dispersed, they went east to 10 India as well as west, all over the continent of Europe, which is why we refer to our common ancestor as *Indo*-European. Many of the languages of northern India, Pakistan, and Afganistan are descended from Indo-European, such as Hindi, Urdu, Punjabi, Assamese, Bengali, and Romany (the language of the Gypsies), as well as many spoken in the lands between Europe and India, such as Persian (the language of Iran), Kurdish, Armenian, and others. The culture of the people who speak these languages is frequently more like that of their non-Indo-European neighbors than like their linguistic relatives in Europe. The Moslem Iranians share much of the culture of their Arab neighbors, who speak a language from the Semitic family. Then again, the Semitic family also includes Hebrew, the language of a people whose culture is vastly different from either the Arabs or the Iranians. Misunderstandings of the differences between language, culture, and race help to heat up political disputes. Part of the old Nazi antagonism toward Jews was based on a misinterpretation of just this principle. The name "Aryan" that the Nazis appropriated for themselves was once used as a synonym for "Indo-European." And as some Nazi leaders believed, without scholarly support, that Germans were the purest descendants of the ancient Aryans (or Indo-Europeans), they assumed that Jews had to be "different" (i.e. inferior) because Hebrew was not an Indo-European language.

The Asian branches of the Indo-European family of languages have contrib- 11 uted relatively few words to Modern English, and even the cognates of these languages are so distant from English that only a specialized etymological dictionary or *The Oxford English Dictionary* is likely to list them.

Closer ties to English can be found, understandably, in the languages ac- 12 tually spoken in Europe. Some of these, such as Greek and Albanian, are single branched families, not closely related to any of their neighbors. Although vastly different from English in structure, even in alphabet, Greek has given thousands of words to English, a legacy of the great flourishing and prestige of Greek culture and philosophy. Some Greek words, such as *hubris*, used in the study of the drama, have come into English directly, transcribed phonetically, with virtually the same definition as the original. Words that come directly, in this manner, from other languages are called *loan words*. Other words have passed through several languages on their way from Greek to English and have undergone changes in spelling and meaning. Take for example the Greek word *geōmetrein*, "to measure land," from *geo-* "earth," and *metrein*, "to measure." The word acquired its modern meaning as it passed from Greek to Latin, where it was spelled *geōmetria*. Over the centuries it passed into Old French as *geometrie*, and then went into Middle English and finally Modern English as "geometry." Still other words have been fabricated in Modern English from Greek parts, especially in the sciences. A good example is "stroboscope" from *strobos*, "a whirling about," and *skopos*, "watcher."

Most of the languages of eastern Europe, excluding Hungarian and Ruma- 13 nian, belong to the Slavic family of languages, which, in turn, is divided into three branches, Eastern, Western, and Southern. The Baltic family, Lithuanian, Latvian, and Old Prussian, appears to have been allied with Slavic in earlier centuries, although they have been distinct for a long time. Family relationships among the Slavic languages are closer than in other families, so that a speaker of Serbo-Croatian, a language of Yugoslavia, would find Russian quite accessible.

Cognates in the Slavic languages are quite distant from English, and, until 14 recently, few loan words have made their way to English from any of the Slavic languages. The considerable migration of peoples from Slavic eastern Europe to North America has not induced many linguistic borrowings. What few words English has taken from any Slavic language come mostly from Russian and generally in the past fifty years, words like "sputnik," "kolkhoz," "agitprop," etc. Needless to say, they are not in wide usage.

The languages of western Europe are divided into three branches, each of 15 which has made considerable impact on English. These are the Romance, Celtic, and Germanic families of languages.

The "Romance" is so called because of the Roman Empire, not because any 16 of the languages is useful in matters of the heart. They include, first, Latin, and from it the languages of lands where Latin was widely used: French, Spanish, Portuguese, Catalan (spoken in northwestern Spain). Provençal (spoken in southwestern France), and Rumanian.

Although English is not of the Romance family, it has been influenced by 17 most of the languages in it (Rumanian excepted). Because Latin was once the language of learning in all fields, the studies of law, medicine, theology, physical and life sciences, philosophy, etc., have borrowed from Latin as they have continued to develop. Most of the "technical" words a student learns in college are of Latin origin. They are characteristically multisyllabled and a trifle stiff. The familiar "school" is of native English origin, but "university" and "institution" come from Latin.

As French culture, taste, and design has had the greatest prestige in Europe 18 since the renaissance, French words have migrated into every one of the Indo-European languages, English included. French-speaking nobles ran England during the middle ages, so English has borrowed more words from French than any other single language.

• • •

In part because the Iberian Peninsula is remote from the British Isles, 19 Spanish and Portuguese contributed fewer words to the English spoken on the far side of the Atlantic. The establishment of Spanish and Portuguese empires in the New World, however, brought Iberian experience in closer association with American and Canadian English. Practically all our terms with life on the ranch are of Spanish origin: "bronco," "lariat," "buckaroo," "stampede," "mustang," etc., as well as dozens of names for western topography: *mesa, arroyo, canyon,* etc. Still others, like "cafeteria," are so much a part of our life they don't "sound" Spanish at all.

The Celtic (pronounced "keltick") family of languages is almost extinct now, 20 but at one time, before the rise of the Roman Empire and the subsequent invastions by the barbaric hordes, it was spoken by more people in western Europe than any other. All of what is today France, northern Italy, southern Scandinavia, Germany, Spain, Poland, Czechoslovakia, Hungary, Austria, and Great Britain was inhabited in the time of the Caesars by Celtic-speaking populations. As the Celts were conquered by or allied with the Romans, their languages were thought to have disappeared at the end of the classical era. It was not until about 1700 that scholars determined several modern languages spoken on the fringes of Europe were descended from ancient Celtic. Those that survived bordered the English speaking world and were divided into two branches; Goidelic, including Irish, Scottish Gaelic, and Manx (spoken on the Isle of Man until 1975, when the last speaker died); and Brythonic, including Welsh, Breton (spoken in northwestern France) and Cornish (spoken in Cornwall until the middle of the eighteenth century).

Only a handful of words from the ancient British, a Celtic language, survived 21 in English. Over the centuries few words have been borrowed from the nearby Celtic languages until recent times, and most of them have come from Irish and Scottish Gaelic, e.g., "slogan," "galore," "creel," "bog," "whisky," etc. But if we were to include colloquialisms and dialect words such as "smashing" (from the Scottish Gaelic *Is math sin*, "That's good!"), "shebang," "kibosh," "shindig," "donnybrook," "acushla," etc., the Celtic contributions to English would number more than a thousand.

The last principal branch of the Indo-European family of languages to be 22 considered is the largest in terms of numbers of speakers, the Germanic. As they were used by many of the invaders at the fall of Rome, the various Germanic languages have heavily influenced the vocabularies of other languages, including some outside Europe. Several older Germanic languages have disappeared, their speakers having been subsumed into other languages, such as Italian, French, and Spanish. The entire Eastern branch, of which only Gothic was ever written, disappeared in the middle ages. The two surviving branches, the Northern and Western, are in robust good health. The Northern branch includes all the Scandinavian languages, excluding the non-Indo-European Finnish. These are Danish, Norwegian, Swedish, Icelandic, and Faroese (spoken by the 35,000 inhabitants of the Faroe Islands).

All of the North Germanic languages are closely related to one another so 23 that the speaker of one finds another easy to learn. The total number of speakers of all five languages is rather small, about 17 million. During the middle ages all five of the modern languages could be classed as one language with different dialects, Old Norse. Because English and North Germanic languages belong to the same larger family, they share a number of cognates. As both North Germanic and English speakers have been maritime peoples sharing the same waterway in the North Sea, it is not surprising that hundreds of Norse words have entered English over the centuries, most extensively during the times of the Viking raids, as we shall see shortly.

The third branch of the Germanic family of languages is the Western, which 24 includes High and Low German (until recently considered two distinct languages), Yiddish (derived from High German), Dutch, Afrikaans (spoken by Dutch settlers in South Africa and derived from Dutch), Flemish, Frisian (spoken by about 300,000 people in northern Holland and parts of northern Germany; the nearest relative of English), and, finally, English.

The languages of the West Germanic branch are not as closely related to one 25 another as those of the Northern branch, even though many of them grew one from the other. The pattern by which Yiddish developed from High German or Afrikaans grew out of Dutch was anticipated by English fifteen centuries earlier when it grew into a distinct language from three Germanic dialects spoken by the Angles, Saxons, and Jutes. Because of this traceable family relationship, English finds an extensive number of cognates with other West Germanic languages, especially Dutch and Frisian. This is not to say that an English speaker finds these languages extraordinarily easy to learn. The unique history of the English language has kept it separate from its near relations since about 450 A.D., when Britain was invaded by those Angles, Saxons, and Jutes. Subsequent developments in Britain /England have made the structure of English entirely different from its sister languages. Quite apart from the cognates, both Dutch and German have contributed many words to English. Dutch words started entering

English at an earlier date, in part because many English books were at one time printed in the Netherlands and also because the two countries were trade rivals, not only in Europe but literally around the globe. German words began to enter English in large numbers by the eighteenth century and have continued at a steady pace ever since, particularly in medicine, philosophy, psychology and political science.

The Old English language, or Anglo-Saxon, as it used to be called, devel- 26 oped slowly from the West Germanic dialects of the invaders. After four centuries it was not so much a single language as a union of four dialects spoken in the England of that day: Kentish, West Saxon, Mercian, and Northumbrian. Most speakers of Modern English find Old English difficult to learn for several reasons. Unlike Modern English, but like most other Indo-European languages, Old English was an inflected language, that is, each word had a different ending according to its case, gender, place in the sentence, and so on. More troublesome for the modern reader, Old English, the largely unwritten language of a warlike, rural people, employed concepts which cannot be translated into any twentieth century Indo-European language, including Modern English. Such an elementary concept as "earth" becomes in Old English *middangeard*, "middle-yard/enclosure." With intensive study, however, many modern students can gain a halting knowledge of Old English, and almost any native speaker of English can spot the family relationship in a passage of Old English prose. Here, transcribed to modern letters, is a passage from the Gospel of Saint Mark, chapter 12, verse 1:

Sum monn him plantode wingeard and betynde hine and dealf anne gettimbrode anne stiepel and gesette hine mid eorthtilium and ferde on eltheodignesse.

In Modern English the passage would look something like this:

A certain man planted a vineyard for himself and enclosed it (him) and dug a pit and built a tower (steeple) and people-d (set) it (him) farmers (earth-tillers) and went into a foreign country.[1]

Old English, unlike its modern derivative, was not receptive to new vocabu- 27 lary from other languages. Instead of borrowing, Old English characteristically made up words for new concepts by jamming together smaller words. Such combinations are called *kennings*, and a few of them have survived to become words in Modern English. When we see a river dropping down a precipice we are more likely to call it a "waterfall," from the Old English, than a "cascade," from Latin via Italian and French.

The England in which Old English was spoken (c.500-1100) was nothing 28 like the stable nation-state of modern times. Just as the Angles and Saxons invaded the island and wrested power from the Britons, so, too, later invaders arrived over the centuries, hoping to make a prize of the country. The first were the Norsemen or Vikings, who started to come to England in 787 and at intervals for the next 300 years. We have been used to think of the Vikings as brutal

---

[1]Suggested by Morton W. Bloomfield, "A Brief History of the English Language," *The American Heritage Dictionary of the English Language* (Boston: Houston Mifflin, 1969), page xv.

savages, perhaps, as some scholars now say, because the accounts of the invaders were written by clergymen; the pagan Norsemen went after the rich churches and monasteries for their first plunder. In time, many of the Norse invaders settled in Great Britain and merged with the native population, especially in the northeast of England and the Lowlands of Scotland. As the North Germanic languages, beginning then to separate into Danish, Norwegian, and Swedish, were fairly closely related to Old English, the Norse invader-settlers never had to make a great effort to learn the native language. Instead, they continued to speak their own languages, making themselves understood in English as best they could, probably with shouting, gestures, and grimaces. By this process a a large number of Norse words entered English. When those Norse words were cognates of Old English their meanings were somewhat altered. A good example of this is the name for the standard garment that both the Anglo-Saxons and the Norsemen wore; both called it by a similar name, Old English *scyrte*, and Norse *Skyrte*. In time the Old English form gave us "shirt" and the Norse "skirt." When Anglo-Saxons and Norsemen dug a hole in the ground they called it a *dic*, which in the Anglo-Saxon interior gives us the word "ditch." Along the seacoast where the Norsemen lived, the dug hole and the dirt from it were considered to be the same thing, and so in time the Norse pronunciation of the word gave us "dike." When two cognates denoted the same thing, the Norse form tended to take a less attractive connotation. The Norsemen and Anglo-Saxons had comparable words for a bad odor, but the Norse word became "stink" and the Anglo-Saxon the more elegant "stench." Another pattern to notice is that Norse-derived words tend to have the harder sounds: s*k*irt, di*k*e, and stin*k*, whereas the Old English have the softer: *sh*irt, di*tch*, and sten*ch*.

A more traumatic invasion of England began in 1066 when the French- 29 speaking Normans came across the Channel and drove out or exterminated most of the native English aristocracy. Actually, the Normans looked very much like the Norsemen, as they themselves had come from Scandinavia to France only a generation earlier. But in the short time they had been in France they had acquired the French language and somewhat superior manners, or so it seemed to the Anglo-Saxons. For the next 300 years in England, French was the language of the royal family, the courts, most business, and of well-furnished country estates. The Norman invaders did not want to bother learning English, considering it a coarse, lower-class language. When English emerged again as the written language of the privileged classes about the time of Chaucer, 1360-1400, it was vastly transformed. Aspects of the language that the Normans refused to learn simply disappeared, such as most of the inflections and genders. Instead, English became a highly idiomatic language, one in which words were put together in highly individual, sometimes erratic ways, a language easy to start to learn but difficult to master. More important to our purposes here, the Normans brought the first wave of thousands of French words to come into English. As with the Norse instance, the French words usually had to compete with Anglo-Saxon rooted words already in the language; only this time the native words took the less favorable connotation, or, in the case of many foods, the meaning more associated with the countryside as opposed to the great house.

The key example of this pattern is always the word for the place we live. The English-derived word is, "house," and the Norman-derived word, from the French *maison*, is "mansion." Significantly, the word *maison* in French does not denote anything especially grand, but when it was borrowed into English by someone who lived in a great *maison* it acquired a new connotation.

A good indication of the social distinctions between the Anglo-Saxons and 30 the Normans is their contrasting names for food and the animals who produced it. Initially, both French and English had one word to serve both purposes. Thus the Old English word *cu* meant both the beast in the fields and the butchered, cooked meat upon the table. Alas, many Anglo-Saxons were not eating much *cu*, but the Normans were, calling it *boef*, giving us the modern word "beef." Other such counterparts are:

ANGLO-SAXON	NORMAN FRENCH
sheep	mutton
pig	pork
calf	veal
chicken	pullet

With these in mind we should not be surprised that the ordinary "steak" is of Germanic background, actually from the Old Norse *steik*, whereas "sirloin" is Norman French.

The reader will notice that the Anglo-Saxon derived words tend to be 31 shorter, simpler, and more familiar. This is not absolutely the case, as many Anglo-Saxon forms have been replaced by foreign borrowings and have been forgotten, or have become dialect words, and so seem quite unfamiliar in a modern context. Nevertheless, the pattern that Anglo-Saxon words should be shorter and blunter is reliable. The pattern finds its extreme in the so-called "four-letter words," that collection of a half-dozen or so salty expressions every English speaker learns sometime before adolescence and which can be found on the walls of almost every public lavatory in the English-speaking world. All are Anglo-Saxon except the ultimate one, which is borrowed from Dutch, apparently an inheritance from sailors during the seventeenth century trade rivalries. But not a one is Latinate or multisyllabled. Somehow Latin or French words, even when they are raucus in their own languages, don't sound pungent or "dirty" in English. There was a time, not distant, when the more delicate parts of the body could only be referred to in writing in Latin terms, presumably because anyone educated enough to read Latin could not be corrupted by seeing them in print. This emotional effect still applies in English: Latinate words usually have less impact on the reader or listener.

The English language continued to be hungry for new words all through the 32 Middle English period (c. 1150-1500), and on into Modern English (c.1500 to the present). Far from getting its fill of new words, the language continues the absorb more each year at a steadily increasing rate. More new words have appeared in English for the first time in the past twenty-five years than in any other twenty-five year period of its history. Many of these words are used only in the sciences or are ephemeral colloquialisms, but not all are. The words "elitism" and "elitist," so often used in conversations in North American colleges today, go back only to 1969, although their root, "elite," is several centuries old. Depending on what one counts as a distinct word (are "hot," "rod," and "hot rod" three words or two?), there are presently somewhere over 800,000 words in the English language, more than any one brain can hope to remember without assistance.

Once a word is established and used in the language, whether it is an ancient, 33 native word or a recent borrowing, it frequently refuses to sit still and mean the same thing century after century. The usual pattern is for a word to pick up new definitions while retaining the old. Take for example "mule," that beast of burden which is a sterile hybrid of a male donkey and a female horse. As one of the first things a breeder would notice about a mule was that it couldn't reproduce itself, the first acquired meaning of the word is "any hybrid which is sterile," even one so different physically as one crossbred from a canary and another bird. Another definition accrues from the people who work with mules and notice that they are sometimes intractable. Those people gave us the informal definition of "mule" as a "stubborn person," a figurative application of the first definition. Because the mule is often asigned tedious and difficult labor, it has given its name, again figuratively, to two machines, one that makes thread or yarn from fibers and another that hauls freight over short distances, as in a mine. Quite apart from these is the definition of "mule" as a "backless, strapless slipper." This "mule" is an entirely different word that just happens to be spelled and pronounced the same way. A good dictionary will list it as "mule²" to distinguish it from the "mule" we have been talking about. We call such verbal coincidences *homonyms*.

Sometimes the pattern of a word's acquired meanings will be clear and 34 logical. The word "plumb" comes, via Old French and Middle English, from the Latin *plumbum*, "lead." Even today the weight we tie at the end of a plumb line might well be lead. Because a plumb line would be used to establish the exact, true vertical, anyone who is utterly in the state he occupies is, colloquially, "plumb," as in "plumb crazy," or the western movie favorite, "plumb loco." Taking another line from *plumbum*, a man who works with lead to repair leaking pipes, though not necessarily with a plumb line, is a *plumb*er.

At other times the transition will be harder to explain. How did "harlot," 35 which referred to a male vagabond or a male servant in Middle English, come to denote a female of ill-repute? How did "fix" start out meaning "fasten securely" but come to mean "repair," "bribe," or "take heroin intravenously"?

Language historians are interested in determining the pattern of change in a 36 word's definition. Some words start out their lives perfectly respectable and admired, but something sullies them and they acquire unseemly connotations and even denotations. The most often cited example of this process is "villain," which meant merely "serf" in Middle English, its root going back to the Latin *villa*, "country house." The change in the word's meaning may indicate something about the behavior of many of those serf/villains or, more likely, the perception of them. A similar fate befell "salon" as it became "saloon," although in Britain a "saloon" still describes a place where a respectable lady might be found. The downgrading of a word's meaning is called *pejoration*. Its opposite is *amelioration*, the general improvement in a word's denotation and connotation. A "marshal" was originally a groom or stable servant, but now it may describe an officer in a royal household, one of high rank in an army, or, in the U.S., a Federal law officer. Some words ameliorate because they are used so often they lose their bite. "Naughty" was a foul, insulting term in Shakespeare's time, but it had barely enough stamina to frighten a child in even Victorian times. Similarly, many men would not now consider the epithets "rogue" and "scoundrel" grounds for a duel.

The study of word history, etymology, is nowhere near as simple as this short sketch would imply. It is, at best, an inexact science, somewhat more reliable than weather forecasting. We can find the origin of a word only if it has been recorded. Many quite common words have histories which cannot be traced or are disputed, such as the American colloquialisms, "finagle," "lollapalooza" (it only *looks* Italian), "phony," and "raunchy." Some other etymologies are fabricated, either by cocksure dictionary makers or by vain, would-be genealogists who would like to inflate the histories of their families. A case in point is the word "schooner," once thought to have been named by Captain Andrew Robinson of Gloucester, Massachusetts, in 1713. The only evidence for this came from a letter written by the captain's descendants seventy-seven years later. Although *The Oxford English Dictionary* records the etymology with a skeptical note, most other dictionaries pass on the origin as fact. The pretension and imprecision that once characterized the study of etymology provoked a famous parody from Mark Twain. The origin of "Middletown" is easy to trace, he asserted. The "M" is from "Moses" and the "iddletown" will be found shortly.

DISCUSSION QUESTIONS

As is not the case with most of the other essays in this book, it is difficult to talk about some of the implications of what Chisholm has to say without another reference in your hands: the dictionary of your choice.

1. Where do most of the words you use come from? Take the first ten words from some writing of yours, preferably something informal, such as your journal, and look up the origins of the words. How many of the words are of Anglo-Saxon origin as opposed to Latin or French? Compare this with the first ten words from a textbook, especially one you find difficult reading.

2. Bergen Evans has pointed out that many slang words repeat the etymologies of their more formal synonyms. For example, "exaggerate" comes from the Latin ex-, "out," and agger, "heap," fairly close to "heap it on," the slang term. Is there a comparable pun in "to impose" and "to put something over on," "to apprehend" and "to catch on," "to converse" and "to go around with," "to excoriate" and "to take the hide off," "to be ecstatic" and "to be beside oneself"? Can you find others?

3. Explain why most dictionaries give the Latin, or taxonomic, names for plants, animals, and birds even though few readers understand them.

4. Look up the following words in your dictionary and explain whether the etymology is a useful guide to current meaning: "buxom," "gossip," "leash," "pledge," "silly," "torrent," "write." Compare the pattern of those words with: "conversation," "glide," "lapse," "metropolis," "peel," "sophomore."

5. One aspect of etymology that Chisholm neglected was the number of words which have entered English from non-Indo-European origins. All of the following words have come from outside the Indo-European family: "tomato," "chocolate" "coyote," "hara-kiri," "jukebox," "okra," "yams," "potato." Does their "exotic" origin make them feel "foreign"? Why or why not?

6. Some words have simply been made up and do not derive from any root in another language. Does this make them feel "different"? Some of these are: "radar," "snafu," "laser," "blimp," and "quark."

7. Here is a list of prefixes and "combining forms" from Greek and Latin that are used as word parts in the formation of English words, mostly of a learned character. A combining form is one that cannot be used alone but only in combination with other forms. Linguists call such forms bound morphemes. Consult your dictionary to see how many words have been built with them.

Combining Form	Meaning	Example
	GREEK	
1. aster astro	star	astronomy
2. biblio	book	bibliography
3. ec eco	earth	ecology
4. gyn gyno gyne gyneco gynous	woman	gynecology
5. mega	great; million	megaton
6. mis miso	hatred	misogynist
7. orth ortho	straight; upright	orthodoxy
8. phil philo phile	love; loving	philosophy
9. phot photo	light	photography
10. zo zoo	animal	zoology
	LATIN	
11. ad	to; toward	admit
12. circum	around	circumvent
13. com con	with	compose, convene
14. cor	heart	coronary
15. inter	among	interstate
16. intra	within	intramural
17. mare	sea	mariner
18. port	carry	portable
19. uni	one	uniform
20. voc	call	vocation

LAWRENCE VAN GELDER
"The Ketchup Connection."

Although *The Oxford English Dictionary* may have been compiled to aid the loftiest scholarly enterprises, its thousands of pages give us so much information that we can use it to answer all kinds of questions about the way we live as well as about the way we think. By using the OED and other reference works, Van Gelder shows us that ketchup is more exotic than chili sauce and older than hamburgers. From time to time it may have more things thrown into it than are in hot dogs. It even gives us a handle on trying to find the right spelling for the word.

What's red, originated in the Far East and sometimes seems to be taking over   1
the world?

Chinese Communism is, of course, the wrong answer.   2

The red tide in question here is one of those products that is so literally under   3
everybody's nose (and sometimes on the chin, fingertips and other repositories for drippings as well) that nobody ever seems to wonder how it got here.

Yet without it, the Big Mac might have suffered from stunted growth; french   4
fries might have seemed like small potatoes; and more than a few palates might—just—have managed to adjust to the pristine delights of steak, the unadorned blandishment of eggs and—at the presidential level—even unalloyed cottage cheese.

The subject is ketchup, a subject that leaves lexicographers and culinary   5
encyclopedists in a certain amount of disagreement.

Ketchup seems to be the preferred spelling these days, but "catsup" and   6
"catchup" are not unknown, and the unabridged *Oxford English Dictionary* even takes note of "kitchup."

Not only are the experts less than united on orthography, they also seem   7
bereft of certitude in determining precisely where ketchup came from. *Larousse Gastronomique*, with the sort of high Gallic contempt that prompts the French to blame the English for syphilis, also holds the cross-Channel barbarians accountable for the affliction of ketchup.

"Condiment of English origin," asserts Larousse in one of its entries, "widely   8
used in both England and U.S.A."

Everyone else seems to disdain this French connection and although there is   9
some indication of a Roman relation, there is widespread agreement that ketchup, unlike chop suey, really did come out of the Orient. The disagreement concerns the precise source. China has its adherents, and so does Indonesia.

The *Oxford English Dictionary*, which notes a reference to ketchup as early   10
as 1690, leans in favor of China. It cites the Chinese *koe-chiap* or *ke-tsiap* as well as the Malay *kechap*, which it says, the Dutch spelled *ketjap*.

This early version is defined as a brine of pickled fish or shellfish, which   11
Theodora Fitzgibbon in 'The Food of the Western World' likens to a Roman relish called garum or liquamen.

Made from the salted entrails of dried fish, like anchovies, which were later 12
flavored with vinegar, oil or pepper, garum was popular enough to give rise to
precursors of H.J. Heinz.

'The Food of the Western World' notes, "Several towns were famous for their 13
factory-made garum and in the ruins of Pompeii a small jar was found bearing
the inscription 'Best strained liquamen. From the factory of Umbricus Agath-
opus.' "

Despite the boasts of Umbricus, quite a few years had to pass before the real 14
ketchup boom began. According to the people at H.J. Heinz, which has just
begun its second century of processing ketchup, which it used to call catsup, it
was English seamen who brought back from Singapore an affection for a tangy
compound of fish brine, herbs and spices they knew as kechap.

But lacking some of the native ingredients, they were compelled to cast about 15
for substitutes. Among them were mushrooms, walnuts, cucumbers and tomatoes.

The Oxford English Dictionary notes that by 1748, in her 'Housekeeper's 16
Pocketbook,' Mrs. Harrison was counseling readers not to be without "Kitchup."

More than a century later, similar advice was being dispensed by Isabella 17
Beeton's 'Book of Household Management.' With regard to ketchup, she wrote,
"This flavouring ingredient, if genuine and well prepared, is one of the most
useful store sauces to the experienced cook, and no trouble should be spared in
its preparation."

Her book included recipes for mushroom, oyster and walnut ketchups.   18

In 1876, some 15 years after the first bound edition of Mrs.Beeton's manual 19
was published, Henry J. Heinz became one of the first commercial processors of
ketchup in the United States. He had founded his company seven years earlier.

Like their English counterparts, American seafarers had developed a taste for 20
the condiment, too. But they added to it tomatoes from Mexico or the Spanish
West Indies.And the families of Maine seafarers began planting tomato seeds so
they could make their own ketchup. According to the H.J. Heinz company, the
making of tomato ketchup was an arduous process, which required long hours of
stirring over a hot fire to make certain the tomato neither burned nor stuck. So it
was natural for Henry Heinz to think of making ketchup commercially. The
company notes that its ketchup recipe is the only one that is not altered by its
affiliates around the world to appeal to the taste of a particular country.

Heinz, followed by DelMonte, Hunt and regional packers, dominates the 21
ketchup market. Heinz U.S.A., a division of the H. J. Heinz company, says that
with 65 percent of the restaurant market and 40 to 45 percent of the consumer
market, it sells 300 million bottles of ketchup a year, or nearly 1½ bottles a
person.

And life, lips, laps and lapels would hardly be the same without it.   22

DISCUSSION QUESTIONS ·

1. Most people think of ketchup as a distinctly American product. Does
this article suggest that it is really foreign?

2. Do you know of any other words which have passed around the

world as much as "ketchup"? Could they also find a home in North America?

3. How does the history of the word explain the unsettled spelling the word has today—even on the bottles of different manufacturers?

4. Does the history of "ketchup" help explain its widespread popularity?

5. Can you explain how the information in this essay is not widely known, even though it is in the OED? In short, how did we happen to forget that ketchup originated in the Orient?

Student Essay
Hunting a "Deer"

The word "deer" is not like the words for other animals. For one thing, it is ₁ usually spelled the same way plural as singular, not like those irregular words, "mouse" and "mice" or "goose" and "geese." The deer is one animal that has been common in both the British Isles and in North America and is therefore a beast we have had a chance to make up our mind about. It brings out feelings of tenderness in women and raises the hot, *machismo* juices of the great hunter in men. What I did not know until I looked up "deer" in *The Oxford English Dictionary* is that the word once referred to any animal that breathed. Over the years the meaning of the word has changed so that it refers only to that special, graceful animal in English and American forests.

"Deer" comes from an Old Teutonic substantive and has been in the English ₂ language for a long time. It has cousins in many of the languages related to English, such as German, Dutch, Frisian, Swedish, Danish, and Icelandic. These related forms of "deer" look a bit like the English word but are always spelled a little bit differently. For example, there is a word in Dutch and Low German, *dier*. Some other spellings look quite different from English, such as the Swedish *djur* and the Icelandic *dýr*. These related forms are called cognates and do not always mean the same thing as the English word. "Deer" does not have cognates in other Indo-European families; the *OED* lists nothing, for example, from French, Latin, Greek, or Russian.

The word "deer" first began to appear in English back in the Dark Ages, ₃ when the monks were spending their time copying and recopying old manuscripts. Not surprisingly, some of the first examples of the word "deer" in English are in translations of the Bible, such as the *Lindisfarne Gospels* from about 950 A.D. The spelling of "deer" was in dispute, or so it would appear. From 950 to about 1700 it was spelled more than a dozen ways, including *dior, deor, der, dor, dier, duer, dur, dure, deure,* and others. Our spelling "deer" did not become the most popular until about 1400. Through all of this, though, the singular and the plural forms were usually the same.

The biggest change that has occurred to the history of the word "deer" is that ₄ it used to refer to any animal before it came to mean specifically the deer we now call by that word. Most of the examples of "deer" referring to any animal are very old, beginning in 950 and mostly from before 1250. The last was recorded in 1481, and there were none before that for 200 years.

The switch in the meaning of the word "deer" is something like what hap-   5 pened to *anima* in Latin. Originally *anima* meant "soul" or "breath." In this sense it gives us the English words "animation" and "animate." Eventually, though, it gave us the word "animal," apparently because it singled out the characteristic of the living things that were not plants or vegetables. The original root of "deer" meant "to breathe" also, but it was made more specific twice.

Once the speakers of English decided that "deer" means what we define it as   6 today, they didn't add any more meanings to it. The oldest use of "deer" the way we usually define it is from 893, actually before the first definition, but many more are from the thirteenth and fourteenth centuries. It did not seem to lend itself to figurative uses.

On the other hand, "deer" has lent itself to a large number of derived forms,   7 some of which are directly related to the deer of the forest, such as "deer bed," which, sure enough, is a bed for deer. Many others are unrelated, however. The long, sleek racing dog known as the "deer hound" is more like a greyhound or a borzoi than an actual deer. The people who named it must have been thinking of the graceful neck and the speed.

Checking into other dictionaries, I found that all of them were in general   8 agreement with the *OED*, but most of them had at least one bit of different information. Not a one was even a quarter the size of the entry in the *OED*, although *Webster's New International Dictionary, Third Edition*, came the closest. *WNID-3* includes cognates from Lithuanian and Sanskrit and also gives two definitions not in the *OED*, "deer" as "deer meat," or venison, and the color "deer," very much like "camel." *The Random House Dictionary* adds nothing, but *The Standard College Dictionary* gives a collateral, scientific name for "deer," *cervine*. *Webster's New World Dictionary* says "deers" is an occasional plural for "deer," but *The American Heritage Dictionary* says it is an alternate plural without calling it "occasional." *American Heritage* also gives "deer" another definition: other small, deerlike animals such as the mouse deer, a kind of goat found in Africa and Asia.

In the thousand and more years that English speaking people have talked   9 about deer we have had more to say than "Kill!" or "This is the sweet story of Bambi." The different spellings of such a simple word as "deer," and the differ-ent concepts for such a familiar animal as the deer, give us a capsule history of the English language.

RHETORICAL ANALYSIS

1. Outline the topics of the nine paragraphs in the essay. How would you describe the order the student author has chosen in putting this essay together?

2. What other kinds of order are available in an essay which gives a

history? Could the student author have covered the same topics with a different organization?

3. What is the topic of paragraph 3? Is it a unified paragraph?

4. Paragraphs 4, 5 and 6 outline different definitions of the word "deer" from the middle ages on. What transitional devices has the student author used to help distinguish the differences in the definitions?

5. Does the substance of the paper justify the first sentence of the opening paragraph? Is "deer" really unlike the words for other animals?

6. Are the student author's comments about killing deer and Bambi justified in the conclusion? Might she have done better to place them in another part of the paper?

POINTS OF DEPARTURE

A. Putting Your Hands into *The Oxford English Dictionary*

Although much of the reading in this chapter encourages you to be critical in using and reading a dictionary, you may have noticed that one dictionary seems to stand above criticism, the incomparable *Oxford English Dictionary*.[1] If your instructor has not assigned the article by Roberts earlier in this chapter, you will find it worthwhile to review the sections on the *OED*, pages 289-292. As it was produced with much donated effort and underpaid academic labor, the dictionary would be impossible to duplicate in the present age, even with our rapid technological management of information. Then again, there is a sense in which the *OED* was never completed. Scholars are at work now to bring the entries up to date. The first of a three-volume corrected supplement appeared in 1972.

The *OED* is incomparable not only in the way it was produced but also in the ways you can use it. It would never serve, for example, as a substitute for a desk-sized college dictionary. Those 16,400, triple-columned pages of tiny print make it too bulky, no matter how well it is packaged; besides, it nearly always provides too much information for handy reference. Nevertheless, anyone who wants to know how the English language works will consult it many times. One immediate reason is to define obscure words, especially if they appear in older English literature. All the words in Shakespeare, for example, are treated thoroughly. A more common reason for consulting the *OED* is to trace the changing definitions of words, especially more common words we already think we know.

Once you have mustered the strength to lift one of the massive volumes down from the shelf and have opened it, you may be somewhat intimidated by the density of the print and the frequency of abbreviation. But these problems can be

---

[1] The title page in current editions reads, *The Oxford English Dictionary on Historical Principles* and is therefore usually abbreviated as *OED*. As the first edition read *The New English Dictionary on Historical Principles* it is sometimes abbreviated as the *NED* or the *HED*. Less commonly, it is sometimes "Murray's Dictionary," after its first editor, Sir James A. H. Murray.

overcome. The *OED* may be a monument of scholarship, but it is not a monolith. It was intended to be accessible to anyone with the background of, say, a college freshman. As any dictionary, the *OED* provides a guide to its use placed immediately after the title page, listing five symbols and 233 abbreviations employed throughout the text. Most of the abbreviations are self-explanatory and widely used in writing, such as *Math.* for "mathematics" and "unkn." for "unknown," but a few are a bit less obvious, such as "LXX" for "Septuagint," the name for the Greek translation of the Old Testament made in the third century B.C.

An entry often used to show how the *OED* works is the one for "deer." As you begin to read the entry you will notice the editors have been conscientious in listing variant spellings, which, in the case of "deer,"run to more than a dozen, all but one long out of use. To keep order among the different spellings, the editors decided to number them according to the century of their appearance in writing, beginning with 1 for all spellings found before 1100 A. D. Thus 2 stands for the twelfth century, 1100-1200, 3 for the thirteenth century, and so on down to 7 for the seventeenth century, by which time most spellings had stabilized. You will notice that the modern spelling "deer" became dominant in the fourteenth century. And from the beginning of the word's usage the plural form has tended to be the same as the singular.

Following the survey of the spelling comes the etymology, set off with square brackets, generaly in the same paragraph. The etymology gives not only the immediate ancestors of the word but also its cognates in the different Indo-European languages. The root of "deer" was a common Germanic or Teutonic substantive, appearing in Old and Middle English before continuing in Modern English. When you get to the actual definitions below, you will notice that the *OED* does not separate Old and Middle English forms and definitions from Modern ones, but instead treats the language as a single continuity. After the immediate ancestors, the entry lists a wide range of cognates in most of the North and Western Germanic languages, including Old Saxon, Old Frisian, Middle Dutch, etc.

Then, still within the brackets, there comes a note in smaller type which tells us that "deer" is believed to go back to (an Indo-European) root *dhus*, "to breathe," which, in turn, invites a comparison with the Latin *anima*, "breath" or "soul," which gives us the word "animal." The essential meaning of both "deer" and "animal" seems to suggest something breathing.The conclusion of the etymology advises us that the word "dear" seems to be related to "deer," but that the Greek word for "wild beast" is not.

Only a few advanced students will ever need this information, but you should know, first, that it exists. A knowledge of the etymology of a word is not always as esoteric as it might seem. You may very likely encounter questions of the origin of words in philosophy, psychology, and other fields of study. Such information is often called to bear on the legal definition of a word.

Following this begin the actual definitions of the word, each numbered. The first is marked with a dagger (†), one of the conventional symbols of the *OED*, indicating that the sense given here is now obsolete. The word "deer" once

Deer (di•ɪ). Forms: 1 díor, déor, 2–3 deor, (2 dæer), 2–4 der, (2–3 dor, 3 dier, 3–4 duer, 4 dur, 5 dure, deure), 4–6 dere, (4–7 deere, 5, 7 diere, 5– (*Sc.*) deir, 6–7 deare), 4– deer, (5 theer). *Pl.* 1–9 normally same as sing.; also 2 deore, deoran, 2–3 -en; 3–4 deores, dueres, 7–9 *occas.* deers. [A Comm. Teut. sb.: OE. *díor*, *déor* = OS. *dier*, OFris. *diar*, *dier* (MDu. and Du. and LG. *dier*), OHG. *tior* (MHG. *tier*, Ger. *tier*, *thier*):–WG. *dior*, ON. **djúr* (Icel. *dýr*, Sw. *djur*, Da. *dyr*); Goth. *dius*, *diuz-*:–OTeut. *deuzoᵐ*:– pre-Teut. *dheuso·m*.

Generally referred to a root *dhus* to breathe (cf. *animal* from *anima*), and thought by some etymologists to be the neuter of an adj. used subst. Cf. DEAR *a.*². (Not connected with Gr. θήρ wild beast.)]

†1. A beast: usually a quadruped, as distinguished from birds and fishes; but sometimes, like *beast*, applied to animals of lower orders. *Obs.*

c 950 *Lindisf. Gosp.* Luke xviii. 25 Se camal þæt micla dear. *a* 1000 *Boeth. Metr.* xxvii. 24 Swa swa fuȝl oððe dior. *c* 1000 ÆLFRIC *Voc.* in Wr.-Wülcker 118/31 *Fera*, wild deor. *Bellua*, reðe deor.. *Unicornis*, anhyrne deor. **1154** *O. E. Chron.* (Laud MS.) an. 1135 Pais he makede men & dæer. *c* 1200 ORMIN 1176 Shep iss..stille der. *Ibid.* 1312 Lamb iss softte & stille deor. *a* 1250 *Owl & Night.* 1321 Al swo deth mani dor and man. *c* 1250 *Gen. & Ex.* 4025 Also leun is miȝtful der. **1481** CAXTON *Reynard* (Arb.) 18 The rybaud and the felle diere here I se hym comen.

β. plural.

c 1000 ÆLFRIC *Gen.* i. 25 And he siȝ ofer þa deor. *c* 1175 *Lamb. Hom.* 43 Innan þan ilke sea weren un-aneomned deor, summe feðerfotetd, summe al bute fet. *Ibid.* 115 þene bið his erd ihened..on wilde deoran. *c* 1200 *Trin. Coll. Hom.* 177 Oref, and deor, and fishshes, and fugeles. *Ibid.* 209 Hie habbeð geres after wilde deore. *Ibid.* 224 Of wilde diere. *c* 1250 *Gen. & Ex.* 4020 On ilc brend eft twin der. *Ibid.* 4032 Efte he sacrede deres mor. *a* 1310 in Wright *Lyric P.* xiii. 44 Deores with huere derne rounes. *Ibid.* xiv. 45 In dounes with this dueres plawes. *c* 1340 *Gaw. & Gr. Kt.* 1151 Der drof in þe dale..bot heteily þay were Restayed with þe stablye.

2. The general name of a family (*Cervidæ*) of ruminant quadrupeds, distinguished by the possession of deciduous branching horns or antlers, and by the presence of spots on the young: the various genera and species being distinguished as *rein-deer*, *moose-deer*, *red deer*, *fallow deer*; the MUSK DEER belong to a different family, *Moschidæ*.

A specific application of the word, which occurs in OE. only contextually, but became distinct in the ME. period, and by its close remained as the usual sense.

[*c* 893 K. ÆLFRED *Oros.* I. i. (Sw.) 18 He [Ohthere] hæfde þa ȝyt ða he þone cyningc sohte, tamra deora unbebohtra syx hund. þa deor hi hatað hranas.] *a* 1131 [see *der fald* in 4]. *c* **1205** LAY. 2586 To huntien after deoren [*c* **1275** after deores]. **1297** R. GLOUC. (Rolls) 9047 He let [make] þe parc of Wodestoke, & der þer inne do. *c* **1325** *Song on Passion* 59 (*O. E. Misc.*) He was todrawe so dur islawe in chace. **1375** BARBOUR *Bruce* VII. 497 [He] went..to purchase venysoun, For than the deir war in sesoun. *c* **1420** *Anturs of Arth.* (Camden) iv, Thay felle to the female dure, feyful thyk fold. **1464** *Mann. & Househ. Exp.* 195 A payr breganderys cueryd wyth whyte deris leder. **1470-85** MALORY *Arthur* x. lxi, He chaced at the reed dere. **1538** STARKEY *England* I. iii. 98 A dere louyth a lene barren.. ground. **1601** SHAKS. *Jul. C.* III. i. 209 Like a Deere, strocken by many Princes. **1611** CORYAT *Crudities* 10 A goodly Parke .. wherein there is Deere. **1774** GOLDSM. *Nat. Hist.* (1776) III. 80 An hog, an ox, a goat, or a deer. **1855** LONGF. *Hiaw.* III. 169 Where the red deer herd together.

b. occasional plural *deers.*

c **1275** [see **1205** in prec.]. **1674** N. Cox *Gentl. Recreat.* II. (1677) 58 The reasons why Harts and Deers do lose their Horns yearly. **1769** HOME *Fatal Discov.* III, Stretch'd on the skins of deers. *c* **1817** HOGG *Tales & Sk.* II. 89 The place of rendezvous, to which the deers were to be driven.

† c. *Deer of ten*: a stag of ten, i. e. one having ten points or tines on his horns; an adult stag of five years at least, and therefore 'warrantable' or fit to be hunted. *Obs.*

1631 MASSINGER *Emp. of East* IV. ii, He will make you royal sport, He is a deer Of ten, at the least.

3. *Small deer*: a phrase originally, and perhaps still by Shakspere, used in sense 1; but now humorously associated with sense 2.

14.. *Sir Beues* (1885) p. 74/2 (MS.C.) Ratons & myse and soche smale dere, That was hys mete that vii yere. **1605** SHAKS. *Lear* III. iv. 144 But Mice, and Rats, and such small Deare, Haue bin Toms food, for seuen long yeare. **1883** G. ALLEN in *Colin Clout's Calender* 14 Live mainly upon worms, slugs, and other hardy small deer.

transf. **1857** H. REED *Lect. Eng. Poets* x. II. 17 The small deer that were herded together by Johnson as the most eminent of English poets.

4. *attrib.* and *Comb.*, as *deer bed, herd, -hide, -keeper, kind, life, -sinew, -snaring,* etc.; *deer-like, deer-loved* adjs. [Several already in OE., as *déor-fald* an enclosure or cage for wild beasts in the amphitheatre, or for beasts of the chase, a deer-park, *déor-edisc* deer-park, *déor-net* net for wild animals, etc.]

1835 W. IRVING *Tour Prairies* xi, The tall grass was pressed down into numerous *'deer beds', where those animals had couched. *a* **1000** *Ags. Gloss.* in Wr.-Wülcker 201 *Cauea, domus in theatro,* *deorfald. *a* **1131** *O. E. Chron.* an. 1123 Se king rad in his der fald [æt Wudestoke]. **1860** G. H. K. *Vac. Tour.* 123 Peaks..where the scattered remnants of the great *deer herds can repose in security. **1814** SCOTT *Ld. of Isles* III. xix, Goat-skins or *deer-hides o'er them cast. **1849** JAMES *Woodman* vii, I have got my *deer-keepers watching. **1875** LYELL *Princ. Geol.* II. III.

xxxix. 359 Animals of the *deer kind. **1860** G. H. K. *Vac. Tour.* 122 The shepherds..see a good deal of *deer life. **1840** Mrs. Norton *Dream* 127 The dark, *deer-like eyes. **1876** Geo. Eliot *Dan. Der.* IV. liv. 114 Deer-like shyness. **1831** Lytton *Godolph.* 23 The *deer-loved fern. *c* 1000 Ælfric *Voc.* in Wr.-Wülcker 167 *Cassis*, *deornet. **1856** Kane *Arct. Expl.* II. vii. 79 To walk up Mary River Ravine until we reach the *deer-plains. **1866** Kingsley *Herew.* I. vi. 178 Sea-bows of horn and *deer-sinew. **1862** S. St. John *Forests Far East* II. 34, I have been out *deer-snaring in this neighbourhood.

b. Special comb. : **deer-brush,** an American shrub in Arizona ; **deer-cart,** the covered cart in which a tame stag to be hunted is carried to the meet ; **deer-dog** = DEER-HOUND ; **deer-drive,** a shooting expedition in which the deer are driven past the sportsman ; so *deer-driving* ; **deer-eyed** *a*, having eyes like deer, having soft or languid eyes ; **deer-fence,** a high railing such as deer cannot leap over; **deer-flesh,** venison ; **deer-forest,** a ' forest ' or extensive track of unenclosed wild land reserved for deer ; † **deer-goat,** an old name for the capriform or caprine antelopes ; **deer-grass,** species of Rhexia (N.O. *Melastomaceæ*) ; **deer-leap,** a lower place in a hedge or fence where deer may leap ; **deer-meat** = *deer-flesh* ; **deer-neck,** a thin neck (of a horse) resembling a deer's ; **deer-park,** a park in which deer are kept ; † **deer-reeve,** a township officer in New England in the colonial days, whose duty it was to execute the laws as to deer ; **deer-plain,** a plain inhabited by deer ; **deer-saddle,** a saddle on which a slain deer is carried away ; **deer's eye** = BUCK-EYE (the tree); **deer's foot** (*grass*), the fine grass *Agrostis setacea* ; **deer's hair** = DEER-HAIR ; **deer's milk,** a local name of the wood spurge, *Euphorbia amygdaloides*; **deer's tongue, deer-tongue,** a N. American Cichoraceous plant, *Liatris odoratissima* ; **deer-tiger,** the puma or cougar; **deer-yard,** an open spot where deer herd, and where the ground is trodden by them.

1883 W. H. Bishop in *Harper's Mag.* Mar. 502/2 The *' deer brush ' resembles horns. **1840** Hood *Up the Rhine* 186 The hearse, very like a *deer-cart. **1814** Scott *Ld. of Isles* v. xxiii, Many a *deer-dog howl'd around. **1882** *Society* 21 Oct. 19/1 Setting out for a *deer-drive. **1860** G. H. K. *Vac. Tour.* 143 Mr. Scrope..was a great hand at *deer-driving. **1884** Q. Victoria *More Leaves* 14 The gate of the *deer-fence. *a* **1300** *Cursor M.* 3603 (Cott.) If þou me *dere flesse [*v.r.* venisun] ani gete. **1854** *Act* 17–8 *Vict.* c. 91 § 42 Where such shootings or *deer forests are actually let. **1892** E. Weston Bell *Scot. Deerhound* 80 Probably not more than twenty deer forests, recognized as such, were in

existence prior to the beginning of the present century. **1607**
TOPSELL *Four-f. Beasts* (1658) 93 Of the first kinde of Trage-
laphvs which may be called a *Deer-goat.   **1693** SIR T. P.
BLOUNT *Nat. Hist.* 30 The Deer-Goat .. being partly like a
deer partly like a Goat.   **1866** *Treas. Bot.* 972/2 Low perennial often bristly herbs, commonly called *Deer-grass, or
Meadow-beauty, [with] large showy cymose flowers. **1540-2**
Act 31 *Hen. VIII*, c. 5 To make *dere leapes and breakes
in the sayde hedges and fences.   **1838** JAMES *Robber* i, In
front appeared a *deer-park.   **1860** G. H. K. *Vac. Tour.* 172
It is no light business to get our big stag..on the *deer
saddle.   **1762** J. CLAYTON *Flora Virginica* 57 *Æsculus
floribus octandris* Linn. .. *Dear's Eye, and Bucks Eyes.
1883 *Century Mag.* XXVI. 383 Among the lily-pads, *deer-
tongue, and other aquatic plants.   **1880** *7th Rep. Surv.
Adirondack Reg. N. Y.* 159 We reached an open forest
plateau on the mountain, where we were surprised to find
a *' deer-yard '.   Here the deep snow was tramped down by
deer into a broad central level area.

meant a "beast: usually a quadruped, as distinguished from birds and fishes," but
it does no longer. This meaning is given first, nonetheless, because all the
evidence indicates that is what the word originally meant and continued to mean
until at least 1481. Some students who know German will recognize that this
definition survives in the German cognate *Tier*, and thus a *Tiergarten*, "animal
garden," is a zoo. The meaning is not wholly lost to English, as we can see in the
word "wilderness," which comes from the Old English *wildēornes*, "a wild beast
place."

The next paragraph gives the citations of usage, all somewhat abbreviated.
The first is from the *Lindisfarne Gospels*, a document written down in about 950
A.D., translated from St. Luke, chapter 18, verse 25. The passage is the familiar
one about the camel going through the eye of the needle, although here the
camel is a *dear*. The rest of the citations may not be as easy to decipher, but
generally they are as clear as they need to be. In the cases of Old and Middle
English texts, any student could find the full title by consulting a handbook to
the literature of those times. In more modern citations, the references to better-
known writers are easy enough to decipher, and lesser-known ones can be ignored; often the date and the fact that the word was used at all are enough.

Definition 2 shows a dramatic narrowing down of the meaning of the word to
what we know it as, although the scientific name for the family, *Cervidae*, may
be unfamiliar. But then, most native speakers already know what a deer is, and
the lexicographer is hard pressed to find other words to define the animal. Notice
that the last citation for this definition comes from "Longf. *Hiaw*.," identifiable
as Longfellow's *Hiawatha*, 1855, an indication of the editors' attempt to include
usages from those parts of the English-speaking world outside Britain.

Under definition 2 are two subheadings, which should be self-explanatory.
Subhead b records that the word has occasionally been spelled with the plural -s,
and when it was it meant the same thing as the singular spelling. And under
subhead c, the editors record that deer having ten-pointed antlers were once
known as "deer of ten," although this usage was now obsolete.

The relationship of definition 3 to earlier definitions is given in lucid note. A reference to the citations will help the reader to understand how the editors decided the order of the definitions. Definition 2 may have one citation, from 893, that is actually older than definition 1, but the bulk of them are later and continue until modern times. Citations for definition 3 do not begin until 1885.

Definition 4, as a note helpfully reminds us, are attributive and combinative uses of the word, growing out of the earlier definitions of the word given under number 2. These are given alphabetically instead of chronologically, so that "deer bed," recorded in 1835, from the American author Washington Irving, is given before Sir Walter Scott's "deer-hides" of 1814. Notice that all the cited words in the first part of definition 4 are preceded by an asterisk, an indication that the word defines itself. (When an asterisk is used in an etymology, however, it indicates that the spelling is speculative and not actually found in writing.) Under subhead b we find some forms of the word which do not explain themselves. Who, for example, could know that the now obsolete "deer-reeve" once referred to a township officer in colonial New England?

The entry for "deer" is among the simpler ones in the OED. As it lacks the philosophical or political implications found in some other entries, it is most likely to be read only by students with a well developed interest in the history of the language. But some one of the half-million or so words in the dictionary may have more to offer the individual student. Not long ago a popular magazine published OED entries for the words "democracy," "republic," and "populism," side by side, as a commentary on the argument over these words in contemporary affairs. Strangely, the entries which seem so long and crowded when compared with entries in other dictionaries seemed in that context to be elegantly terse.

When you feel you can read the OED without trepidation, you should also consult the two dictionaries which offer the same kind of information for words found only on this side of the Atlantic. The first of them was compiled by Sir James Craigie and James R. Hulbert, *Dictionary of American English on Historical Principles* or *DAE* (Chicago: University of Chicago Press, 1938). Craigie had been the last editor-in-chief of the OED and when his work there was complete, he began again with a remaining stock of American words. The DAE was followed by another dictionary which dealt with phrases as well as words, Mitford M. Mathews's *Dictionary of Americanisms on Historical Principles* (Chicago: University of Chicago Press, 1951). Both of these later works may be read the same way the OED is.

B. How to Pick Your Own Dictionary of Usage

The reader will have noticed by now that the hottest question with which a dictionary must deal is usage. Indeed, no aspect of language study is as touchy as usage. Many of us assume the "right" usage is the one we grew up with and that deviations from that norm are either a sign of undesirable bearing or simply "wrong." Part of any nightclub comic's repertory is the shuffling of different usages; lower-class and regional usage becomes "dumb," the butt of jokes, and upper-class or overprecise usage becomes a model for travesty. Modern linguistic science has tried to calm the seas of anxiety that produce these tensions by pointing out that many questions of usage are determined by the dialect group in which we live, and that one dialect can communicate hunger, love, danger, fear, or compassion as well as the next.

This is not to say that one usage is as good as another in all contexts. Many questions of usage are based on a genuine concern for clarity. Although "hang" and "hung" are frequently confused, there is an immeasurable difference between being suspended, "hung," and executed, "hanged." Similarly, the resolution of many arguments over usage can improve the style of the writer, resolving ambiguity, deflating verbosity, and reducing redundancy. And those who live in a society with diverse tastes and styles eventually acquire an unconscious recognition of different usage areas; one simply does not talk the same way in a court of law or a church as in a grease pit or a gymnasium.

The continuing problem with usage is in knowing what to do in writing. The bulk of published writing, exclusive of dialogue in novels and plays, is still in Edited Standard English, a subject considered at some length in the first chapter of this book. Language resists the surface democracy of, say, dress. An author may appear at a publisher's office wearing patched jeans and work boots, a costume ostensibly aping the clothing of the lower classes, but the manuscript the author submits will encounter hostility if it includes such expressions as "irregardless," "educationwise," or "hassle" or if the manscript has too many split infinitives, confuses "lay" and "lie," and includes such redundancies as "The reason the train was late was because of a tie-up." All of these examples are widespread in speech but they have not overcome the resistance of editors.

There are thousands of such questions in English, and for that reason most people who plan to do much writing, professionally or not, usually have at their hands a dictionary of usage. A good dictionary of usage will not only provide an answer to questions of usage, it should also give a bounty of practical advice about writing. The problem is, just as with general dictionaries of the language, not all dictionaries of usage say the same things. With this in mind we would like to reproduce a sample entry from each of the leading seven dictionaries of usage on the North American market. The sample entry is for "unique," in part because it is usually a fairly short one and also because it does give an idea of the diversity of advice available. As the seven dictionaries are not absolutely uniform in design and purpose, this survey will necessarily give some an advantage. It is not our purpose to recommend one against the other but to aid you to choose. The titles are given here in order of the date of first publication.

The most widely used and often cited of these works is Henry Watson Fowler's *Modern English Usage*, first published in 1926 and revised twice.[1] Like any Englishman, Fowler faced less ambiguity about usage as his country has a recognized upper class, a House of Lords, and a definable standard of usage. Quite fittingly, an earlier work of Fowler's on usage was called *The King's English*[2] offering a model for common English citizens to emulate. Thus Fowler

---

[1] London: Oxford University Press, 1926. Margaret Nicholson adapted the work for American readers in 1957 (New York: Oxford University Press), and Sir Ernest Gowers gave the work a fuller revision in 1965.

[2] With his brother, F. G. Fowler (London: Oxford University Press, 1906).

has no difficulty in disposing of "unique": it is "nonsense" to use "unique" to mean "rare or unusual," although he can provide contrary examples from writers who were, presumably, neither fools nor incompetents.

> **unique.** A watertight definition or paraphrase of the word, securing it against confusion with all synonyms that might be suggested, is difficult to frame. In the first place, it is applicable only to what is in some respect the sole existing specimen, the precise like of which may be sought in vain. That gives a clean line of division between it and the many adjectives for which it is often ignorantly substituted—*remarkable, exceptional, fabulous, rare, marvellous,* and the like. In the qualities represented by those epithets there are degrees; but uniqueness is a matter of yes or no only; no unique thing is more or less unique than another unique thing, as a rare thing may be rarer or less rare than another rare thing. The adverbs that *u.* can tolerate are e.g. *quite, almost, nearly, really, surely, perhaps, absolutely,* or *in some respects;* and it is nonsense to call anything *more, most, very, somewhat, rather,* or *comparatively u.* Such nonsense, however, is often written: *What made Laker's achievement all the more unique was. . . . / I am now at one of the most unique writers' colonies imaginable. / I have just come across the production of a boy aged seven which is, in my experience, somewhat unique. / Sir, I venture to send you a copy of a rather unique inscription on a tombstone. / A very unique child, thought I.*
>
> But, secondly, there is another set of synonyms—*sole, single, peculiar to,* etc.—from which *u.* is divided not by a clear difference of meaning, but by an idiomatic limitation (in English though not in French) of the contexts to which it is suited. It will be admitted that we improve the two following sentences if we change *u.* in the first into *sole,* and in the second into *peculiar: In the always delicate and difficult domain of diplomatic relations the Foreign Minister must be the unique medium of communication with foreign Powers. / He relates Christianity to other religions, and notes what is unique to the former and what is common to all of them. Unique* so used is a GALLICISM.

If the quoted entry seems a trifle stiff it gives a misleading impression of what fun can be had in reading *Modern English Usage.* Two generations of writers have made Fowler bedside reading, taking one of the longer entries as a witty essay on style. Some of the entries, such as "Elegant Variation," "Genteelism," "Love of the Long Word," or "Pedantry," are still frequently reprinted. In his time Fowler was something of a rebel, vigorously attacking the "right/wrong" approach of the rigid schoolmarmism inherited from Victorian times.

The first work to employ an entirely different approach from Fowler's was Bergen and Cornelia Evans's *Dictionary of Contemporary American Usage* in 1957.[3] Bergen Evans has been a Professor of English at Northwestern University and a television performer (the host of several word-game shows in the 1950s and 1960s). Cornelia Evans, his sister, is a Washington-based author of fiction and nonfiction. The implications of their modifiers "contemporary" and "American" are not to be overlooked. The Evanses reflect the judgments of American academic linguistic thinking that usage cannot be based on one authoritarian dictate, no matter how gracefully and wittily presented. Instead, they try to

---

[3]New York: Random House, 1957.

describe usage among the most admired contemporary writers. This means, in fact, that although the Evanses often quote Fowler they frequently give precisely the opposite advice. In describing rather than prescribing, the Evanses take a position very much like that of the *Webster's New International Dictionary, Third Edition.* [4] Bergen Evans defended the new dictionary most eloquently in an essay titled "But What's a Dictionary For?" a work still reprinted as an answer to Dwight Macdonald and other critics.

As we can see, the Evanses perceive a contemporary usage strikingly different from Fowler's in regard to the word "unique."

> **unique** once meant "only," as in *his unique son.* It can no longer be used in this sense. Today *unique* may mean "in a class by itself," but it more often means "unparalleled" or simply "remarkable." In this, it is following the pattern of *singular.* In all its current senses *unique* may be used with words that imply degrees, such as *more unique* and *quite unique.* Some people believe that there is something about the meaning of *unique* that makes expressions of this kind "illogical" or improper, but these expressions are used freely by outstanding writers and educators today. One grammarian, commenting on the much condemned *quite unique* points out that the word here means "unparalleled" and that we certainly do say *quite unparalleled.* He then says of the word *unique* itself:"I don't see anything quite unique in it."
>
> **unique; singular; exceptional.** *Unique* and *singular* may be used as synonyms, but *singular* is more often used in the sense of extraordinary, remarkable *(The child has a singular inability to comprehend the simplest instruction).* *Exceptional* also may be used as a synonym for *unique* in its sense of forming an exception, or forming an exceptional or unusual instance. However, it is more often used, like *singular,* to mean simply unusual or extraordinary.

A work of much narrower scope is Margaret M. Bryant's *Current American Usage,* [5] sponsored by the National Council of Teachers of English in 1962. Limiting herself to only 240 entries, Professor Bryant deals with the most debated questions in usage, surveying the work of professional linguists who had worked in the six language areas of the United States and at three definable levels of usage—standard, informal, and dialect. *Current American Usage* is therefore an aid to problem solving for linguists rather than a guide for students or nonspecialist writers. She provides no entry for "unique" but deals with the question of its usage under "Comparisons, Illogical":

> . . . adjectives like *perfect, unique, round, straight, dead, final, black, impossible, complete* are compared freely even though some textbooks contend that these adjectives should not be compared since their meaning is absolute; i.e., they name qualities that do not vary in degree. Yet a famous example comes from the Constitution: "We the people of the United States, in order to form a *more perfect* union. . . ."
> One study found words of this type compared 89% of the time. . . .

---

[4] This dictionary is the great divider among authorities on usage, and for that reason we shall be referring to it again in the next few pages; for convenience we shall use the standard abbreviation WNID-3.

[5] New York: Funk and Wagnalls, 1962.

A more practical and straightforward guide is Roy H. Copperud's *Dictionary of Usage and Style* from 1964.[6] Designed primarily for journalists and editors who need immediate answers to thorny questions, Copperud's *Dictionary* has much to recommend it in brevity and clarity.

> **unique** The doctrine that *unique* is an absolute modifier that cannot be qualified may be a noble one, but it has no connection with the facts of usage. When used without a qualifier, as in "His outlook on the world was *unique*," it means *without a like or equal.* There are so few unique things under the sun that generally the word is used with a qualifier. This simply extends its usefulness without diminishing its force as an absolute when used alone. "So *unique* then was a ship carrying only tourists that port officials greeted them with alarm" and "The college shares with other private schools several points of *uniqueness*" are not open to reasonable criticism. *More unique, most unique, quite unique,* and the like are equally acceptable Yet the fastidious reserve *unique* for the absolute sense. Unique takes *a,* not *an.*

Copperud's directness should not be taken as an indication of his amateur standing. His writing shows a long-term interest in questions of usage. He gave WNID-3 a good review in *Editor and Publisher,* and, six years after the work cited above, produced a survey of a number of different guides on the subject. *American Usage: The Consensus*[7] summarizes the entries of the four usage dictionaries we have considered here, usage dictionaries by Bernstein and Follett which we shall deal with shortly, and also an array of general dictionaries and more discursive studies. These entries take longer to peruse, but they give the judicious writer the fullest advice.

Although there seems to be some agreement among the Evanses, Bryant, and Copperud that "unique" might occasionally be compared, they were followed by two dictionaries which refuted such slippage into permissiveness. The first of these was Theodore M. Bernstein's *The Careful Writer* in 1965.[8] Bernstein was assistant managing editor at *The New York Times* when that newspaper denounced WNID-3 and discouraged its use by *Times* writers. His *The Careful Writer* is more than a response to relaxing standards of usage, it is also a handbook of style for those writers who would like to meet the uncompromising standards of the *Times'* editors. Although Bernstein does not provide an entry for "unique," he does treat with it under the heading "Incomparables." The key phrase in the discussion is probably "literary unwashed":

Incomparables

> When Orwell wrote that "All animals are equal but some are more equal than others," one would have thought the bite of his sarcasm sufficient to destroy the arguments of those who try to justify the use of the comparative and superlative degrees of words that express absolutes. But the arguments persist—as do the misuses. "Perhaps one of the most unique of Austrian exports is . . ."; "Nothing is more fatally

---

[6]New York: Hawthorn Books.
[7]New York: Van Nostrand Reinhold, 1970.
[8]New York: Atheneum.

dangerous to the G.O.P. . . ."; "His rule of the party is more absolute than that of any of his predecessors."

It is not necessary or desirable to draw up a long list of words that do not seem to admit of comparison, because if one goes hunting for such words he will find himself in a philosophical predicament and a literary straitjacket. He will find himself questioning quite innocent words: A thing is either smooth or it is not smooth (he will find himself saying), therefore how can one be smoother than another?

. . . If we allow the literary unwashed to determine that "more unique" is correct usage, the meaning of *unique* becomes eroded. What word will we then have to convey the meaning of "the only one of its kind"? Shall we have to coin another word for this idea—"scrumpish," for example? If we do, you can be sure that it will not be too long before the unwashed are using "more scrumpish," then we shall have to coin still another word. . . .

The dismissal of the usage standards in WNID-3 was mild compared with the virulent denunciation of them in *The Atlantic Monthly* by Wilson Follett, chief compiler of *Modern American Usage*.[9] His review, titled "Sabotage in Springfield," accused the editors of WNID-3 of being "out to destroy . . . every obstinate vestige of linguistic punctilio, every surviving influence that makes for the upholding of standards, every criterion for distinguishing between better usage and worse."[10] Follett obviously hoped that his *Modern American Usage* might help stem the tide. He does not have an entry for "unique" and "deals with it only briefly under "Absolute Words":

Absolute Words

Some words exclude comparison or partition; they denote what is superlative or complete, and they must be handled accordingly. The most familiar example is *unique*: something can be *almost unique* but not *rather unique*.

The most recent contribution to the discussion of usage in America is William and Mary Morris's edition of *The Harper Dictionary of Contemporary Usage*.[11] As the editor of *The American Heritage Dictionary*, William Morris presided over the usage panel employed to determine controversial questions there. Although the panel for *The Harper Dictionary* is larger than that for *The American Heritage*, several authorities appear on both. The testimonials gathered by the Morrises can hardly be expected to end the discussion on the question, but they certainly do demonstrate to the reader and writer how high emotions still run on the matter of "unique":

[9]New York: Hill and Wang, 1966. Follett died during the writing of *Modern American Usage*, and his work was completed by Jacques Barzun, a sympathetic colleague, and a panel of distinguished authorities.
[10]*The Atlantic Monthly* (January 1962), 74.
[11]New York: Harper & Row, 1975.

unique

Usage Panel Question

Unique is regarded by grammarians as one of the "absolute" adjectives, one not possessing a comparative or superlative form. Yet one often sees expressions like "a rather *unique* apartment" and "a most *unique* occasion." Would you approve such expressions?

In writing   Yes: 11%. No: 89%

In casual speech   Yes: 24%. No: 76%

Michael J. Arlen: "No. It's dumb."

Isaac Asimov: "No. I am a slight perfectionist in this respect. (Joke.)"

W. H. Auden: "No. Do, do use 'perfect.' "

Stewart Beach: "I stick by the absolute meaning. There are plenty of other adjectives which have proper comparatives and are more accurate in the examples."

Saul Bellow: "In speech, I'd tolerate it."

Jules Bergman: "The mass of words spoken over the radio, TV—books, and the unbelievable events of our era have already left 'unique' by the wayside. Its strength has ebbed."

Barry Bingham, Sr.: "Why spoil a highly specific and exact word by stretching it all out of shape?"

Hal Borland: "This practice is inexcusable in anyone with even a high school education."

Heywood Hale Broun: "No. Muddying of exact meaning makes communication even more difficult."

Anthony Burgess: "No. The word must not be weakened into a comparative. It has a unique meaning."

Ben Lucien Burman: "No. This was thought up by the same person who invented 'Pizza Pie.' "

Abe Burrows: "This comes from the weakening of a great and useful word. Or perhaps I should say a 'most divine' word and 'most perfect.' "

John Ciardi: "No. Not while 'distinctive' is so readily available."

Robert Crichton: "Yes. No one means 'unique' uniquely any more."

Robert Cromie: "No. 'Unique' means *one* with no rivals and nothing comparable."

Gerold Frank: "No—but perhaps permissible in casual speech."

John K. Hutchens: "In casual speech—yes—but a bit uneasily."

Helen L. Kaufmann: "No—no more than 'more' or 'rather' perfect."

Pinckney Keel: "No. 'Unique' *should* denote one-of-a-kind."

Walt Kelly: "No. This sort of thing, softening the precise, is useful in comic writing when you want to show the speaker to be a boob."

Irving Kolodin: "No. This is an abuse of 'unique,' which is degraded to 'unusual' or 'uncommon.' "

Robert Lipsyte: "No. You lose the word."

Russell Lynes: "Yes—grudgingly."

Dwight Macdonald: "Etymology makes this un-possible."

David McCord: "What corpse is ever 'a trifle dead'?"

Herbert Mitgang: "No. Too basic."

Edwin Newman: "No. I deliver unwelcome lectures on this subject to colleagues and have discussed it on the air."

Orville Prescott: "An indefensible outrage!"

Peter S. Prescott: "Never, because it is meaningless. How about a 'somewhat unicorn'?"

Francis Robinson: "No. It's like 'one of the greatest.' "

Berton Roueché: "I think we should oppose anything that diminishes the language by destroying a word."

Vermont Royster: "Is it unique or isn't it? Or is it rather unusual, different, or impressive?"

Harrison Salisbury: "Down with 'unique'!"

Leonard Sanders: "Each time a word is misused, its value is diminished to some extent, and the language has lost that degree of clarity."

Charles E. Silberman: "I would accept 'rather unique' but not 'most unique.' "

Elvis Stahr, Jr.: "Unique *is* absolute, not merely 'regarded by grammarians' that way."

Rex Stout: "Yes. Oh well."

Frank Sullivan: " 'Most unique' is wrong but the radio and television announcers use it so much that I suppose it's pedantic to hold out against it. It's 'in.' "

Howard Taubman: "No. Only the other day a good writer spoke of 'the most perfect.' Like 'unique,' can there be anymore more than perfect?"

Davidson Taylor: "No. It is not comparable."

Earl Ubell: "Let's hold out for the meaning of this unique word."

Although the members of the panel, not all of whom have contributed to this entry, are "established" writers of one kind or another, they are by no means stuffed shirts. Many are quite popular figures. Walt Kelly, for example, used to draw the *Pogo* comic strip. Isaac Asimov is the prolific author of science fiction with a wide readership among college students. Heywood Hale Broun, Jules Bergman, Robert Cromie, and Edwin Newman are television personalities. Gerold Frank has written popular biographies of movie stars. Michael J. Arlen's *Passage to Ararat* was a best seller in 1975-76. Anthony Burgess, Dwight Macdonald, and Edwin Newman have contributed to this text.

WRITING ASSIGNMENTS

Essays

1. With what you have learned from the Classroom Exercise and the various readings in this chapter, write an estimate of the dictionary you use. Does it have all the important features a good college dictionary should have? Does it provide information on usage? What is its usage label for "ain't"? Has it failed to provide information on words you have found in your reading for this year? What kinds of words did it not include? Does it have words of recent coinage such as "clone" and "cloning"? Does it give biographical information on controversial or contemporary figures?

2. Write the history of an English word, using *The Oxford English Dictionary*. Pick some word at random, perhaps one close in spelling to your family name. Try to take one at least one column long but no more than three columns. Has the word changed in meaning over the years? Or has it,

like "deer," stayed pretty much the same? Why? In your conclusion, make a cross reference to a more contemporary dictionary.

3. Pick a word you have described as bad usage such as "ain't," or "irregardless." Look it up in a number of dictionaries, including dictionaries of usage; your college library should have several of those described in the section on usage dictionaries. What is the origin of the word? How long as there been argument over its usage? What are your conclusions after checking all the sources you can find?

4. What are some of the words you were discouraged form using as you were growing up? What do they have in common in terms of etymology, history, or usage taboos? *The American Heritage Dictionary* and the 1975 edition of *The Random House College Dictionary* list many words that previous dictionaries deleted. If need be, you might consult a dictionary of slang. The work of Eric Partridge in England and Harold Wentworth and Stuart Berg Flexner in America are highly recommended.

5. Write a definition of a current slang word that is not sufficiently covered in the dictionaries. Try for example, "laid back," "hassle," "bummer," "boss," or "funky." In what contexts do you find these words? Where did you first hear or read them? Who would most likely use them? Can you assume anything about their origin—drug culture, or black musicians, or Estonian carpenters? Do the words have more than one definition according to context?

6. Consult copies of *Webster's Third* or *The American Heritage Dictionary*. Review the attacks of Macdonald and Kilburn on the respective volumes. Are their charges warranted? After examination of either volume, write a defense of one of them, answering charges with evidence.

JOURNAL KEEPING

1. Ask yourself how there could possibly be a controversy over something as apparently gray as a dictionary. As you read through the chapter, record your reactions to what the different authorities say.

2. Many of the inferior dictionaries on the market, characteristically sold at discount prices in supermarkets and variety stores, are called "Webster's," a name the publishers may use legally, as explained in this chapter. If you tried to use one of those to complete the classroom exercise you very likely found it impossible. To see more fully how one of these dictionaries measures up, compare one page—taken at random—of one of these with one of the list of quality college dictionaries given earlier in this chapter. What is missing from the poorer dictionary?

3. Reading this chapter can provide you with means to expand your vocabulary. Simply by attending college classes and keeping up with the reading, you will encounter thousands of new words. You may find it difficult to stop to look up each one of them as you encounter it, especially when the meaning is clear in context. On the other hand, if you make no

effort to record the words, you may not retain their usage and definition. One method of building your vocabulary would be to write down each of these words as you find them, perhaps on a slip of paper acting as a book-mark. This will allow you to look them all up at the same time. If you anticipate using some of the words again, keep a record of them, with definitions, in your journal. If you are finding a large number, you might set aside another journal just to keep track of them, perhaps with subdivisions according to subject, alphabetization, etc. By continuing this method for four years of college you will expand your vocabulary tremendously; the words you have will be more useful than those taken at random from news-paper or magazine "vocabulary building" columns.

4. You can improve your spelling by a comparable method. Keep a record, perhaps in the back pages of your journal, of all the words you find difficult to spell or which are marked misspelled on papers you submit to classes. Don't think of it as a humiliation that you have misspelled them; rather, be glad you have isolated the words you don't know. Most people who think of themselves as "bad spellers" regularly misspell only about 100 words; they would consult a dictionary before trying "Czechoslovakia" or "Schenectady." Once you have identified the words you don't know, try writing them out, ten at a time, on a card or a sheet of paper that you can carry in a shirt pocket or a purse. If you continually refer to the list, perhaps while waiting for a doctor's appointment, an interview, etc., you will quickly reduce the 100 words you most often misspell.

To the Student

As *Speaking of Words* was written and edited for you, we think you should have a chance to tell us how useful you found it. Please help us by filling out this questionnaire and returning it to us at: Holt, Rinehart, & Winston, College English Office, 383 Madison Avenue, New York, N.Y. 10017.

College_____

Instructor's name _____

1. Did you like reading *Speaking of Words*? _____

2. Which essay did you like best?_____

   _____

3. Which essay did you like least? _____

   _____

4. Was the book too easy? _____Too difficult?_____

5. Which chapter did you like best? _____

   _____

6. Which chapter did you like least? _____

   _____

7. Did our Discussion Questions lead to real discussions? _____

8. Could you actually write papers following our suggested writing topics? __

9. Did you keep a journal following our suggestions? _____

10. Did you like the book's physical appearance? _____

11. Do you feel your instructor should assign this book again next year? ____

12. Will you keep the book for your personal library? _____

13. Would you like to tell us something we forgot to ask?_____

_____

_____

May we quote you in our promotion efforts for this book?

_____Yes_____No

Date_____Signature_____

Address_____

Thanks for your help.